D0206332

Teaching Models
in Education of the Gifted

Teaching Models in Education of the Gifted

SECOND EDITION

C. June Maker

Aleene B. Nielson

pro·ed
8700 Shoal Creek Boulevard
Austin, Texas 78757

pro·ed

© 1995, 1982 by PRO-ED, Inc.
8700 Shoal Creek Boulevard
Austin, Texas 78757-6897

Library of Congress Cataloging-in-Publication Data

Maker, C. June.
  Teaching models in education of the gifted / C. June Maker, Aleene
B. Nielson. — 2nd ed.
     p.   cm.
  Includes bibliographical references and index.
  ISBN 0-89079-609-2
  1. Gifted children—Education. I. Nielson, Aleene B. II. Title.

LC3993.M293 1995   94-17650
371.95—dc20   CIP

This book is designed in Sabon with Universe Condensed.

Production Manager: Alan Grimes
Production Coordinator: Adrienne Booth
Art Director: Lori Kopp
Reprints Buyer: Alicia Woods
Editor: Tracy Sergo
Editorial Assistant: Claudette Landry

Printed in the United States of America

2   3   4   5   6   7   8   9   10   99   98   97   96

To Dan and Tom

Contents

Preface

PURPOSE OF THE BOOK

More than 10 years have passed since the first edition of this review of teaching-learning models appropriate for education of the gifted was first published. Our purpose has not changed, but many changes have occurred in the field of general education and, particularly, in our field. New program models have been developed specifically for gifted students, more research has been done, and new materials have been published. In many areas, special programs are in jeopardy or have been eliminated. Greater emphasis has been placed on the development of programs to serve diverse populations, and "mainstreaming" all children into heterogeneous classrooms is practiced widely. The value of some of the thinking process models in the education of all students has been recognized as well. Some of the models reviewed in this book also are recommended to all teachers who want to create a more effective learning environment in their classrooms. This book provides a comprehensive review of teaching-learning models that can be used in the development and implementation of a curriculum for gifted students. In providing this review, the authors hope to supply enough information to teachers, prospective teachers, program coordinators, and curriculum development specialists to enable them to (a) assess critically the match of the assumptions in a model with their own philosophies; (b) evaluate the validity of a model for the purpose for which they intend to employ it; (c) apply the model appropriately in any situation; and, most importantly, (d) implement the model with gifted students. Because of its focus on implementation, the book provides many examples of the use of different models with gifted students of several ages.

This book also serves as a companion volume to *Curriculum Development for the Gifted* (Maker, 1982). In that volume, modifications of the regular curriculum content, processes, products, and learning environment to make it more appropriate for gifted students were discussed. Suggestions for curriculum development, along with several examples of appropriate curricula, also were provided. To implement such a curriculum, however, more specific teaching strategies, more examples, and more in-depth discussions of the variety of approaches available for teaching gifted students are needed. In effect, this book provides a variety of alternatives for implementing the general principles described in *Curriculum Development for the Gifted*. No single model or way of teaching the gifted can provide the comprehensive curriculum needed by the students. Therefore, this book is focused on the development of a comprehensive understanding of a variety of approaches. Once these approaches have been understood, curricula can be designed that consider the following important factors: (a) the philosophies of the teacher, school, and community on purposes of education for the gifted; (b) the underlying assumptions of the theoretical and practical approaches and how these assumptions mesh with the philosophies of everyone concerned; (c) the varied characteristics and interests of the children; (d) parental concerns; (e) the teaching style, strengths, and preferences of the teacher; and (f) the physical setting of the school. The product, a functional curriculum for gifted children, may have an emphasis on the use of one main model, one model as a framework with supplementary models, or the integration of several models into a framework constructed by the curriculum developers.

The models described were chosen for several reasons. The first was a concern for their demonstrated or potential success with gifted children. Each principle described in *Curriculum Development for the Gifted* (Maker, 1982) was considered in this selection process. Second, these models were selected because of their widespread use in programs for the gifted or the integration of most of the recommended modifications into their structure. A third and final concern was variety and complementarity. No one model can encompass all the content, process, product, and learning environment changes necessary for a comprehensive curriculum to be established. No one model will be attractive to all teachers, and no one model will fit every situation. For these and related reasons, models were chosen that could be combined in a variety of ways to enhance their effectiveness and increase the chances that teachers will find a combination to fit their preferred styles of teaching and their students' preferred styles of learning.

ORGANIZATION OF THE BOOK

The first chapter provides an introduction to teaching-learning models and their role in programs for the gifted. The main body of the book consists of separate chapters about each model. These chapters follow a consistent outline containing a discussion of the model, a teaching unit developed from it, an analysis of the unit, and a listing of additional resources. The outline for each chapter is as follows:

A. Overview of the Model
B. Assumptions Underlying the Model
   1. About Learning
   2. About Teaching
   3. About Characteristics and Teaching of the Gifted
   4. Other
C. Elements/Parts
   1. Dimensions, Thinking Levels, or Steps
D. Modification of the Basic Curriculum
   1. Content
   2. Process
   3. Product
   4. Environment
   5. Examples of Teaching Activities/Strategies
E. Modifying the Approach
F. Development
   1. How
   2. By Whom
G. Research on Effectiveness
   1. With Nongifted
   2. With Gifted
H. Judgments
   1. Advantages
   2. Disadvantages
I. Conclusion
J. References
   1. Background Readings
   2. Curricular Materials

The final chapter is a discussion of how a comprehensive approach might be developed by combining and integrating more than one of the models described.

Chapter 1

The Role of Teaching-Learning Models in Curriculum Development for the Gifted

THE NATURE OF TEACHING-LEARNING MODELS

A teaching-learning model is a structural framework that serves as a guide for developing specific educational activities and environments. A model can be highly theoretical and abstract, or it can be a more practical structural framework. Regardless of how theoretical or practical, the distinguishing features common to teaching-learning models are (a) an identified purpose or area of concentration, (b) underlying explicit and implicit assumptions about the characteristics of learners and about the teaching-learning process, (c) guidelines for developing specific day-to-day learning experiences, (d) definite patterns and requirements for these learning activities, and (e) a body of research surrounding their development or an evaluation of their effectiveness.

Joyce and Weil (1986) identified more than 80 models of teaching and divided them into families based on common viewpoints about teaching and learning. The first group, social interaction models, has an emphasis on the relationship of the individual to society and to other groups and is focused on the individual's ability to relate to others, engage in democracy, and work productively within society. Information-processing models, the second group, are focused on the ways people handle information, organize data, sense problems, and generate solutions to problems. The third family, personal models, shares an orientation toward the development of self-concept. Behavior modification and cybernetic models, the fourth group, are focused on changing observable behaviors based on efficient sequencing of learning tasks along with manipulation of antecedents and consequences. Most of the models presented in this volume fall into the first and second families, although some could be considered personal models.

The area of concentration of focus in the model can be very broad or quite narrow. Renzulli's *Enrichment Triad,*[1] for example, was developed as a total enrichment program for the gifted, integrating content knowledge, a wide range of intellectual skills, and the development of an investigative attitude. The Parnes model, on the other hand, was developed to enhance problem solving and creativity, a more narrow range of intellectual and affective skills. Because the Renzulli model has many components, each practice is explained in less depth than the practices in the Parnes model.

Although the different models have different purposes or areas of concentration, they are not focused exclusively on one aspect of learning. For example, the information-processing models, such as Parnes and Taba, also have an emphasis on the development of social relationships and an integrated, well-functioning self. The social interaction models, such as Betts or Sharan and Sharan, also have an emphasis on the development of information-processing skills.

In each model some theoretical assumptions must be made regarding the nature of the learner (for example, learning, motivational, intellectual, and emotional characteristics) and the nature or effectiveness of certain teaching methods. These assumptions can range from highly theoretical and complicated ones, such as Kohlberg's assumption that all individuals progress through identifiable, invariant stages in their development of moral reasoning, to one of Taylor's simple assumptions that a variety of talent exists in individuals. The "proof" of these assumptions also varies from model to model. A related aspect of assumptions is how clearly they are stated. Some authors clearly reveal the assumptions they reject and state the ones they accept, while others describe some assumptions and omit other critical ones. Still other authors say nothing about either their implicit or explicit assumptions, and teachers must search for the underlying ideas.

The third and fourth aspects of models comprise their guidelines for development of specific learning experiences. With these guidelines, certain requirements or standards by which their appropriateness is judged necessarily follow. The Bloom and Krathwohl *Taxonomies,* for example, provide definitions of cognitive and affective behaviors at each level in the hierarchy. One requirement or standard associated with the implementation of the models is that each lower level behavior is necessary before the higher level behavior can be executed effectively. Associated with the Taba *Strategies* is a broad range of teacher attitudes and competencies that involve much more than simply knowing what sequences of questions to ask the children.

---

1. Specific references for each model can be found in the individual chapters on each model.

All teaching-learning models have some basis in research, either as a background for their development or as a justification for use because of their effectiveness. Extensive research has been done on the elements included in the Parnes program, for instance, along with numerous longitudinal and experimental studies of its effectiveness with various groups. The Taba *Strategies* were developed and evaluated over a period of approximately 10 years. On the other hand, little research has been done on the effectiveness of Betts' model in achieving the stated purposes. Renzulli's model was developed out of his experience in evaluating programs for the gifted and based on reviews of research on the characteristics of gifted individuals. Ongoing research also is being conducted to determine its effectiveness in creative and affective outcomes.

THE CURRICULUM FOR GIFTED STUDENTS[2]

Qualitative Differences

The phrase most frequently used to describe the appropriate school curriculum for gifted students is "qualitatively different from the program for all students." This phrase implies that the basic curriculum must be examined, and changes or modifications must be made so that the most appropriate curriculum is provided for the gifted students. Modifications must be quality changes rather than quantity, and they must build upon and extend the characteristics (both present and future) that make the children different from other students. To make the basic curriculum more appropriate for gifted students (Gallagher, 1975), an educator can modify the content (what is learned), the process (the methods used and the thinking processes students are expected to use), and the learning environment (the psychological and physical environment in which the learning is to occur). Renzulli (1977) added product (the end products expected of children as a result of the processes used) as a dimension that must be considered.

Content Modifications

The content of the curriculum consists of the ideas, concepts, descriptive information, and facts that are made available to students in school settings.

---

2. The material presented in this section represents a brief review of information contained in Section I of *Curriculum Development for the Gifted* (Maker, 1982). Readers who are not familiar with the concepts as presented by Maker should read this more comprehensive discussion of curriculum development for the gifted.

Curriculum may be structured in a variety of forms that can differ in degree of abstractness, complexity, organization, and subject areas covered.

Abstractness

The major focus of discussions, presentations, reading materials, and lectures in a gifted program should be on abstract concepts, themes, and theories—ideas that have a wide range of applicability or potential for transfer both within and across disciplines or fields of study. Concrete information and factual data are intended as illustrations or examples of the abstract ideas rather than as the major focus.

Complexity

Abstract ideas usually are complex as well but vary in the degree of complexity or richness. For gifted students, these ideas need to be as complex as possible so that children can work at their challenge level rather than at or below comfort level. The complexity of an abstract idea can be determined by examining the number and complexity of concepts involved, the number and complexity of the disciplines or traditional content areas that must be understood or integrated to comprehend the idea, and the variety of possibilities for student exploration.

Variety

In past years variety has been the definition of enrichment and, in many programs, is the only content modification made for gifted students. The concept of variety suggests that ideas and content areas not taught in the regular curriculum should be taught in a gifted program. A related suggestion is that gifted students work on different aspects of a broad theme and that the curriculum include ideas of interest to students with varied gifts and abilities.

Organization for Learning Value

Since knowledge in most areas increases and changes at an alarming rate and since gifted students have a limited amount of time to spend in the educational program, every learning experience must be the most valuable that can be offered. To achieve economy, content must be organized to facilitate transfer of learning, memory, and understanding of abstract concepts and generalizations. According to Bruner (1960), these results can be achieved if the content is organized around the key concepts or abstract ideas to be learned, rather than arranged in some other fashion.

Study of People

Gifted students are likely to become scholars; leaders; and creative, productive individuals in the future. They also enjoy reading biographies and autobiographies. For these reasons and their need to learn how to deal with their own talents and possible success, gifted students should study creative and productive individuals. An analysis of problems these individuals faced, the way they handled their problems, their personal traits, their career or professional characteristics, and their social interactions can stimulate social and psychological development of gifted students.

The Study of Methods

Gifted students should study the methods of inquiry—the investigative techniques—used by scholars in different disciplines. They need practice in using these methods, and they should learn a variety of techniques. Such studies can contribute to a better understanding of the content area and enhance the independence of the students.

Process Modifications

The process aspect of the curriculum involves the way new material is presented, the activities in which the students engage, and the questions that are asked. Process includes teaching methods and the thinking skills or processes developed by the students.

Higher Levels of Thinking

The methods used in programs for the gifted should stress the use rather than acquisition of information. Since gifted students can acquire information rapidly and almost effortlessly, they should apply it in new situations, use it to develop new ideas, evaluate its appropriateness, and use it to develop new products.

Open-endedness

Questions and activities for gifted students should include many more open than closed questions and learning activities. The principle of open-endedness indicates that no predetermined right answer exists. The questions or activities are provocative in that they stimulate further thinking and investigation about a topic. Openness stimulates more thought, permits and encourages divergent thinking, encourages responses from more than one child, and contributes to the development of an interaction pattern in which learning, not the teacher, is the most important focus.

Discovery

The activities designed for gifted students should include a great many situations in which students use inductive reasoning processes to discover patterns, ideas, and underlying principles. Such guided discovery has several advantages for gifted children: (a) increased interest through involvement in learning; (b) use of their natural curiosity, their desire to figure out the "how and why of things" (Renzulli, Smith, White, Callahan, & Hartman, 1976), and their desire to organize and bring structure to things; and (c) increased self-confidence and independence in learning by showing they are capable of figuring things out for themselves.

Evidence of Reasoning

Another important process modification for use with gifted students is to ask them to express not only their conclusions but also the reasoning that led them to these conclusions. This aspect of teaching is especially important when using a discovery approach, developing higher levels of thinking, and asking open-ended questions. Using this strategy, students learn different reasoning processes from other students, and they are encouraged to evaluate both the process and products of others' thinking. Listening to students' reasons and evidence also is an effective way for teachers to assess the students' levels of thinking.

Freedom of Choice

Whenever possible, gifted students should be given the freedom to choose learning experiences and topics. Their interest and excitement in learning will be increased by such techniques. However, not all gifted students are independent learners, so some students may need assistance in making and executing their choices.

Group Interaction

Structured activities and simulation games as well as unstructured opportunities to interact should be a regular part of the curriculum for gifted students to enable them to develop social and leadership skills. These activities should include rule-structured games and open-ended group investigations among a small group of students, peer evaluation, and self-analysis or critique. Both peer evaluation and self-analysis will be more effective if the activity has been videotaped or audiotaped for students to review.

Pacing and Variety

The final two process modifications serve mainly as facilitators for the success of other changes. *Pacing* refers to how rapidly new material is presented to the students. Research (George, 1976) and experience have indicated that rapid pacing often is important to maintain the interest of the students and provide a challenge. Rapid pacing, however, does not refer to the amount of teacher wait-time needed during discussions. *Variety* simply suggests that the teacher use various methods to maintain the interest of the children and to accommodate the different learning styles of the students.

Product Modifications

Products are the "ends" of instruction. They can be tangible or intangible, sophisticated or unsophisticated. Sophisticated products involve detailed, original work, while unsophisticated ones involve paraphrasing or copying. Products can include reports, stories, plays, dances, ideas, speeches, pictures, and illustrations. The products expected from gifted students should resemble the products developed by professionals in the discipline being studied (Renzulli, 1977). These professional products will differ from typical student products in the following ways:

- *Result from real problems*—The products developed by gifted students should address problems that are real to them. Students can be encouraged to choose a specific area of concern within a certain field of study and design an investigation around that area.

- *Addressed to real audiences*—To the extent possible, the products developed by gifted students should be addressed to real audiences, such as the scientific community, the city council, or a government agency. At other times, the real audience consists of classmates or other students in the school. The gifted students should not be developing products that are seen or heard only by the teacher.

- *Transformation*—Gifted students' products should represent transformations of existing information or data rather than mere summaries of others' conclusions. Original research, original artwork, and other such products should include the collection and analysis of raw data. If students use higher levels of thinking, they must produce a product that is a true transformation.

- *Variety*—Gifted students should be encouraged to learn about and use a variety of types of products and to consider carefully what is the most appropriate representation of their content to the proposed audience. Variety in products allows students with different intellectual and creative strengths to demonstrate their competence with appropriate media. They also need practice using varied product options to meet the same goal.

- *Self-selected format*—Gifted students must be allowed to decide which formats to use in presenting their solutions to problems real to them. Student interests, strengths, and prior experiences all may influence these choices. Certainly teachers can provide assistance in the selection of a format and may encourage students, at times, to try a format new to them; however, students should be allowed to make the final choices.

- *Appropriate evaluation*—Often, student products are directed toward and evaluated by the teacher only. The products of professionals are evaluated by the audiences for whom they were intended. Products of gifted students should be evaluated by appropriate audiences, including audiences of peers. Students also should be encouraged or required to complete an extensive self-evaluation of their own products.

Learning Environment Modifications

The learning environment is the setting in which learning occurs and includes both the physical setting and psychological climate of the school and classroom. Many dimensions of learning environments are important; different individuals have different preferences for certain aspects (for example, amount of sound and light or presence of color). The learning environments appropriate for gifted students resemble the environments appropriate for all children but differ in degree. All environment modifications presented in this section were chosen because they meet the following three conditions: (a) they are preferred by most gifted students; (b) they are necessary for implementing the content, process, and product modifications advocated; and (c) they build on characteristics of gifted students.

Learning Centered Versus Teacher Centered

Environments for gifted students should include a focus on the students' ideas and interests rather than those of the teacher. Student discussions rather than teacher talk should be emphasized, and patterns of interaction seldom should have the teacher as the central figure or focus.

Independence Versus Dependence

The degree of tolerance for and encouragement of student initiative is the main idea in this dimension of the environment. The focus is on having students work to solve their own problems, including those related to classroom management, and make their own decisions instead of depending on the teacher.

Open Versus Closed

The physical environment should be open to permit new people, materials, and things to enter. The same is true of the psychological environment. New ideas, diverse values, exploratory discussions, and the freedom to change directions to meet new situations must be encouraged.

Acceptance Versus Judgment

The three major elements of this dimension are: (a) attempting to understand students' ideas, (b) the timing of value judgments, and (c) evaluation rather than judgment. Before teachers can assess student ideas, they must accept and understand those ideas; that is, they must attend or listen actively, accept the ideas, and then request clarification, elaboration, and extensions of the ideas before approving or challenging them. Timing refers to the stage of creative production or problem solving when evaluations occur. Idea production, for example, is one of the most inappropriate times. *Judgment* implies rightness or wrongness, while *evaluation* implies an assessment of both the strengths and limitations of a product or person. Evaluation should be emphasized rather than judgment, and students also should be taught to respond to each other in nonjudgmental ways.

Complex Versus Simple

As a dimension of classroom climate, complexity versus simplicity refers to both physical and psychological environments. A complex physical environment, necessary for the gifted, includes a variety of materials; sophisticated and varied "tools," references, and books; a representation of varied cultures and intelligences; and a variety of databases and electronic resources. A complex psychological environment, also necessary for gifted students, includes challenging tasks, complex ideas, and sophisticated methods.

Varied Versus Similar Groupings

Grouping arrangements in programs and classes for the gifted should be varied and fluid rather than identical and static. The types of tasks and the purposes of learning experiences will be varied; therefore, the groupings needed to accomplish these purposes also must be different. Groupings should approximate real-life situations, and students need to be allowed to make choices about how the groups are set up.

Flexibility Versus Rigidity

One of the most important elements of both physical and psychological environments is flexibility. Flexibility is needed in scheduling, requirements to be met, criteria for evaluation, and some teacher values. Learners often need extended periods of time to become engaged in complex projects or activities of interest; they also need to work on these projects long enough to achieve a sense of personal satisfaction. In addition, some events outside the school environment (e.g., death of a friend, outstanding achievement of an individual or the group) may be of such paramount importance to students that class time must be used for discussion of the event. If student time is rigidly and tightly scheduled and students always are expected to follow the teacher's predetermined schedule, student autonomy and internal motivation are not allowed to develop. Extreme frustration may be the result in highly motivated or caring students.

High Mobility Versus Low Mobility

The amount of movement allowed and encouraged is the most important aspect of this dimension of the environment. If gifted students are to develop professional products, have freedom of choice, and be allowed to develop the autonomy necessary for exploration and investigation, the environment must allow movement in and out of the classroom and access to different environments, materials, and equipment.

Summary

The changes advocated in this section have been chosen to meet, collectively and individually, two basic criteria that are different in quality from the regular curriculum and based on the unique characteristics of gifted students. The chosen elements were based on the group traits of gifted students; not all children will possess every characteristic. Thus, the curriculum must be tailored to fit the needs of each child based on an assessment of that child's characteristics, needs, and interests.

ADAPTING AND SELECTING MODELS

The construction of a curriculum that incorporates the content, process, product, and learning environment modifications recommended for gifted children requires an approach in which educators provide specific strategies for accomplishing these changes. Several factors must be considered before selecting an approach: the setting (the school, the school district, and the community), the students, the teachers, and the model(s) to be emphasized.

In other words, a match must exist between what a model can offer and what is needed in a specific program for gifted students.

Assessing the Situation

The first step in adapting or selecting models is to assess factors related to the setting, teacher, and students that would influence the choice of a model or models. One of the situational factors, for example, is the kind of grouping arrangement used for the program, such as a regular classroom with a consulting teacher, resource rooms in each building, resource centers across the district, or a self-contained classroom. Another factor is the attitude of regular classroom teachers toward the program. If a particular approach requires the cooperation of teachers who will not cooperate, a different choice must be made. Factors related to the students would include their common characteristics (average) and the range of those characteristics (differences), their ages, areas of giftedness, achievement levels, interests, background experiences, and learning style preferences.

Research on the effectiveness of educational approaches shows that the single most important variable in determining success is the teacher. If the teacher does not have the skills necessary to implement the approach and does not believe in its value, the program cannot be effective. Teacher factors to consider can be separated into three groups: philosophical, personal, and professional. Philosophical characteristics include those pertinent to education for the gifted, its purpose and implementation. Personal traits include creativity, intelligence, motivation, and self-confidence. Professional characteristics include the skills possessed by the teacher, educational background, and past experiences. Factors related to the model include all items discussed at the beginning of this chapter. All these factors must be considered carefully when selecting or adapting a teaching-learning model (or models) for a program.

Assessing the Model

The next step in choosing an approach is to assess the appropriateness of the model based on the situational factors identified. Five general criteria have been selected for evaluating a model: (a) appropriateness to the situation, (b) comprehensiveness as a framework for curriculum development for the gifted, (c) flexibility or adaptability, (d) practicality, and (e) validity. Others could be added. Some specific questions can be asked during this assessment:

Appropriateness to the Situation

- To what extent do the purposes of the model match the needs of the students, the school philosophy, parental values, and teacher characteristics?

- To what extent do the underlying assumptions made in the model fit reality? (For example, if assumptions are made about the characteristics of gifted students, are these characteristics true of students in the program?)

Comprehensiveness

- What content modifications are provided by the model?
- What process modifications are provided by the model?
- What product modifications are provided by the model?
- What learning environment modifications are provided by the model?
- Which of the modifications not actually provided by the model easily could be generated by or integrated into the approach?

Flexibility or Adaptability

- How easily can the model be adapted to all content areas or subject matter covered in the program?
- How easily can the model be adapted to the present administrative structure of the school and program?
- How easily can the model be combined with other models to provide a comprehensive program?
- How easily can the model be used with the age levels of children served by the program?
- How adaptable is the model to individual differences among gifted children?

Practicality

- What materials or services are available to implement the approach?
- What is the cost of the materials or services?
- How much training of the special teacher or regular classroom teacher is needed to implement the model effectively?
- How easily could the approach be implemented in the present situation?

Validity

- Was the model developed using appropriate methods?

- How much research is available to show its effectiveness as an educational approach?

- How much research is available to show its effectiveness as an approach for use with gifted students?

- How much evidence is available to indicate that the model is internally valid (or structurally sound)?

- Is the approach defensible as a qualitatively different program for gifted students?

Two worksheets have been designed to facilitate the process of assessing models. On the first worksheet, the criteria and questions are listed on one side, and the models are listed at the top (see Figure 1.1). Using the system of 1 = poor, 2 = average, and 3 = excellent, a rating should be assigned to each model on each criterion. Next, the ratings for each should be totaled to indicate the model's overall appropriateness.

The second worksheet provides a structure for assessing the criterion of comprehensiveness (see Figure 1.2). On this worksheet, the curricular modifications presented earlier are listed as criteria, and the models are listed at the top. A check mark is placed in the column and row if the modification is made; the column is left blank if it is not. The totals for each column can be used to indicate the comprehensiveness of the model. Information from this worksheet also can be used to examine the different models and determine how they complement each other.

Combining the Models

The final step in the process of adaptation/selection is to decide whether one approach can serve as the only model used or whether the models should be combined, used together, or used in different situations.

The models presented in this book are different in their purposes as well as in the ways content, process, product, and learning environment modifications appropriate for the gifted are directly addressed. For example, Bruner's approach modifies content by suggesting that it be organized around basic concepts. His approach also addresses the process of discovery, although its major modifications are in the area of content. The *Cognitive* and *Affective Taxonomies,* on the other hand, provide modifications only in the process area and only in one aspect of process, the development of higher levels of thinking.

Guilford's theory provides a unifying model for changes in content, process, and product as dimensions of a learning task. However, it does not make all the suggested curricular changes in any of the areas. Thus, even though this theory is more comprehensive than many others, it alone would not provide a complete curriculum.

Assign a rating to each model on each criterion using the following code:
1 = Poor   2 = Average   3 = Excellent

Criteria and Questions	Betts	Bloom	Bruner	Guilford	Kohlberg	Krathwohl	Parnes	Renzulli	Sharan	Taba	Taylor	Treffinger	Williams	Total	Comments
Appropriateness to the Situation															
To what extent do the model's purposes match needs of students, school philosophy, parental values, and teacher characteristics?															
To what extent do underlying assumptions made in the model fit the situational reality?															
Flexibility/Adaptability															
How easily can the model be adapted to all content areas or subjects covered in the program?															
How easily can the model be adapted to present administrative structure of school and program?															
How easily can the model be combined with others to provide a comprehensive program?															
How easily can the model be used with the age levels of children served by the program?															
How easily can the model be adapted to individual differences among gifted children?															

(continues)

Figure 1.1. Worksheet for overall curriculum design. Adapted from *Curriculum Development for the Gifted* by J. Maker, 1982, Austin, TX: PRO-ED. Adapted with permission.

Assign a rating to each model on each criterion using the following code:

1 = Poor 2 = Average 3 = Excellent

Criteria and Questions	Betts	Bloom	Bruner	Guilford	Kohlberg	Krathwohl	Parnes	Renzulli	Sharan	Taba	Taylor	Treffinger	Williams	Total	Comments
Practicality															
What materials and services are available to implement the model?															
What is the cost of these materials or services?															
How much staff development is needed for the special teacher or regular classroom teacher to implement the model effectively?															
How easily could the approach be implemented in the present situation?															
Validity															
Was the model developed using appropriate methods?															
What research is available to show its effectiveness as an educational approach?															
What research is available to show its effectiveness as an approach to education of gifted children?															

(*continues*)

Figure 1.1. *Continued*

Assign a rating to each model on each criterion using the following code:

1 = Poor   2 = Average   3 = Excellent

Criteria and Questions	Betts	Bloom	Bruner	Guilford	Kohlberg	Krathwohl	Parnes	Renzulli	Sharan	Taba	Taylor	Treffinger	Williams	Total	Comments
Validity (cont.)															
How much evidence is available to indicate that the model is internally valid or structurally sound?															
How defensible is the approach as a qualitatively different program for gifted students?															
TOTALS															

Figure 1.1. *Continued*

Rate each model on each criterion by placing a ✓ in the column if the modification is made in the model. If modification is not made, leave the space blank.

Curricular Modifications	Betts	Bloom	Bruner	Guilford	Kohlberg	Krathwohl	Parnes	Renzulli	Sharan	Taba	Taylor	Treffinger	Williams	Total	Comments
CONTENT															
1. Abstractness															
2. Complexity															
3. Variety															
4. Organization for Learning Value															
5. Study of People															
6. Study of Methods															
PROCESS															
7. Higher Level Thought															
8. Open-endedness															
9. Discovery															
10. Evidence of Reasoning															
11. Freedom of Choice															
12. Group Interaction															
13. Pacing															
14. Variety															

(continues)

Figure 1.2. Worksheet for overall curriculum design. Adapted from *Curriculum Development for the Gifted* by J. Maker, 1982, Austin, TX: PRO-ED. Adapted with permission.

Rate each model on each criterion by placing a ✓ in the column if the modification is made in the model. If modification is not made, leave the space blank.

Curricular Modifications		Betts	Bloom	Bruner	Guilford	Kohlberg	Krathwohl	Parnes	Renzulli	Sharan	Taba	Taylor	Treffinger	Williams	Total	Comments
PRODUCT	15. Result from Real Problems															
	16. Addressed to Real Audiences															
	17. Transformation															
	18. Variety															
	19. Self-Selected Format															
	20. Appropriate Evaluation															
LEARNING ENVIRONMENT	21. Learner Centered															
	22. Encourages Independence															
	23. Openness															
	24. Accepting															
	25. Complexity															
	26. Varied Groupings															
	27. Flexibility															
	28. High Mobility															
	TOTALS															

Figure 1.2.   *Continued*

The same is true of Renzulli's *Triad*. Although it can provide a comprehensive framework for an overall approach, other process models need to be added, such as Bloom, Taba, Taylor, Kohlberg, and Krathwohl, to guide the development of Type II activities. Treffinger's developmental approach to self-direction or Betts's *Autonomous Learner Model* can provide the teacher with methods for moving students toward the development of their Type III investigations.

Some similarities also should be noted. Most of the models modify process, and few consider content changes at all. In fact, many of them make similar process changes because of their emphasis on higher levels of thinking and on development of creative or divergent thought processes. Most also emphasize the thinking skill of evaluation (for example, Bloom, Krathwohl, Guilford, and Parnes) or decision making (for example, Taylor).

If these models are combined or used separately, their similarities and differences must be considered. In other words, they must be combined so that the total curriculum is comprehensive, but the degree of overlap also should be considered. Placing undue emphasis on process skills would not be desirable simply because more methods and materials are available for use.

Chapter 2

George Betts: The Autonomous Learner Model

P rograms for highly able students in secondary schools, when they do exist, frequently consist of advanced placement classes, acceleration in a specific content area, or concurrent enrollment in college classes. Advanced placement, accelerated content, and concurrent enrollment do have a place in the education of gifted students but offer few opportunities for young people to develop creative potential. Nor do these options, with a primary focus on content learning, foster independent learning abilities, creativity, or self-awareness.

Renzulli and Gable (1976) found that independent study or self-directed learning is highly successful with gifted students; however, not all gifted students have the self-regulatory strategies essential for independent study (Zimmerman & Martinez-Ponz, 1990). Goal setting, planning strategies to reach the goal, and self-evaluation of progress and quality of work are essential to the success of self-directed learning, but few gifted students reported using those strategies. When gifted students are taught how to use strategies, however, they learn to use the strategies more efficiently and also are able to transfer them to new tasks (Scruggs & Mastropieri, 1988). The implication, from a review of research on self-regulatory strategies and metacognitive development, is that designing activities that help gifted students develop self-regulatory learning strategies is an effective and productive way to help highly able students. Teaching self-regulatory strategies may be particularly important to "underachieving gifted" students who are not living up to their potential (Risemberg & Zimmerman, 1992).

One major goal of differentiated education for the gifted is to help highly able students realize their potential and experience a sense of personal fulfillment or self-actualization (Feldhusen & Treffinger, 1980). Another goal is to help these students understand their uniqueness (develop intrapersonal awareness) and cultivate the interpersonal skills needed to work effectively with others. The *Autonomous Learner Model* (ALM) was designed to meet the diverse social–emotional and cognitive needs of potentially gifted students and to help them to develop strategies and attitudes necessary for independent learning. Autonomous learners are those individuals who have the ability to be responsible for development, implementation, and evaluation of their own learning (Betts, 1985). Becoming an autonomous learner is not an easy task; self-direction requires a new orientation to learning, development of cognitive and interpersonal skills, self-awareness, and formative experience in designing and conducting independent projects. As students develop needed skills, concepts, and attitudes through class activities, they also explore topics, information sources, careers, and other resources that might stimulate ideas for further research. Changing orientation and attitudes to move away from highly structured, traditional classes toward autonomous learning is an incremental process that takes time, energy, goals, patience, and support. The ALM is an ongoing program with a minimum 3-year commitment. While students are enrolled in ALM, they also are taking required and elective courses in areas of interest. When the model is implemented in elementary schools, the recommendation is that students attend a resource room program at least 2 half-days per week. ALM students participate in curriculum decisions and evaluate effectiveness of the model. Student ownership is an important element of the program.

Betts and Knapp (1981) define an autonomous learner as one who solves problems or develops new ideas through a combination of divergent and convergent thinking and who functions with minimal external guidance in selected areas of endeavor. With that definition as a guide, the *Autonomous Learner Model* was designed to help students meet eight emotional, social, and cognitive goals (Betts, 1985, p. 4).

1. Develop more positive self-concepts.

2. Comprehend their own giftedness in relationship to self and society.

3. Develop the skills appropriate to interact effectively with peers, siblings, parents, and other adults.

4. Increase their knowledge in a variety of subject areas.

5. Develop their thinking, decision-making, and problem-solving skills.

6. Participate in activities selected to facilitate and integrate the cognitive, emotional, and social development of the individual.

7. Demonstrate responsibility for their own learning in and out of the school setting.

8. Ultimately become responsible, creative, independent learners.

ASSUMPTIONS UNDERLYING THE MODEL

A program for gifted students must be multifaceted. "All five dimensions of the *Autonomous Learner Model* [orientation, individual development, enrichment activities, seminars, and in-depth study] are essential for the development of an individual autonomous learner. If we look at the environment, either in or out of school, we see all five dimensions being experienced by the individual who has become an autonomous learner" (Betts, 1985, p. 3). The ALM is designed explicitly to integrate the emotional, social, and cognitive aspects of learning. One underlying assumption is that as these needs are met, gifted students gradually will become autonomous learners able to plan, implement, and evaluate their own learning. "You are able to continue into the unknown for your security is carried within" (Betts, 1985, p. 31). A related assumption is that a high level of support is necessary in the early stages of the developmental process. Becoming an autonomous learner takes time, relevant experiences, effort, and support.

The goal of education must be to facilitate change and learning. "The only man who is educated is the man who has learned how to learn; the man who has learned how to adapt and change; the man who has realized that no knowledge is secure, that only the process of seeking knowledge gives a basis for security" (Rogers, 1983, p. 120).

About Teaching

The teacher/facilitator must be dedicated to the goal of helping students become autonomous learners. "Besides being a dispenser of knowledge, a teacher must become a facilitator of the learning process. A teacher facilitates, guides, questions, and supports, but does not direct, specify, or restrict" (Betts, 1985, p. 28).

As many activities in this model are designed to help students develop self-understanding and interpersonal skills, an implied assumption is that the teacher/facilitator also needs some counseling expertise, a repertoire of group-building strategies, and discussion skills. The teacher/facilitator must provide activities to help students develop skills and attitudes needed to work effectively in small groups. In addition, the teacher/facilitator must have excellent organizational and interpersonal skills, a broad knowledge of community resources, and the ability to recruit appropriate guest speakers and mentors. Mentors are essential to the pursuit of in-depth studies.

Finally, the teacher also must be an autonomous learner. "The *Autonomous Learner Model* should not be used directly as it is presented. Each teacher/facilitator should review the model, look at the situation of the school, review the characteristics and needs of the students and then begin to develop a plan of action" (Betts, 1985, p. 4).

About Learning

Betts (1985) emphasizes the importance of experience as a catalyst to learning. "Learning is a process of discovering what is important, what is available, and what can be created" (p. 42). Learning is not merely acquisition of prescribed information; it involves a transformation of information and experience. "Learning incorporates the learner, the process, and the materials into new and unique products" (p. 43).

Developing products or ideas new and unique to the learner is a necessary, but not sufficient, goal for autonomous learners. Real audiences are essential when gifted students have created new products. "Once something is learned there is a need to share and present the new information . . . with the appropriate audience" (p. 52).

Developing cognitive skills alone does not prepare a student to become productive or self-actualizing. Social and emotional skills also must be learned. Processes to enhance reflective thinking, self-awareness, metacognition, and interpersonal skills must be a part of an autonomous learner's repertoire of skills. The ability to work as a member of a group is essential. "You cannot control how the world handles you, but you can control how you handle your world" (p. 17).

Students must be involved in guided, open-ended learning experiences prior to initiating an in-depth independent study. Teacher/facilitators must model the attitudes and skills needed for independent study and teach explicitly strategies such as planning, decision making, organization, analysis, and synthesis. "Learners incorporate the useful ideas of teaching into their own approach to learning. . . . An internal frame of reference helps learners in their quest for knowledge and understanding" (p. 65).

Learners must be able to investigate real-world problems and work toward real solutions. "In-depth studies are life-like for they provide an opportunity to go beyond the usual time and space restrictions of most school activities" (p. 55).

Learners need opportunities to explore new ideas and gain awareness of the broad scope of possibilities for investigations and creative production. "Seventy percent of a learner's time can be spent in In-Depth Study, but the remaining thirty percent needs to be involved with the development of new areas of exploration, new skills, concepts and attitudes, and the development of activities which further develop the autonomy of the individual" (p. 56).

About Characteristics and Teaching of the Gifted

The natural curiosity of gifted, creative, and talented children is a powerful motivational factor. Gifted students want to know, explore, and become active learners. Learning experiences should be interactive, challenging, and real. Potentially gifted and creative individuals need interactive experiences to learn essential self-regulation strategies such as self-monitoring, goal setting, and decision making. Emphasis must be placed on the development of the skills, concepts, and attitudes that will enable gifted students to become lifelong learners.

Curriculum must be based on the interests of the gifted students. "Prescribed content" is needlessly limiting to students who possess skills and strategies for learning different from those of average students. Many highly able children are frustrated by a surface approach to knowledge and need the freedom and support to go "in-depth" in their learning. Participation in planning and evaluating learning experiences and curriculum is important to the success of a program for gifted students. "Gifted students know what they need to help them meet their cognitive, emotional, and social challenges. Ask them, listen closely, and the program will become appropriate" (p. 23). Learning in the company of highly able peers facilitates social, emotional, and cognitive development. Gifted and talented students also benefit from working together. Interaction with intellectual peers is a powerful stimulus to personal growth.

ELEMENTS/PARTS

The model has five dimensions that contribute to emotional, social, and cognitive development and guide a student toward autonomous learning.

Orientation

The first dimension is designed to provide students with opportunities to build a basic understanding of the concept of giftedness, their own interests and abilities, and the *Autonomous Learner Model,* and to learn about the opportunities and responsibilities they will have as members of the program. This dimension has four components: (a) Understanding Giftedness, (b) Group Building, (c) Self-Understanding, and (d) Program Opportunities and Responsibilities.

Understanding Giftedness

Few gifted students have had opportunities to develop understanding of the concepts of *giftedness, intelligence, creativity, talent,* or *potential.* Experiences, activities, readings, discussions, and interviews with gifted and creative

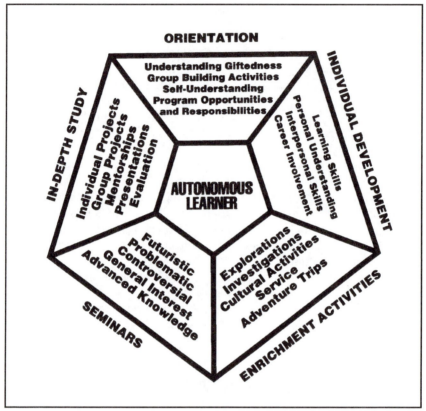

Figure 2.1. Dimensions of the Autonomous Learner Model. From *The Autonomous Learner Model for the Gifted and Talented* by G. Betts, 1985, Greeley, CO: Autonomous Learning Publications and Specialists. Reprinted with permission.

individuals are a major part of this component of the Orientation Dimension. Students do research on gifted persons, role-play an eminent individual in simulations, listen to speakers who are gifted, and conduct interviews with gifted persons in the community to broaden and deepen their understanding of their own giftedness.

Group Building Activities

Students explore the dynamics of group process, apply group processes in their environments, and participate in group building activities to learn more about themselves and others. The functions of groups, roles necessary for successful group interaction, and the importance of learning to work together are taught through classroom activities and special projects. Students have opportunities to make connections with other gifted and talented students and become increasingly comfortable with and supportive of each other as a result of group building activities.

Self-Understanding

Students explore their interests and aptitudes, review the information and procedures used to select them for the ALM class, do a learning style inventory, discuss "nurturing" and "toxic" behaviors to become more aware of how their actions affect others, and brainstorm the different roles of "student" and "learner." As a result of this involvement, students begin to develop concepts and ideas about themselves, their unique abilities, and their potential as learners.

Program Opportunities and Responsibilities

Students learn about the goals, objectives, dimensions, and activities of the model. Expectations of participants in the program are delineated, and students are provided with necessary information to help them make thoughtful decisions about their future educational program. As a culminating activity, each student develops a Student/Learner Growth Plan as a guide to further participation in the model.

Individual Development

Dimension Two of the model is designed to provide activities and experiences to facilitate development of many, varied learning skills, greater personal understanding, improved interpersonal skills, and career exploration.

Learning Skills

A variety of cognitive skills (e.g., creative thinking, organizational strategies, research methods, higher level thinking) are essential for students to become autonomous learners. Students learn the importance of the skills and participate in activities designed for students to practice the skills, acquire the concepts, and develop the attitudes that are featured in this component.

Personal Understanding

This component is a continuation of the self-understanding initiated in the first dimension of the model. Through discussions, reflection, and personal analysis activities, students learn more about themselves and their feelings.

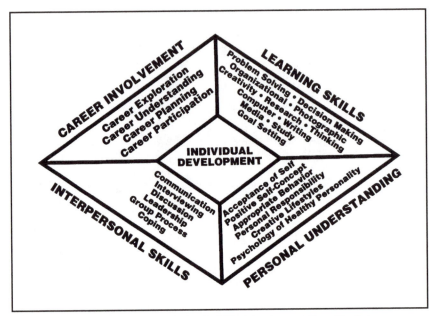

Figure 2.2.   Components of Dimension Two: Individual development. From *The Autonomous Learner Model for the Gifted and Talented* by G. Betts, 1985, Greeley, CO: Autonomous Learning Publications and Specialists. Reprinted with permission.

Interpersonal Skills

Appropriate interaction skills are identified, and students have opportunities to improve skills in communication, discussion, group processes, and interviewing others. Effects on the group of appropriate and inappropriate behaviors are examined as students are involved in role-playing, group discussions, and group activities. Participation in an optional "coping group" allows students to discuss feelings and frustrations with peers and share ideas or receive support for dealing with problems.

Career Involvement

Students explore questions such as "What do I want to do with my life?" After presentation of information about a broad range of possible careers, students choose specific careers to investigate, interview individuals in the selected career fields, and intern with an adult in a chosen career. This component of the model often helps students develop interests and identify possible mentors for in-depth studies.

Enrichment Activities

The main goal of Dimension Three is to help students discover what is "out there" to be learned. Students are now becoming "student/learners" and are capable of increased responsibilities in the selection and direction of their own learning experiences. Components of this dimension are Explorations, Investigations, Cultural Activities, Service, and Adventure Trips.

Explorations

Explorations are opportunities for student learners to discover what resources are available in the community, learn how to retrieve various kinds of information, develop areas of interest, and make contacts with individuals, businesses, and agencies with expertise in an area of interest. They may visit information centers such as university and public libraries, search online computer databases, and visit museums. They also may identify commercial establishments such as media production centers, graphics production companies, art studios, and advertising agencies with resource persons who are willing to share their knowledge or work with a student intern. Nature conservancy areas, astronomical observatories, botanical gardens, zoos, and similar facilities also can be sources of information. The scope of a specific exploration is dependent on the resources of the community and the amount of time students have to discover what is available.

Investigations

An investigation is a mini in-depth study about a topic selected by the student/learner. Each participant prepares an informal proposal outlining the topic and purpose of the investigation, activities planned, resources needed, a time line, and a plan for final presentation. The scope of a mini in-depth study usually is more limited than an in-depth study. In addition, the student/learner is serving an apprenticeship in the process of planning, implementing, and evaluating her or his own work. Most student/learners must complete several investigations before they are ready to begin an in-depth study.

Cultural Activities

Through this component, individuals become more aware of the variety of cultural opportunities available to them in the community. They visit museums, attend plays and concerts, visit art shows, and participate in seminars. Any event that involves a worthwhile new experience for a student may qualify as a cultural activity. Individuals or small groups of students select events they propose to attend and, with the approval of the teacher/facilitator, also make arrangements for "behind the scenes" visits to learn how the events are planned and organized.

Service

Participation in an activity that benefits the community is intrinsic to developing an understanding of oneself as a contributing member of a larger society. Each student/learner in the program completes a service unit every year. Students select their own activities and may work with agencies such as the Red Cross or the Salvation Army, in hospitals, with elderly citizens, or one-to-one with an individual who has special needs. The experience is a practical application of interpersonal skills that builds an appreciation of the rewards of sharing and satisfaction gained by unselfish giving.

Adventure Trips

Students may elect to participate in a yearlong project to plan, organize, finance, and implement trips that promote growth in cognitive, emotional, social, and/or physical skills. Destinations and topics of study are selected by participants and may include excursions to large cities, national parks, wilderness areas, or other places that offer intellectual, physical, social, and emotional challenges.

Seminars

In Dimension Four of the model, emphasis is on "production" of new knowledge. Individuals are evolving into self-directed learners with greater opportunities and greater responsibilities. In small groups, learners select and research a topic selected from one of five areas: futuristic, controversial, problematic, general interest, and advanced knowledge. Then they plan and implement a three-phased seminar that includes presentation of factual information, group discussion or activity, and the concept of closure. Learners participate in self-evaluation, discuss the concept of a seminar, evaluate the effectiveness of the presentation, and discuss ways to enhance future seminars.

In-Depth Study

Dimension Five is the most challenging in the ALM. Students have become learners with a repertoire of skills, abilities, and attitudes necessary to conduct independent investigations. Individually or in small groups, learners develop an In-Depth Study Contract; they identify the topic of the study, objectives, activities, questions to be investigated, a list of resources needed, a time line, and a plan for interim and final presentations. An in-depth study ranges in length from 2 months to 2½ years; learners are more than 90% responsible for their own studies. Support from teacher/facilitators and mentors is still important, however. A sample In-Depth Study Contract for an advanced autonomous learner with an interest in genetic research is given in Exhibit 2.1.

EXHIBIT 2.1.   Sample Contract for In-Depth Study

Name _Rachel McCarthy_   Date _January 27, 1994_

Title_ Gene therapy for muscular dystrophy: Promise and problems_

Brief description: *Gene therapy may promise a cure for muscular dystrophy in humans within a decade. Laboratory research with mice has proved successful, but many problems must be solved before the procedure can be tested in human subjects. This study will focus on the work of Dr. Jeffrey Chamberlain and his research associates at the University of Michigan, investigate the procedures used in gene therapy, and identify the problems and the promise of gene therapy.*

Rationale and purpose: *Many serious diseases are of genetic origin and presently have no cure. One of these diseases, muscular dystrophy, afflicts thousands of boys, including my cousin. Recent developments in genetic research hold promise of curing this disease through genetic manipulation. As my career goal is to become a research geneticist and participate in gene therapy research, I believe a study of the principles and practices of genetic therapy, particularly those related to muscular dystrophy, will further my goals of understanding the procedures, potential benefits, and controversies surrounding gene therapy.*

Questions to be answered:
1. *How does a defective gene cause muscular dystrophy?*
2. *What are the differences between types of muscular dystrophy?*
3. *How can a defective gene be "cured"? Through what processes is DNA altered?*
4. *What practical problems must be solved before Dr. Chamberlain's research can be applied to human subjects?*
5. *What ethical problems must be solved in order to use gene therapy with human subjects?*

(continues)

EXHIBIT 2.1. *Continued*

Objectives to be obtained:
1. *Expand my own knowledge of the genetic causes of muscular dystrophy and the principles, procedures, and problems associated with gene therapy.*
2. *Gain "frontier" experience in my chosen career field.*
3. *Prepare a television documentary for presentation to the MDA and others.*

Detailed activities:
1. *Intensive research at the Health Sciences Library.*
2. *Research internship with Dr. John Snow, a former graduate assistant of Dr. Chamberlain's who is now pursuing postdoctoral research at the university.*
3. *Consultation with Eva James, research coordinator of the Muscular Dystrophy Association.*
4. *Attendance at a symposium on gene therapy at the university and reading of symposium proceedings.*
5. *Attendance at a series of discussions of ethical issues associated with medical breakthroughs.*
6. *Synthesis of research results and my personal reflections.*

Time line (per grading period):
1. *Emphasis on research in the library and through Med-line and other databases to expand my background knowledge of the techniques and procedures of gene therapy.*
2–3. *Internship, including symposia and seminars. Conducting interviews.*
4. *Writing final draft of technical report and assisting in editing documentary. Preparation of presentation.*

Resources: *My content advisor is Jerry Graves, science specialist. My mentor will be Dr. John Snow. Facilities will include the University Health Sciences Library and Dr. Snow's research lab. Research materials will be obtained through the library, on-line database searches, the Muscular Dystrophy Association, and in Dr. Snow's laboratory.*

Final product: *Ben Silver and I will collaborate to produce a television documentary; in addition, I will write a technical report detailing the results of my research.*

(continues)

EXHIBIT 2.1. *Continued*

Plans for final presentation: *The television documentary will be presented to an audience of fellow classmates, representatives of the Muscular Dystrophy Association, and other interested persons. A copy of the documentary will be presented to MDA for their resource center. My primary responsibilities are (1) preparation of the script, conducting interviews with representative individuals who have muscular dystrophy, their parents, physicians, researchers, and medical ethicists; and (2) making arrangements for computer-generated graphics and electron microscope images to be included in the documentary. Location and dates of the presentation will be determined with members of the science seminar group during third term.*

Evaluation criteria (per grading period):

1. *Progress reports, submitted at the end of first and second trimesters, show efficient use of time and participation in all planned activities.*

2. *Drafts of technical report show growth in knowledge, use of process, and writing skill.*

3. *Evaluations by Dr. Snow indicate growing skill in use of laboratory procedures.*

Signatures:

Learner _____

Teacher/Facilitator_____

Content Specialist _____

Mentor _____

Final date of completed contract: May 10, 1995.

Basic Principles of the Model

The implementation of the *Autonomous Learner Model* is guided by the following basic principles (Betts, 1985, p. 6):

- Emphasis is placed on the emotional, social, and cognitive development of the individual.

- Self-esteem is encouraged and facilitated.

- Social skills are developed and enhanced.

- Curriculum is based on the interests of the students.

- Students are involved in guided open-ended learning experiences.

- Responsibility for learning is placed on the student/learners.

- Students need experiences which allow them to become life-long learners.

- Teachers are facilitators of the learning process as well as dispensers of knowledge.

- Learning is cross-disciplinary.

- Students develop a wider area [range] of basic skills.

- Higher-level thinking skills are integrated, reinforced, and demonstrated in the learning process.

- Students develop appropriate questioning techniques.

- Varied responses are sought from the students.

- Content topics are broad based, with emphasis on major themes, problems, issues, and ideas.

- Time and space restrictions for schools are removed for in-depth learning.

- Students develop new and unique products.

- Students use various resources in the development of in-depth studies.

- Cultural activities provide new and unique growing experiences.

- Seminars and In-Depth Studies are an essential component of the learning process.

- Mentorships provide adult role-modeling, active support, and individual instruction and facilitation.

- Completion and presentations of In-Depth Studies are integral in the learning process.

IMPLEMENTING THE MODEL

The ALM is designed to be implemented as a one-period-per-day elective class in secondary schools; a 3-year commitment from gifted students is recommended. During the first year of implementation, students continue to take regular content and elective classes for the remainder of the day. In subsequent years, a learner, with the cooperation of a teacher/facilitator, a content-area teacher, and community resource persons or mentors, may develop In-Depth Study Expansions for one or more content areas. If an elective class is not feasible, ALM may be integrated into a content course (e.g., language arts, science, social studies); the regular curriculum is compacted into 2 or 3 days per week and curriculum for the autonomous learning is implemented in the other days. When the teacher/facilitator and individual student believe the necessary level of thinking/learning and intrapersonal skills have been developed, an individual Personal Growth Plan is prepared by the student with the cooperation of teacher/facilitators, content teachers, counselor (if available), and parents. The Personal Growth Plan provides direction for learning growth in the next 2 or 3 years and identifies what activities/investigations (in school and community) are planned, how the student will be involved, and where the activities/investigations will take place. Figure 2.3 illustrates the suggested time line for implementation of the *Autonomous Learner Model.*

At the elementary level, the ALM can be implemented in a resource room program in which students are involved for a minimum of 2 half-days per week. The suggested scope and sequence emphasizes Dimensions One,

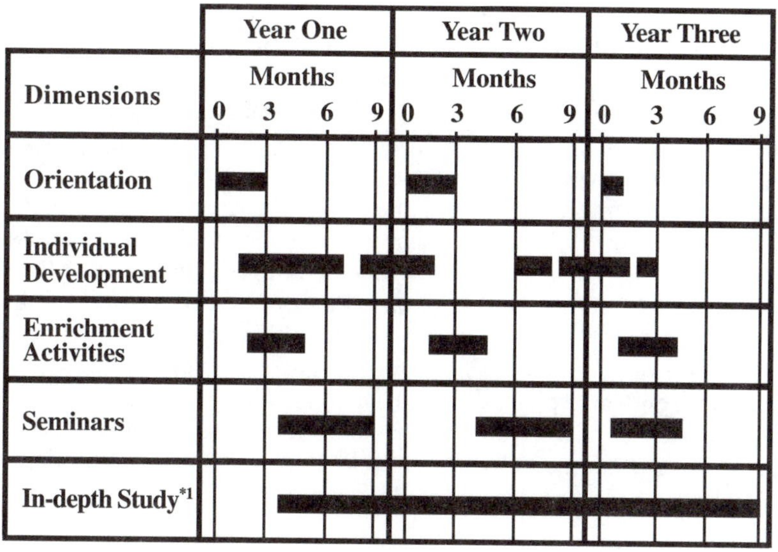

*Some students may begin in-depth study immediately.
[1]After the third year, the majority of time would be concentrated on in-depth study expansion and out-of-school experiences.

Figure 2.3. Suggested time line for implementing the model. From *The Autonomous Learner Model for the Gifted and Talented* by G. Betts, 1985, Greeley, CO: Autonomous Learning Publications and Specialists. Reprinted with permission.

Two, and Three in elementary schools. Students in Grades 4 and 5 also are introduced to Dimensions Four and Five, but few students are ready to develop seminars and in-depth study prior to Grade 6. Betts does recommend, however, that if students are ready (intellectually, socially, and emotionally) for involvement in an in-depth study, they should not be restricted by expectations of what is age appropriate or "best" for the gifted.

Betts suggests areas of emphasis in each dimension. Table 2.1 shows examples of possible activities within each component of the ALM.

MODIFYING THE APPROACH

The *Autonomous Learner Model* provides a comprehensive framework for curriculum modification appropriate for gifted students in all areas. As with the Renzulli *Enrichment Triad Model,* the content, process, product, and learning environment modifications suggested by Maker (1982) are incorporated within the framework.

Content Changes

The content modifications of abstractness, complexity, variety, and study of people are incorporated into recommended activities and principles. The modification of organization for learning value is suggested in the principle that content topics are broad based with emphasis on major themes, issues, and ideas. One recommendation to strengthen this component is to organize guided investigations and enrichment activities around abstract concepts and generalizations, as recommended by Bruner (see Chapter 4), to facilitate transfer of learning and cognitive development. Recommended student activities also include numerous opportunities to develop general methods of inquiry. A comparison of methods of inquiry used in various disciplines would complement the enrichment activities and better prepare learners for in-depth studies. When students are learning to conduct investigations and present seminars, the *Group Investigations* model (see Chapter 7) provides an excellent way to structure content and help students develop essential cognitive and social skills needed for group collaboration.

Process Changes

Process modifications stressed in ALM include higher levels of thinking, open-endedness, freedom of choice, discovery, group interaction, pacing, and variety. As evidence of reasoning is not explicitly stressed in ALM, inclusion of Taba questioning strategies among the thinking skills developed in Dimension Two would incorporate this important element into the model very easily.

TABLE 2.1. Summary of Teacher and Student Activities and Roles in the Autonomous Learner Model

Step, Type, or Level of Thinking	Student		Teacher	
	Role	Sample Activities	Role	Sample Activities
Understanding Giftedness	Active participant Observer Inquirer Synthesizer	Do biographical research on a gifted individual. Role-play the gifted individual at a news conference or open house. Read and discuss books and selected articles about gifted people. Brainstorm questions for guests. Interview gifted people in the community. Do an informal survey on attitudes about giftedness or creativity. Participate in discussions. Develop own definition of giftedness.	Resource Facilitator	Plan experiences to put students in contact with gifted individuals. Encourage students to visit the library and use a variety of resources to research aspects of giftedness. Arrange visits, field trips, guests. Model interviewing skills and provide a resource list of at least 25 gifted persons in the community that students can interview. Plan group and individual exercises to develop survey questions and skills.
Group Building	Active participant Friend Interviewer Planner	Conduct a personal interview with a fellow student. Nurture a "secret" friend. Participate in a "Starve your vulture" campaign to build self-esteem. Use Taba conflict resolution strategy to resolve interpersonal problems. Participate in group discussions about your own and others' feelings and perceptions about being part of the group. Use Creative Problem Solving to design and implement a project to benefit the group, school, or community.	Resource Facilitator Planner	Demonstrate and help students to analyze varied group process skills. Model esteem-building behaviors. Plan individual and group activities to develop thinking/feeling processes students can use for varied purposes. Plan process experiences to meet both individual and group needs. Ask thought-provoking questions. Model active listening and communication skills. Assist students in the development of plans and acquisition of resources for special projects.

(continues)

TABLE 2.1. *Continued*

Step, Type, or Level of Thinking	Student		Teacher	
	Role	*Sample Activities*	*Role*	*Sample Activities*
Self-understanding	Active participant Self-analyzer Synthesizer	Review identification information and procedures for selection to the program for the gifted. Analyze and discuss "nourishing" and "toxic" behaviors and how they affect oneself and other people. Do a learning style inventory. Brainstorm differences between role of a student and role of a learner. Keep a journal of personal thoughts. Design and implement a project to synthesize new self-understandings.	Facilitator Resource Discussion leader	Plan and implement activities to assist students in understanding identification procedures. Plan group and individual exercises to increase students' awareness of behavior patterns and effects. Provide resources for inventories of learning styles and interests. Share results of inventories with individual students. Facilitate a discussion of autonomous learner characteristics.

(continues)

TABLE 2.1. *Continued*

Step, Type, or Level of Thinking	Student		Teacher	
	Role	Sample Activities	Role	Sample Activities
Program Opportunities and Responsibilities	Active participant Observer Inquirer Presenter Planner	Learn the dimensions, structure, and goals of the ALM. Analyze presentations of various speakers and own abilities to discover topics of interest for seminars and/or in-depth studies. Individually or in small groups, explore libraries and community resources for possible seminar and in-depth study topics. Prepare and present an oral report to classmates on possible topics. Develop a "personal growth plan" that includes activities, resource people, in-school participation, and out-of-school participation. Include skills, concepts, and attitudes necessary to become a lifelong learner.	Researcher Planner Presenter Facilitator Resource	Do a "program search" to identify all activities available for gifted students in the school and community. Identify potential advisors, resource people, and possible mentors. Develop a presentation on *Autonomous Learner Model* for students and all interested persons. Implement individual and group activities to assist students in development of skills and attitudes needed for lifelong learning. Plan guest speakers, discussions, and exploratory experiences to put students in contact with topics of interest and possible mentors. Provide information and a format to assist students in the development of individual Student Growth Plans.
Learning Skills	Active participant	Participate in thinking skill activities. Do research skill activities. Develop goal setting and organizational skills. Develop skills in computer use. Develop skills in photography and/or multimedia production. Do activities designed to improve writing and communication skills.	Facilitator Trainer Resource	Guide varied problem-solving, creativity, and thinking activities to develop skills students can use in investigations. Provide activities to develop goal-setting, decision-making, research, and organization skills. Facilitate activities to help students develop skills in writing, the use of computers, photography, and media production.

(continues)

TABLE 2.1. Continued

Step, Type, or Level of Thinking	Student		Teacher	
	Role	Sample Activities	Role	Sample Activities
Personal Understanding	Active participant Reflective thinker Inquirer	Periodically complete open-ended questions from *Journeys Into Self* exercises in self-exploration. Participate in role-playing simulations and subsequent discussions of behaviors. Explore creative lifestyles and the advantages and disadvantages of varied occupations. Synthesize all information/ideas developed in these activities.	Facilitator Resource	Provide structured self-exploration exercises to students three or four times yearly. Conference with students to discuss similarities and differences in responses to the same questions. Plan and implement activities in which students role-play appropriate and inappropriate behaviors; facilitate discussion of experiences.
Interpersonal Skills	Active participant	Participate in activities designed to develop skills in communication, interviewing, discussion, leadership, group processes, and coping. Participate in a "coping group," if desired, to discuss issues and problems of concern. As a group, plan and implement a closure activity for this unit.	Facilitator Resource Trainer	Plan and implement activities to assist students in the development of skills in each of the target areas (e.g., reflective listening and congruent sending in communications). Plan and implement role-playing simulations in which students develop interview skills. Provide expertise and support for coping group meetings.

(continues)

TABLE 2.1. *Continued*

Step, Type, or Level of Thinking	Student		Teacher	
	Role	**Sample Activities**	**Role**	**Sample Activities**
Career Involvement	Inquirer/ researcher Intern Synthesizer	Participate in activities designed to develop awareness of a broad range of careers. Investigate career(s) of choice in depth. Participate in an internship in a career of choice. Plan a closure activity to synthesize new career knowledge.	Facilitator Resource Coordinator	Plan and implement activities to encourage students to learn about many, diverse careers. Invite guest speakers to discuss specific careers. With students, identify individuals and/or businesses for student internships. Provide support as needed in research skills and internship behaviors.
Explorations	Active participant Inquirer/ researcher Synthesizer	Individually, or in small groups, brainstorm topics of possible interest. Individually identify "passion areas" for possible in-depth study. In small groups, plan and conduct an exploration of different facets of a chosen topic. Individually, plan and conduct three to five explorations of chosen topics using multiple resources. Select a format and share information about the topic with the group.	Facilitator Resource	Plan and implement a group exploration activity to review research skills/strategies and help students develop the concept of information retrieval from multiple resources. Provide assistance to small groups and individuals, as needed, during explorations. Provide a structure for the sharing of information learned.

(continues)

TABLE 2.1.   *Continued*

Step, Type, or Level of Thinking	Student		Teacher	
	Role	Sample Activities	Role	Sample Activities
Investigations	Active participant Investigator Presenter Reflective thinker	Individually, select a topic and prepare a proposal for an investigation. Conduct the proposed investigation. Evaluate the investigation. Synthesize the results and prepare a presentation for an appropriate audience. Compare/contrast an exploration, an investigation, and an in-depth study.	Facilitator Resource Advisor	Plan and implement activities designed to help students develop an investigation proposal. Review proposal with each student. Meet with individual students weekly during the investigation to discuss progress. As needed, review specific skills and provide support to investigators. Provide appropriate audiences for presentations.
Cultural Activities	Observer Participant	In small or large groups, prepare a proposal for participation in after-school, evening, or weekend cultural events (e.g., visits to museums, plays, concerts, speeches, historical events) and go "behind the scenes" to see how events are set up. Synthesize the experience in a summary paper after each event.	Facilitator Resource	Review proposals. Assist students in making "behind the scenes" arrangements. Facilitate discussions of appropriate behaviors for attendance at cultural activities.
Service	Active participant	Plan and conduct research on an individual humanitarian. Share research with group. Brainstorm common characteristics of humanitarians. Plan and complete a service project in the community.	Facilitator Proposal evaluator Resource	Guide a discussion on the concept of humanitarianism. Compile a list of agencies or organizations that provide humanitarian services in the community. Confer with individual students to review proposals prior to approval.

(continues)

TABLE 2.1. *Continued*

Step, Type, or Level of Thinking	Student		Teacher	
	Role	Sample Activities	Role	Sample Activities
Adventure Trips	Decision maker and planner Active participant Evaluator	Participate in decision making to decide destination, purpose, goals, and the focus area of study. Participate in planning all aspects. Participate in trip activities. Participate in evaluation focused on both academic and group process aspects of the adventure trip.	Facilitator Resource	Plan a meeting for interested members of the group, parents, and other teachers to explore possibilities and make decisions. Advise student planners. Coordinate student efforts in fund-raising, travel arrangements, and administrative requirements. Conduct "debriefing" for evaluation.
Seminars	Active participant Planner Researcher Presenter Evaluator	In small groups, develop a seminar on some aspect of a broad topic such as futuristics, controversial issues, social problems, or advanced knowledge in a field. Prepare contract for seminar. Conduct research. Prepare and present factual information about topic. Conduct discussion or involvement activity.	Facilitator Resource	Plan activities to help students understand the purpose and structure of seminars. Negotiate seminar contract with each group. Provide appropriate audiences for the seminars. Guide an evaluation discussion.

(continues)

TABLE 2.1.   *Continued*

Step, Type, or Level of Thinking	Student		Teacher	
	Role	**Sample Activities**	**Role**	**Sample Activities**
In-Depth Study	Active participant Inquirer Producer Presenter Evaluator	Select a topic for in-depth study. Design a learning plan; select a mentor. Conduct the in-depth study. Make progress presentations. Develop the product(s). Evaluate the experience.	Facilitator Resource Advisor	Confer with individuals on in-depth study proposals. Approve proposals when complete. Help mentors define role and responsibilities. Answer questions or provide support as needed. Monitor student progress. Provide appropriate audiences for presentations. Guide evaluation discussions.

Teacher/facilitators also could ask members of discussion groups to state reasons and support for inferences or decisions. Several higher level thinking processes are implicit, but specific techniques for developing higher level thought are not identified. A recommended change is to use Bloom's *Taxonomy*, Parnes' *Creative Problem Solving*, Taba's questioning strategies, and Taylor's *Multiple Talent Model* as process models in enrichment activities. The value of guided discovery also is addressed implicitly in the Investigation component of Dimension Three, but teachers could enhance this component by encouraging learners to use Taba's interpretation of data strategy to discover patterns, ideas, and underlying principles as an integral part of synthesizing the results of investigations.

Product Changes

One of the strengths of the model is that product modifications recommended for gifted students (Maker, 1982) are specifically identified in the ALM basic principles and in most recommended activities. Students deal with real problems (e.g., community traffic patterns near the school that represent a danger to students), and solutions are presented to real audiences (e.g., a better traffic plan presented to the city council).

Transformation is assured by an emphasis on products that are new and unique to the learner, and self-evaluation is an integral part of all activities in the ALM. When students select their own topics for investigations, seminars, and in-depth study, teacher/facilitators can encourage choice of a topic related to issues, problems, and areas of concern.

Learning Environment Changes

The basic principles of the ALM assure that the program will be learner centered, promote independence, and involve students in decisions regarding curriculum, special activities, and evaluation. High mobility is required; many activities are planned that encourage students to leave the classroom to explore or investigate in other parts of the school and community. Complexity is assured through offering challenging tasks, teaching advanced strategies, and involving learners in the planning, implementation, and evaluation of such activities as field trips, service projects, seminars, and in-depth study.

Summary

The *Autonomous Learner Model* provides a framework for long-term development of potentially gifted and creative students with the goal of developing gifted and creative lifelong learners. The modifications recommended for gifted students either are intrinsic to the model or can be made easily through the integration of specific process models and the organization of skill development activities or investigations around complex, abstract concepts and generalizations.

DEVELOPMENT

The *Autonomous Learner Model* grew from a program designed by teachers at Arvada West High School in Jefferson County, Colorado, in the late 1970s. One of the first enrichment programs developed for secondary students, the program deliberately emphasizes emotional and social development in conjunction with cognitive development. Dr. George Betts, then director of Gifted and Talented Learning at Arvada West, was responsible for the design and implementation of the program. The present model was developed in 1980 following evaluation by a team of professionals and participants in the program. Betts, now director of the Center for the Study of Gifted, Talented, and Creative at the University of Northern Colorado, does not cite the theoretical foundations of the model; nor has any large-scale, empirical research been conducted to assess the overall effectiveness of the model.

Originally developed as an elective class for gifted and creative students in secondary schools, the model has been expanded to include a framework for a comprehensive, resource room–based program for elementary-age students as well. A scope and sequence of elements in each dimension suggests appropriate grade levels for awareness, introduction, development, and application of each element. The elementary school program has a focus on Dimensions One, Two, and Three; because of their complexity, Seminars and In-Depth Study dimensions generally are limited to gifted students in secondary schools.

RESEARCH ON EFFECTIVENESS

No empirical research on the effectiveness of the model has been conducted. Formative program evaluations have been conducted at several sites but results are not available. Traditional measures of student growth, in which content knowledge is emphasized, are not appropriate for assessing the effectiveness of this model. However, substantial research is needed to support the belief that the program is effective. Are all five dimensions of the model essential for the development of autonomous learners? What are graduates of the program doing now? What effect did participation in the program have on their career decisions? How did it affect their lives? A well-designed longitudinal follow-up study of program participants, at periodic intervals following graduation from high school, may be the most valid research for this complex model. The multitude of interaction variables among participants, teachers, community resource persons, mentors, and sites for investigations may make comprehensive empirical research impossible. However, participants can be compared with nonparticipants at several sites to obtain needed information about possible effects of the model.

JUDGMENTS

Advantages

One outstanding advantage of the *Autonomous Learner Model* is that it was designed by teachers specifically for gifted, creative students in secondary schools. The extension of the scope and sequence of the model to K–12 is an added plus. Unlike Renzulli's *Enrichment Triad Model*, task commitment is not assumed and specific activities and experiences are designed to help potentially gifted learners develop the social, emotional, and cognitive strategies that will enable them to become autonomous learners. Another advantage is the emphasis on student independence and choice. Not only do learners choose their own topics for investigations, seminars, and in-depth study, they also make decisions about culminating activities and plan, implement, and evaluate those activities. Another advantage is that the model can be incorporated into the framework of secondary schools and includes procedures for cooperative planning with content teachers and community resource persons to allow in-depth study expansions in content area classes. As the suggested time line (see Figure 2.3) illustrates, the model is flexible. Some students may spend more time in developmental activities; others may begin in-depth study almost immediately. A suggested scope and sequence, from awareness through introduction, development, and application of each component in all five dimensions is provided for grades K–1, 2–3, 4–5, 6–8, and 9–12.

Learners who have developed the essential cognitive, emotional, social, and organizational skills through involvement in the *Autonomous Learner Model* in earlier grades may engage in in-depth studies throughout the majority of their high school experience.

Another advantage is that the model is flexible and can be adapted to the needs of the school, the characteristics and needs of gifted students, the talents/gifts of teachers/facilitators, and the resources of the community. Most of the skills emphasized in the Individual Development Dimension are appropriate to all students and could be included in heterogeneous classes. With some adaptation, the model also could be used as a guide for assisting highly able students in smaller schools or communities to develop the skills and attitudes for participation in seminars and in-depth study investigations.

Disadvantages

One obvious disadvantage of the model is the lack of research on the effectiveness of the approach. The complexity of interactions among participants, along with the variations among content areas, study sites, mentors involved, and activities selected for Personal Growth Plans, makes empirical research difficult and may preclude comparative effectiveness studies with other approaches for gifted individuals. However, research has been conducted on the importance of developing strategic self-management (or metacognitive) skills and on the effectiveness of self-directed study with gifted students. Other research (e.g., Schneider, 1987) also has validated the importance of facilitating the development of social competence by gifted children. Unfortunately, Betts has not identified the philosophical, theoretical, or research bases of the *Autonomous Learner Model*, nor is information available about the demographic or personal characteristics of students who successfully make the transition to autonomous learner. What are the characteristics of students selected for participation in the model? What are the effects of the program on special populations of gifted students? What has happened to program participants in the years following high school graduation? What is the "durability" of the program (e.g., How long do adopting school districts maintain the implementation)? What cognitive, social, and emotional characteristics and skills are essential for successful teacher/facilitators? Many questions remain to be answered.

Another disadvantage of the program is the complexity of the instructional, management, and interpersonal skills required of teacher/facilitators. The flexibility of the model, which may be an advantage for some dedicated teachers who also are autonomous learners, may not provide the support tools necessary for a less assured teacher/facilitator. The scope of skills to be developed in Dimension Two alone requires the teacher/facilitator to have an extensive knowledge of learning skills, group processes, and counseling skills to facilitate students' personal understanding and career exploration. Comprehensive staff development, including strategies for involving community resource persons and mentors, is essential for the implementation of the model. Teacher/facilitators must have a variety of resources available, skill in the use of the resources, and time to locate both human and material resources. The few books available on the model are not comprehensive and present only a framework and suggested activities for implementation. Few materials necessary for implementation of units (e.g., lesson plans, teaching strategies, organizational or management tools) are available.

CONCLUSION

The *Autonomous Learner Model,* with its five dimensions, is designed to provide comprehensive learning experiences that will enable students dependent on teacher direction to become autonomous learners capable of self-directed, lifelong learning. The goals, assumptions, and basic principles in the model are based on needs of gifted students identified by leaders in the field (e.g., Clark, 1983; Feldhusen & Treffinger, 1980; Renzulli, 1977; Treffinger, 1978). Educators who wish to adopt or adapt this approach may need intensive staff development to acquire the process, management, and interpersonal skills necessary to implement the model. With these reservations, the model is recommended as particularly appropriate for secondary school programs for gifted students.

RESOURCES

Background Information

Betts, G. T. (1985). *Autonomous Learner Model for the gifted and talented.* Greeley, CO: Autonomous Learning Publications and Specialists. The principles, dimensions, and framework of the model are condensed into less than 100 pages. Scope and sequence charts are included for all components of the model, and suggested activities are outlined briefly. On the first reading, this book seems to lack the information needed for the reader to construct a mental image of the model. For teachers with little experience in the field of education of the gifted, more information is essential. More experienced educators will find that the volume is densely packed, and suggestions for activities can be expanded with the help of suggested references, which, unfortunately, are somewhat dated. The Year One Summary, Years Two and Three Summary, and an example of a transcript letter show the progression of a gifted high school participant in the program. Forms for planning a seminar and an in-depth study are included.

Allen, J. (1992). Meeting the needs of Australian rural gifted children: The use of curriculum enrichment projects (CEPPS) for primary schools in western Australia. *Gifted Education International, 8*(1), 23–31. In this article, the author describes the development of materials that can be used with gifted students to initiate and guide independent learning. The materials, framework for development, and examples are provided. The reference list contains sources for these materials.

Bodnar, J. A. (1993). High school internship program. In C. J. Maker & D. Orzechowski-Harland (Eds.), *Critical issues in gifted education: Vol. III. Programs for the gifted in regular classrooms* (pp. 342–373). Austin, TX: PRO-ED. Bodnar describes an internship program for high school students implemented in Albuquerque, New Mexico, as a career-exploration program for high school students. The article includes several forms for student application, identification of mentors, management, and evaluation.

Burns, F. D. (1993). Independent study: Panacea or palliative? In C. J. Maker & D. Orzechowski-Harland (Eds.), *Critical issues in gifted education: Vol. III. Programs for the gifted in regular classrooms* (pp. 381–399). Austin, TX: PRO-ED. Burns, an experienced teacher and coordinator in programs for gifted students, discusses three models recommended for use in independent study programs (Betts, Renzulli, and Treffinger). She contrasts them and discusses how they can be combined.

Friedman, R. C. J., & Gallagher, T. (1993). Reaction to "independent study." In C. J. Maker & D. Orzechowski-Harland (Eds.), *Critical issues in gifted education: Vol. III. Programs for the gifted in regular classrooms* (pp. 400–412). Austin, TX: PRO-ED. A reaction to Burns's chapter from a different perspective, the article provides additional insights into the use of the three models.

Nash, W. R., Haensly, P. A., Scobee-Rodgers, V. J., & Wright, N. L. (1993). Mentoring: Extending learning for gifted students. In C. J. Maker & D. Orzechowski-Harland (Eds.), *Critical issues in gifted education: Vol. III. Programs for the gifted in regular classrooms* (pp. 313–330). Austin, TX: PRO-ED. The authors explore the historical bases of mentoring relationships and identify the functions of such relationships in enhancing creativity, shaping careers, role-modeling, and shaping personal growth. Necessary elements of school-based mentorship programs and examples of mentoring programs also are discussed.

Seghini, J. B. (1993). An expanded view of internships. In C. J. Maker & D. Orzechowski-Harland (Eds.), *Critical issues in gifted education: Vol. III. Programs for the gifted in regular classrooms* (pp. 374–380). Austin, TX: PRO-ED. Seghini, a veteran educator, notes that counseling for educational needs and planning is a critical issue for gifted students. She briefly reviews some models and concludes that the *Autonomous Learner Model* is an excellent program for this purpose. Educators address career planning and personal development (social, emotional, and academic) early in the program and revisit these dimensions on a regular basis. As the developmental nature of autonomy is recognized, this planned approach can increase the number of students who can (will) benefit from an internship in one or more areas of career interest.

Torrance, E. P. (1984). *Mentor relationships: How they aid creative achievement, endure, change, and die.* Buffalo, NY: Bearly Limited. The development, growth, and change of mentoring relationships is emphasized in this useful book with its focus on how and why mentoring produces positive benefits for both partners.

Instructional Materials and Ideas

Betts, G. T. (1985). *Journeys into self.* Greeley, CO: Autonomous Learning Publications and Specialists. A tool for facilitating introspective thinking, values clarification, and personal understanding.

Dalton, J. (1992). *Creative thinking and cooperative talk in small groups.* Portsmouth, NH: Heinemann. In this book packed with activities, the author provides clear strategies for developing thinking skills and developing interpersonal skills students need to do cooperative work in small groups, develop management skills, and evaluate their own progress.

Fleisher, P. (1993). *Changing our world: A handbook for young activists.* Tucson, AZ: Zephyr Press. From his experience as a teacher and social activist, the author has prepared a step-by-step guide for young people interested in social justice issues. Suggestions for developing effective leadership skills and historical information about activists also are included.

Galbraith, J. (1983). *The gifted kids survival guide for ages 11–18.* Minneapolis: Free Spirit Publishing. A book that can be given to young people so they can explore the development of giftedness and grow in self-understanding.

Galbraith, J. (1984). *The gifted kids survival guide for ages 10 and under.* Minneapolis: Free Spirit Publishing. An excellent guide to help gifted students understand themselves and their potential and to build their self-esteem.

Garvin, K. (1989). *Primary activities: A treasure chest of primary-level ALM exercises.* Greeley, CO: Autonomous Learning Publishers and Specialists. This autonomous learner guide contains activities and forms for implementing several components of ALM Dimensions One, Two, and Three in primary grades. The emphasis is on group building, self-understanding, creativity, problem solving, goal setting, choosing appropriate behaviors, and interpersonal skills.

Gross, R. (1983). *The independent scholar's handbook.* Boston: Addison-Wesley. A valuable manual for helping students move toward the role of learner or independent scholar, this book includes guides for research design and final products, research techniques, and strategies for self-regulation.

Kunz, C. (n.d.). *Brainstrains: Creative problem-solving and logical thinking.* Victoria, Australia: Down Under Books. The author combines fiction with facts about the lives of eminent individuals to pose problems that promote creative mathematical problem solving and logical thinking. Designed for grades 3 through 8.

Scott, J. (n.d.). *Teach thinking strategies.* Victoria, Australia: Down Under Books. Based on Bloom's *Taxonomy of Cognitive Objectives,* this book contains ideas for teaching higher level thinking skills for students in grades 7 through 12. Photocopyable resource pages are designed to help students reflect on and write about their thinking strategies.

Udall, A. J., & Daniels, M. A. (1991). *Creating the thoughtful classroom: Strategies to promote student thinking.* Tucson, AZ: Zephyr Press. Classroom tested and classroom ready, this is a guide that teachers can use to help develop students' thinking skills in grades 3 through 12. Methods of assessment also are included.

von Oech, R. (1983). *A whack on the side of the head: How to unlock your mind for innovation.* New York: Warner Books. A humorous exploration of 10 mental "locks" that block creativity and innovation, the book presents activities to free oneself from a mental straitjacket of "right" thinking. An equally appealing book by the same author is *A Kick in the Seat of the Pants.* Both books will be enjoyed by, and useful with, older gifted students.

Autonomous Learning Publications and Specialists (Greeley, CO) also publishes a number of other books for use with ALM, including *Community Search, Future Studies, Images of Greatness, Discovering Who's Who in Our Community,* and *Research Skills for Beginners.* The ALPS catalog includes a number of other resources recommended for use in this model. The address is: ALPS, P.O. Box 2264, Greeley, CO 80632.

Chapter 3

Benjamin Bloom and David Krathwohl: The Cognitive and Affective Taxonomies

O ne model frequently used for the development of higher level thinking skills is the *Taxonomy of Educational Objectives.* The model is an integral part of many programs for the gifted as well as many thinking skills programs. Although both the *Cognitive* and *Affective Taxonomies* were developed by essentially the same group of educators and psychologists, the cognitive usually is referred to as *Bloom's Taxonomy,* and the affective as *Krathwohl's Taxonomy.* In this chapter they will be referred to as *Cognitive Taxonomy* and *Affective Taxonomy.*

The purpose of the taxonomies is to provide a set of criteria that can be used to classify educational objectives according to the level of complexity of the thinking required. They are generic in that they apply to any academic subject area and level of instruction from kindergarten through adult education (including graduate school). The two taxonomies have a different focus; one is on cognitive, or intellectual, behaviors, while the other is on affective, or "feeling," behaviors. Although their focus and levels are different, most of their underlying assumptions, their development, and their use are similar. The basic reference for the *Cognitive Taxonomy* is Bloom (1956); for the *Affective Taxonomy,* Krathwohl, Bloom, and Masia (1964) is the basic reference.[1]

The taxonomies were developed to facilitate communication between psychologists and educators in such areas as test construction, research, and

---

1. Because these are the only references used in descriptions of the taxonomies, they are not cited each time. Whenever their general development, use, and essential elements are described, the sources are the basic ones unless otherwise specified. In discussions of their use or applicability in programs for the gifted, the information and perceptions have come from the authors' experiences in education of the gifted.

curriculum development. At the time of their development, probably no one anticipated the widespread use of the classifications to develop teaching activities. However, they provide a simple, easy-to-learn structure for developing teaching-learning activities that take students through a sequential process in the development of a concept or the learning of relationships. Recently, the taxonomy has been criticized for the emphasis on microlevel skills (French & Rhoder, 1992), the vagueness of its concepts, and the lack of criteria for evaluating performance in the use of the skills (Ennis, 1985). A major concern is that the assumption of a one-way hierarchy of thinking skills disregards the complexity of interrelationships in thinking processes (Paul, 1985). Another criticism is that the focus on basic, discrete skills may draw attention away from the complex process strategies such as reflective thinking, problem solving, and decision making (French & Rhoder, 1992). With the caveat that discrete thinking skills should be taught in the context of their use, the *Cognitive Taxonomy* is "the best available inventory of micro-thinking skills we should be teaching" (Beyer, 1984, p. 556).

ASSUMPTIONS UNDERLYING THE MODEL

About Learning

The most basic assumption made by the developers of the taxonomies is that they are hierarchical. Each higher level depends on all the levels below it. Thus, application, the third level in the *Cognitive Taxonomy*, cannot be achieved without knowledge and comprehension. If students are to be able to solve a problem they have never seen before, they must know and understand whatever principles or computational methods are necessary for its solution. The fourth level, analysis, which often is required of students on exams (for example, compare and contrast the following ideas . . .), cannot be reached adequately unless the student has applied the ideas to a situation never before encountered. Students cannot be expected to develop a system of values unless they have first considered whether they value certain things, and how two or more of their values would compare. In short, the implications of this assumption are important to the instructional process. Teachers must make certain that their students are able to perform the behaviors at the lower levels before expecting them to function at the higher levels.

Related to this assumption is the implication that all learners are capable of the thinking and feeling processes described at each level of the taxonomies. In other words, if given enough time, all children are capable of the thinking processes of analysis, synthesis, and evaluation, as well as the feeling processes of valuing, organizing values, and internalizing values. The authors state that if students are provided with proper teaching conditions and allowed enough time, 95% can master any learning task. Teachers must have a view of the final level to be attained and concentrate on movement toward that goal in a fashion that helps students achieve mastery.

Another underlying principle of the taxonomies is that thinking or feeling processes or teaching objectives can be defined behaviorally and, when defined, can fit into one of the classifications of the taxonomies. In other words, certain types of thinking can be observed and classified. Implicit in this assumption and the methods used to develop the taxonomies is the belief that educators and psychologists working together can develop a logical classification that approximates reality.

About Teaching

Basic to the use of the taxonomies as a teaching tool, but not proposed by their developers, is the view that by designing activities that evoke the types of thinking at each level of the hierarchies, thinking and feeling processes can be improved. Through systematic emphasis on each of the levels from the lowest to the highest, students ultimately will be better thinkers at the higher levels. An aspect of this idea is that teaching activities can be developed that evoke certain types of thinking and teachers can be reasonably accurate about the underlying processes that go into a particular activity. For example, in designing a factual or knowledge question (the lowest level of the *Cognitive Taxonomy*), the teacher assumes a child has had prior contact with the information being requested. If the child has not, the question requires a higher level of thinking than knowledge. To answer the question, the student may have to think about some related information, put it together in a new fashion, and develop a possible answer. Similarly, when teachers design questions to evoke a higher level of thinking, such as evaluation, which requires students to make a judgment, they must assume that when the students give their answers, they are giving their own judgments rather than simply recalling judgments made by someone else (that is, knowledge level). Often questions of the appropriate form calling for higher levels, such as evaluation, are asked. (For example, what do you think are the advantages and disadvantages of this approach?) However, the students are being expected to list the pros and cons that previously have been presented by the teacher. In these cases, the students must operate at the lowest level rather than the highest.

A related idea is that any learning task can and should be broken down into smaller units or steps. The step-by-step approach assumes a skills-based model of learning. An underlying assumption is that all people learn in the same way and, as a result, an appropriate sequence can be developed for all learners. This idea is directly opposed to the belief that each individual thinks differently and comes to learning encounters with different experiences and the related view that people often learn through a process of intuitive leaps rather than sequential steps.

About Characteristics and Teaching of the Gifted

The authors of the taxonomies do not make statements directly related to their use with gifted children. They believe that all children are capable of the various processes. However, educators of the gifted assume that more time should be spent at the higher levels with these children because they are already capable of high-quality thinking and feeling at the lower levels. Although this observation usually is valid due to the wide range of information the children possess, the need for knowledge and comprehension often goes unrecognized, and these important steps are neglected. When attempting to concentrate on the higher levels, educators often forget to check the children's knowledge and understanding of the concepts involved. A related assumption is that gifted students should spend more time at the higher levels because this type of thinking is more challenging for them.

ELEMENTS/PARTS

Dimensions, Thinking Levels, or Steps

The *Cognitive Taxonomy* consists of six levels: knowledge, comprehension, application, analysis, synthesis, and evaluation. The *Affective Taxonomy* consists of five levels: receiving or attending, responding, valuing, organization, and characterization by a value complex. Although the two taxonomies usually are viewed as parts of two different domains, human behavior, especially at the higher levels, is impossible to separate into two different components. Affective processes, particularly those related to the value placed on learning, will affect greatly children's motivation to develop the thinking processes required of them. Affective behaviors, then, can be viewed as one of the necessary means for attaining cognitive objectives. On the other hand, cognitive objectives can be seen as one of the necessary means for attaining affective objectives. For an individual to develop a value complex, for example, the person must be able to evaluate available choices (including by implication, prior knowledge, comprehension, analysis, and synthesis related to these choices). More will be said about the relationships between the taxonomies after each is explained separately.

The Taxonomy of Cognitive Objectives

Knowledge

The first level, labeled *knowledge,* requires no transformation of the information an individual receives. This level might be more properly labeled *rote recall* (Ennis, 1987; Paul, 1985). Students must remember what has been read, heard, or observed. The knowledge level consists of remembering the following: (a) specifics, including terminology and specific facts; (b) ways and means of dealing with specifics, including conventions (for example, characteristic ways of treating or presenting phenomena), trends and sequences, classifications and categories, criteria, and methodology; and (c) universals and abstractions in a field, consisting of principles, generalizations, theories, and structures.

Comprehension

In the second level, comprehension, an individual is at a fairly low level of understanding of a concept or process. The person is able to make use of information that has been acquired and restate ideas in her or his own words. Comprehension might be compared to Piaget's definition of assimilation; information can be incorporated into existing conceptual structures with little change in information or conceptual frames. Comprehension is made up of three related skills: translation, interpretation, and extrapolation. *Translation* involves paraphrasing or restating an idea without changing its meaning. *Interpretation* is explaining or summarizing a communication and can involve reordering or rearranging its parts. *Extrapolation,* the highest level of comprehension, involves the extension of trends or tendencies beyond the given data. Immediate implications or effects are predicted on the basis of known facts.

Application

Putting abstractions or general principles to use in new, concrete situations involves the third level of cognitive behavior, application. Principles or abstractions can be in the form of general ideas, rules of procedure, technical procedures, or theories.

Application, like comprehension, requires that students use previously learned ideas, procedures, or theories. Unlike comprehension, however, rules or procedures are not used in the context in which they were learned. At the application level, students are not told which rule is the proper one nor shown how to use a principle or rule. Instead, they must draw on past experience to select relevant principles or procedures that apply to new problems or new situations. Application may require students to accommodate or modify conceptual schemes to cope with new information or problems.

Analysis

The fourth level, analysis, involves the breaking down of a complex whole into its elements or parts so that the nature of the components is made clear and the interrelationships between the parts are made explicit. Analysis has as its purpose a greater understanding of the underlying structure, effect, or theoretical basis of ideas or systems. Included in this level are such behaviors as recognizing unstated assumptions (that is, analysis of elements), checking the consistency of hypotheses with existing information (that is, analysis of relationships), and recognizing the use of propaganda techniques (that is, analysis of organizational principles).

Synthesis

Synthesis is, in many ways, the opposite of analysis. It involves the putting together of parts to form a whole. These pieces or elements are rearranged or combined so that they make a pattern or structure not there before. In other words, the products of synthesis are new and unique, as distinguished from the comprehension-level skill of interpretation, which simply involves reordering or rearranging the parts to demonstrate an understanding of the idea. The products of interpretation are not really new. Synthesis, however, includes the following elements: (a) producing a unique communication either through writing or through speaking; (b) producing a plan or proposed set of operations, for example, a proposal, a unit of instruction, a blueprint for a building; and (c) derivation of a set of abstract relations, including classification schemes, hypotheses, and inductive discovery of mathematical principles or abstract generalizations. One justification for the use of discovery learning is that the intellectual skills involved in discovery are at the synthesis level, whereas in a deductive approach, in which principles are given and then applied, the intellectual skills involved are at only the application level.

Evaluation

According to the taxonomy, the highest cognitive skill is evaluation, or making judgments about the value of something (for example, materials, methods, ideas, theories) for a given purpose. These judgments can be based on criteria chosen by students or criteria given to them, and can be either quantitative or qualitative. Also included in evaluation are judgments based on either internal or external evidence.

Internal evidence consists of criteria such as logical accuracy or consistency, while external evidence consists of comparing a work with other recognized works of high quality or with standards of excellence established in a particular field, or assessing the worth of an idea in terms of a particular theory. Most of the critical thinking skills discussed by Ennis (1987) involve evaluation. These judgments can be made through application of internal criteria, as in judging whether a statement follows from the premises.

External evidence would be involved in judging whether an observation statement is reliable by using a set of principles from the fields of law, history, and science (that is, a statement is more reliable if the observer is unemotional, alert, and disinterested; is skilled at observing the sort of thing observed; and uses precise techniques).

Table 3.1 gives a summary of teacher and student roles and activities at each level in the model.

The Affective Taxonomy

Receiving

At this level, the learner is simply sensitive to the fact that certain things exist. Awareness and sensitivity also include a willingness to attend, although they do not imply a judgment. Each student has had experiences that will influence this willingness either positively or negatively.

Receiving is divided into three subcategories on a continuum from a passive role on the part of the learner to the point at which the learner directs his or her own attention. *Awareness,* the lowest level, includes being conscious of something and taking it into account. This level does not imply that the individual can verbalize what has caused the awareness. The second level, *willingness to receive,* involves a neutrality or suspended judgment toward the phenomenon, but the student is inclined to notice it. An individual will not necessarily seek out something but is not actively seeking to avoid it. The highest level of receiving is *controlled or selective attention,* in which the student selects a favored stimulus and attends to it despite competing or distracting stimuli.

Responding

The second level, responding, includes most "interest" objectives. At this level, students are so involved in or committed to a subject or activity that they will seek it out and gain satisfaction from participation. Responding also includes three subcategories: (a) acquiescence in responding, (b) willingness to respond, and (c) satisfaction in response. *Acquiescence in responding* can be described as obedience or compliance. Students are passive in the sense that they do not initiate the behavior, but they do not resist or yield unwillingly. *Willingness to respond* implies that students will do something "on their own" and that they choose to do an activity or participate in the learning process. At the next higher level, *satisfaction in response,* the element of enjoyment is included. Students have a feeling of satisfaction, pleasure, or zest when participating in an activity.

TABLE 3.1. Summary of Teacher and Student Activities and Roles in the Taxonomy of Cognitive Objectives

Step, Type, or Level of Thinking	Student		Teacher	
	Role	Sample Activities	Role	Sample Activities
Knowledge	Passive recipient Memorizer Active recipient	Pay attention to information read or heard. Answer questions almost verbatim about specific facts. Answer questions requiring recall or memory.	Provider of information and resources Questioner Organizer of learning activities Evaluator	Present information about a subject. Provide students with resources on a topic. Ask questions to check whether students know the information presented to them. Assist students in finding information identified as necessary or desirable.
Comprehension	Active participant	Answer questions or do activities that require: (1) translation of information (e.g., explain a metaphor); (2) interpretation of information (e.g., After you read the paragraph, what did you think the meaning was?); and (3) extrapolation of existing information (e.g., What do you think will happen next in space exploration?)	Provider of information and resources Organizer of learning activities Evaluator	Check to see if students have the knowledge required for the task. Ask questions to see whether students can paraphrase, extend, and/or make inferences based on the information. Provide sequential activities that first require the student to translate, then interpret, then extrapolate meanings from the given information.

(continues)

TABLE 3.1. *Continued*

Step, Type, or Level of Thinking	Student		Teacher	
	Role	**Sample Activities**	**Role**	**Sample Activities**
Application	Active participant	Use some previously learned rule or method in a new situation. Decide which method to use or which principle to apply to a new task. Based on an understanding of a task and its requirements, select an appropriate procedure to complete the task.	Provider of information and resources Assigner of tasks Questioner Evaluator	Check to see if students have the knowledge and comprehension necessary for the task. Provide students with a new problem or situation in which they can apply principle(s) or method(s) previously learned. Ask questions to determine student understanding of requirements of the task. Provide feedback to students on their performances (e.g., You chose a good method to solve that problem *or* You used the right method but need to do this step differently *or* This method would be better for solving that problem).
Analysis	Active participant	Break down a whole (e.g., plan, communication, proposal, system) into its parts (e.g., What are the unstated assumptions in the planned goals?) Identify the relationships between parts of a whole (e.g., Is the hypothesis consistent with the assumptions given?) Identify the arrangement or structure of a complex whole (e.g., Chart the pattern(s) of meaning in a literary work).	Provider of information and resources Questioner Organizer of learning activities Evaluator	Ask questions to determine whether and how students have analyzed elements, relationships, and organizational principles. Provide feedback to students (e.g., That is a clear analysis that contains all the necessary steps *or* You may have overlooked an element (relationship) that you need for a complete analysis *or* In your hypothesis, you seem to have incorrectly identified the underlying principles).

(continues)

TABLE 3.1.   *Continued*

Step, Type, or Level of Thinking	Student		Teacher	
	Role	Sample Activities	Role	Sample Activities
Synthesis	Active participant	Combine elements in a new way so that a different pattern or product is developed. Organize and write original statements or narratives. Develop a plan, research proposal, or new product. Formulate or modify a theory.	Provider of information and resources Questioner Organizer of learning activities Evaluator	Check to see whether students have the knowledge, comprehension, and application skills necessary to do the task. Design sequential learning activities to develop the component skills of identifying the elements of a whole, analyzing the relationships among elements, and recognizing the organizational principles involved. Provide feedback to students on their products (e.g., You've arranged your essay effectively so that others can understand your ideas *or* Check the steps in your plan carefully; you may have left something out *or* Show me how your theory is consistent with the general principles of this discipline).

(continues)

TABLE 3.1. *Continued*

Step, Type, or Level of Thinking	Student		Teacher	
	Role	**Sample Activities**	**Role**	**Sample Activities**
Evaluation	Active participant	Make judgments about the value of information, materials, or methods for a given purpose. Select or develop appropriate criteria for making a judgment for a given purpose. Use internal and external criteria as a basis for judgment. Use quantitative and qualitative data in making judgments.	Provider of information and resources Questioner Organizer of learning activities Evaluator	Check to see whether students have the knowledge, comprehension, application, analysis, and synthesis skills necessary to do the task. Structure situations in which students must evaluate products based on different kinds of evidence (logical, internal, external, qualitative, quantitative). Provide criteria for evaluation of some activities or products; invite students to develop criteria for evaluation of some activities or products. Devise learning activities to help students select/develop criteria for evaluation (e.g., logical principles for evaluating arguments). Give students specific feedback on their performances (e.g., strengths demonstrated, suggestions for improvement, and mini-lessons on a specific skill, technique, or principle needed).

Valuing

Of all the levels in the *Affective Taxonomy,* valuing has received the most attention in educational practice. It includes three levels or subcategories: ascribing worth, demonstrating preference, and making a commitment. *Valuing* simply means deciding that a person, thing, phenomenon, or idea has worth or importance. Behavior at this level is consistent and stable and has taken on the characteristics of a belief or an attitude. Actions resulting from values are motivated by a commitment to the underlying value rather than by the desire to comply or obey.

Acceptance of a value, the first subcategory, includes a consistency of behavior enabling the underlying value to be identified but is at the lowest level of commitment. Individuals have a tendency to behave in a certain way but would probably be more willing to reevaluate their position than at the higher levels. The second level of valuing, *preference for a value,* includes not only a willingness to be identified with a value but also an intent to seek out or want that value. *Commitment,* the third subcategory, implies beliefs that are certain beyond a shadow of a doubt. Individuals who are committed will act in ways that further the particular value, will try to convince others, and will try to deepen their own involvement with it.

Organization

As values are internalized, situations that involve more than one value arise. People then must organize these values, determine the relationships among them, and establish the pervasive ones. Two subcategories are included in this level. The first, *conceptualization of a value,* is developing a view that enables an individual to see how a particular value relates to other values already held or to new ones being developed. At the next level, *organization of a value system,* students bring together a set of attitudes, beliefs, and values into an ordered relationship with each other. Some of these values may be quite different or in opposition to one another in certain situations. The individual must synthesize these into a value complex that, if not harmonious and internally consistent, is at least in dynamic equilibrium.

Characterization by a Value or a Value Complex

At this level, values already have been internalized and organized into a hierarchy and have controlled behavior long enough for the individual to adapt to behavior this way. The subcategories, *developing a generalized set of values* and *characterization,* represent two aspects of the individual's consistent behavior. A generalized set of values is a basic orientation, a persistent and consistent reaction to a family of related situations or things. This usually unconscious set guides action without an individual deliberately considering alternatives beforehand and can be thought of as an attitude cluster. At the characterization level, behavior results from a philosophy of life, a broad range of behaviors constituting a world view. Objectives included in this subcategory are broader or more inclusive than those considered a part of the generalized set, and emphasis is placed on internal consistency.

Table 3.2 gives a summary of teacher and student roles and activities in the implementation of this model.

Examples of Thinking Levels

To illustrate the differences among the types of thinking generated in specific levels, consider the lessons described in Table 3.3 and Table 3.4 based on the *Cognitive* and *Affective Taxonomies.*

In any activity, complete separation of the cognitive and affective domains is impossible. Three basic kinds of relationships seem to exist. The most important is that, explicitly or implicitly, a cognitive component can be found in every affective objective and an affective component in every cognitive objective. At every level of the *Cognitive Taxonomy,* the affective behavior of receiving or attending is a prerequisite. Responding is required if a student is asked to answer a question or participate in an activity. At every level of the *Affective Taxonomy,* with the possible exception of receiving, the cognitive behavior of knowledge is prerequisite to responding, and comprehension is prerequisite to valuing and organizing values.

A second relationship between the domains is that educators often use one of the domains to achieve objectives in the other domain. Usually, cognitive objectives are used as a way to achieve affective objectives. Students are given new information with the hope that an attitude change will result. In the example provided, students were given information about other societies and people's reactions to them as a way to help them examine their own feelings and values. The relationship can go the other way, however. Affective goals can be used to achieve cognitive goals. Educators can develop students' interest in something as a way to increase their knowledge of a phenomenon. Krathwohl et al. (1964) suggest that guided discovery methods provide a way to use an individual's drive for competency (an affective behavior probably at the valuing level) to enhance the possibility that children will discover or develop necessary cognitive abilities.

The third relationship is only slightly different; affective and cognitive goals can be achieved simultaneously. Again, Krathwohl et al. (1964) refer to discovery learning as an example. In Suchman's (1965) inquiry training, children are presented with a puzzling event. They ask questions, in a manner similar to the 20-question game, of the teacher, who acts only as a data giver. Teachers observe the pattern of the students' strategies and offer suggestions for improving them. In this way, the cognitive goal of improving the

TABLE 3.2.   Summary of Teacher and Student Activities and Roles in the Taxonomy of Affective Objectives

Step, Type, or Level of Thinking	Student		Teacher	
	Role	*Sample Activities*	*Role*	*Sample Activities*
Receiving	Passive recipient to active recipient	Attend to what is being presented. Be aware. Be willing to take notice. Choose one stimulus over others.	Provider of stimuli Organizer Presenter Covert evaluator	Present learning activities or information to capture the attention of the learner. Check to see if learner is aware of the stimuli. Plan sequential activities that will lead the student through the levels of awareness, willingness to receive, and selected attending.
Responding	Passive respondent to active, pleased respondent	Comply with suggestions. Voluntarily seek out activities of interest. Enjoy activities chosen.	Provider of stimuli Organizer Presenter Covert evaluator	Check to see if students have attended to relevant stimuli. Plan activities designed to stimulate interest (pleasure in responding). Ask questions regarding student response (feelings) toward activities, ideas, people, objects.
Valuing	Chooser	Accept a value; be willing to be identified with that value. Act consistently so that others can identify preferences as values. Choose a position and seek it out. Attempt to convince others that your value choices are important.	Provider of stimuli Organizer Questioner Presenter	Check student's response to a phenomenon, idea, or other people. Organize activities in which students can make value choices. Provide situations in which students can exhibit and discuss their value choices. Assist students in clarification of their values with provocative questions.

(continues)

TABLE 3.2. *Continued*

Step, Type, or Level of Thinking	Student		Teacher	
	Role	Sample Activities	Role	Sample Activities
Organization	Chooser Believer Organizer of beliefs	Identify the essential characteristics of values held. Figure out the relationships between values. Synthesize parts of values into a new value complex.	Provider of stimuli Organizer Questioner Presenter	Check what values students hold. Arrange situations in which students must choose between competing values they already hold. Assist students in the examination of relationships between their values by asking questions. Help students to develop equilibrium in their value systems.
Characterization by a Value or Values Complex	Internalizer of values	Act consistently in accordance with internalized values. Act consistently in accordance with a total world view. Develop a consistent philosophy of life.	Provider of stimuli Organizer Questioner Observer	Check to see that students have organized and examined their values. Arrange situations in which students can demonstrate internalized values. Assist students in the identification of the values they have internalized.

TABLE 3.3.   Examples of Thinking Levels: Cognitive Domain

To illustrate the differences between the levels of thinking in the *Taxonomy of Cognitive Objectives*, consider this sample lesson. The purpose of the lesson is to work toward the development of the following generalization:

Every society has rules, written or unwritten, through which social control over individual conduct is maintained.

Level of Cognitive Taxonomy	Activity	Questions
Knowledge	Information about three civilizations—Roman, Cherokee, and Industrial American—is presented to students in print and audiovisual formats. Students view, listen to, and read data about the three civilizations.	What were some of the written rules in Roman civilization? . . . in Cherokee communities? . . . in industrial America? How were these laws used to control behavior? [Each of these questions can be answered directly from presented information.]
Comprehension	Students present a sociodrama depicting their interpretation of an event about which they have read. The class is divided into three groups so that one sociodrama is presented for each civilization. A discussion follows each sociodrama.	What were some of the written rules governing each situation presented in the sociodrama? What were some facts that contributed to individuals' reactions to these laws or rules? What do you think will happen next? Why do you think so?
Application	Students view a videotape or film about a trial in a different society (e.g., American frontier, Japan, South Africa, Egypt). Discussion follows. Students draw a diagram to illustrate the relationship between social characteristics of a society and its criminal laws.	Based on what you know about other societies and cultures, what might be some characteristics of this society? What reasoning led you to make that conclusion? Draw a diagram to illustrate how the social characteristics of this society may have affected the development of its criminal laws.

(continues)

TABLE 3.3. *Continued*

Level of Cognitive Taxonomy	Activity	Questions
Analysis	Students reflect, in writing, on unwritten codes of conduct that they follow in everyday life. Discussion follows.	What were some unwritten codes of conduct, mores, and values in the [Roman/Cherokee/Industrial American] civilization? In your opinion, why were these unwritten codes? How did the unwritten codes differ from written laws? Why do you think that is so? How did unwritten codes differ among the three civilizations? What factors might have contributed to the differences? How were the unwritten codes among the three civilizations similar? In your opinion, why were these codes similar in that way?
Synthesis	Students are grouped in two teams; each team develops laws and codes for its own hypothetical civilization. Students in each team then devise a way (e.g., skit, visual representation) to present the legal structure of the civilization to the other team without actually specifying the laws and social codes.	How might you represent the social codes of your civilization through a skit? Why would that be a good way? What is another way to present your ideas? What important data do you want your audience to understand?

(continues)

TABLE 3.3. *Continued*

Level of Cognitive Taxonomy	Activity	Questions
Evaluation	Following a team presentation, the audience is asked to assess the consistency of the presentation with the legal structure the team has created for the hypothetical civilization.	What evidence did you see in the presentation that helped you to identify [written/unwritten] laws in this civilization? In what ways was the presentation [consistent/inconsistent] with the identified structure of the civilization? What items/actions in the presentation led you to believe the team [identified/failed to identify] some important codes of conduct or values?
	Teacher presents the lesson generalization following the evaluations of both team presentations. Discussion follows.	Think about the validity of this statement: *Every society has rules, written or unwritten, through which social control over individual conduct is maintained.* Why do you [agree/disagree] with it? What would you change about the statement to increase your agreement? Why would this change make the statement more agreeable to you?

TABLE 3.4.   Examples of Thinking Levels: Affective Domain

To illustrate the differences between the levels of thinking in the *Taxonomy of Affective Objectives*, consider this sample lesson. The purpose of the lesson is to work toward the development of the following generalization:

Every society has rules, written or unwritten, through which social control over individual conduct is maintained.

Level of Affective Taxonomy	Activity	Questions
Receiving	Information about three civilizations—Roman, Cherokee, and Industrial American—is presented to students in print and audiovisual formats. Students view, listen to, and read data about the social and political structures of the three civilizations.	What were some of the [events/acts] you saw happen in the film? What were some of the reactions of the people when their leader spoke to them? What did you see that led you to say that?
Responding	Students and teacher continue to discuss the information presented about the three civilizations.	What were your feelings when you [watched the film/read the story]? When [you/someone you know] [were/was] involved in a similar situation, what are some of the things that happened? How did you feel about that situation? What did you [read/see] that helped you understand how an individual of the [Roman/Cherokee/Industrial American] civilization might feel about its laws? How did it make you feel? As you participated in the sociodrama, what were some of your feelings? What are some social controls that you have experienced? Why do you think you reacted [positively/negatively] to that control?

(*continues*)

TABLE 3.4. *Continued*

Level of Affective Taxonomy	Activity	Questions
Valuing	The teacher presents an attitude/value continuum to the students: no control <-----------------> strict rules and enforcement Students are asked to indicate their judgment about how much social control a society needs by placing an X at some point on the line.	Where on this continuum would you stand? Why do you feel that way? What are some things that have happened to make you feel that way? In the sociodramas, what were some of the values of the characters involved? What led you to think that [specify value] was valued by that person?
Organization	Students brainstorm and list all the means of social control currently in effect in their own society and those they learned about in the three civilizations studied. By group consensus, students select five of the most important in each society; then each student individually ranks those five according to (a) desirability and (b) effectiveness.	In what ways are your values (as expressed in the social continuum activity) different from those you discovered in the three civilizations we studied? In what ways are the values similar? Why do you think your values are [different from/similar to] those of citizens in the other civilizations (i.e., What experiences have you had that contribute to the formation of values [similar to/different from] citizens in the other societies?
Organization by a value complex	After a discussion of the team presentations in the cognitive evaluation activity, each student individually develops an ideal set of social controls for the society.	How would you describe your ideal society? What social controls are absolutely necessary to the operation of the society? What social controls are just desirable? What do you believe about the necessity for social controls? Why do you believe that?

child's inquiry skill is achieved in a situation that engages the child's interest. By providing a critique of the strategy, the teacher also builds motivation to use the skill in other situations.

According to the authors of the *Affective Taxonomy*, the closest relationships between the taxonomies can be found between receiving and knowledge, analysis/synthesis and conceptualization, and evaluation and organization/characterization. At the lowest levels, the relationship is clear: Learners must attend before they will know, and they can develop knowledge only if they have a willingness to pay attention. Thus, in the examples of thinking levels in Tables 3.3 and 3.4, students must attend affectively to information in a film or videotape to develop cognitive knowledge about the reactions of people in each of the three societies. At the higher levels of analysis/synthesis and the related affective levels of conceptualization (the first level within organization), the cognitive ability of analysis is needed as students "break down" the common elements of values or of situations in which they are involved and put the elements back together (synthesis) into a value that is important to them. In the example, students must analyze the presentations of other teams, as well as their own, and then relate their own behaviors to the presentations.

The cognitive skill of evaluation clearly is involved in both the organization category of a value system and in the highest affective level, characterization by a value complex. To develop a total philosophy of life and to weigh one value or way of behaving against situational considerations requires that an individual be able to make defensible judgments. The criteria for making these judgments become internalized to the extent that the individual behaves almost automatically in some situations. In the example, students are asked to develop their ideal society, which requires them to evaluate the other societies on the basis of some criteria and to put into their ideal those aspects that are consistent with their own philosophy.

Williams (1971) presents a slightly different, somewhat simple view of the relationship between the cognitive and affective domains. He relates them almost directly in the following way:

- Receiving corresponds to knowledge through information an individual wants to receive.

- Responding relates to comprehension through the willingness to understand information.

- Valuing relates to application through the appreciation of information that is relevant and useful.

- Conceptualization relates to analysis and synthesis in that an individual forms a value system by integrating bits of information into a new and unique combination.

- Internalization relates to evaluation through an individual's judging how something fits into a way of life.

Although this expression is more simplistic than the relationships described earlier, it corresponds roughly and can be used as a guide for integrating the two domains. Further support for the use of this scheme can be found in the fact that teacher and student roles (see Tables 2.1 and 2.2) correspond roughly as the higher levels of both taxonomies are reached. The student moves from the role of a passive recipient who remembers to an active learner who makes judgments. The teacher provides the information and develops the experiences and then moves to a more facilitative role as the student takes an increasingly active part in the learning situation.

MODIFICATION OF THE BASIC CURRICULUM

In programs for the gifted, the *Cognitive* and *Affective Taxonomies* have been used mainly as systems for making one process modification: development of higher levels of thinking. Although they were developed as schemes for classifying objectives or specified outcomes of instruction, what is described or classified is student behavior, either thinking (cognitive) behavior or feeling (affective) behavior. As such, the taxonomies provide ways to classify the thinking and feeling processes that children use as they participate in a learning activity or answer a teacher's question.

The taxonomies do, however, have other valuable uses in making certain curriculum modifications for the gifted. They can be used as structures for evaluating the sophistication of products and as systems for classifying content according to its complexity and abstractness.

Content Modifications

Although seldom used for this purpose, the knowledge level of the *Cognitive Taxonomy* contains a scheme for classifying content according to its type as well as its abstractness and complexity. Three types of knowledge are described: (a) specifics, (b) ways and means of dealing with specifics, and (c) universals and abstractions in a field. These categories can be used in a variety of ways to make content changes for the gifted.

Knowledge of Specifics

This category is considered to be at the lowest level of complexity and abstraction. It includes the facts or specific information about a field of study. These specifics, the basic elements the learner must know to become acquainted with a field, include knowledge of terminology and knowledge of specific facts. Each field contains a set of terms that serves as the basic language of that field and both verbal and nonverbal symbols that have particular referents. Some examples are terms associated with work in science, definitions of geometric figures, and important accounting terms. Each field also has a large number of dates, events, people, places, and research results that are known by specialists in the field and used in thinking about specific topics and defining certain problems. Examples include significant names, places, and events in the news; knowledge of the reputation of a particular author; and recall of facts about a certain culture.

Knowledge of Ways and Means of Dealing with Specifics

Information in this category includes ways of organizing, studying, judging, and critiquing ideas, events, and phenomena in a field. Methods of inquiry, patterns of organization, and standards of judgment within disciplines would be included in this category. These are different from specifics in that they are the operations necessary for dealing with specifics. Included in this section are five subcategories: (a) conventions, (b) trends and sequences, (c) classifications and categories, (d) criteria, and (e) methodology.

Knowledge of conventions includes the characteristic ways of treating and presenting ideas and phenomena that scholars or workers in a field use because they suit their purpose or fit the phenomena. Examples include rules of etiquette, correct form and usage of English in speaking and writing, and standard symbols used on maps and charts.

Knowledge of trends and sequences includes trends involving time sequences as well as cause–effect relationships that are emphasized by scholars and workers in a field. Some examples are the following: (a) the evolutionary development of humans, (b) effects of industrialization on the culture of a nation, and (c) trends of government in this country during the last 50 years.

The third group, knowledge of classifications and categories, includes the classes, sets, or divisions that are considered fundamental or useful in a particular field. These classification systems are used to help structure and systematize the phenomena being studied. Objectives in this group include types of literature, the classification of elements in chemistry, and the classification of living things in biology.

Knowledge of criteria includes the standards by which facts, principles, opinions, and behaviors are tested or judged. This includes standards such as those used to judge the nutritive value of a meal, the aesthetic value of a work of art, or the validity of sources of information. Knowledge of methodology includes methods of inquiry, techniques, and procedures that characterize a particular field and those usually employed in investigating certain problems. Examples include the steps in a scientific method, attitude surveys, and procedures for conducting health and medical research.

Knowledge of Principles and Generalizations

The most abstract and complex of the groups, this category of knowledge includes the major ideas, schemes, and patterns that dominate a field and serve as organizing themes for the other information available. Universals and abstractions bring together a large number of facts and events and describe the relationships among them. The category includes two subgroups: (a) principles and generalizations and (b) theories and structures. Knowledge of principles and generalizations includes abstractions that summarize observations of phenomena and are valuable in explaining, describing, or predicting. These include such items as fundamental principles of logic, generalizations about cultures, biological laws of reproduction and heredity, and principles of learning.

Theoretical knowledge is the result of a body of principles and generalizations interrelated into a structure that has broad explanatory and predictive power. Knowledge of theories and structures corresponds to the "thought systems" described by Taba (1962) as the characteristic modes of thinking employed by scholars in a particular field. Some examples include the theories of relativity, evolution, social learning, and philosophic bases for judgment.

For example, chemistry is not simply a study of elements and compounds, with their characteristics and interactions. Rather, a "language" or body of knowledge common to practitioners in the field embodies specific facts, classifications, inquiry methods, symbol systems, and conventions for reporting research and communicating findings to others.

Abstractness and Complexity

To use this classification system in providing the content modifications of abstractness and complexity, the major emphasis or focus would be placed at each level of the taxonomy on the third category, principles and abstractions. Of course, knowledge and understanding of specifics are important to understanding abstract ideas, but the focus should be on the principles and abstractions. At the knowledge level, specifics would perhaps be as important as the generalizations and abstractions, but as an individual moves up the levels of the taxonomy, specifics assume much less importance.

Variety

The curricular modification of variety also can be provided by using this scheme for classifying knowledge. In a program for the gifted, an important strategy is to sample systematically from a variety of types of knowledge to make certain that students have been exposed to a range of ideas in a particular field or across several fields (Maker, 1982). Bloom's system could be used as a scheme for viewing the knowledge in each field of study and for making certain that gifted students have received exposure to all types of knowledge available in each field, that is, the specifics, the methods, and the theories.

Methods of Inquiry

The classification scheme proposed by Bloom brings attention to the fact that within each field of study certain conventions, techniques, and strategies are unique. When teaching gifted students methods of inquiry, this system can be used to suggest methods that might otherwise have been forgotten.

The Affective Taxonomy

Because of its concentration on aspects of behavior that are traditionally considered only a small part of the educational process, the *Affective Taxonomy* also could be considered a vehicle for making content changes by deliberately including affective components in the curriculum. This idea relates especially to the content change of variety. However, no system of classification of affective content exists in the affective taxonomy like the one contained in the cognitive one.

Process Modifications

One critical point should be made clear. Even though the taxonomies have enjoyed widespread use as schemes for making process modifications for the gifted and for seriously considering process in the regular curriculum, the developers did not intend them to be used in this way. As they developed the systems, they were attempting to make each description neutral. They did not suggest, for example, that everyone should develop activities at all levels of the taxonomies or that specified amounts of time be spent at the various levels. The developers did not even suggest that learning objectives or activities be arranged sequentially according to the levels of the taxonomies. All knowledge is not at a lower level than all analysis, for example. Knowledge of specifics, strategies, and generalizations in theoretical physics may require a higher level of thinking than analyzing the components of a chemical solution. The authors implied a sequential arrangement with their statement that the *Cognitive Taxonomy* is arranged from the most simple to the most complex intellectual behavior. All these uses and implications have been added by those who subsequently have applied the taxonomies to their educational situations.

The *Cognitive Taxonomy* provides a useful way for educators of the gifted to develop learning activities that require higher levels of thinking or more complex intellectual activity, one of the most basic goals of curriculum modification for the gifted. The implication that follows is that more time is spent at the higher levels with the gifted when perhaps an equal amount of time would be spent at all levels with most students.

The *Affective Taxonomy,* though not particularly intended for this purpose, can be used as a means for making process changes emphasizing greater complexity or higher levels. Since intellectual activity cannot be separated entirely from its affective components, this taxonomy can be incorporated into the methodology as a way to develop higher levels of feeling. Although the concept of complexity was not used as an explicit organizing principle in this taxonomy as it was in the cognitive one, the behaviors are arranged in a developmental order (for example, a person must be aware of something before developing a preference for it or before it can become a part of a total world view). Since the behaviors are arranged in this way, the taxonomy can provide a framework for devising learning activities that systematically develop affective processes, for designing learning center tasks to lead students to more complex thinking, or for creating games for the same purpose. The taxonomies also are useful in preparing auto-instructional programs or as the basic structure in learning contracts.

Product Modifications

Because of the arrangement of thinking behaviors ranging from simple to complex, the *Cognitive Taxonomy* can be used to evaluate the complexity of student products, particularly in assessing whether they involve a mere summary of prior information (comprehension level) or reflect a higher level involving reordering, reinterpreting, and recombining information (synthesis level). Students can be taught to use the taxonomy in evaluating their own products.

Learning Environment Modifications

Neither of the taxonomies provides specific guidelines for the development of appropriate learning environments. However, the *Affective Taxonomy* provides the teacher with some suggestions for developing an effective psychological climate, particularly in the dimensions of learner-centeredness and independence. Teachers can structure their own behaviors in such a way that the students can reach the higher levels. Teachers must respect the learner's prior level of feeling about a situation and build upon these feelings in the learning process.

MODIFYING THE APPROACHES

In addition to the curricular changes directly suggested by the taxonomies, other modifications important in programs for gifted students can be made by combining the taxonomies with other models or by using them in ways other than those suggested by the authors.

Content Changes

Abstractness, Complexity, and Organization for Learning Value

Both taxonomies can be combined easily with Bruner's ideas about "teaching the structure of a discipline." To combine the models, the first step would be to identify or develop the abstract themes that will be used to unify the content. These ideas and the key concepts contained in them will serve as the content organizers. Then specific information and facts to be taught are selected as examples of the concepts. When designing learning activities, data or specific facts serve as the basis for the lowest levels of the taxonomies, and the concepts and themes become more important at the higher levels.

In the examples presented earlier in this chapter, a general statement was used as the content organizer. At the knowledge and receiving levels, students were presented with data about three different civilizations. The questions they were asked were designed to check their memory of this information, in other words, to check whether students "attended" and "received" the information they would need to use later.

At the responding level in the *Affective Taxonomy* and at the comprehension level in the *Cognitive Taxonomy*, the data continue to be important, but concepts are entered into the process. For example, when students present the sociodrama, they demonstrate their understanding of some underlying concepts, such as written rules and people's reactions to rules, and they predict what might happen next based on this understanding. At the responding level of the *Affective Taxonomy*, the students indicate their responses to some of the concepts and describe personal experiences with these aspects of social control. At the valuing level, the value placed on the concepts also is important.

At the application level of the *Cognitive Taxonomy*, general statements and themes assume importance as the students apply a rule or principle in a new situation. The rule or principle can be a concept (category) or a statement of relationships between certain concepts. Analysis can include examining different aspects of concepts or examining several concepts to learn how they relate to each other to form a generalization. Of course, students are dealing with information, but they use it as examples or proof for ideas. Synthesis involves developing new generalizations or new products through combining encountered ideas in a new way. At the evaluation level, all types of content are important. Students judge the accuracy or appropriateness of information and the validity of concepts and general statements. In the two highest levels of the *Affective Taxonomy*, the major emphasis is on generalizations, with some focus on concepts and how they are related.

In both examples presented in this chapter, the element of complexity is included, since both the affective and cognitive processes are used. Complex ideas or thought systems as described by Taba (1962) consist not only of facts, principles, and concepts but also of methods and characteristic ways of thinking about ideas, objects, or phenomena, including value systems. To aid in fully understanding others' feelings about an idea, method, or phenomenon, students can be led through a process of examining their own affective behavior related to the same idea, method, or phenomenon.

To achieve maximum learning value, in addition to organizing content around key concepts and themes, an educator could begin the learning process at the application level as a way of discovering what is not known and thus needs to be taught. In this way, previous learning would not be repeated. The same process could be used with the *Affective Taxonomy* by beginning at the valuing level.

Variety

Because of its emphasis on affective content, Krathwohl's *Taxonomy* suggests the incorporation of content usually not taught in the regular curriculum. To achieve variety of content with the *Affective Taxonomy*, the suggested procedure and worksheet presented in the discussion of Bruner's approach would be appropriate. (See Table 3.4.)

Study of People

To incorporate this content modification, the taxonomies could be used as a structure for studying the lives and accomplishments of eminent individuals. A teaching approach that uses the taxonomies concurrently would be especially appropriate in this context. Students could be led through a process of examining the individuals and their characteristics, and also could study the reactions of other people. The gifted students could then examine their own lives, including value systems, and compare themselves with the individuals studied.

Methods of Inquiry

The taxonomies can be used easily as structures for studying different methods of inquiry. The taxonomies themselves are methods and, as such, can be taught to the students. The taxonomies are classification systems to facilitate communication between professionals in the behavioral sciences. Students can use them in the same way that professionals do.

Process Changes

Open-endedness and Evidence of Reasoning

These two process modifications are incorporated easily into teaching strategies that use the taxonomies as a basis. To achieve open-endedness, an educator should simply design all questions and learning activities so that they will encourage varied perceptions and be provocative. Stimulating, divergent activities and questions can be designed easily at the higher levels of the taxonomies but may be more difficult at the lower ones. Asking students to explain their reasoning or cite examples as evidence to support their conclusions is incorporated easily by asking for these explanations when answers are given at the higher levels of the taxonomies. Such explanations also may be appropriate at the responding and comprehension levels depending on the content and activities.

In the examples presented earlier in this chapter, all questions were designed to be open-ended and to stimulate further activity or thought. The examples also included questions calling for explanations of reasoning or logic when appropriate. For instance, one question at the responding level was "What are some of the social controls you have experienced? What were your reactions?" After this second question, a question calling for support is appropriate: "Why do you think you reacted that way?"

Discovery

Incorporating discovery learning into the use of the taxonomies is difficult if they are used as a strict hierarchical model. If the assumption is accepted that activities must be presented at each level of a taxonomy, beginning with knowledge and receiving and then progressing to comprehension and responding, the learning sequence would be deductive rather than inductive. With the *Cognitive Taxonomy,* for example, students are given the information needed to solve a problem (that is, the rule or principle) at the knowledge level, learn how to use the principle at the comprehension level, and are given a new problem and expected to apply the rule or principle in solving the problem at the application level. Following this, they analyze or break down the problem or solution, create something new, and then evaluate. This is essentially a deductive learning sequence.

To incorporate an inductive or discovery approach, one must reject the assumption that activities must be presented sequentially at each level of the taxonomies and make a major adaptation of the approach. Since research data are not adequate to indicate that sequential presentation is necessary, and support is available for the idea that inductive approaches work well with gifted students, such an adaptation seems justified. One way that the taxonomies can be adapted for the gifted is by presenting the first activities at the application level rather than beginning at the knowledge level.

One obvious advantage of this approach is that the teacher does not reteach what the students already know. A new problem or situation is presented to the students, and they attempt to solve it. If they do solve the problem, the teacher asks them to explain how they arrived at the solution. If they can explain the principle involved, as well as the process, further activities can be presented at the higher levels of the taxonomy. When students are unable to solve the problem, the teacher has several options. He or she can change to a deductive approach and present some applicable rules and principles, show how they are used, and then present more new problems. The teacher also can continue with an inductive approach and present several new problems that illustrate the rules or principles to be learned and, through questioning, lead the students to discover these underlying principles.

Freedom of Choice

With regard to students' freedom to choose learning activities and topics of study, the *Cognitive* and *Affective Taxonomies* can be used effectively. The teacher can design a variety of learning activities at each level and allow the students to choose ones that are of the most interest. The taxonomies could be presented to the students and used as a structure for designing their own learning activities. Students could choose their own topics of study and structure their learning about the topic so that mastery of each level of the taxonomy is demonstrated.

Group Interaction and Variety

To use the taxonomies in providing the curricular modification of group interaction, an educator can design activities for small groups using the taxonomies as the structure. Activities can be designed at the higher levels that will be challenging to students. Analysis activities are suited to the examination of tapes or other observational data, while synthesis activities are appropriate for designing plans for improving a group's interaction patterns. Evaluation is particularly appropriate for assessing individual and group participation and guiding plans for improvement.

The *Affective Taxonomy* is helpful as a procedure for examining each individual's participation in the group activities. Observers can, for example, examine and discuss the differing values of the individuals involved and how these values may have influenced their interaction in the group. In this same context, this taxonomy could be used as an observation tool. Observers could look for behaviors and statements that indicate the stage of development of certain values in the individuals being observed. In other words, does a person's behavior indicate that she or he has incorporated a particular belief to the extent that it has become a part of a philosophy of life? Also, does he or she always behave consistently with that belief (that is, characterization by a value or value complex)? Or is the person simply willing to be identified with that belief (that is, valuing level)?

To provide the curricular modification of variety, the taxonomies can be used to develop a variety of activities. For example, a structured series of questions for use in a class discussion would lead students gradually through the levels of thinking. They can be used to design learning center tasks that would lead students to higher levels of thinking. The taxonomies can be used in designing games, as a part of contract learning, and as the basis for auto-instructional programs. Creative readers can generate many more uses for these adaptable classification systems.

Pacing

The most important aspect of pacing with regard to the taxonomies is that movement through the lower levels must be as rapid as possible since students can acquire the needed knowledge quickly and learn to put it to use rapidly. They must be allowed to move to the next level as soon as they have demonstrated competence at a particular level.

Product Changes

Neither of the taxonomies provide specific suggestions for product modifications, though the *Cognitive Taxonomy* provides a useful way of assessing whether a product is a transformation of existing information or merely a summary. With regard to the evaluation of products, however, both classifications can be used by the students in self-evaluation and can be used by other audiences to evaluate the products. When using them as evaluation schemes, the evaluator examines the product in two ways. First, he or she attempts to determine whether the student who produced the product used all levels of thinking in the development process or whether the person used only the lower levels. In other words, the product as a whole is evaluated to determine its level in the taxonomy scheme. The next assessment represents an attempt to determine the quality and accuracy of the product with regard to each level. For example, at the knowledge level, "Does the product contain accurate and complete information?" At the comprehension level, "Are the trends and implications that are presented valid?" And at the characterization level, "Are the values presented consistent with the attitudes and behaviors described?" These are questions that can be asked to determine the quality and accuracy of the product.

Learning activities at the analysis level can be valuable in helping students decide upon problems to investigate or narrow an area of study so that a solvable problem or researchable question is posed. Teachers can assist in this process by helping students to design their own activities for use in this context.

The evaluation level of the taxonomy can be used as a guide for developing criteria for simulated audiences to use in evaluating the product. Activities at this level also can be used to generate possible criteria that a real audience would use in product evaluation.

Learning Environment Changes

All the learning environment changes advocated for gifted students are important facilitators of the successful use of the taxonomies as they would be modified. If learners are to achieve the objectives of reaching the highest levels, the environment must be centered around their ideas and interests. They must be encouraged to be independent; the environment must be open and must include complex tasks and materials. If students are allowed the freedom to choose activities at all levels, they will need flexibility, varied grouping arrangements, and high physical mobility.

One aspect of the environment that is particularly critical in the development of higher levels of thinking is the accepting versus judging dimension. If students do not believe they are free to express their ideas, they will respond only at the lower levels by repeating what the teacher or someone else has said, rather than take a risk by generating their own ideas. Since expressing feelings is riskier than expressing ideas, this dimension of the environment is more important with the *Affective Taxonomy* than the *Cognitive Taxonomy*. The hierarchy of teacher behaviors presented by Maker (1982) that moves from attending through accepting, clarifying, and challenging is especially critical.

The authors of the taxonomies do not make suggestions about the kind of learning environment that should be established when the taxonomies are used. Their comments do not address the environmental dimensions important at different levels of the classification schemes.

Summary

By combining the *Cognitive* and *Affective Taxonomies* with Bruner's content suggestions, and by using the taxonomies differently (for example, not rigidly progressing through each level), many of the content, process, and product modifications appropriate for the gifted can be made. Two major adaptations of the models have been suggested: (a) teaching the taxonomies to gifted students so they can apply the ideas to their own investigations and (b) beginning each learning sequence at the application level rather than at the knowledge level so that learning is not repeated and inductive learning is facilitated.

DEVELOPMENT

In 1948, at an informal meeting of college examiners attending the American Psychological Association (APA) convention (Bloom, 1956), the idea for developing a theoretical framework for classifying educational objectives was proposed. This meeting became the first of a series of informal annual meetings of college examiners. The members were not always the same, but a core group usually was present. Early in the process, the group decided that the major purpose of the taxonomy should be to facilitate communication between educators. To fulfill this purpose, it would need to have at least the following four characteristics:

1. It should be an educational taxonomy and, whenever possible, should be related closely to the decisions educators must make.

2. The classification system should be logical; it should define terms as concisely as possible and should use them consistently.

3. It should be consistent with psychological theories and principles that are accepted widely and are relevant.

4. It should avoid value judgments, being neutral about principles and philosophies so that objectives from many different orientations could be classified.

The committee of approximately 30 people began its work by collecting a large list of educational objectives, dividing each objective into intended behavior and content of the behavior, and then attempting to group the behaviors according to their similarities. In an attempt to develop an order from simple to complex, the committee looked for a psychological theory that could be used as an overall framework. They found none, so they developed their own logical system. After developing the categories and definitions of the categories, the committee members attempted to classify additional objectives independently using the system and to compare their separate classifications. In this way, they could clarify ambiguities and further refine the system.

At the outset, the committee's intent was to develop taxonomies in three domains: (a) cognitive, (b) affective, and (c) psychomotor. Since the cognitive domain was most central to their work, it was the first area to be developed and was the only taxonomy completed by the basic committee. A subcommittee responsible for the affective domain finally completed its work and published that taxonomy without submitting it to the original committee for review (Krathwohl et al., 1964). Thus, the *Cognitive Taxonomy* has been subjected to more critical reviews both by the committee and by other educators.

After the committee completed its work, a preliminary edition of 1,000 copies was published and sent to college and secondary teachers, administrators, and research specialists, who were asked to read and offer suggestions. Their critiques and ideas were incorporated into the final version of the *Cognitive Taxonomy*. The *Affective Taxonomy*, although read by a wide variety of educators, has not received the same depth of criticism.

RESEARCH ON EFFECTIVENESS

With Nongifted

Research on the use of the taxonomies, because of their nature as hierarchies, must concentrate on three related issues: (a) the validity of the hierarchical arrangement (Are they actually arranged from simple to complex? Do the higher levels actually include the lower levels?), (b) their clarity and comprehensiveness (If two or more independent observers classify an objective or a question, will they put it in the same category? Can every educational objective be classified according to the taxonomy?), and (c) the effectiveness of the taxonomy's use with students (By participating in learning activities designed according to the taxonomies, are students more capable of behaving competently at the higher levels?) Most research to date has concentrated on the first two issues, although some evidence is available on the third.

Whether or not the *Cognitive Taxonomy*'s hierarchical arrangement is valid is a question that still has not been resolved. Some evidence exists (Ayers, 1966; Bloom, 1956; Chausow, 1955; Dressel & Mayhew, 1954; Stoker & Kropp, 1964) that the complex behaviors at the higher levels are more difficult than those at the lower levels. In other words, fewer students will perform as well on tests of the higher abilities. Each individual's performance will decrease as the tasks become more complex. The level that usually seems out of place, however, is evaluation. It does not appear to be the most difficult intellectual behavior (Solman & Rosen, 1986; Stoker & Kropp, 1964).

In general, the research supports the *Cognitive Taxonomy*'s comprehensiveness and clarity when used by both practitioners and researchers (Bloom, 1956; Buros, 1959; Dressel & Nelson, 1956; Gabbert, Johnson, & Johnson, 1986; Lessinger, 1963; McGuire, 1963; Morris, 1961; Stanley & Bolton, 1957; Stoker & Kropp, 1964; Tyler, 1966). The first test of the taxonomy's clarity and comprehensiveness was made by its developers when they independently classified additional objectives using their system. They identified only a few objectives that could not be classified. In subsequent studies of its use, considerable agreement exists among raters attempting to classify objectives, as well as conclusive evidence that almost no objectives exist that do not fit into the system. Factor analytic studies of its structure (Milholland, 1966; Stoker & Kropp, 1964; Zinn, 1966), however, indicate that the categories are not mutually exclusive—a student's general ability and motivation appear to be the factors determining his or her achievement of objectives at all levels.

Relative to the use of the *Cognitive Taxonomy* as a basis for developing sequential learning activities, some empirical support can be found in studies of the effectiveness of asking higher level questions before, during, and after a student reads a passage of material. In most of these studies, subjects are given questions at some or all levels of the taxonomy to guide in their reading or recall of the information, and they are tested later to see how effective their learning has been. For example, when students study materials containing either knowledge-level or evaluation-level materials and then are given test questions at all levels of the taxonomy, students who receive evaluation questions during instruction do better on evaluation questions on the posttests.

Those who are given inferential questions do better overall and significantly better on the questions calling for new inferences about old groups than do those given only factual questions. In some studies using classifications of cognitive questions other than the taxonomy (Dapra & Felker, 1974; Felker & Dapra, 1975; Watts & Anderson, 1971), the results indicate that when students have practice at a certain level, they do better on posttests at that level. Practice at the lower levels does not seem to improve performance at the higher levels. Other studies (Andre, 1978; Holland, 1965) however, have not provided support for this area.

In research of a different nature, results indicate that certain types of learning activities improve performance at the higher levels. Knowledge objectives may be learned equally well under both lecture and discussion conditions, but performance at the higher levels is facilitated by discussions and laboratory experiences in which students engage in problem solving and are helped to see how their skills can be improved. Gabbert, Johnson, and Johnson (1986) found that first-grade students ($N = 52$) who were randomly assigned to either cooperative or individual learning conditions on a series of 10 Bloom higher level thinking tasks, from comprehension through synthesis and analysis, showed improvement in higher level thinking, but the productivity of students in cooperative learning groups was significantly higher than that of students working alone. Since discussions, laboratory experiments, and cooperative learning projects usually require learning activities similar to those designed to develop the higher levels of thinking, while lectures do not really encourage their use, this research provides some indirect evidence for the use of the *Cognitive Taxonomy* in designing learning experiences.

Relative to the *Affective Taxonomy,* no studies have been found that address any one of the three issues identified earlier. Perhaps this lack of research is due to a general lack of interest in affective outcomes. It also could be due to the ambiguity often found in affective objectives or the emotional aspects of dealing with values or value-laden subjects. Regardless of the causes for this lack of research, the widespread use of this taxonomy implies a need for some tests of its validity.

With Gifted

When searching for information about the possible effectiveness of curricula based on the *Cognitive* and *Affective Taxonomies* with gifted children, researchers find that the picture is even more bleak. Although programs with curricula based on the *Cognitive Taxonomy* have generally been effective as evidenced by their evaluations, one cannot determine the role of the taxonomy in producing these results. Their effectiveness could simply be due to the fact that gifted students are identified, thus enhancing the students' perceptions of themselves as capable individuals. Similarly, programs based on or using the *Affective Taxonomy* have shown success, but the program evaluations have not shown that this success is attributable to the use of the taxonomy.

JUDGMENTS

Advantages

The most obvious advantages for use of the taxonomies, particularly the cognitive one, stem from their widespread use and acceptance in educational circles. The taxonomy project certainly has achieved its goal of facilitating communication through developing a useful system of classification. Because the system is known, understood, and used in numerous classrooms as a part of the regular curriculum, building on this regular curriculum by concentrating on a greater number of experiences at the higher levels is easy. Communication with other teachers and the administration is enhanced by having the same language. Also due to this widespread use, many classroom materials based on the *Cognitive Taxonomy* are available.

A second advantage of the taxonomies is their relative simplicity and applicability. They are not difficult for teachers to learn and use and can be applied in all content areas and at all levels of instruction. The taxonomies are comprehensive enough to include most objectives that have been developed. Research shows that the hierarchy is valid except for the possible misplacement of the evaluation level.

In addition to its use as a way to develop learning activities that improve students' higher levels of thinking and feeling, the taxonomies have certain related uses (Limburg, 1979). First, they help teachers develop more precise, measurable objectives. If teachers have in mind a general objective, such as "understands concepts involved in . . . ," the *Cognitive Taxonomy* can be used to suggest a more quantifiable statement of the objective. Second, the taxonomies can be used as guides for the development of better teacher-made tests, tests that will sample a variety of levels of thinking or feeling. A related use is evaluating standardized tests for measuring the success of programs for the gifted. Often, even though the program is designed to facilitate the higher levels of thinking, achievement tests that assess recognition and recall are the only instruments used to evaluate their success. In construction of evaluation measures, the taxonomies provide a useful way of matching the instructional emphasis according to levels with the emphasis in evaluative procedures.

Important to the effective use of the taxonomies is the availability of a practical reference source for the teacher. Both systems have comprehensive handbooks available that describe the various categories, relationships among the categories, and numerous specific examples of items included in each category. The handbooks also include self-assessment sections to aid the reader in learning the system.

Disadvantages

On the negative side, the most important considerations are the lack of research on effectiveness with learners, particularly gifted ones, and the limited scope in providing a structure for curricular modification for the gifted. This review of research has not resulted in evidence that the use of the taxonomies will have the hypothesized effect of improving higher levels of thinking. No research even touches on the validity of the categories or the hierarchical arrangement of the *Affective Taxonomy,* and the research on one level of the *Cognitive Taxonomy,* evaluation, suggests that it may not be placed at the right level.

The assumption of a sequential approach to levels of thinking in the *Cognitive Taxonomy* can be misleading. Curriculum developers and test makers find that constructing activities that focus on specific knowledge or recall of information is relatively easy. At all other levels of the taxonomy, an interplay of many types of thinking seems to occur. Comprehension, for example, is an interactive process that includes recall of information, analysis of the relationship of the information to one's existing knowledge base, and evaluation of its potential usefulness. Beyer (1987) characterized the elements in the *Cognitive Taxonomy* as microthinking skills or building blocks for more complex operations such as conceptualizing, problem solving, and decision making. While the *Cognitive Taxonomy* is a useful tool for structuring some learning activities for gifted students, educators would be wise to include activities at several thinking levels in most lessons for gifted students.

The third disadvantage, a limited scope, was discussed earlier, along with the description of curricular modifications suggested by the models. Curricular adaptations made possible through use of the taxonomies are mainly in the areas of process (for example, the development of higher levels of thinking and feeling) and content (for example, developing objectives that focus on the principles and abstractions in a particular discipline). Use of the *Affective Taxonomy* facilitates content changes by suggesting ways to integrate "feeling" content into academic areas and providing a structure for doing so. Some psychological environment modifications also are facilitated by the use of the *Affective Taxonomy*. However, the taxonomies must be combined with other models or used differently to provide a framework for a total approach to curriculum development for gifted students.

CONCLUSION

The *Taxonomies of Educational Objectives* cannot be defended as a total approach to curriculum development for gifted learners and are sometimes difficult to justify at all due to their widespread use in regular education. However, they can be used as one aspect of a program for gifted students, particularly to show the relative emphasis on higher- versus lower-level thinking and feeling processes. Associated uses (i.e., evaluation, development of teacher-made tests, evaluation of standardized tests, construction of more quantifiable objectives) and modifications of the taxonomies can make them more defensible as models to be used in programs for the gifted.

RESOURCES

Background

Roberts, C., Ingram, C., & Harris, C. (1992). The effect of special versus regular classroom programming on the higher cognitive processes of intermediate elementary aged gifted and average ability students. *Journal for the Education of the Gifted, 15*(4), 332–343. In this study, gifted and average-ability students in a special treatment group were given thinking skill training based on Bloom's *Taxonomy* and Guilford's *Structure of Intellect*. Control groups of gifted and average-ability students studied the same content without the addition of thinking skills training. Gains from pretest to posttest on the *Ross Test of Higher Cognitive Processes* significantly favored the two treatment groups.

Solman, R., & Rosen, G. (1986). Bloom's six cognitive levels represent two levels of performance. *Educational Psychology*, 6(3), 243–263. Based on a study with more than 300 Australian secondary school students, the authors conclude that Bloom's levels of analysis and synthesis require greater cognitive maturity than do the other four levels. They argue that synthesis is the highest level of the taxonomy and that little evidence can be found to support the hierarchical arrangement of the six taxonomic levels.

Instructional Materials and Resources

Gangi, J. M. (1990, January/February). Higher level thinking skills through drama. *G/C/T*, pp. 16–19. The author presents a potpourri of activities for children that develop both dramatic talents and thinking skills.

McAlpine, J., Jeweler, S., Weincek, B., & Finkbinder, M. (1987, January/February). Creative problem solving and Bloom: The thinking connection. *G/C/T*, pp. 11–14. A Saturday program for gifted students in grades 7 through 9 in which the transfer/applications of a study of CPS and Bloom's *Taxonomy* were developed in the context of invention or futuristics is described.

Scott, J. (n.d.). *Teach thinking strategies*. Victoria, Australia: Down Under Books. Based on Bloom's Taxonomy of Cognitive Objectives, this book contains ideas for teaching higher level thinking skills for students in grades 7 through 12. Photocopyable resource pages are designed to help students reflect on and write about their thinking strategies.

TNT: Talented and thinking: A complete program for gifted students. Buffalo, NY: D.O.K. This series includes four reproducible workbooks based on Bloom's Taxonomy. Titles are *Creative Communication, Science and Invention, People and Places,* and *Intriguing Endeavors.* The teacher's handbook contains specific objectives for each activity (grades 2 through 8).

Udall, A. J., & Daniels, M. A. (1991). *Creating the thoughtful classroom: Strategies to promote student thinking.* Tucson, AZ: Zephyr Press. Classroom tested and classroom ready, this is a guide that teachers can use to help develop students' thinking skills in grades 3 through 12. Methods of assessment also are included.

Chapter 4

Jerome Bruner: The Basic Structure of a Discipline

O f all the teaching-learning models discussed in this book, Bruner's is the most philosophical. The *Basic Structure of a Discipline* is not actually a framework but a way of approaching the development of a framework. Bruner's ideas have contributed to many of the other models presented and to the authors' views of curricular modifications appropriate for gifted learners. The "basic concept" idea assumed great importance in several innovative curricula developed in the 1960s and 1970s (for example, *Man: A Course of Study* [MACOS; Education Development Center, 1970]) that proved to be very effective with gifted students.

At the same time, many of these curricula were not enjoying the same degree of success with average students. One school district in Illinois, for example, attempted to implement a social studies curriculum based on the "structure of a discipline" concept in all its regular social studies classrooms because of its success as an innovation in the program for the gifted. Much to the educators' disappointment, the curriculum had to be "watered down" so much that most of the original form was lost. As an aside, they also felt that to teach the curriculum effectively, the teacher needed to be gifted. Gallagher (1966), who was involved in the development of the Illinois program, also notes the value of Bruner's approach for the same reasons. Taba, in the development of both her theory of curriculum development (1962) and her *Teaching Strategies* program (1964, 1966) draws heavily upon the concept of teaching the "basic structure" of a discipline as a way to organize and structure the content to be taught. Teaching the methodology and "thought systems" of the various disciplines, an associated idea attributed to Bruner, also influenced Taba, as it did Renzulli (1977) in the conception of his "Type III Enrichment" activities. Students acting as "real inquirers" is another Brunerian concept influencing curricular practices in education of the gifted.

Many ideas in this chapter are actually a result of the now-famous "Woods Hole" Conference on education in science, sponsored by the National Academy of Sciences and directed by Jerome Bruner. In the report from the conference, *The Process of Education* (Bruner, 1960), five areas of education are discussed: (a) the importance of structure, (b) readiness for learning, (c) intuitive and analytic thinking, (d) motives for learning, and (e) aids to teaching. Although four of these areas will be discussed, the importance of structure is of most interest in this book because of the influence these ideas have had on practices in the field of education of the gifted. The basic reference for the ideas is Bruner (1960), and the implications for curriculum development for the gifted are the authors' unless otherwise noted.

ASSUMPTIONS UNDERLYING THE APPROACH

About Teaching and Learning

One assumption has formed the basis for most of Bruner's ideas: "Intellectual activity anywhere is the same, whether at the frontier of knowledge or in a third-grade classroom" (1960, p. 14). The difference is in degree, not in kind, and the best way to learn history is to do it by behaving the way a historian would. Thus instead of focusing on the conclusions in a field of inquiry, the focus should be on the inquiry itself. Most of Bruner's ideas follow from this basic conviction. A person more nearly approximates an inquirer if the basic ideas of that discipline are understood and are of concern, if concepts are "revisited" as understanding increases, if a balance is established between intuition and analysis, and if a long-term commitment to intellectual activity and the pursuit of knowledge is clear.

The Importance of Structure

The theme underlying Bruner's approach is that the aim in education should be to teach the basic structure of academic disciplines in such a way that this structure can be understood by children. This basic structure consists of certain concepts (for example, biological tropisms in science; revolution in social studies; supply and demand in economics; and commutation, distribution, and association in mathematics) and the important relationships between them. In addition to basic concepts, themes, and theories, each discipline has characteristic patterns of inquiry or strategies for research and information management. For example, Figure 4.1 illustrates key generalizations from social science disciplines and the varied approach practitioners in the discipline take toward the problems of world poverty and hunger.

Key Social Science Generalizations	
Discipline	*Generalizations*
History	Wherever human beings have lived, conflicts between individuals, groups, and nations have arisen. A historian's view of the past is influenced by the availability of evidence, his or her personal biases and purposes for writing, and the society and times in which he or she lives and writes.
Sociology	All characteristically human behavior is learned from other human beings through group interaction. The group exerts social control over its individual members through the use of sanctions.
Anthropology	Cultures use a diversity of means to attain similar ends and to satisfy common human needs. Cultural exchange takes place when groups with diverse cultures come into prolonged contact. Cultural change may disrupt a society.
Geography	The physical environment influences how a culture develops and how it solves the problems of survival. An individual's perception of his or her physical environment is influenced by his or her culture and experiences within that environment.
Political science	In every society and institution, regulations and laws emerge to govern the behavior of individuals and groups. Rules and laws reflect the basic values within a society or institution.
Economics	Every individual and society faces a conflict between unlimited wants and limited resources. All members of society are interdependent. Individual producers of goods and services exchange with others to get the goods and services they need to satisfy their basic wants.

Figure 4. 1.   Social sciences. From *Teaching Strategies for the Social*   (*continues*)
Studies: Inquiry, Valuing, Decision-Making (4th ed.) by J. A. Banks, 1990,
New York: Longman. Reprinted with permission.

Perspectives on Global Hunger and Poverty

Historian
Analyzes events that culminated in global hunger and poverty; illuminates similarities between hunger and poverty today and in previous historical periods.

Economist
Studies the economic factors that contributed to the development of global hunger and poverty. Suggests that the standards of living in the world's affluent nations will have to be reduced if the problems of global hunger and poverty are to be solved.

Political scientist
Studies the political consequences of a world that is made up of "have" and "have not" nations. Suggests that power struggles and war might result if the world's scarce resources are not more equally distributed among the rich and poor nations.

Sociologist
Analyzes the effects of hunger and poverty on the norms, values, and socialization practices among the victims of hunger and poverty. Suggests that severe hunger and poverty has a cogent impact on socialization practices.

Psychologist
Analyzes the nature and extent of aggression and frustration that develop among people who are victims of severe hunger and poverty.

Anthropologist
Studies how the responses to severe poverty and hunger are alike and different in various cultures. Concludes that responses to hunger and poverty are influenced by both cultural and biological factors.

Geographer
Studies how hunger and poverty influence people's perceptions of their physical environment and their interactions with it.

Figure 4. 1.   *Continued*

Such concepts and relationships, when understood, enable the learner to understand most of the phenomena in that discipline. Understanding the basic structure means that an individual not only has learned a specific thing but also has learned a model for understanding similar things that may be encountered. A phenomenon is recognized as a specific instance of a more general case. Carefully developed understanding also should permit the student to recognize the limits of applicability of the generalizations.

When developing this theme, several assumptions were made. These beliefs have varying degrees of acceptance or proof in the psychological and educational literature. The first assumption is that the first object of learning is service in the future; whatever people learn should allow them to go further more easily. Learning serves persons in the future through both specific and general transfer. By definition, Bruner argues, basic concepts or ideas have wider applicability and thus greater transfer to future situations. By learning underlying ideas, the student can master more of the subject more quickly, and since educators have little time and much to teach, these basic ideas will go much further.

Related to this idea is the belief that memory is facilitated if a structure is learned. Bruner states that research on memory has shown that unless details (for example, facts or data) are placed in a structured pattern, they are forgotten easily. Once the structure is learned, these facts or details can be remembered more easily or reconstructed if necessary. Another underlying assumption is that by teaching basic structure the gap between basic and advanced knowledge can be narrowed. One difficulty faced by learners from elementary schools through universities is the necessity of "relearning" because traditional information-based curricula often lag far behind new developments in a field of study.

For the teaching of structure to be effective, the curriculum must be rewritten and materials devised so that the most basic ideas are taught. This can best be done by scholars and competent persons in their respective fields. Another requirement is that the materials and presentation must be matched to the abilities of children at different grade levels. This can be done only by those familiar with and experienced in working with children.

Certainly problems are involved in these two assumptions. A major problem is difficulty in achieving agreement among scholars about what constitutes the structure or the most basic ideas that should be taught. Indeed, several attempts to define these basic ideas have resulted in the development of thousands of ideas due to the lack of agreement.

Readiness for Learning

The theme of this section can be summed up in Bruner's bold statement that ". . . any subject can be taught effectively in some intellectually honest form to any child at any stage of development" (1960, p. 33). This statement implies that the form in which the basic structure is taught must be matched to the level of intellectual development of the child and that the basic concepts involved should be revisited as time goes on and the child becomes capable of understanding more of the complexities of the concept.

Underlying the ideas about readiness for learning is the basic assumption that Piaget and other developmentalists are right in saying that at certain stages of development children have a characteristic way of viewing and explaining the world. A young child learns through direct sensory and motor experiences, while children in the next stage—concrete operations—no longer need direct trial-and-error experiences. They now can learn through mentally carrying out activities. At the concrete operational stage, internalized cognitive structures or "schema" are developed that guide the child's perception of reality. However, at this stage the child still must deal only with present reality or direct experiences from the past. Only after children have reached the stage of formal operations can they deal with hypothetical propositions.

The obvious implication of a developmental view of learning readiness is that in the stage of concrete operations, for example, understanding of a basic concept would need to be developed by providing the child with direct concrete experiences. Learning can be accomplished through exercises in manipulating, classifying, and ordering objects, but attempting a formal, logical explanation of the principles involved would be futile. After students have reached formal operations, they are able to understand a formal logical proof or explanation and also develop logical explanations.

One assumption that Bruner makes, however, is somewhat different from Piaget's emphasis. Although Piaget recognizes the role of the environment in the learning process, he does not encourage manipulation of the environment. Instead, he suggests that the normal course of development be allowed to occur. Bruner, on the other hand, suggests that children be "tempted" into the next stages of development by presenting them with challenging and usable opportunities to move ahead.

When educators consider what concepts to teach a child, in addition to the methods used and the consideration of the act of learning, they also must consider whether, when fully developed, these concepts would be valuable for an adult to know. This requirement underlies the idea of a spiral curriculum. As time goes on, the learner returns to these basic concepts, building on them and making them more complex. The learner also relates them to more complex stimuli, so the concepts must be valuable to know.

In his discussion of readiness, Bruner also includes the assumption that learning a subject involves three almost simultaneous processes. First, the learner must acquire information. The information may replace, enhance, contradict, or refine present knowledge. Then comes transformation, the process of manipulating knowledge to make it fit new tasks. Learners transform knowledge in a way that will enable them to go beyond it. A third process is evaluation, checking to see whether manipulation or transformation of information was adequate. In each learning "episode," which may be brief or long and contain many or few ideas, all three processes are present. What is not known, and what Bruner makes no assumptions about, is the amount of emphasis that should be placed on each process in a learning episode, the length and intensity of an episode, what techniques can increase motivation to learn in each episode, and how to achieve a balance between intrinsic and extrinsic rewards to enhance learning in each episode.

Intuitive and Analytic Thinking

Although the nature of, predisposing conditions for, and techniques of measuring intuitive thinking are unknown or undeveloped, intuition is an important complement to analytic thinking and should be developed to the fullest extent possible. The two thinking processes are almost direct opposites. In contrast to analytic thinking, intuitive thinking does not proceed in a step-by-step order with full awareness of the information and operations needed. Rather, it involves maneuvers based on implicit perception of the total problem with little or no awareness of the process used. An individual who uses intuition appears to make seemingly careless, big leaps instead of smaller, measured steps.

According to scholars in various academic fields, the effectiveness of intuition lies in an individual's knowledge of a subject. Through familiarity with the subject, individuals feed their intuition or give it something with which to work. After making an "intuitive leap" and coming up with a solution or hypothesis, the individual can then check or prove its validity through more careful analytical means. The nature of intuitive thinking, ways of measurement, possible predisposing characteristics, and factors affecting the process are areas in which further study is needed. Davidson and Sternberg (1984) developed a subtheory of insight as intellectual giftedness comprised of three separate, but related, processes: selective encoding, or the process of sifting relevant from irrelevant information; selective combination, or blending pieces of relevant information into a unified whole; and selective comparison, or relating newly acquired information to knowledge acquired in the past. They devised varied tasks to assess the level of intuition among gifted and nongifted learners and also to discover whether an insight training program would be feasible for students of at least average ability. The results of their research did indicate that gifted students appeared to solve insight problems more efficiently and with fewer cues than nongifted students. Additionally, gifted students profited little from the training program, while average students improved performance significantly after training. The results of the experiments were consistent with the information-processing theory of insight but, as selective encoding, selective combination, and selective comparison can exist in the absence of insight, additional research is needed with more consequential problems to discover the nature of the processes that constitute insightful thinking. Bruner does make some observations about them but does not assume he is correct. He believes, for example, that effective intuitive thinking requires self-confidence and courage on the part of the student. Mistakes can be made easily by relying on intuition, so a certain willingness to take risks is important. When drawing a parallel with business and industry, where the increasing importance and novelty of a situation causes a decrease in the tendency to think intuitively,

Bruner suggests that the present system of rewards and punishments (usually in the form of grades) actually may discourage intuitive thinking. When considering the development of this process of thinking, educators also must recognize the problems involved. Teachers must be sensitive enough to differentiate between an ignorant answer and an answer from an interesting wrong leap. They must have a thorough knowledge of subject matter, and they must be able to give both approval and correction to a student at the same time.

Motives for Learning

Motivation, an important step toward a pursuit of excellence, must be a happy medium between frenzied activity and apathy. One of the important goals of education must be to arouse long-term interest, or a continuing commitment to learning and the world of ideas, rather than a commitment to capturing the short-term interest of children necessary for learning a "lesson." Bruner believes that the pursuit of excellence should be emphasized through education and that one way to facilitate this pursuit of excellence is through a continuing interest in learning. Along with interest will be a high regard for intellectual activity.

Students have varied and mixed motives for learning, including approval of parents, teachers, and peers, along with their own sense of mastery. To foster the development of interest, educators can develop better exams and counseling techniques, improve teaching methods, and improve subject matter.

About Characteristics and Teaching the Gifted

In his book, Bruner makes several references to the gifted that are interesting in the light of subsequent application of his ideas to the education of gifted children. The first statement he makes is "Good teaching which emphasizes the structure of a subject is probably even more valuable for the less able student than for the gifted one, for it is the former rather than the latter who is most easily thrown off the track by poor teaching" (1960, p. 9). By this statement he does not mean that the content or pace of courses should be the same, but means that if good teaching occurs, even the slowest students can achieve. What he did not take into account with this statement, however, is that not all students would be able to handle or learn the basic concepts identified. Many concepts important to the understanding of a discipline are abstract and highly complex; reasoning and inferential powers sufficient for dealing with complex concepts may not have developed in some students.

From this statement, one assumption seems clear: the conference participants, who were themselves scholars in academic disciplines, were assuming that all learners could profit from the kind of inquiry activities they themselves profited from. Indeed, they stated their central conviction that "intellectual activity anywhere is the same, whether at the frontier of knowledge or in a third-grade classroom" (1960, p. 14). What literary critics or students studying literature do in reading a literary work is the same if they are to achieve understanding. This assumption may be true for all learners, but perhaps it is true only of those who are able to achieve a complete understanding of the basic abstract concepts that form the structure of an academic discipline.

Bruner also should consider his requirement that each concept taught to students be subjected to the test of whether it will be useful to them as adults. Some students, for example, may not need a deep understanding of algebraic principles, the principles of logic, or even the idea of biological tropism. Only those who choose to pursue further study in a field will be interested in these ideas or use them as adults.

A second reference to the gifted is in the speculation that improvements in the teaching of science and mathematics may accentuate the gaps between children of differing ability levels. This possibility, though, should not deter educators from making modifications that will allow learners to develop their reasoning powers fully. Democracy and leadership will have a better chance of surviving if the top quarter of this nation's students are not neglected as they have been in the past.

Bruner states that the pursuit of excellence should not be limited to gifted learners. On the other hand, teaching should not be aimed simply at the average student. The curriculum should contain something for everyone. The challenge is to develop materials that are difficult enough for the most able learners without destroying the confidence of those who are less able— an almost impossible task!

Although not made by Bruner, an assumption made by those who implement his ideas is expressed in the above discussion related to which children need to learn (or will use as adults) the basic ideas or concepts in academic areas. Basic modes of inquiry, the "thought systems," and certain abstract ideas necessary for complete understanding of a field of study will most likely be of use to potential scholars, who often are gifted learners.

ELEMENTS/PARTS

Rather than explaining how an individual can implement each of the five themes expressed by Bruner, which would require volumes, the parts of his approach appearing to have the most potential for success with gifted children are selected and explained. Selection of the ideas to be explained is based not only on the first author's experience but also on the recommendations of other educators of the gifted (for example, Gallagher, 1975; Renzulli & Reis, 1985; Ward, 1961).

Modifications of Content

The most important curricular suggestions made by Bruner are changes in content or what is taught. His major theme is that what should be taught is the "basic structure" of a discipline. Incorporated into his definition of basic structure are several of the recommended content modifications: abstractness, complexity, organization for learning value, and the teaching of methods of inquiry in each discipline. In fact, the only content modifications not addressed in his approach are variety and the study of people. The first three concepts (i.e., abstractness, complexity, and organization) are, from Bruner's point of view, implications resulting from the teaching of basic structure and necessary requirements for its successful implementation. All of these will be discussed together since they are related. The recommendation for teaching methods of inquiry will be discussed as a process or method modification, since his suggestion is that students learn history the way a historian would or learn science the way a scientist would.

The first suggestion Bruner makes is related to the first task in curriculum development: What should be taught? In other words, what are those basic ideas that form the structure of a subject? Which ideas or concepts, when understood, will have the widest applicability to new situations? Which concepts will be needed by students as adults? The people qualified to make these decisions are the scholars in various disciplines. Only they have a complete enough understanding of their discipline to decide what is basic. Since the problem involves not only what concepts should be taught but also how they can be translated into a form that children at different levels of development can understand, Bruner suggests curriculum committees made up of both scholars and child development specialists. These committees can address both questions simultaneously.

A problem with this suggestion is the apparently erroneous assumption that scholars can agree upon the basic concepts that should be taught. Some of the earlier curriculum development projects that grew out of this suggestion included lists of as many as 3,500 generalizations in the social sciences. This phenomenon defeated the purpose of the project since teachers still had to make the major decisions about what was most important. All of these general ideas could not be taught. One can, however, force the issue; ideas agreed upon by the majority can constitute the basic or required curriculum, while those with lesser degrees of agreement can make up the optional or extended curriculum.

The idea of organization for learning value is a significant one in implementing a basic concept approach. Since children have only a limited amount of time in school and an almost unlimited number of things to learn, educators must make each learning experience a valuable one and each concept important. As a guiding principle for implementing this idea, Bruner suggests as criteria the following dual consideration: (a) When fully developed, is it worth being known by an adult? and (b) having known it as a child, does a person become a better adult? According to Bruner, "If the answer to both is negative or ambiguous, then the material is cluttering the curriculum" (1960, p. 52).

A related principle, implicit in Bruner's discussions but not stated as such, is that of organizing the content so that it will facilitate the discovery or development of a basic idea. Using the methods of a scholar and studying phenomena with the potential to increase the chances that a basic idea will be discovered is at the heart of this approach. By structuring activities so that discovery is facilitated, the teachers also develop the interests of learners and capitalize on their natural curiosity and excitement.

One example of the organization of content or learning experiences to facilitate discovery is Bruner's classic example of a basic concept in the area of biology. Presented as an example of a basic idea and how it can transfer to a new situation, it also illustrates how content can be organized.

> Take first a set of observations on an inchworm crossing a sheet of graph paper mounted on a straight line. We tilt the board so that the inclined plane or upward grade is 30°. We observe that the animal does not go straight up, but travels at an angle of 45° from the line of maximum climb. We now tilt the board to 60°. At what angle does the animal travel with respect to the line of maximum climb? Now, say, he travels along a line 75° off the straight-up line. From these two measures, we may infer that inchworms "prefer" to travel uphill, if uphill they must go, along an incline of 15°. We have discovered a tropism, as it is called, indeed a geotropism. It is not an isolated fact. We can go on to show that among simple organisms, such phenomena—regulation of locomotion according to a fixed or built-in standard—are the rule. There is a preferred level of illumination toward which lower organisms orient, a preferred level of salinity, of temperature, and so on. Once a student grasps this basic relation between external stimulation and locomotor action, he is well on his way toward being able to handle a good deal of seemingly new but, in fact, highly related information. The swarming of locusts where temperature determines the swarm density in which locusts are forced to travel, the species maintenance of insects at different altitudes on the side of a mountain where crossbreeding is prevented by the tendency of each species to travel in its preferred oxygen zone, and many other phenomena in biology can be understood in the light of tropisms. (Bruner, 1960, pp. 6–7)

First, the student can be asked to make observations of the behavior of the inchworm when the board is horizontal. Next, the student should observe under the conditions of a 30°, 45°, 60°, and 75° angle and record the behavior of the inchworm. Students can be asked to make similar observations about preferences of animals for environmental conditions, such as illumination, level of salinity, and temperature. In this way, the teacher has organized the content or the specific facts and data to be used around a concept. By having experiences arranged within a definite time period, the teacher facilitates discovery of the underlying principle of tropism. Organization around basic ideas also facilitates selection of the data to be used. Economy is achieved at the same time, since fewer experiences will be needed if arranged closely together to facilitate more rapid transfer.

Process Modifications

Although mainly a theory suggesting content changes, Bruner's ideas include the three following process modifications appropriate for gifted students: (a) higher levels of thinking, (b) discovery, and (c) open-endedness. Underlying the development of the concept of teaching basic structure is the idea that all intellectual activity is the same regardless of the level and that the best way to learn is to act the way a scholar would act or "create" knowledge in the way that someone on the frontier of knowledge would create it. Even though this underlying assumption contributed to the development of Bruner's basic structure theme, it also suggests a method for the effective teaching of structure. The suggestion is an obvious one: Methods of teaching should put the learner in the role of a scholar or inquirer in each subject area being taught.

In the physical sciences, the child should behave as a physicist, chemist, or engineer. In the natural sciences, the child should behave as a biologist, herpetologist, or geologist. In literature he or she should act as a poet, a short-story writer, a literary critic, or a playwright. Teachers must be familiar with the data and basic ideas of a discipline and also know its characteristic methods of inquiry. Alternatively, teachers need to make arrangements for skilled mentors who can work with students in a disciplined inquiry and give them suggestions for improving methodological skills. When a child acting as a sociologist is conducting an attitude survey, for example, the teacher must be prepared to give specific suggestions for designing better questions, analyzing the data, conducting interviews, scaling, and other data collection or evaluation methods.

Because of Bruner's emphasis on putting the learner in the role of a scholar or inquirer, the three process modifications are made. When children behave as scholars they will use, rather than simply acquire, information. Information gained will be applied in practical situations, evaluated, and used to form products new to the students. While using professional methods, the learners also are participating in open-ended activities that are provocative in nature. Discovery is an integral part of Bruner's approach, and he makes many suggestions for implementing it to allow the learner to behave as a scholar or professional. Aspects of open-endedness not included as part of Bruner's approach, however, relate to the questions asked of students while engaged in inquiry.

The following are three important aspects involved in implementing guided discovery: (a) organization and selection of data to be used in facilitating the child's discovery of some basic idea, (b) the use of questions or activities that will guide students in their process of inquiry, and (c) ways of teaching that will develop in the child an excitement about learning that will translate into an "inquiry attitude." Bruner does not give specific suggestions for implementing the approach, but he does provide general guidelines. First, a balance needs to be established between an approach in which the basic idea is first stated by the teacher with students providing the proof (a deductive approach), and an inductive or discovery approach. Presenting all of what a student needs to know through a discovery approach would be too time-consuming. However, with gifted learners the approach does not take nearly as much time as with other students. If an inductive approach were used exclusively, though, it no doubt would get boring, and learners would not get practice in a deductive approach. In short, a balance is necessary between the two types of approaches, but just what constitutes balance is as yet unknown. Bruner makes no assumptions about the relative emphases.

Discovery approaches need not be limited to formal subjects such as mathematics. They can and should be used in social studies, language arts, and the sciences.

Related to the use of a discovery approach is the theme of intuitive versus analytic thinking. Intuitive thinking, which proceeds by a series of "jumps" rather than in an analytical step-by-step fashion, often is the scientist's or scholar's way of making an important new discovery. In mathematics, for example, individuals are said to think intuitively when they suddenly achieve a solution but still have not provided the formal proof. Another example of intuition in mathematics is the ability to make good, quick guesses about the best possible approaches to take in solving a problem. The phenomenon of intuition as described by Bruner is similar, if not identical, to the "Aha!" experience described by Parnes (see Chapter 5). In an "Aha!" experience, an individual suddenly understands and/or has a great idea. This experience usually comes after a period of incubation in which the person has been working on a problem subconsciously. Suddenly things click, and the person knows the answer but has no idea how the idea came.

According to Bruner, little is known about the nature of intuition and the factors affecting it. He speculates that solid knowledge of a subject helps a person become a good intuiter, but that not all people who are familiar with their subject areas are good intuiters. Thus, a good background in the basic ideas of the subject may be necessary but not sufficient for intuition to occur. Other conditions that may be necessary, or at least increase the probability that intuitive thinking will be developed, include (a) intuitive teachers who can provide a model of effective intuition or a willingness to use intuition, (b) emphasis on the structure or connectedness of knowledge, (c) encouragement of guessing, and (d) a change in grading practices in certain situations so that less emphasis is placed on getting the right answer.

One way to increase the possibility that intuitive thinking will occur is to use a discovery approach. Discovery, if true to its definition, should more nearly approximate the inquiry process of a scholar. In their own fields and in day-to-day work, scholars often make intuitive leaps. Thus, by using an approach that ensures that the learning situation in school is more like the true inquiry process, educators increase the probability of intuitive thinking. In the day-to-day work of a scholar, intuitive thinking often is used to come up with a hypothesis that can be tested by analytical means. When using a discovery approach, this aspect of the inquiry process can be incorporated. Learners can be encouraged to use intuition to make guesses about underlying principles and then check their guesses through research. Constructive evaluation can be given on the student's use of intuition in forming the hypothesis and assessment can be based on the methods of proof chosen to test the hypothesis.

Product and Learning Environment Modifications

Although Bruner does not specifically address curricular modifications in the areas of product and learning environment, modifications of products are implied (and, in fact, required) by his approach. Because students are acting as real inquirers and scholars, their products address real problems and involve transformations rather than summaries of existing ideas or information. The involvement of real audiences and the realistic evaluation of products are ideas not implied or addressed by his approach.

With regard to the learning environment, Bruner makes no specific suggestions. Some of his comments imply that the environment would need to resemble the environments of professionals. This idea is related to the dimensions of centering on learning, encouraging independence, complexity, varying grouping options, flexibility, and high mobility. However, since no mention is made of the environment, these modifications are not really addressed. To provide a way for the reader to integrate the underlying themes expressed in Bruner's book with the following example of the use of his approach, the basic ideas relating to curriculum development for the gifted are summarized in Table 4.1. In this table, student roles and activities and teacher roles and activities are related to each major theme.

TABLE 4.1. Summary of Teacher and Student Activities and Roles in Bruner's Basic Structure of a Discipline

Step, Type, or Level of Thinking	Student		Teacher	
	Role	Sample Activities	Role	Sample Activities
Basic Concepts	Inquirer Data gatherer Analyzer Synthesizer	Using primary sources, study some phenomenon by collecting "raw data." Using secondary sources, study the conclusions or ideas of others about some phenomenon. Acquire, transform, and evaluate new information.	Organizer Facilitator Methodological consultant Resource	Choose concepts or basic ideas identified as most important by scholars in a field. If those ideas are not already available in a discipline, form a committee made up of scholars and child development specialists to develop ideas and suggestions how the ideas can best be learned by children. Subject each concept to be taught to the tests of usefulness to an adult. Select the data and plan learning experiences that are the "richest" and most economical in developing concepts and basic ideas.
Inquiry as a Scholar	Inquirer Data gatherer Analyzer Synthesizer	Be a professional in a discipline (e.g., scientist, mathematician, social scientist, writer, playwright, artist, musician).	Organizer Facilitator Methodological consultant Resource	Provide students with constructive feedback on their inquiry skills. Provide students with feedback on the validity of their conclusions and/or logic in reaching them.

(continues)

TABLE 4.1. *Continued*

Step, Type, or Level of Thinking	Student		Teacher	
	Role	**Sample Activities**	**Role**	**Sample Activities**
Discovery	Inquirer	Try to figure things out; make sense of phenomena, observations, data. Make hypotheses and test them.	Organizer Facilitator Resource Stimulator	Organize content and plan learning experiences that will facilitate students' discovery of basic concepts. Provide a balance between discovery (inductive) and deductive approaches. Develop discovery techniques in all content areas.
Intuitive Thinking	Hypothesizer Risk taker	Make guesses intuitively and then check hypotheses by analytical methods. Hypothesize (guess) about solutions as well as about the best approaches for investigation.	Supporter Facilitator	Help children develop good solid knowledge of a discipline to enable them to become good intuitive thinkers. Model the use of intuitive thinking by making hypotheses. Encourage students to make hypotheses. Emphasize the structure and connectedness of knowledge. Change grading practices so that "wrong hunches" are not unnecessarily detrimental.

Examples of Teaching Activities

A prime example of Bruner's activities and strategies is found in *Man: A Course of Study* (MACOS). Through this social studies curriculum, children learn a set of key concepts, acquire new information, and then are led to generalize from these newly assimilated facts and to evaluate their generalizations. Through a series of films that simulate field study and a set of 30 booklets, the children assimilate information about animal and human behavior arranged around a few basic themes. Much of the learning comes from the work of Irven DeVore, Jane Goodall, and Niko Tinbergen, all admired scientists and specialists in their fields who devoted their energies to long-term investigation. By studying the works of such people, children develop an understanding of and appreciation for ongoing scientific investigation. Through independent and small-group study and through group discussion, children arrive at generalizations about the essence of being human.

The most basic theme of MACOS is "What makes man human?" This conceptual question forms the basis for organizing the course, which is concerned with the nature of humans as a species and the forces (for example, tool making, language, social organization, management of prolonged childhood, and the urge to explain the world) that shape and have shaped humanity. Nine conceptual themes are explored through both primary and secondary data sources using the inquiry methods of scholars in the major fields that are associated with the themes: biologists, psychologists, sociologists, and anthropologists. Table 4.2 gives a summary of conceptual themes, data sources, classroom techniques, and learning methods used in the MACOS curriculum.

One of the introductory lessons suggested to teachers, shown in Exhibit 4.1, concerns how an anthropologist studies behavior.

MODIFYING THE APPROACH

Bruner's model does not suggest curricular modifications appropriate for the gifted in the following areas: (a) content—variety and the study of people; (b) process—evidence of reasoning, freedom of choice, group interaction, pacing, and variety; (c) product—real audiences and appropriate evaluation; and (d) learning environment—no changes are made. Since his approach is so comprehensive, it can almost be used as a total curriculum. However, if the elements described in the following sections were added, his approach would be more appropriate for gifted learners.

TABLE 4.2. Summary of Conceptual Themes, Data Sources, Classroom Techniques, and Learning Methods in *Man: A Course of Study*

Conceptual Themes	Data Sources	Classroom Techniques	Learning Methods
Life cycle (including reproduction)	1. Primary Sources	Examples	Inquiry and/or investigation: problem defining, hypothesizing, experimentation, observation, literature searching, summarizing and reporting
Adaptation	Student experiences Behavior of family	Individual and group research (e.g., direct observation or reading of texts)	
Learning	Behavior of young children in school		
Aggression	Behavior of animals	Large- and small-group discussions	Sharing and evaluating interpretations
Organization of groups (including group relationships, the family, the community, division of labor)	2. Secondary Sources	Games	Accumulating and organizing information for retention
	Films, slides, videotapes	Role play; simulations	Exchanging opinions, defending opinions
Technology	Recordings Anthropological field notes	Large- and small-group projects such as art, construction, drama	
Communication and language	Written data on humans, other animals, diverse environments	Writing songs, poems, stories, plays	Exploring individual feelings
World view			Exposure to and experience with diverse aesthetic styles
Values			

Note. Adapted from *Man: A Course of Study* by J. P. Hanley, D. K. Whitla, E. W. Moo, and A. S. Walter, 1970, Newton, MA: Education Development Center. Adapted with permission.

EXHIBIT 4.1. **Lesson B: The Study of Human Beings from an Anthropological Perspective**

Materials

A selection from:

lipstick	road map	notepad
aspirin	magazine	pencils or pens
address book	photographs	spoon
newspaper	calendar	eyeglasses
tissues or handkerchief		wallet with some contents
letter from a friend		candy bar or gum

I. Introducing the Task

Before class, fill a pocketbook, briefcase, or desk drawer with several of the items listed above and/or other common items. In a brief introduction to the class, explain that the students are to pretend that they have just discovered these items and do not know anything about the person to whom they belong or the place or time the person lived in. What can they learn about the person's way of life from these belongings? What can they guess about the society the person lives in? What does the person seem to care about? Which items seem necessary for survival? What questions would they like to ask this person?

After examining one item together, small groups can take other items and examine them in light of some of the questions raised. (You might reproduce the questions for each group; the class could then compile their guesses on a chart.)

II. Focusing on Ways of Studying Human Beings

After students have discussed what they think they know about the owner of the items and the society to which he/she belongs, you can explain that, in some ways, they have been acting as anthropologists, scientists who study human beings. They have been using available evidence to inquire into the nature of human beings and the societies in which they live. Students should think about some of these questions:

- What would you have to know about another group of people to understand their culture?
- How would you keep records of what you learn?
- Are some of the ways you study about human beings similar to the ways you study other animal species?
- How is the study different?

In response to the last question, it should be clear that we can observe human beings to try to see what is important to them, but we can also ask them questions and ask them to give their opinions. What can be learned through observations? What cannot be learned through observation alone? To focus on these questions, students can list their responses and develop a chart similar to the one that follows. The chart points out the different kinds of things we can learn about human beings, based upon our ability to speak with each other.

(continues)

EXHIBIT 4.1. *Continued*

Learned Through Observation	Learned Through Talking
What they look like	What they did yesterday and will
How they meet basic needs	do tomorrow
How they act toward one	How they like what they do
another	What their favorite color is
How they play	What they think or feel about an
How the young act with the old	event in another part of the world
How parents act with offspring	What they believe in
What they do not like to eat	What they think is funny

III. A Visit from an Anthropologist

Students may be interested in learning more about anthropology as a field of study and about what anthropologists do. The teacher might make a statement such as the following:

Some anthropologists look mostly at the physical structure of human beings; others examine traces of human beings from the past. Still others are what we call cultural anthropologists; they look at what a group of people share in common: their beliefs, their tools, the ways they define their relationships with each other, their language, the way they raise their children, and so on. Anthropologists call all the things that people share their culture. Cultural anthropologists often study groups of people who share a culture, such as the Netsilik Eskimos, the people whose way of life is the focus of the course.

Students might think about what an anthropologist visiting their classroom would observe. How does an anthropologist decide what to record? Would every anthropologist record the same things? This question can lead to a discussion of the bias of different anthropologists. How might a woman's view differ from a man's? Suppose one anthropologist was an artist as well as an anthropologist, and another was a school teacher as well as an anthropologist. How might this affect the way they look at a group of people? How would you feel about having your customs recorded by a person taking notes on your activities and talking with you? (Possible conflict over individual privacy versus scientific study could come out of a discussion of this question. How does a real anthropologist answer that question?)

Students will better understand anthropology as a professional field if they indeed meet and speak with an anthropologist. Frequently, colleges and universities have departments of anthropology with professors or graduate students who enjoy talking with young people about their field. You could probably locate such a person through a call or note to the head of a nearby anthropology department.

Note. From *Man: A Course of Study.* Reprinted with permission.

Content Changes

Variety

To add the element of variety, a person simply needs to assess the regular curriculum to determine what is being taught and make certain that the content in the program for the gifted is different. In so doing, however, the educator must continue the organization of content around key concepts as Bruner suggests. To illustrate this process, Maker (1982) developed a worksheet for assessing content plans (see Figure 4.2). The generalization to be discovered is written at the top of the worksheet, and the concepts contained in the generalization are listed below it. Each concept is analyzed separately. On the left, the data and information pertaining to the concept that is taught in the regular curriculum are listed. On the right side, the teacher lists what additional data need to be taught for the students to achieve a full understanding of the concept's use. In the example, the generalization and concepts pertain to the scientific method and its use. Two concepts—observation and organization of data—are analyzed. The process should be continued until each concept contained in the generalization is analyzed.

Study of People

This content modification would be interesting and fun as an adjunct to Bruner's model and is easy to incorporate. When considering each key concept to be developed, the teacher could, as a part of the process of deciding what data to teach, also choose a person or persons who have contributed significantly to the development and explanation of that concept. Learners could examine the ideas and methods of those individuals and attempt to trace the evolution of their ideas. At the same time, they can examine how these individuals' methods differed and how the different methods may have contributed to the development of different theories or ideas.

As learners are using the methods of scholars and investigators, they can engage in discussions of the different investigative techniques and examine the lives of eminent individuals who developed and used these methods. In addition they can discuss the creative/productive accomplishments of these individuals and others' reactions to these discoveries or accomplishments.

Process Changes

The most effective way to modify Bruner's approach would be to combine it with the Taba *Strategies,* with Betts's *Autonomous Learner,* and with Renzulli's *Enrichment Triad.* The Taba *Strategies* could be used to guide class discussions of key concepts and methods, and the Betts and Renzulli models could be used to help students structure and implement independent

Generalization No ___1___ : The growth of knowledge in science occurs through questioning, observation, experimentation, manipulation of materials, observation of results, and revision of original theories.

Key concepts to be developed:

Observation*	Organization of data*	Control groups
Prediction	Classification	Hypothesis
Environment	Inferences	Energy
Scientific method	Contamination	Variable
	Raw data	Brainstorming

Data taught in the regular curriculum	Data needing to be taught in the special curriculum
Observation Ways to observe and record changes in temperature The importance of careful observation	*Observation* Different kinds of observations that can be made: checklists, coding schemes, timed observation, use of microscope, changes in color from use of chemicals Types of measurement for observations: weight, length, color, density, temperature Experimental and control observations Examples of incorrect inferences resulting from careless observations
Organization of Data Keeping records of observations in notebooks Grouping like observations together	*Organization of Data* Types of graphs: bar, line Choosing units for graphs Separating experimental from control observations

*Concepts developed in this worksheet

Figure 4.2. Worksheet for overall curriculum design (Worksheet #6b: Building Content Plans upon the Regular Curriculum). From *Curriculum Development for the Gifted* by J. Maker, 1982, Austin, TX: PRO-ED. Adapted with permission.

or group investigations. Another useful model to combine with Bruner's approach would be Sharan and Sharan's *Group Investigations* (see Chapter 7).

Since many of Taba's ideas were influenced by Bruner, the two approaches are compatible. For example, in planning a Taba discussion, the teacher could begin with a concept or generalization and plan a series of focusing questions to stimulate the students' interaction with each other, through which they eventually will reach their own statement of a generalization or organization of information around a concept.

Betts's, Renzulli's, and Sharan and Sharan's models also are compatible with Bruner's approach. Bruner suggests that children use investigative techniques; however, in many cases, the teacher tells them what techniques to use and what problems to study. With gifted students, a more effective approach would be to assess their level of self-direction and either guide their investigations or serve as a resource for their study of a problem of interest to them. The teacher can retain the organization of content around key concepts by encouraging investigations related to a particular concept. The teacher also can suggest that students attempt to use a variety of methods selected from the many investigative techniques available to them.

With the use of Taba's techniques, the teacher would be certain of the systematic development of higher levels of thinking, the use of open-ended questions, and the use of questions calling for explanations of reasoning and logic. An element of variety (class discussions) would be added, and specific suggestions for pacing would be included. If the other process models are followed, freedom of choice would be added, as would other elements of variety.

Pacing

In addition to the pacing of discussions, when using Bruner's ideas or the curricula developed from his ideas, teachers must realize that gifted learners need only a few examples (or specific facts) to enable them to discover a principle or understand a concept. Thus, an important aspect of implementation is to select only a few examples and to move quickly from one concept to the next, depending on how quickly learners grasp the ideas, rather than teaching everything contained in the curriculum.

Variety

In addition to the variety added by Taba discussions and varied investigative techniques, learning experiences should include field trips to observe scientists, poets, or other professionals at work. Methods also can include learning centers for investigations, lectures, demonstrations, and simulations.

Group Interaction

Adding simulations and interaction techniques to the basic methods suggested by Bruner will add interest and stimulate student participation. In fact, such an addition would not represent a great amount of deviation from his suggestions. For instance, the example in which students behave as anthropologists is similar to the activities contained in the simulation game

Dig, in which two teams of students develop a culture, create the artifacts of the culture, and bury them. The teams then uncover and analyze the artifacts developed by the other team and attempt to recreate the culture. This sort of activity is the type that would satisfy Bruner's requirements for learning situations.

This simulation offers many excellent opportunities for interaction and for self- and peer-analysis of the process. The digging process, the analysis, and other activities could be videotaped, and participants then could analyze their own and others' performances, not only looking at their interactions with each other but also critiquing the scientific (or unscientific) methods used. If videotaping equipment is not available, observers can serve the same purpose. All the students can take turns observing and recording their observations of interactions or methods being used.

Product Changes

Although the problems studied when using Bruner's approach are "real," some may not be of interest to individual learners. Using Betts's *Autonomous Learner* or Sharan and Sharan's *Group Investigations* model would provide the structure for student selection of problems to investigate.

Real Audiences

Adding this element to Bruner's approach is easy. As the emphasis in his method is on use of the techniques of professionals, the teacher can extend this idea by asking Renzulli's (1979) "Key Question" about the research: What do anthropologists do with the results of their research? What do creative writers do with their poems, short stories, novels, or plays? The answers to these questions suggest what the students should attempt to do with their products. This aspect of product development can mesh well with the study of people, as the students can use these people's products and audiences as a way to stimulate their own ideas.

Appropriate Evaluation

Building on the previous example, students can be asked another Key Question: How are the anthropologist's products judged? How do different audiences view these products? A study of eminent individuals also can provide answers to these questions. The products and the reactions of different audiences to the products can be examined. An analysis of the reactions of eminent individuals to their varied audiences and critics would add interest and help students to gain a greater understanding of the assessment of real products.

Learning Environment Changes

Even though Bruner does not address directly the question of what kind of learning environment a teacher should establish, environments similar to those described for gifted learners are essential if Bruner's ideas are to be implemented effectively. For students to function as real inquirers, the focus must be on student ideas and learning activities; teacher talk must not dominate the classroom. The environment must permit a high degree of mobility to enable students to carry out their investigations. The following techniques can be used to make the environment more appropriate.

Learner Centered

If Bruner's approach is combined with the Taba *Strategies* as suggested earlier, discussions will be learner centered. Teachers will talk very little, the teacher will not be the center of a discussion, and the teacher will not serve as an authority figure. The classroom can become even more learner centered if Betts's, Sharan and Sharan's, and Renzulli's suggestions are followed; student ideas and topics of investigation will be emphasized rather than those of the teacher.

Encouraging Independence

This aspect of classroom climate extends the emphasis on independence into the nonacademic realm as well as the academic one. Bruner's objectives of having students learn as professionals can be achieved simultaneously with this one. If, for example, the teacher has been having difficulty with classroom management but does not want to impose solutions on the students (an important aspect of this dimension), the next topic of study could become "government," and the students could begin to learn how government works by establishing their own classroom government, electing their own officials, and developing and enforcing their own laws. Thus, they learn the system, while at the same time they solve their own problems.

Openness and Flexibility

The classroom environment must be open to allow learners to make "wrong" intuitive leaps during the discovery process, to make their own hypotheses, and to test them with experiments. The teacher must let them make their own mistakes and learn from them. Students must be allowed to pursue solutions without interruptions to do the teacher's tasks. Other people, including content experts, should be brought into the classroom. Teachers must make few restrictions on the areas of study, the methods used, and the timing of activities.

Accepting

This dimension of the classroom climate is particularly important in the discovery process. The teacher must be careful to avoid both positive and negative judgments of student ideas during the discovery process. If one student has developed a hypothesis that the teacher knows will "work," the teacher should avoid praising the student until after the hypothesis has been accepted by other students. This gives that learner the opportunity to explore his or her own ideas and other students equal opportunity to develop and test their own ideas rather than using the hypothesis praised by the teacher. Acceptance does not imply nonevaluation. In fact, evaluation is necessary to the process. Learners must be assisted in examining their hypotheses to determine both the accurate or valid aspects and the inaccurate ones. They also must examine the appropriateness of their methods.

Complexity

To enable gifted students to learn as a scholar does and to facilitate their discovery of abstract, complex ideas, the classroom must include a variety of sophisticated references, equipment, and environments. They need environments that simulate those used by professionals in as many ways as possible.

High Mobility and Varied Grouping Arrangements

A high degree of mobility also is necessary. If reference materials are not available in the classroom, students must have the independence to leave the class to find them. They also must be allowed to leave the classroom and school to conduct their investigations. They must be able to work individually, in small groups, and in flexible groupings during the activities in which they are engaged. Such provisions are essential if the approach is to work.

Summary

Bruner's approach, while mainly a content model, emphasizes discovery and techniques and processes used by practicing professionals in each discipline. His ideas can be combined effectively with the strategies of Sharan and Sharan, Taba, Betts, or Renzulli to achieve a comprehensive, complementary program. Bruner's approach also could be combined with other thinking/learning models such as Bloom's, Krathwohl's, or Parnes's.

DEVELOPMENT

After the conference in Woods Hole, Jerome Bruner began his massive task of synthesizing the major points made by the conferees after their 10 days of discussion and debate. The members of the conference had been divided into five work groups and as each of these groups had prepared a lengthy report to present to the rest of the participants for debate, this task was not easy. In an attempt to reflect as accurately as possible the major themes, conclusions, and disagreements, the chairman of the conference first prepared a draft report based on the conference papers. Copies were then sent to all participants for their comments and critiques. The final draft, which incorporated as much of the flavor of the meetings and comments as possible, became a classic book in curricular reform.

Bruner's ideas have continued to develop along the lines suggested in the conference report. Subsequent writing and research have extended and refined many of them. In the massive social studies curriculum, *Man: A Course of Study,* Bruner incorporated and extended his ideas into an exciting, effective learning program; however, the curriculum was sharply criticized by conservative groups and others who considered the materials too difficult or inappropriate for children. Finding copies of this superb curriculum may be difficult but is well worth the search.

RESEARCH ON EFFECTIVENESS

With Nongifted

In a comprehensive evaluation of MACOS, Hanley, Whitla, Moo, and Walter (1970) found the curriculum to be highly effective in achieving its goals with children and in effecting desirable changes in the teachers who used it. In the teachers, a noticeable shift occurred from didactic to interpersonal modes of teaching and learning. After teaching the course, teachers talked less and were less dominating, allowed students to give longer responses, raised more issues for discussion, and engaged in more student-to-student interaction. In comparisons of control and experimental groups, several differences favored the classes using MACOS. Following are some of the desirable outcomes for students:

- They had increased desire and ability to work independently.

- The wide range of course materials seemed to modify students' views of traditional data sources.

- Children learned a lot of information and methods of investigation. They began to understand the meaning of serious investigation.

- Children were personally involved in and reflective about the course ideas.

- Interdependence of species members was a concept that began to be fully understood.

Evaluation of the course materials and relative effectiveness for achieving the goals of the course yielded the following results:

- The materials and methods were enjoyable, exciting, and interesting to the students.

- Children tended to become much more aware of the similarities between humans and animals than of the differences.

- Ability to master and use the concepts in the course correctly seemed to depend heavily on the quality and number of examples given.

- Students became impatient with obvious repetition in material but also were disturbed when ideas were not presented in a thorough manner.

- The Netsilik unit (the section on humans) was the favorite of the majority of the children.

- The hunting games were highly successful teaching devices, but youngsters must reflect on their play to learn much from it.

In addition to MACOS, many other curricula have been based on Bruner's approach. Most were developed and evaluated in the 1960s, some of them quite extensively.[1] In a large-scale evaluation of the University of Illinois Committee on School Mathematics (UICSM) math program involving almost 2,000 students, Tatsuoka and Easley (1963) found significant gains in the experimental over the control group on a traditional test of algebraic concepts. Others (Begle & Wilson, 1970; Grobman, 1962; Wallace, 1962) found that when progress was measured by traditional tests of achievement, which usually measure factual information, curricula built on Bruner's approach were not as successful as traditional curricula. On tests constructed

---

1. For a list of some of these projects, along with names and addresses, see the resource list at the end of this chapter.

by the developers of the curricula, however, the experimental groups were similar. Most of this research says what a person would logically predict. The traditional approaches are better at doing what they intend to do, while the new approaches are better at doing what they intend to do.

Bruner (1985) observed that developing a curriculum involves political decisions on the nature of learning and learners based not simply on data but also on ideals and cultural conditions in which the learning is to take place. The best approach is one that requires reflection and inquiry on whether the "script" imposed on learners is there for the stipulated reasons or whether the activities or curriculum serve other purposes. "We would do well to equip learners with a menu of their possibilities and, in the course of their education, to arm them with procedures and sensibilities that would make it possible for them to use the menu wisely. . . . The appreciation of that variety is what makes the practice of education something more than a scripted exercise in cultural rigidity" (Bruner, 1985, p. 8).

With Gifted

Some research has compared the achievement of different ability levels of children when using Bruner-type curricula. Generally, however, these comparisons have been more or less afterthoughts except for two well-designed studies. In another evaluation of the UICSM material stressing the discovery method, Lowman (1961) compared this method with a traditional algebra class. He found a significant difference favoring the UICSM materials for students in the top third in ability, but not for the middle and lower thirds. In a 3-year study of six curricular approaches with more than 1,500 gifted junior high students, Goldberg, Passow, Camm, and Neill (cited in Gallagher, 1975) found that the ranking of these programs was as follows: (1) School Mathematics Study Group (SMSG)—accelerated (4 years of SMSG in a 3-year period); (2) UICSM—normal; (3) UICSM—beginning earlier; (4) SMSG—normal; (5) traditional accelerated; and (6) traditional enriched. Thus, the new curricular approaches were superior to traditional ones, and the most superior was one of the new approaches taught in a more concentrated period of time.

In other evaluations, gifted and high-ability students seemed to profit more from learning abstract concepts and using a discovery approach. In evaluations of *Biological Sciences Curriculum Study* (BSCS) materials, Wallace (1962) and Grobman (1962) concluded that high ability was an important factor in the mastery of the concepts presented and that low intelligence was a negative factor. Others (Mayor, 1966; Proviss, 1960; Suppes, 1969) have concluded that modern math students do as well as students in traditional programs in arithmetic fundamentals and do better at conceptualization.

For the gifted, the difference in conceptualization is even greater. The MACOS evaluation showed that intelligence quotients (IQs) made no difference in the amount of learning from pretest to posttest in the animals unit but did make a difference in the Netsilik unit. Some of the important differences between the two units include the following: (a) The animal unit has much more repetition of the basic ideas and concepts through returning to them each time a new animal is studied; (b) more inferential skill and transfer of concepts is needed in the Netsilik unit because children compare humans with all the animals studied to "discover" important similarities and differences; and (c) the unit on humans requires the most speculation and reflection on how all the learned concepts contribute to and affect personal lives.

Throughout all these evaluations, a consistent trend emerges. Gifted students enjoy dealing with abstract, complex ideas and can handle them more easily than other students. They need fewer examples to learn the concepts, and they need to revisit the ideas much less frequently in the learning process. In fact, when the curriculum includes too many examples and too many returns to the ideas, they get "turned off" and do not achieve as well as when the content is accelerated or economically chosen.

Characteristics of Gifted

Added to their high ability are two other characteristics that indicate the reasons for the success of Brunerian-based curricula. One is that gifted and creative people prefer to use their intuition in searching for deeper meanings rather than using direct sensory data in forming impressions and making decisions. Another is that they tend to learn in a series of intuitive leaps.

Support for the idea that gifted persons prefer to use an intuitive mode for gathering information and making decisions comes from research with the *Myers-Briggs Type Indicator* (Myers & Briggs, 1976), a personality assessment tool based on Karl Jung's (1923) theory of psychological types. According to the theory, a major dimension of personality is an individual's preferred way of gathering information. The two opposite psychological types are called sensing and intuitive. A sensing person prefers to get information directly through the five senses and to stick with the verifiable facts. An intuitive person relies on the deeper meanings and possibilities obtained through intuition, based on hunches and perceptions rather than verifiable facts. Although the general population includes fewer intuitive than sensing types (that is, approximately 75% are sensing while 25% are intuitive), an extremely high percentage of intellectually gifted and creative individuals can be classified as intuitive types (Myers & Briggs, 1971). In fact, in Mac-Kinnon's (1962) studies of creative people, 90% of the creative writers, 92% of the mathematicians, 93% of the research scientists, and 100% of the architects were classified as intuitive types.

Studies of concept formation (Osler & Fivel, 1961; Osler & Troutman, 1961) have provided the basis for saying that the gifted tend to learn through a series of intuitive leaps. The learning curves of the higher ability subjects showed a series of dramatic increases interspersed with an almost flat progression. Lower ability subjects showed a steady progression over a series of trials. Osler and her associates interpreted the results to mean that the high-ability subjects were forming hypotheses and then testing them. When they hypothesized correctly, their performance increased dramatically. The periods when learning curves were flat occurred while subjects were operating on the basis of incorrect hypotheses. Another finding in the study was that the high-ability subjects were more distracted by certain kinds of irrelevant cues than were those of lower ability. The interpretation of this finding was that those of higher ability were attempting to use all of the situational cues in forming their hypotheses, while the trial-and-error learning of the other subjects did not require their use of these cues.

Educators and researchers have continued to be interested in thinking, problem solving, and learning strategy differences between gifted and other children, searching for those "qualitative" differences that will justify special programs. Generally, however, most research has revealed that gifted students use strategies and demonstrate cognitive traits similar to non-gifted, older individuals (Carter & Ormrod, 1982; Scruggs & Mastropieri, 1988; Scruggs, Mastropieri, Monson, & Jorgensen, 1985). Such results are not surprising since IQ tests are designed such that those who are "developmentally advanced" have higher scores. Shore and Dover (1987) suggest that gifted students possess and use more metacognitive strategies but their process of assessment depends on the ability to explain (verbally) their strategies. We do know, however, that gifted students usually learn differently from their same-age peers.

JUDGMENTS

Advantages

Bruner's approach has a number of important characteristics to recommend its use with gifted students. First, it is a total approach that provides a framework for most if not all the curricular modifications suggested earlier. The majority of the adaptations are addressed directly by the approach (for example, content changes of abstractness, complexity, organization, methodology; process changes of varied methods, higher levels of thinking, discovery), while others are suggested indirectly (for example, process modifications of pacing, open-endedness, expressing logic or reasoning; product changes of real problems and use of raw data; learning environment changes of available resources and equipment, free expression). Those not addressed, such as freedom of choice of topics, choice of method, real audiences, and appropriate evaluation, can be incorporated easily into the approach and would no doubt enhance its effectiveness.

A second major advantage is that evaluations have shown its effectiveness with gifted students, although its effectiveness with other students is less consistent. They seem to be unable to handle the abstract concepts without numerous examples that often are repeated. The advantage to educators, then, in answering the tough question, "But isn't that good for all children?" is that in this case, for once, the answer is no. Some of the other methods are good for all children to some degree, so the "no" answer given in other situations must be qualified endlessly.

Another practical advantage is that a variety of materials and comprehensive curricula are built on this approach. Although some have been revised so that other learners can be successful in using them, some are still available in their original forms. Selective use of the material is possible. Usually, in using commercial materials with the gifted, the teacher must add to the materials by introducing higher level content, more challenging ideas, and so on. However, since the problem with some of the Bruner-based curricula is that often too many examples and activities are given for the abstract concepts, teachers have an easier task leaving out rather than making up activities. Another way to be selective is to revisit each concept less often or fewer times. This helps avoid the unnecessary repetition that causes boredom in gifted students.

Building on the unique characteristics of gifted students while preparing them for the roles they will be likely to assume in society is one final advantage of the basic structure approach. Gifted students will need the inquiry skills and the abstract concepts. Most importantly, the attitude toward discovery—a love of learning—can carry over into their lives as adults, regardless of whether they become scholars or leaders.

Disadvantages

The major disadvantage in using Bruner's approach is that teachers have a tough role. They not only must keep up on the latest informational and theoretical developments in a field but also must be knowledgeable enough in the methods of inquiry to be able to give children assistance in their investigations. To teach these high-level concepts adequately, the teacher must understand them. Many, if not most, elementary teachers are not knowledgeable enough about the academic areas because child development and teaching methods (for example, techniques for individualizing instruction) have been viewed as a more important part of teacher education than academic understanding. This emphasis is probably valid in most cases. However, teachers of the gifted must be special persons. They may need to go back to school or in some way develop academic understanding before teaching in the way Bruner would suggest. Of course, one person cannot be an expert in every academic area or even all the major ones, no matter how much he or she studies or how gifted a teacher he or she is.

Another problem is that even the scholars in a field have difficulty deciding what the basic concepts are that should be learned. Certainly, if scholars disagree, others will have difficulty reaching consensus.

CONCLUSION

Based on the available research, the basic structure approach combined with teaching methods emphasizing inquiry and discovery rather than didactic ones can be highly successful with gifted students. Although the teaching of structure and abstract concepts is a difficult task for the teacher, materials and comprehensive curricula are available as aids. With Bruner's approach, the advantages greatly outweigh the disadvantages.

RESOURCES

Background Information

Adler, M. J. (1981). *Six great ideas*. New York: Collier Books. These great ideas we judge by and act on can be used as unifiers in interdisciplinary programs or simply as "food for thought" for gifted minds.

Banks, J. A. (1990). *Teaching strategies for the social studies: Inquiry, valuing, and decision-making* (4th ed.). White Plains, NY: Longmans. A classic text for teaching social studies, this book includes many tables, charts, and teaching strategies useful with gifted students. Although Banks does not cite Bruner's theoretical approach, the author's basic assumptions are in harmony with the *Basic Structure of a Discipline*: (a) that students must develop the ability to use scientific knowledge in a reflective way to resolve personal problems and help to shape public policy through intelligent social action; (b) that individuals can be taught to reflect thoughtfully about problems before taking action to resolve them; and (c) the main components of decision are scientific knowledge, value analysis, and the selection of a course of action through synthesis of knowledge and values. The text includes sections on various methods of social inquiry, essential components of decision making, products of social inquiry, and questioning strategies. In addition, strategies for organizing concepts, generalizations, and theories of social science disciplines into interdisciplinary units and curricula are stressed. Also included is a section on assessment and evaluation of inquiry, decision making, and social action projects.

Gallagher, J. J., Oglesby, K., Stern, A., Caplou, D., Courtright, R., Fulton, L., Guiton, G., & Langenboch, J. (1982). *Leadership unit: The use of teacher-scholar teams to develop units for the gifted.* New York: Trillium Press. Developed using Bruner's ideas for combining the expertise of teachers and scholars, these units are excellent resources for the teacher.

Instructional Materials and Resources

Aicken, F. (1991). *The nature of science* (2nd ed.). Portsmouth, NH: Heinemann. The nature of scientific thinking is explored in a series of essays that stress the value of scientific thinking as a tool for solving problems. In the essays, Aicken presents commentaries on issues that can provoke students toward further exploration. Some simple thought-provoking experiments and notes for further reading also are included.

Carin, A. A., & Sund, R. B. (1985). *Teaching science through discovery* (6th ed.). Columbus, OH: Charles E. Merrill. This classic text, in which the principles and theoretical bases of discovery learning are stressed, includes many basic problems in science disciplines, practical suggestions for setting up learning centers, and other teaching techniques. Hundreds of experiments that children can do comprise most of the text. Useful appendices include a historical summary of science education and an update on science curriculum projects.

Hyde, A. A., & Hyde, P. (1991). *Mathwise: Teaching mathematical thinking and problem solving.* Portsmouth, NH: Heinemann. In this book, written for teachers in elementary grades, the authors suggest a number of activities in which students are actively involved in problem solving and working on authentic problems. The problem-solving approach builds connections between students' lives and key concepts of the mathematics curriculum.

Kramer, S. (1987). *How to think like a scientist.* New York: Crowell. In an easy-to-read (grades 2 through 5) introduction to the scientific method, the author gives examples of the steps in the scientific method: asking a question, collecting data/information, forming a hypothesis, testing the hypothesis, and reporting the results.

Michaelis, J. U. (1985). *Social studies for children: A guide to basic instruction.* Englewood Cliffs, NJ: Prentice-Hall. This attractive text includes an emphasis on the core social science disciplines, methods of inquiry in each discipline, and suggestions of ways to incorporate broad themes and/or issues of concern into the curriculum. Concepts, generalizations, and the spiral development of concept clusters are explained clearly through text and illustrations in the chapter "Teaching Knowledge and Developing Thinking Ability." Another helpful chapter is titled "Developing Creativity Through Expressive Experiences." Numerous strategies and examples of lessons are included.

Tinkler, D. (1989). *Social education for Australian primary schools: The humanities core curriculum (HCC): A "futures" perspective* (rev. ed.). Melbourne, Australia: Macro-View Educational Publications. Tinkler outlines four constructive approaches to curriculum development, defines the functions of social education in the classroom, and includes both teaching strategies and ideas for improving methods of teaching and learning. His work is based on the theories and ideas of Dewey, Piaget, Bruner, Taba, and Ausubel and influenced by the methodology of Montessori, Cuisennaire, and Gategno. The author's purpose is to provide a curriculum relevant to the needs of children that can be adapted readily in elementary schools and support classroom teachers with practical ideas and strategies. The HCC includes aspects of anthropology, sociology, economics, politics, life sciences, earth science, applied sciences, mathematics, history, and geography integrated in a logical, sequential spiral development model for students from K–6. Twelve strands are grouped into five clusters: conceptual, self and society, natural, technological, and social–emotional–geographic. Although the curriculum was designed for Australian children, the structure and the twelve strands are universal and can be adapted easily by teachers in all parts of the world.

Simulations

A number of excellent scenarios for interactive simulations in varied disciplines are available for elementary and secondary students from Interact: Learning Through Involvement at P.O. Box 997, Lakeside, CA 92040.

Excellent interactive simulations available on computer disks include the *Decisions Decisions* series from Tom Snyder Productions. Topics include the tradeoffs and responsibilities of industrial growth, the environment, federal budgets and spending, colonization, revolutions, foreign policy, media ethics, prejudice, immigration policies, political campaigns, substance abuse, and AIDS. The issues are interdisciplinary and involve small groups of students performing as professionals, doing research, making decisions, resolving conflict, and evaluating the effects of their decisions.

Maxis produces a variety of simulations including *Sim-City, Sim-Farm, Sim-Ant,* and *Sim-Earth.* In *Sim-City,* for example, each player assumes the role of urban planner. Each simulation has multiple levels of difficulty and can be used by gifted students from upper elementary grades through graduate school.

Other Sources

Professional societies of specific disciplines often have curriculum guidelines and/or materials. For example:

National Council for the Social Studies
3501 Newark Street NW
Washington, DC 20016

National Council of Teachers of English
1111 Kenyon Road
Urbana, IL 61811

National Council of Teachers of Mathematics
1906 Association Drive
Reston, VA 22091-1593

National Science Teachers Association
1742 Connecticut Avenue NW
Washington, DC 20009

Chapter 5

Sidney Parnes: Creative Problem Solving[1]

O ne approach that has been used widely in programs for the gifted is the *Creative Problem Solving* model developed by Sidney J. Parnes, director of the annual Creative Problem Solving Institute (CPSI) held at the State University of New York (SUNY) at Buffalo. Influenced greatly by the work of Alex Osborn (1963) in applying imagination to the practical problems encountered in the business and professional worlds, Sidney Parnes attempted to develop the most comprehensive process possible for stimulating the use of imagination in practical situations. He used his own applied research on the development of creative thinking in the program at SUNY, along with the applied and theoretical research of others, to come up with a process that would be comprehensive, theoretically sound, and above all, effective. He and others are involved continually in the modification of this process as new information becomes available. His institutes are attended yearly by many of the most widely known researchers and theorists in creativity development and by individuals just beginning to be interested in their own or others' creative development.

The Parnes *Creative Problem Solving* model provides a structured method for approaching problems in an imaginative way. It is different from the usual problem-solving methods in its emphasis on generating a variety of alternatives before selecting or implementing a solution. In each of the steps of the process, the problem solver defers judgment during ideation or generation of alternatives to avoid inhibiting even the wildest possibilities, which may turn out to be the best ideas. Judgment then is exercised at a more appropriate time.

The purpose of the model is twofold: (a) to provide a sequential process that will enable an individual to work from a "mess" to arrive at a creative,

---

1. Appreciation is expressed to Dr. Sidney J. Parnes for his thoughtful review and support.

innovative, or effective solution; and (b) to enhance an individual's overall creative behavior. Creative behavior, according to Parnes, is "a response, responses, or pattern of responses which operate upon internal or external discriminative stimuli, usually called things, words, symbols, etc., and result in at least one unique combination that reinforces the response or pattern of responses" (1966, p. 2). Creative behavior is a function of knowledge, imagination, and evaluation and results in a product that has both uniqueness and value to an individual or group. In other words, through participation in a process, such as that developed by Parnes, individuals apply their own knowledge, imagination, and evaluation to both internal and external "stimuli" and as a result develop a product (for example, plan, idea, performance, report) that is both unique and valuable. These definitions of creative behavior, although precise and rather dry, provide clear and measurable guidelines for program development and evaluation.

The need for creativity training in all phases of education can no longer be ignored. The current state of the educational process, with its emphasis on "the right way," together with the necessity of dealing with massive amounts of information, a constantly and rapidly changing world, and pressing social concerns, makes the development of creative problem-solving skills imperative. Parnes cites Maslow's (1970) "need for self-actualization" as a goal that can be met through education for creativity. Thus, the kind of education developed from a creative problem-solving perspective would meet both individual and societal needs.

Of the many teaching-learning models currently used in programs for the gifted, the Parnes model provides the most "hard data" showing its effectiveness. It also demonstrates the most versatility based on successful practical application in business, government, the health care professions, and education. The process is taught to university students, teachers, young children, adolescents, parents, artists, managers, scientists, city planners, architects—anyone who is interested—through the Creative Problem Solving Institutes (CPSI). Participants are almost unanimous in their response to these institutes: "It was the most valuable personal and professional experience I've ever had. It's fun and it also works!"

ASSUMPTIONS UNDERLYING THE MODEL

About Learning

A major assumption made by Parnes is that creativity is a behavior or set of behaviors that can be learned. Creativity is not an inborn, fixed characteristic but is present to varying degrees in all individuals. It can be manipulated and cultivated deliberately. Since creativity is learned, a related assumption is that examples and practice will strengthen it and that the methods used in a creative problem-solving course are generalizable to new situations. In other words, all persons can become more creative, and they can apply this creativity in all facets of their lives.

Another assumption is that creativity is related positively to other characteristics of individuals, such as ability to learn, achievement, self-concept, and intelligence. These characteristics, when combined, contribute to a "wholeness" of objective (factual–logical) and subjective (sensing–feeling) aspects of an individual. Inherent in this assumption is the belief by Parnes that knowledge is important in creative productivity. Although factual information must be manipulated and transformed into usable ideas, a person cannot be creative without first having an available store of knowledge. This knowledge, however, can be used more creatively and effectively if initially learned with a "creative" set than if initially learned with a "memory" set.

About Teaching

Since Parnes believes that creative behavior can be learned, he obviously believes that educators can and should teach creative behavior. According to Parnes, when his problem-solving process is taught to students in school or to adults in an institute, a set of skills is developed that can be applied to all kinds of practical problems, for example, improving relationships with others, making decisions about activities or programs, managing resources, and planning personal or career goals. He believes that by participating in the process, creative leaders can learn to use *Creative Problem Solving* (CPS) successfully with groups ranging from elementary school children to adults. In short, Parnes feels that CPS is simple to learn, easy to teach, and highly transferable.

Parnes (1967) makes an important distinction between creative teaching and teaching for creativity. A teacher who is creative will be imaginative in the use of materials (films, posters, tapes) and strategies (demonstrations, unique experiences), while a teacher who teaches for creativity will encourage students to express themselves and stimulate them to develop their own productivity. Consequently, the teacher will listen more than talk and guide rather than direct. Individuals who teach for creativity do not need to be creative in their methods of imparting information. To develop an atmosphere conducive to the learning of creative behavior, a teacher must (a) establish a climate of psychological safety for the free expression of ideas, (b) encourage playfulness, (c) allow incubation, and (d) seek quantity as well as quality of ideas.

About Characteristics and Teaching of the Gifted

Although not stated, an implicit assumption made by Parnes is that individuals who are intellectually gifted have the potential to be more creative than those who are not gifted. Gifted people also can benefit from learning how to use the creative problem-solving method in artistic, social, and scientific areas. Following from this assumption is the recommendation that in teaching the gifted, educators should use a method such as CPS much more frequently and/or earlier because of the greater potential of gifted learners to benefit from its use. Following this line of reasoning, gifted students also have greater amounts of information they must organize, manipulate, and evaluate. As a result, gifted individuals need to use the creative problem-solving process much more often than those who are not gifted.

ELEMENTS/PARTS

Dimensions, Thinking Levels, or Steps

Since he first encountered Alex Osborn's program in 1963, Parnes has worked toward the establishment of the most comprehensive program possible for nurturing creative behavior. Using Osborn's model as a base, he added parts of existing theories and programs he could uncover, as well as new approaches recently developed. At present, the model consists of six steps, usually followed in sequential order. Parnes feels the resulting process is easy to follow, and, once the procedures have been learned, the components of understanding the problem (Steps 1–3), generating ideas (Step 4), and planning for actions (Steps 5–6) are quite flexible and can be adapted to the particular needs of the group and the task (Parnes, 1988). These six steps, along with activities for each step, are described in Table 5.1.

TABLE 5.1. Steps in the Parnes Creative Problem Solving Process

Steps	Activities
1. Mess finding	Analyze what is known about the "mess." List broad objectives, goals, or purposes. Generate criteria for evaluation. Select the best statement(s) or objective(s) to define the chosen task.
2. Data finding	Collect data dealing with the first objective. Act as a camera; observe carefully and objectively. Explore the facts of the situation. Recognize that feelings are part of the facts. Select the data most pertinent to the objective. Repeat the process now (or at conclusion) for other objectives.

(continues)

TABLE 5.1.   *Continued*

3. Problem finding	Prioritize options based on importance and probability of success. Speculate on possible problems. Look at possible problems from different perspectives. Converge on major problem(s). Restate the problem in a form that: (a) states the issue for which you really want to generate ideas, (b) encourages a flow of ideas, (c) expresses the issue in concise terms, (d) identifies the ownership of the problem, (e) is free of criteria, (f) has a stem that opens up the statement to many possible answers (e.g., "In what ways might we . . . ? How might we . . . ?"), (g) uses an action verb to identify the specific action recommended, and (h) has an object that identifies the specific focus of the action.
4. Idea finding	Produce ideas to solve the problem. Generate many, varied, unusual ideas; freewheel. Elaborate on ideas to make them more complete or more interesting. Brainstorm alternatives for various conditions. Defer judgment. Strive for quality. Seek combinations and/or hitchhiking; link new ideas with others.
5. Solution finding	Screen, sort, and select ideas using evaluation criteria. Identify promising solutions. List criteria, using a divergent process, for use in evaluation. Select criteria that are appropriate to the focus of the problem and the needs of the problem owner(s). Analyze, develop, and support tentative solutions. Objectively apply the criteria to each tentative solution. Select the most promising solution based on objective evaluation.
6. Acceptance finding	Consider all audiences who must accept the plan. Brainstorm the concerns and priorities of all these audiences. Develop a plan of action. Try out the plan on a pilot basis to see if the solution is workable. Revise plan, if necessary, and present it to target audience(s). Make contingency plans in case acceptance is not achieved.

Movement through the six steps is illustrated in Figure 5.1. The illustration seems to be of a unitary, linear, sequential process. However, Parnes stresses that the model is flexible and suggests that, for specific purposes, some steps of the model may be used alone.

The diamonds in the figure represent the divergent and convergent thinking that occurs again and again while one moves through the steps (or returns to an earlier step to try a different approach). After listing a variety of ideas (divergent thinking) that identify opportunities or challenges of the "mess" in Step 1, the individual or group rates each idea, on a scale of 0 to 10, on two dimensions: importance and probability of success. Then the two ratings are multiplied together to get an overall rating. A mess statement with a probability of success of 10 and an importance rating of 1 would receive an overall score of 10; another with an importance rating of 5 and a probability of success rating of 5 would receive an overall rating of 25. Thus, a mess statement, or objective, with a high rating of importance and a high to average probability of success is identified as a *promising opportunity*, while options low in importance with an average or high probability of success are identified as *distractions* (Isaksen, Dorval, & Treffinger, 1994). This method helps to eliminate options of average to high importance but little probability of success and those with little importance and low to average probability of success. Problem solvers then can focus on substantial options rather than waste their time with trivial or impossible tasks.

Movement through the steps of the process is aided by some proven techniques for stimulating idea output and development, such as deferred judgment, elimination of fears, extended practice, forced relationships, brainstorming, hitchhiking, checklists, attribute listing, morphological analysis, synectics, and incubation. These are all strategies to assist in getting data out of memory storage and relating it to current situations that require problem solving. Deferred judgment, for example, is a cardinal principle in allowing the expression of as many ideas as possible. When used in a group, the principle is called brainstorming. Supplemental to this process is the procedure of hitchhiking, or building upon and elaborating on the ideas of others. These hitchhikes are accepted simply as additional ideas without discussion or argument as the flow of ideas continues.

Synectics, another example, is a process that involves two basic activities, making the strange familiar and making the familiar strange. It consists of the mental activities of analysis, generalization, and model seeking or analogy. According to Wilson, Greer, and Johnson (1973), synectics is a powerful tool for use with the gifted, as it enables them to "keep pace with the requirements of a rapidly changing world where traditional methods fall glaringly short" (p. 261).

To facilitate movement through the steps, another required skill is asking creative questions that can lead to unconventional solutions. Parnes feels

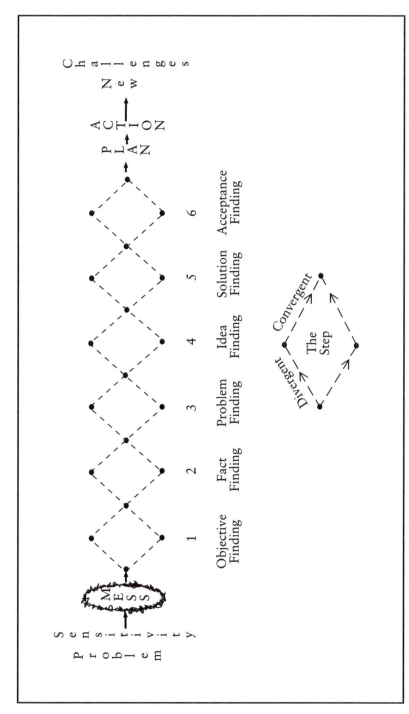

Figure 5.1.   Illustration of the steps in Creative Problem Solving. From *Creative Actionbook* by R. B. Noller, S. J. Parnes, and A. M. Biondi; 1976, New York: Charles Scribner's Sons. Adapted with permission.

this skill takes critical thinking and practice, but once acquired it enables creative problem solving to be accomplished in a minimum amount of time. As John Dewey said, "A problem well put is half solved." Einstein continued, "The formulation of a problem is often more essential than its solution, which may be merely a matter of mathematical or experimental skill. To raise new questions, new possibilities, to regard old questions from a new angle, requires creative imagination and marks real advance in science."

J. W. Getzels, who along with P. W. Jackson (Getzels & Jackson, 1962) started the continuing controversy over the creativity–intelligence distinction in the gifted, describes two types of problem situations, the presented problem situation and the discovered problem situation. A presented problem situation is a problem that has a known formulation, a known method of solution, and a known solution. A discovered problem situation is a problem that does not yet have a known formulation, method of solution, or solution. This latter type stimulates creative problem solving.

Getzels (1975) gives examples of the two types; the story that illustrates them briefly is of a car being driven along a deserted road when its tire has a blowout. The occupants discover they have no jack, and their question is, "Where can we get a jack?" They remember a gas station several miles back and begin walking. Another car is driving on the same road, and it too has a blowout and no jack. The occupants of the second car ask the question, "How can the automobile be raised?" It just so happens they see a deserted barn nearby, and in the barn is an old pulley for lifting bales of hay to the loft. The car is raised, the tire changed, and the occupants are on their way again, while the other people are still walking to the service station. Getzels concludes:

> In effect, the first group dealt with the dilemma as a "presented problem situation" akin to type-case 1: a known problem, a known method of solution, a known solution. The second group dealt with the dilemma as a "discovered problem situation" akin to type-case 3: a situation which could be defined in terms of a variety of problems. (1975, pp. 12–18)

In a discussion of the development of creativity in the gifted, Gallagher (1975) indicates that one of the general principles for encouraging a person to be more creative is to "remove the brakes that stop his associative mechanisms from functioning naturally" (p. 244). He continues by observing that gifted children, who often are concerned about pleasing the teacher and giving a quick answer to questions, will have difficulty inhibiting this first reaction, thinking about the problem, and allowing their associative thoughts to flow. While this is an important observation to make, one also must consider Parnes's principle of deferred judgment. "Removal of the brakes" includes going beyond the first reaction and also requires that problem solvers free themselves from the natural tendency to judge an idea as good or bad before saying or writing it. If the idea gets a bad rating in a student's mind, he or she may decide not to say it because others might laugh or think he or she has stupid ideas. This "wild" idea may be much better than any of the conventional ones that pass the spur-of-the-moment test of value. According to Parnes, taming a wild idea is much easier than "beefing up" a conventional one. Thus, with gifted children who have been successful in school by pleasing the teacher, appearing smart, and not having "stupid" ideas but who have the potential to create the most unique and original ideas of all, practice in using the principle of deferred judgment is essential.

Generating criteria for evaluation of problems, ideas, and solutions frequently is a difficult process for children. Using a divergent process to generate many, varied, and unusual criteria from which to choose will improve the probability of making wise choices. Criteria should be phrased as questions (e.g., "Will it be legal?" "Can fifth-grade students accomplish this task?" "Is this an underlying problem?" "To what extent will . . . result in . . .?") that can be answered with "yes," "no," or a rating. Possible convergent tools (Isaksen et al., 1994) include an evaluation matrix and a paired comparison matrix for group consensus. In an evaluation matrix, possible options are listed along one axis and criteria along the other (see Table 5.2). Each option is rated on an agreed-upon scale (e.g., 1 = low to 5 = high or +1, 0, –1) for each criterion. Points are totaled for each option, and options are ranked in order from high to low. In paired comparison analysis (PCA), each member of the decision

TABLE 5.2. Convergent Decision Matrix (Example)

Options	Criteria				
	1	2	3	4	Total
Wilderness	3	1	4	2	10
Riparian area	4	2	1	4	11
Homes	1	3	1	2	7
State park	3	2	2	3	10
Guest ranch	4	2	0	3	9

Note. As a group, members assign a rating to each option for each criteria. The total is the sum of the ratings given to each option.

group separately completes an evaluation matrix using an identical set of options and an identical scoring system (e.g., 1 = low to 5 = high). A group grid, prepared with options listed along one axis and group members' names along the other, then is filled in and points for each option totaled (see Table 5.3). The purpose of the PCA is to help groups build consensus and establish priorities. The procedure also is an aid to structuring discussions and allowing members of the group to express reasons for their support (or lack of support) of options. Converging on a problem or solution might also be done in steps through using an evaluation matrix to narrow the list of alternatives and then listing advantages (strong points and positive aspects), limitations (concerns or weak points phrased as "How to . . ." questions), and unique qualities (novel aspects, "What does this idea have that no others have?") of the most promising options (Isaksen, 1992).

Another related idea important in the development of creative thinking in gifted children is developing and maintaining a balance between the more freewheeling, playful side of a person and the logical, judgmental, analytical side. When describing the program at SUNY (and this also applies to Parnes's institutes taught in other parts of the United States), he concludes:

> In adapting all of the evolving programs that we have been able to synthesize with our creative problem-solving courses and institutes, we have been trying always to develop a balance in individuals—a balance between the judgment and the imagination—between the open awareness of the environment through all of the senses and the deep self searching into layer

TABLE 5.3.   Paired Comparison Analysis Matrix (Example)

Group Member	Options				
	A	*B*	*C*	*D*	*E*
John	2	15	10	14	5
Sally	11	0	6	8	11
Jessica	13	7	9	12	7
David	1	10	7	15	8
Total Points	27	32	32	49	31

Note. Each group member rates each option on each criteria, totals the points for the option, and enters the total in the grid by her/his name for each option.

upon layer of data stored in the memory cells between the logic and the emotion—between the deliberate creative effort and the incubation—between the individual working with the group and his working alone. The longer I work in this field the more the underlying problem seems to become one of developing this balance between these extremes, by strengthening the weaker aspect, not by stunting the stronger side. (Parnes, Noller, & Biondi, 1967, p. 154)

MODIFICATION OF THE BASIC CURRICULUM

Although the Parnes model provides a setting for modification of content and product, the most significant (and direct) modifications suggested are those of process and learning environment. The approach itself is a process model. Therefore, by using this process or by teaching children to use it, educators modify the usual process of learning. Learners are active rather than passive, teachers are facilitators rather than information disseminators, and learners must separate their use of divergent and convergent thinking so that the flow of ideas is not inhibited while evaluations are made. Each sequential step in the process initially requires divergent thinking and ends with convergent thinking.

Content Modifications

The CPS process suggests content modifications of variety and methods that are appropriate for gifted students. Variety is suggested because the problems that are identified and solved are those practical problems not usually considered in a school curriculum. The CPS method is used to identify and solve a variety of personal, social, and academic problems. The process itself is a method of inquiry; this content modification is made easily. Gifted students should participate in the process in group situations and should be taught how to apply it to the solution of their own problem situations.

Process Modifications

Process modifications appropriate for the gifted are made in the following four areas: (a) higher levels of thinking, (b) open-endedness, (c) freedom of choice, and (d) variety. The development of higher levels of thinking (for example, the use rather than acquisition of information) is facilitated by the six-step process, which proceeds from exploring the mess to generate questions or objectives through identifying facts about the situation, defining the problem, developing ideas for solving the problem, evaluating the ideas, and finally, developing a plan for implementing the solution. Although these steps are sequential rather than hierarchical, they progress from recalling facts (that is, Bloom's knowledge level) to analyzing the situation, creating new ideas (that is, Bloom's synthesis), and evaluating (that is, solution finding), and then "back" to synthesizing (that is, acceptance finding). Openendedness also is an important process modification made by CPS. Both teacher and student questions at all steps of the process must be open-ended to facilitate divergent answers. The process even includes components to assist participants in devising their own open-ended questions at the problemfinding step. As shown in Figure 5.1, each step in the process contains both a divergent and a convergent aspect. Participants are taught through the process when each type of thinking is appropriate for problem solving.

The CPS process encourages freedom of choice and suggests the use of a variety of methods at different steps. With regard to freedom of choice, participants usually are encouraged to choose a problem of interest to them. Although they are expected to follow the basic approach, individual variations are possible, especially at the problem-finding and idea-finding steps. For example, at the idea-finding step, a variety of idea-stimulating questions and techniques are presented, and individuals can later choose those that work best for them in a particular situation. Since many methods are available and are suggested at each step, the principle of variety also is incorporated.

Product Modifications

The Parnes method suggests product modifications in all areas that are appropriate for the gifted. Addressing problems that are real to and interesting for gifted students is very much a part of this method. Although some teachers may be directive in their use of the method with students, the first three steps are designed to assist participants in identifying and stating a problem as they see it. If this product modification is not made, the problem is in the implementation, not the process itself.

A second modification, directing products toward real audiences, is made through the acceptance-finding step. At this step, the problem solver attempts to anticipate how those who must accept the solution will react to it. Based on this analysis, a plan is developed to implement the solution. Some detailed suggestions are given for assessing audiences, developing plans, and implementing solutions.

Another product modification is appropriate evaluation. In the process, both teacher and student learn how to develop criteria for product evaluation and how to apply these criteria to the selection of solutions. When developing criteria for evaluation, for example, problem solvers should consider the problem from the viewpoint of many individuals and judge the possible solutions on criteria other than their own personal preferences. Often decisions and evaluation depend very much on this subjective aspect of judgment. This and other suggested techniques help students develop skills in making appropriate evaluations. The techniques also provide methods for peers and audiences to use in evaluating products presented to them.

Variety and self-selected formats also are essential components of the Parnes model, since the form of the solution must fit the problem definition and is determined solely by the problem solvers.

The final product modification, transformation rather than summary, is made easily through application of CPS. Throughout the process in solving problems, students must manipulate information, seek a variety of new data, combine information in new ways, and view situations from new perspectives. Particularly in the idea-finding step, development of original ideas is emphasized, that is, combining old ideas to form new ones, substituting parts of one idea, and other similar techniques.

Learning Environment Modifications

To facilitate movement through the problem-solving process, the leader must establish and maintain an environment that is similar to that recommended for the gifted in most of the dimensions. The dimensions of particular importance are learner centered, independent, open, and accepting.

The environment must be learner centered. Learners should identify the problems to be solved and generate the ideas for solving them. Selecting solutions and developing plans for implementation also are the responsibility of the students. Appropriate implementation of CPS requires that the leader serve as a facilitator of the process rather than as a person who instructs or "leads" the process. Thus, the teacher asks open-ended questions, plans activities to stimulate idea production, and enforces the rules of brainstorming. Since the teacher is not offering or judging ideas, he or she does not become the center of the discussions. When CPS is implemented in other than a total class setting, the teacher cannot assume control or dominate the group.

Independence is fostered by encouraging individuals and groups to apply the process on their own and to use it as a procedure for solving everyday problems as well as academic ones. Since the ultimate goal of those who teach the process is to see it used by individuals to solve their own problems, this modification is an important aspect of the creative problem-solving process.

Specific guidelines are given by Parnes for the development of an open and accepting environment. For example, the rules of brainstorming should be strictly enforced at all times when generating ideas or when the activity requires divergent production. As a way to assist in the idea-finding step, Noller, Treffinger, and Houseman (1979) provide the following instructions for conducting and participating in brainstorming. These instructions illustrate the learning environment suggestions for implementing CPS.

The teacher must foster a climate of appreciation and understanding of the creative process. For example, the teacher must encourage and appreciate the need for incubation, allowing subconscious concentration on the problem. As students focus on a problem and search for ideas, they consciously will defer judgment and allow free flow to the associative mental processes. These associations also may occur in the preconscious, before a student is aware that they are being formed. By detaching from direct involvement in a problem, preconscious activity occurs, where links that may otherwise be inhibited are allowed to form (Parnes, 1967). Individuals often become consciously aware of these subconscious associations in an "Aha!" experience; a new idea suddenly appears when they are not consciously thinking about the problem. Teachers must not only provide for incubation but also encourage and appreciate the need for it even when it does not fit into the daily lesson plan.

Examples of Teaching Activities

One student used the following steps in solving an everyday problem using CPS (see Exhibit 5.1) (Keisel, 1979).

EXHIBIT 5.1. Arnold's Problem: "How Will I Write My Research Paper?"

Known	Like to Know	Sources
• Only one book has been published on my subject. • I have the book. • I'm not to ask my teacher directly about my paper. • I have access to a Wide Area Telephone Service (WATS) line. • I have notes from two sessions I attended about my subject. • I have only one week to write this paper. • I need to find more information.	• Are any articles published about this subject? • Are other people's notes from the lecture available? • Are there any people in the city who know about my subject?	• Author of technique • People predominant in the field who will know about the model • ERIC search • Other professors at the university • Author's secretary

Note. From *The Creative Problem Solving Model* by S. Keisel, unpublished paper, 1979. (Available from J. Maker, Department of Special Education and Rehabilitation, University of Arizona, Tucson)

Objective Finding: Generate one or more "mess statements."

From the question, "How will I write my research paper?" Arnold identified the purpose(s) of this CPS process.

Fact Finding: Collect all data surrounding the problem.

In an attempt to solve his problem, Arnold developed a chart to help in the gathering of data related to his situation. (See Exhibit 5.1.)

Problem Finding: Restate the problem in a more solvable form.

As Arnold thought about his situation, he decided that the problem seemed to center on ways to get the information in order to write the paper rather than on how to put the words down on paper. He tried the following restatements of the problem:

- In what ways might I write this paper?
- How can I get rid of the teacher who is making me write this paper?
- Who will help me write this paper?
- What information will I use to write this paper?
- In what ways might I get the information to write this paper?

He finally selected the last question as the most appropriate problem to solve.

Idea Finding: Brainstorm and defer judgment in an attempt to develop as many ideas as possible for solving the problem.

Arnold tried asking himself the question, "In what ways might I get the information to write this paper?" He came up with the following ideas:

- Call the author of the technique.
- Call his secretary.
- Call predominant people in the field.

He then tried a few of the idea-spurring concepts suggested by Osborn (1963)—magnify, minify, rearrange, combine, substitute, put to new uses—and applied these to the ideas he had and to the questions resulting from the fact-finding process. He was happier with this result, which follows:

- Reread the book I have.
- Go through all class notes on my subject.
- Go through workshop notes.
- Conduct an ERIC search and look for articles.
- Talk to university professors who might know.
- Talk to people who have researched the author's ideas previously.
- Call one of the author's students.
- Write to one of the author's students.
- Cry, and give up.
- Go to the university where the author teaches and hang around.
- Read the American Psychological Association (APA) manual.
- Read any article on information gathering.
- Check the Education Index.

Solution Finding: Produce (divergent) criteria for evaluating solutions and then select (convergent) the most useful criteria to evaluate each idea or potential solution. Choose the best solution.

Arnold first thought about some possible ways to judge his ideas. He could consider time, cost, effectiveness, safety, acceptability to the teacher, and uniqueness. Based on what he knew about the situation, Arnold decided that the most important criteria were time (he had only one week to finish the paper), effectiveness (it had to work), and acceptability to the teacher (he wanted a good grade). He then developed a grid for rating his possible solutions from the idea-finding step. (See Exhibit 5.2.) He assigned a point value of 1 for the bad ideas, 2 for those in the middle, and 3 for the good ideas. Each idea was rated on each criterion, and the points were totaled. According to this rating, he had several good solutions, including the following: call the author, reread the book I have, go through class notes, go through workshop notes, conduct an ERIC search, and call one of the author's students.

Acceptance Finding: Make the solution more appealing (acceptable) to all parties involved; make it more workable. Plan, implement, evaluate the results, and provide corrective action as needed.

Since conducting an ERIC search and calling one of the author's students seemed to be the most promising solutions, Arnold decided to imple-

EXHIBIT 5.2.   Rating of Arnold's Ideas on Selected Criteria.

Possible Solutions	Time	Effectiveness	Acceptability	Total
Call the author	3	2	3	8
Call his secretary	3	1	2	6
Call predominant people in the field	2	2	3	7
Reread the book I have	3	2	3	8
Go through all class notes	3	2	3	8
Conduct an ERIC search	3	3	3	9
Talk to university professors	2	2	3	7
Talk to people who have researched his ideas previously	1	2	3	6
Call one of his students	3	3	3	9
Write to one of his students	1	2	3	6
Cry and give up	3	1	1	5
Go to the university where he teaches and hang around	1	1	3	5
Read the APA manual	3	1	3	7
Read an article on information gathering	1	2	3	6
Check the *Education Index*	1	2	3	6

Note. From *The Creative Problem Solving Model* by S. Keisel, unpublished paper, 1979. (Available from J. Maker, Department of Special Education and Rehabilitation, University of Arizona, Tucson)

ment these first. Since the only individuals involved would be Arnold and his teacher, he quickly checked with her to determine the acceptability of these solutions. After her approval, he began to develop his plan for implementing the solutions. He first would call a student of the author to get as much information as possible, then he would get a friend to show him how to conduct an ERIC search. After retrieving the available articles, he would decide whether additional information was needed. If so, he would call the author, go through his notes, and reread his book.

In Arnold's situation, as in many others, the most crucial aspect is the statement of the problem. The problem must be stated in an open-ended, solvable way and must be focused on the aspect of the situation that is actually causing a problem. The teacher was not involved in this process at all. She had initially taught Arnold the process, which he had transferred to the new situation.

Table 5.4 provides a summary of teacher and student activities and roles for each step in the CPS process.

MODIFYING THE APPROACH

When modifying the Parnes CPS approach to make it more appropriate for the gifted, educators should make changes mainly in how the approach is used rather than in the method. The majority of suggestions are in the content area, with a few in the area of process. To make these changes, one effective method is to combine Parnes with Bruner, while another would be to make each separate change as described below.

Content Changes

The CPS method does not make content changes appropriate for the gifted in the following areas: abstractness, complexity, organization for learning value, and study of people. CPS can be combined with other approaches to achieve several of these changes. To implement the first content changes, abstractness and complexity, the problem areas selected by gifted learners should involve complex, high-level problem situations rather than mundane or simple problems. Some examples of complex problems involving abstract concepts would be the following: current ecological problems, the current economic situation, talent development in an egalitarian society, rising populations and shrinking land availability, and industrialization or exploitation of underdeveloped countries by world powers. In all of these situations, information or facts need to be gathered from a variety of sources and traditional disciplines for both definition and solution of problems. No one viewpoint or set of information would provide the necessary background. In addition, the concepts involved in understanding the situations and in devising possible solutions are abstract. The materials available from the *Future Problem Solving* (FPS) program (Hoomes, 1986; Torrance,

TABLE 5.4.   Summary of Teacher and Student Roles and Activities in the Parnes Creative Problem Solving Model

Step, Type, or Level of Thinking	Student		Teacher	
	Role	Sample Activities	Role	Sample Activities
Objective finding	Active participant Idea generator	Explore the "mess." List potential objectives. Generate criteria. Select objectives.	Facilitator Resource	Develop or select exercises to lead students in exploration of the "mess" and generation of potential objectives. Develop or select exercises to lead students in generation of criteria. Develop or select exercises to lead students through an evaluation of potential objectives based on selected criteria. Lead students through exercises individually or in groups.
Data finding	Active participant Idea generator	Differentiate what is known from what needs to be known. Collect needed information. Observe carefully. Act as objectively as possible.	Facilitator Resource	Develop or select exercises to assist students in a process of finding out the known and unknown data about a situation. Lead students through exercises individually or in groups. Help students identify new sources of information and select relevant from irrelevant data.

(continues)

TABLE 5.4. *Continued*

Step, Type, or Level of Thinking	Student		Teacher	
	Role	Sample Activities	Role	Sample Activities
Problem finding	Active participant Idea generator Evaluator	Look at the problem from several viewpoints. Generate many potential problems. Select the most important problem(s). Restate the problem in more solvable form.	Facilitator Resource	Help students speculate on possible problems. Develop or select exercises to assist students, individually or in groups, to narrow the problem, select the most important problem, state it in solvable form, and look at it from different viewpoints. Provide examples of action verbs to assist students in structuring a more solvable statement of the problem. Encourage students to use action stems (e.g., "In what ways might I . . . ?" "How might we . . . ?")
Idea finding	Active participant Idea generator	"Incubate" on the problem for an extended time. Generate many, varied ideas. Defer judgment until all ideas are expressed. Hitchhike on ideas of self and others. Strive for quantity.	Facilitator Resource	Develop/select ideas that will assist students, individually or in groups, to generate a wide variety of useful and original ideas. Provide idea-stimulating questions (i.e., "How might we magnify/minify/rearrange/combine/modify . . . ?") to help students generate many, varied, unusual ideas and add to their ideas. Enforce the rules of brainstorming (i.e., quantity over quality, hitchhiking is desired, no evaluation of ideas). Maintain a psychologically safe environment to encourage the free expression of ideas.

(continues)

TABLE 5.4. *Continued*

Step, Type, or Level of Thinking	Student		Teacher	
	Role	Sample Activities	Role	Sample Activities
Solution finding	Active participant Idea generator Evaluator	Develop criteria for solution evaluation. Choose alternatives with the greatest potential for solving the problem. Objectively apply criteria to selected alternatives. Support chosen solution with evidence of reasoning.	Facilitator Resource	Develop/select exercises to enhance students' abilities to (a) generate criteria for judging a solution, (b) select relevant criteria, and (c) objectively apply criteria to selected alternative solutions. Lead students in exercises individually or in groups. Assist in the identification of possible criteria for evaluating ideas. Demonstrate the use of decision matrix or other convergent tools. Ask for support of chosen solutions.
Acceptance finding	Active participant Idea generator Evaluator	Brainstorm ways to gain acceptance of idea/solution. Consider all audiences. Develop a plan of action. Try out plan on a pilot basis. Evaluate and revise plan as needed. Present plan to target audience(s).	Facilitator Resource	Develop/select exercises to help students identify all audiences concerned with the solution. Develop/select exercises to help students formulate an action plan. Develop/select activities to help students implement solutions. Lead students through exercises individually or in groups. Enforce the rules of brainstorming. Maintain a psychologically safe environment.

Williams, & Torrance, 1977), particularly the practice problems, are excellent sources of complex, current, relevant problem situations.

The addition of the process of CPS to any area of study would contribute an element of complexity. Since problem solvers must integrate a variety of information from several points of view in the identification of problems and development of solutions, complexity is introduced automatically. Creative solutions to problems often require that information from seemingly remote fields be brought together in an original way.

The modification of organization for learning value is not suggested by the Parnes approach but can be incorporated readily. If the content is arranged around key concepts or themes, the problem situations to which CPS is applied can involve these concepts directly. For example, in Chapter 3, activities were developed around the following generalization: *Every society has had rules, written or unwritten, by which social control over the people's conduct can be maintained.* Students can, of course, identify many problem situations that are related to this idea and should be encouraged to do so. However, the teacher also can present problem situations for further examination through CPS. Some problem situations related to this generalization are prison riots, the death penalty, government intervention in crisis situations, rehabilitation of prisoners, moral and ethical development through education, the present court system, the juvenile justice system, how to develop appropriate parent–child relationships, and society's changing values.

If the content is not organized already around key concepts and generalizations, it could be organized around problem situations. The CPS process then could be used as the overall method for gathering information, identifying subproblems for study by small groups of students, and combining old information with new ideas to form new, creative solutions. Complex problems involving abstract concepts should be selected as organizers; most current local and national problems would be excellent. The students could identify with the problems, could select subproblems of interest to them, and could develop end products (for example, solutions, research reports) that are directed toward real audiences and represent their creative thinking and original research about a problem area.

The study of creative, productive people can be accomplished through the use of CPS. Students can identify problems faced by these individuals and use CPS to develop solutions for them. They then can compare their solutions with the ones actually developed and implemented by the famous individual. This comparison should definitely include a look at the differences and similarities between the individual studied and the gifted students themselves, along with similarities and differences in the social situation now and during the life of that individual.

Process Changes

Process changes that are not suggested directly by the Parnes model are discovery, evidence of reasoning, group interaction, and pacing. The problem of pacing does not seem relevant to the implementation of CPS with gifted students since new material is not being presented and participants have much opportunity to set their own pace in solving problems. When the process is used in a group setting, however, the teacher should attend to the appropriate pacing of discussions during most of the steps. During idea finding, the teacher should be careful to allow plenty of time for thought since students are producing rather than acquiring or remembering information.

Discovery

Although CPS is not a strategy for discovery learning in the sense that discovery is defined by the authors, it is closely related. The methods employed in the first five steps of CPS also can be used by students to structure their process of discovery or inquiry. For instance, fact finding would be important as a way to gather information from the situation that is relevant to the generation of hypotheses. At the problem-finding step, learners would sift through the information to identify those aspects that are most relevant, and the idea-finding step would be used for the generation of hypotheses. Solution finding would provide a framework and methods for evaluating and selecting hypotheses.

Evidence of Reasoning

Asking students to explain their reasoning or provide evidence for their inferences would be easy to incorporate into the CPS process. However, questions such as these must be asked only at certain times. Otherwise, the idea-production phases of each step would be inhibited. During brainstorming, fact finding, and phases of the process involving divergent thinking, questions calling for explanations of reasoning would be completely inappropriate. During selection of problem statements, selection of criteria for evaluation, and decisions about action plans, however, such questions are highly appropriate and will facilitate understanding of the process and its use in solving problems at any of the convergent stages.

If teachers fear that the asking of "why" questions will inhibit the process, they always can use the procedure in Taba's application of generalizations strategy. In this strategy, students brainstorm their predictions without any interruptions by the teacher except to clarify ambiguous ideas. After the ideas have been listed, the teacher goes back and asks for reasons why each prediction was made. This strategy would not be appropriate at the idea-finding step but would work well at solution finding and acceptance finding.

Group Interaction

If the CPS process is used in a whole-class setting, it can provide a situation for observation and analysis of group interaction. To implement this curricular modification, the teacher should tape the process or appoint observers willing to stay out of the discussion. Through this method, however, only one type of group interaction could be observed, that is, participation in group problem solving. The process also could be used as an adjunct to the observation of group interaction by using it as a method for developing solutions to interaction situations that have been observed.

Learning Environment Changes

Learning environment changes not suggested by the CPS method are complexity and high mobility. These aspects of the environment become important when students are developing sophisticated products and conducting original research. They can be crucial at the fact-finding step of the process if students need to gather information from a variety of sources for the solution of certain types of problems. The environmental dimensions of complexity and high mobility may vary in relation to the type of problem to be solved and the stage of the problem-solving process. If students are preparing a presentation for a real audience (e.g., a legislative subcommittee), mobility is of crucial importance.

Although independence already has been discussed as a learning environment modification made by the Parnes approach, a few more ideas are helpful. The CPS method provides an excellent process for use by students in solving their own problems and in developing solutions to classroom-management problems. Students need to be taught the methods thoroughly, however. This includes working through several sample problems with substantive content, discussing the implementation of the process, learning a variety of facilitative techniques that can be employed at each step of the process, and speculating on the application of CPS in other contexts. This conscious attention to the purpose and procedures of the problem-solving process contributes to metacognitive development and transfer of learning to other situations. Finally, students need supervised practice in the use of CPS in both individual and group situations.

DEVELOPMENT

Sidney Parnes was greatly influenced by Alex Osborn's techniques, which are presented in *Applied Imagination* (Osborn, 1963). Parnes extended and elaborated on Osborn's work through research on identifying and nurturing creativity. He developed a course and later a programmed text that has been highly effective in developing the creative behavior discussed by Osborn. Since launching the interdisciplinary Center for Creative Studies, now called the Center for Studies in Creativity, and developing the Creative Problem Solving Institute, Parnes has continued to incorporate new ideas and research into CPS. In 1985, Isaksen and Parnes proposed a six-step model, which split fact finding into objective finding and data finding. In 1993, the six steps were conceptualized as three components (Isaksen, Dorval, & Treffinger, 1994): problem definition, idea generation, and planning for action.

RESEARCH ON EFFECTIVENESS

With Nongifted

The CPS model has been the subject of extensive research. This research has focused on two different but related issues, creativity and problem solving (James, 1978). As the two terms often are used interchangeably, this leads to confusion and inconsistency in research. Parnes uses CPS to produce a set for solving problems then evaluates its effectiveness using measures of general creativity. Parnes assumes that creativity enhances the whole problem-solving process. Others (see Mansfield, Busse, & Krepelka, 1978) evaluate the effectiveness of the solutions and find that other problem-solving methods are just as effective as the Parnes process. For example, some studies have shown that other methods, such as the use of Program Evaluation and Review Technique (PERT) charts and conventional (nondeferred judgment) methods of problem solving are just as effective in developing ability to solve problems as the Parnes process (Mansfield et al., 1978). However, these other programs do not seem to cause increases in performance on measures of creativity.

In 1957, Parnes began an extensive research effort to evaluate the effectiveness of his program. For the first 10 years, the research was concentrated in the following four areas:

1. the effects of a semester course in stimulation of creativity

2. the relative effects of a programmed course used alone or with instructors and class interaction

3. the effects of extended effort in problem solving

4. the effectiveness of the principle of deferred judgment

In general the results of several studies indicate that the program is highly effective. Some of the major findings were as follows (Parnes, 1975):

- The semester programs resulted in increases in both quantity and quality of ideas produced. These increases (over a control group) held up even when students were tested from 1 to 4 years after taking the course.

- The results of research on the effectiveness of the programmed course also were positive. The instructor-taught groups were superior to the other two groups, while the group using the programmed materials alone was superior to the control group receiving no creativity training.

- Extended effort in idea production resulted in a greater proportion of good ideas among those produced later.

- Individuals instructed to defer judgment during idea production produced significantly more good-quality ideas (criteria included uniqueness and usefulness) than did individuals instructed to judge concurrently with idea production. In addition, subjects trained to use the principle of deferred judgment produced significantly more good quality ideas under the deferred judgment condition than did subjects who were not trained. Groups also produced more and better ideas when using this principle than did either groups or the same number of individuals working independently while using concurrent evaluation.

After these initial studies, which concentrated heavily on development of the process, Parnes and his associates began a longitudinal investigation, *The Creative Studies Project*. They hypothesized that students who complete a four-semester sequence of creative studies courses will perform better in the following areas than otherwise comparable students who do not take the courses: (a) measures of mental ability, problem-solving capability, and job performance; (b) tests measuring the creative application of academic subject matter; (c) achievement in other than academic areas calling for creative performance; and (d) measures of personality characteristics associated with creativity. Parnes (1975) provides the following brief summary of the results:

- Students in the courses are significantly better able to cope with real-life situational tests, including production, evaluation, and development of useful ideas.

- In the semantic and behavioral half of Guilford's *Structure of Intellect* (SI) model of intelligence (Guilford, 1967), students in the courses perform significantly better on three out of five mental operations: cognition, divergent production, and convergent production. Students show significant year-to-year gains over comparable controls and perform similarly to the controls on two of the operations—memory and evaluation—and also in the symbolic and figural half of the model.

- Most of these students believe they have become more creative and productive and that the program has been helpful in other college courses and in their everyday lives. Those continuing for 2 years in the program feel that this improvement is shown in their more active participation in class discussions and in their ability to cope with everyday problems.

- In nonacademic areas calling for creative performance, these students show a growing tendency to become more productive than students not enrolled in the program.

- Measures of personality characteristics show that students taking the courses are changing in ways that make them more like highly creative persons.

- Since the students in both the experimental (Creative Studies Program) and control groups are similar to students at most colleges and universities, the results of this research should generalize to many other situations.

- The *Creative Studies Project* participants also showed improvements in convergent processes and on ultimate criteria, as did participants in several other studies. (Parnes, 1987)

In a review of research on the effectiveness of creativity training programs, Mansfield et al. (1978) report that of all the creativity programs reviewed, the Parnes program is the most effective. They are not as positive as Parnes about the results, as they believe that several of the studies showing gains suffer from serious methodological flaws. Some of the problems include confounding of instructor effects with program effects, massive sample attrition, and volunteer subjects for the instructed but not for the control groups. Parnes and his colleagues, however, do not agree with this assessment except in the case of volunteer subjects in experimental but not control groups in the first study. These concerns were dealt with in other studies. One extensive, well-designed study, however, showed very positive results: high school students in an instructor-taught course performed significantly better on all 10 verbal tests of divergent thinking (four of fluency, two of flexibility, two of originality, and one each of elaboration and sensitivity) than did students in the control group. In the same study, students using the programmed text without an instructor were inferior to the instructor-taught groups but superior to the controls who had no instruction.

Torrance (1972) also reviewed studies testing the effectiveness of programs designed to develop creativity in children. Approaches were separated into nine categories, including CPS and other disciplined approaches, including training in general semantics, complex programs involving packages of materials, the creative arts as vehicles, media and reading programs, curricular and administrative arrangements, teacher–classroom variables, motivation, and testing conditions. Of all these approaches, the Parnes *Creative Problem Solving* process and other disciplined approaches showed by far the highest percentages of success. These approaches achieved 91% and 92% success rates, compared to the next highest percentages—81% for the creative arts as vehicles and 78% for the media and reading programs.

In a meta-analysis of long-term creativity training programs, Rose and Lin (1984) concluded that such training does enhance creativity. Innate abilities can be stimulated and skills can be developed through creative problem solving. CPS training significantly improves the interaction among members of small groups (Firestien, 1990). Members of the trained groups also produce a significantly greater quantity and higher quality of ideas generated for real problems.

In summary, the program does seem to be effective in improving performance on tests of divergent thinking, which may be an important aspect of creativity. Certain specific principles, such as deferred judgment and extended effort, also are effective in producing more and better ideas.

With Gifted

Although gifted students are included in the groups studied by Parnes and his associates, little research has concentrated on the effectiveness of CPS with only the gifted. Schack (1993) investigated the effects of a creative problem solving curriculum on gifted, honors, and average students. The curriculum produced substantial gains in problem-solving ability in all three groups.

A significant body of research related to the topic is concerned with relationships between creativity and intelligence. However, since a review of this literature could fill volumes, only a few of the more significant results will be presented. In a classic study of the creativity–intelligence relationship, Getzels and Jackson (1962) found a low correlation between IQ scores and performance on tests of creativity in gifted students (average IQ 132). They also found that those who scored highest on tests of creativity, but not highest on IQ tests (average IQ 132), scored just as well on achievement tests as did those who were highest on IQ tests (average IQ 150) but not highest on tests of creativity. Wallach and Kogan (1965) also measured the performance of those who were highest on measures of both creativity and intelligence. They found, as did Getzels and Jackson, that the "high creatives" did just as well on achievement tests as the "highly intelligent." However, they also found that the highest achievers and most versatile individuals were those who were both highly creative and highly intelligent. Another important finding of this study is that those who scored high on IQ tests but not on tests of creativity have a "disinclination" rather than an "inability" to perform well on tasks calling for divergent thinking. The subjects appeared to be reluctant or fearful of being original rather than unable to be original.

The results of these studies have important implications for the use of CPS or other such techniques with gifted children. If intellectually gifted but not necessarily creative children have the potential to be more original than they are, and if these children can be more effective achievers when they use both their intelligence and their creativity, then teachers must provide experiences that will increase these children's use of all their potential abilities.

Several researchers have studied the effects of the *Future Problem Solving* (FPS) program, a program for students that is designed to develop problem-solving skills. Torrance (1977) found that those who participated in FPS showed increased concern for the future, future solutions through careers, interdependence of people, and knowledge as a source of power. Tallent (1985) found that the gifted FPS program participants performed better on futuristic ill-structured problems than did those who had not participated. Finally, Tallent-Runnels and Yarbrough (1992) found that gifted fourth-, fifth-, and sixth-graders who participated in FPS differed from those who did not participate in the following ways: perceptions of their control over the future, concerns about the future, and types of concerns cited most frequently. FPS participants were interested in more global issues and were more positive about their control over the future. In general, these are important, positive effects and suggest that gifted students of many ages can benefit from the program.

JUDGMENTS

Advantages

The major advantages of the Parnes model in programs for the gifted are its versatility and validity. The CPS process can be used in any content area, as a method both for learning about the content area and for arriving at creative solutions to significant problems proposed by scholars in that field. The process also can be used to solve the practical problems encountered in classrooms, business, industry, and daily life. The skills transfer easily from one situation to another and can be taught to children of all ages. For the teacher, the advantages also include a wide variety of materials that are readily available, teacher training that is available, fun while using the process, and a personally rewarding experience. The goals of CPS are explained easily and justified to parents or school personnel, and gifted children enjoy participating in the process.

With regard to its validity, although only a few comparative studies have assessed the effectiveness of the method with gifted students, the Parnes model is consistent with the characteristics of gifted learners. It builds on their capability for developing unique products and, at the same time, provides for the development of the "inclination" to use their creative potential. Parnes defines creativity in specific behavioral terms and provides a structure and process for increasing these behaviors. Thus, the goals, procedures, and evaluative measures are clear. Research indicates that when this process is followed, the results are positive. Continuing research and evaluation of the process by Parnes and his associates ensure that new developments will be incorporated into the process to enhance its effectiveness.

A final, important advantage is that many excellent materials are available for use in a variety of situations. Manuals for leaders, sample problems, and how-to books for problem solvers are readily available.

Disadvantages

The major disadvantage of the model is that it was not designed specifically for use with the gifted (and, in fact, may be equally effective with those who are not gifted). For this reason, a gifted program based only on the Parnes model may be difficult to justify as "qualitatively different" from the basic school curriculum that includes CPS. In addition, one cannot even create a rationale for concentrating on particular aspects of the process with gifted students, as with certain other models (for example, Bloom's and Krathwohl's *Taxonomies*). The use of these approaches in programs for the gifted can be justified by the rationale that the educator is concentrating on the higher rather than lower levels of thinking. In this way, the program is qualitatively different for gifted students. On the other hand, with CPS, each step is equally important for all learners. Thus, when used by itself, CPS does not provide a comprehensive, qualitatively different program for gifted students unless it is used as a model for attacking complex, societal problems.

Although the program is supported by extensive positive research, methodological problems are present in several important studies. The major problem is in measuring of creativity. Most studies equate divergent thinking with creativity, even though this type of thought process may be only a small part of creative behavior. A related problem is that most studies use standardized measures of creativity as the criterion, rather than long-term assessment of transfer effects. For example, a critical question involving the transfer effect of risk taking might be "Will students who engage in creative problem solving exhibit fluency, flexibility, and originality in situations in which their ideas may be subject to criticism?" (Bodnar, 1974, p. 4).

For many years, advocates of the *Creative Problem Solving* model tended to overemphasize the inspiration and imagination required in the idea-generation phases of the process and neglected the actual implementation phase, with its requirements of high degrees of motivation, self-discipline, self-criticism, and hard work. If the model is used alone as the basis of a program for gifted students, this emphasis on the divergent phases of the process can be a real disadvantage. Recently, however, a few authors (e.g., Isaksen, Dorval, & Treffinger, 1994; Lewis, 1991) have focused on planning for action and implementing proposed solutions in the real world. With that approach, the emphasis on inspiration and imagination in the Parnes process adds a positive and enjoyable dimension to a comprehensive program for gifted students.

CONCLUSION

As a total approach to curriculum development for the gifted, the Parnes (CPS) model is difficult to justify as qualitatively different or comprehensive. However, the model can be combined easily with other approaches in a way that can minimize or eliminate its disadvantages. Teachers also can emphasize different uses of the process, complex societal problem solving, and application of the process in interdisciplinary studies to make CPS more appropriate as a strategy in program development for gifted students.

RESOURCES

Background Information

Feldhusen, J. F., & Treffinger, D. J. (1985). *Creative thinking and problem solving in gifted education* (3rd ed.). Dubuque, IA: Kendall/Hunt. This revision of a classic resource book includes information on varied program models and their relationships to creativity and problem solving. Techniques for nurturing creative thinking and critical thinking in the classroom are a major feature. Reviews and descriptions of more than 50 curriculum resources also are included.

Isaksen, S. G., Dorval, K. B., & Treffinger, D. J. (1994). *Creative approaches to problem solving*. Dubuque, IA: Kendall/Hunt. This book is a large, comprehensive manual that includes theoretical background, development, implementation, research, and evolution of the *Creative Problem Solving* process. The intended audience is any individual, whether in education or in other occupations, who has an interest in using and teaching the process. Chapters include "Conceptions of Creativity," "Creative Problem Solving," "Personal Orientation to CPS," "Situational Outlook for Creativity,"

"Preparing for CPS," "Understanding the Problem," "Generating Ideas," "Planning for Action," and "Applying CPS." Numerous charts, checklists, illustrations, and support materials enhance the lively text and add to its usefulness. A glossary of terms and extensive bibliographies for "extending your learning" make this a truly comprehensive resource.

Parnes, S. J. (Ed.). (1992). *Source book in Creative Problem Solving: A fifty year digest of proven innovation processes.* Buffalo, NY: Creative Education Foundation Press. Dr. Parnes has produced a distillation of the best ideas about creative problem solving.

Treffinger, D. J., & Isaksen, S. G. (1992). *Creative Problem Solving: An introduction.* Sarasota, FL: Center for Creative Learning. For first-time users of CPS, this is an easy-to-understand introduction to all the steps in the process and tips for implementing them in your own programs. Methods and techniques are provided as guides to (a) recognize opportunities and challenges; (b) identify data necessary to problem solving; (c) design problem statements and identify appropriate problems or subproblems for investigation; (d) encourage fluent, flexible, original thinking; (e) select and use criteria for evaluation of promising alternatives; and (f) develop and implement specific action plans. As the focus is on creative thinking, no modifications for gifted students have been included.

Instructional Materials and Ideas

Eberle, R. F. (1977). *Scamper: Games for imagination development.* Buffalo, NY: DOK Publishers. The purpose of this book is to assist children to maintain and improve their imaginative ability through behaviors such as substitution, combination, magnification or minification, and elaboration. The book contains 10 games such as New Zoo, in which children imagine new animals by combining parts of familiar ones. Appendices include ideas to encourage children to scamper (run playfully through one's mind) alone or with adults. A related book, also published by DOK, is *Scamper On.*

Eberle, B., & Stanish, B. (1980). *CPS for kids: A resource book for teaching creative problem solving to children.* Buffalo, NY: DOK Publishers. This book, along with *Be a Problem Solver* by the same authors, includes a variety of options for teachers and students to use to improve abilities to sense problems and challenges, find facts, define problems, find ideas, decide on solutions, and gain acceptance for solutions. Exercises are relevant to students, and most involve real-life situations.

Elwell, P. (1990). *CPS for teens.* Buffalo, NY: DOK Publishers. Designed for students in grades 6 through 12, this is a practical resource for teaching older students the *Creative Problem Solving* process. Many of the practical activities include reproducible materials for use in the classroom.

Kobert, D., & Bagnall, J. (1991). *Universal traveler: A guide to creativity, problem-solving, and the process of reaching goals* (7th ed.). Menlo Park, CA: Crisp Publications. This new revision of a classic book on creative problem solving is in the format of a travel guide, as the authors see the development of the creative process as a journey to be planned carefully. The book includes background information on the skills required for creativity and the design process and numerous activities that outline the necessary steps in the creative problem solving process and supplementary "Side Trips." The theme, illustrations, and layout are unique; teachers and students will enjoy using this appealing teaching-learning tool.

Kunz, C. (n.d.). *Brainstrains: Creative problem-solving and logical thinking.* Victoria, Australia: Down Under Books. The author combines fiction with facts about the lives of eminent individuals to pose problems that promote creative mathematical problem solving and logical thinking. Grades 3 through 8.

Lewis, B. A. (1991). *The kid's guide to social action: How to solve the social problems you choose—and turn creative thinking into positive action.* Minneapolis: Free Spirit Publishing. This practical handbook is a treasure for teachers of gifted, socially aware students. A rationale for getting involved in social action is followed by specific examples of significant ways that gifted kids have influenced social/political actions. Chapters include "Power Skills" in telephoning, letter writing, interviewing, speeches, surveys, petitions, organizing, and protesting; "Initiating or Changing Laws"; "Resources," including hundreds of addresses, contact groups, and a select list of children's books on legislative processes; and "Tools," a group of reproducible forms for student use in social action problem solving. The author is an award-winning teacher of inner-city gifted students, and many of the recommendations and illustrations in the book are drawn from experiences of her students.

McAlpine, J., Jeweler, S., Weincek, B., & Finkbinder, M. (1987, January/February). Creative problem solving and Bloom: The thinking connection. *G/C/T,* pp. 11–14. A Saturday program for gifted students in grades 7 through 9 in which the transfer/applications of a study of CPS and Bloom's *Taxonomy* were developed in the context of invention or futuristics is described. The importance of open-ended questions, asking "why" questions, and evaluation are stressed.

Noller, R. B., Treffinger, D. J., & Houseman, E. D. (1979). *It's a gas to be gifted or CPS for the gifted and talented.* Buffalo, NY: DOK Publishers. This short book presents a simulation, concerning the Froop Oil Company, to involve students in solving the problem of how best to use a gas station that has been closed by the oil company. The major purpose is to develop a wide variety of creative thinking processes such as observation, seeing new relationships, sensing problems, and discovering ideas. The major steps for the CPS process and guidelines for implementing the simulation are included.

Parnes, S. J. (1981). *The magic of your mind.* Buffalo, NY: Bearly Limited.

Parnes, S. J. (1988). *Visionizing: State of the art processes for encouraging innovative excellence.* Buffalo, NY: D.O.K. An extension of the principles of creativity and creative problem solving, this is a guide for translating dreams into reality. The book integrates effective materials from earlier Parnes books (e.g., *The Guide to Creative Action, Creative Actionbook, Creative Behavior Guidebook, Creative Behavior Workbook*) and adds newly developed course materials for future creative problem solving. The approach is a blend of imagery and analogy processes with the CPS process and provides resource materials for all kinds of creativity development, including self-study. A *Visionizing* audiocassette also is recommended for initiating the experience of deep relaxation and intense imagery that evokes visionizing and helps the visioneer commit to an action plan to actualize the vision.

Two international programs that provide students with experience with the creative problem-solving process are *Future Problem Solving* and *Odyssey of the Mind.* Coaches training is available in most of the United States and many other countries. Students work in teams to solve realistic problems, develop creative solutions, and construct action plans to implement the solutions. Results are submitted to trained evaluators who provide formative feedback so that students can improve their problem-solving skills. State, national, and international competitions are conducted annually.

Future Problem Solving Program
315 West Huron, Suite 140-B
Ann Arbor, MI 48103-4203

Odyssey of the Mind
P.O. Box 27
Glassboro, NJ 08028

Chapter 6

Joseph S. Renzulli: The Enrichment Triad

E ducators of the gifted and critics of special provisions for the gifted have long been concerned about providing "qualitatively different" learning experiences for these students; therefore, Renzulli presents an enrichment model that can be used as a guide in developing defensible programs for the gifted.

Unlike most teaching-learning models considered in this volume, the *Enrichment Triad Model* (Renzulli, 1977) was developed specifically to provide differentiated education for gifted students. The first two components of the triad, general exploratory activities and process thinking, are deemed appropriate for almost all children, and the third component, individual or small-group investigation of real problems, is seen as most appropriate for gifted learners. As most gifted students spend the majority of their time in regular classrooms, Renzulli and Reis (1985) have adapted and expanded the *Enrichment Triad Model* to create the *Schoolwide Enrichment Model* (SEM), a plan to promote educational excellence and school reform. The major difference between the two models is that the SEM involves a much greater number of teachers and children in Types I and II enrichment activities and requires that all personnel at a participating school buy into the philosophy of the triad model. An added benefit is that the involvement of almost all students in Types I and II activities seems to lessen the charges of elitism often directed toward gifted students who are involved in special projects.

Renzulli (1978) proposes a three-ring conception of giftedness as the interaction of above-average intellectual ability, creativity, and task commitment. Creativity and task commitment, in his theory, are developmental objectives to be fostered in intellectually able students. He proposes that *gifted* be used as an adjective and avers that gifted behaviors also are contextual;

creative and/or gifted performances are dependent on the interaction of people, circumstances, time, and place. As a result, the *Enrichment Triad Model,* designed to move gifted students through awareness (Type I activities), learning of processes (Type II activities), and development of *real-world* projects (Type III activities), was complemented by the *Revolving Door Identification Model* (Renzulli, Reis, & Smith, 1981), in which 15% to 20% of the students in a school are identified as a *talent pool,* those who have well above average ability either in a general sense or in a specific performance area. Students in the talent pool participate in Type I and Type II activities, as do almost all students in SEM programs, and may revolve out for a period of time to do qualitatively different Type III projects of interest to them.

Qualitatively different, according to Renzulli, means more than freedom of choice, lack of pressure, absence of grading, and individualization of rate or pace, although all of these are important in programs for the gifted. Modifications also need to be made in such areas as content, learning style, and teaching strategies.

The simplest form of enrichment, sometimes referred to as vertical enrichment or acceleration, consists of introducing gifted students to advanced courses early. This practice takes care of the gifted student's need to be challenged and to interact with equally advanced peers and a more specialized instructor. Thus, through accelerated placement the advanced ability of the learner is considered. However, according to Renzulli, two other dimensions of learning in enrichment activities must be respected: the student's content interest and his or her preferred style of learning. These are important components of Renzulli's model.

Two main program objectives are recommended for guiding the education of gifted and talented students and are incorporated into the *Triad* approach (Renzulli, 1977):

1. For the majority of time spent in gifted programs, students will have an opportunity to pursue their own interests to whatever depth and extent they so desire; and they will be allowed to pursue these interests in a manner that is consistent with their own preferred styles of learning. (p. 5)

2. The primary role of each teacher in the program for gifted and talented students will be to provide each student with assistance in (1) identifying and structuring realistic, solvable problems that are consistent with the student's interests; (2) acquiring the necessary methodological resources and investigative skills that are necessary for solving these particular problems; and (3) finding appropriate outlets for student products. (p. 10)

Superior intelligence, or an extremely high ability score on a test, has been the major criterion for admitting students into programs for the gifted in the past. Renzulli offers a rationale for using more than one criterion. According to Renzulli, three clusters of characteristics are important in students who can benefit from his model: (a) above-average intelligence, (b) above-average creativity, and (c) task commitment (motivation-persistence). The interaction of these three clusters results in superior performance.

ASSUMPTIONS UNDERLYING THE MODEL

About Teaching and Learning

In developing his model, Renzulli (1977) states that he makes major assumptions about the regular curriculum and about enrichment activities. Inherent in his approach and following from his stated premises are implicit and important assumptions that must be recognized and accepted before the approach can be appropriately implemented.

The following assumptions are clear from discussions of the model's development.

1. Certain basic competencies should be mastered by all students so they can adapt effectively to the culture in which they live. This mastery process should be as exciting, relevant, and streamlined as possible.

2. Talent pool students are capable of mastering one or more subjects in the regular curriculum at a faster pace than average or slower students. "Curriculum compacting" (Renzulli & Reis, 1985) should be used to enable able students to progress through the basic curriculum as rapidly as possible.

3. A student's content interests and style of learning must be respected in any enrichment situation. Student interests should be the point of entry for all enrichment activities. Educators must take the time and develop the skills to assist students in the discovery of areas of true interest.

4. Enrichment experiences and activities may be integrated with regular curriculum themes but must be above and beyond the scope of the standard curriculum. Exploratory activities (Type I enrichment) allow students to interact with a particular person, concept, or piece of knowledge, stimulate interest, and open up opportunities for exploration. Varied thinking processes and information-management strategies (Type II enrichment) must

be learned to enable students to conduct self-directed investigations and/or develop products and ideas.

5. Enrichment experiences can take place in almost any setting and involve one child or many children. Any student with superior potential for performance and a sincere interest should have the opportunity to pursue the topic(s) in depth.

Most of these assumptions are concerned with the educator's concept of providing "enriching experiences" for gifted students. All children participate in the regular curriculum, but gifted students need experiences that are above and beyond those experiences provided for all children. Renzulli assumes that gifted students should participate in the regular curriculum for some part of their school experience, or they should at least demonstrate the minimum competencies that are required as a part of this regular curriculum. An implication of this assumption, very important for those planning to implement Renzulli's ideas, is that the *Triad* model may need some major modifications if it is to be used as a basis for curriculum planning in a self-contained program for the gifted.

The last assumption about the physical setting carries with it some important considerations that go beyond the usual concerns in a classroom setting. To implement appropriately the model and its requirement that ". . . if a particular student has a superior potential for performance in a particular area of sincere interest, then he or she must be allowed the opportunity to pursue topics therein to unlimited levels of inquiry" (Renzulli, 1977, p. 17) means that administrative flexibility is absolutely essential. Enrichment activities could take place in the regular classroom, in a special resource room, in an independent study carrel in the library, or in the community. They could involve one child or several children and must not be limited to any one place. For example, students should be able to study with a college professor if that is the best way for them to pursue their topics to "unlimited levels of inquiry."

About Characteristics and Teaching of the Gifted

The major assumption Renzulli (1978) makes about the characteristics of the gifted follows from his reviews of the research on characteristics of successful or eminent individuals. He reviews the research of Roe (1952), Wallach (1976), Terman and Oden (1959), Hoyt (1965), and MacKinnon (1965). From these and other studies, he concludes that gifted individuals possess three interlocking clusters of traits, which he calls the "three-ring conception" of giftedness. The clusters are (a) above-average general and/or specific ability, (b) above-average task commitment, and (c) above-average creativity. Renzulli and Reis (1985) stress that gifted behavior is a result of interaction among these three clusters and is contextual; it occurs in certain people at certain times and under certain circumstances. The clusters may not be equally important in all instances. Someone with great task commitment may be able to compensate for average ability and someone with superior creativity may produce a superior product without superior task commitment. Interaction among the clusters, not one single cluster, is what is necessary for creative/productive accomplishment.

Above-Average Ability

Above-average cognitive abilities include those characteristics often measured by intelligence, aptitude, or achievement tests. However, Renzulli is highly critical of a unitary conception of giftedness (IQ) and argues that gifted behaviors also include other abilities not measured on traditional tests (e.g., superior performance in a specific ability area). In the selection of students for a talent pool, Renzulli recommends selection of all students who score at or above the 92nd percentile (using local norms) on one or more subtests of standardized instruments. Teachers then are asked to nominate additional students whose academic or creative performance may not be assessed accurately by psychometric instruments. Additional students are identified through a case study approach to ensure that highly able students from divergent populations will not be excluded. Renzulli does not define clearly the concept of *above-average ability* but points out that approximately 20% of students can profit from the enrichment activities often reserved for those who score at or above the 95th percentile on standardized tests.

Task Commitment

Of the three clusters, task commitment is the newest concept and seems to be the most misunderstood by individuals attempting to implement the *Triad* model. Educators seem to equate the concept of task commitment with either a global concept of motivation or a more specific concept of a child who is "motivated" to do a teacher-chosen task. What Renzulli has in mind is different. The kind of motivation he discusses is a refined or focused commitment and ability to take energy and concentrate it on something very specific (e.g., a problem situation, a creative project, a research project). Some of the characteristics included in this cluster are the following: persistence in the accomplishment of goals; integration toward goals; drive to achieve (Terman, 1959); enthusiasm; determination; and industry (MacKinnon, 1965). An important point to emphasize is that these characteristics were observed when the individuals were involved in work of their own choosing—their life work—not in a teacher-designed task.

Renzulli's task commitment cluster seems similar to the concept of continuing motivation (CM) discussed by Maehr (1976). Continuing motivation is defined as "the tendency to return to and continue working on tasks away from the instructional content in which they were initially confronted" (p. 443). Included in this definition are several important ideas, for example, returning to a task in different circumstances without external pressures and when other alternatives are available. To justify the value of this concept, Maehr cites some research suggesting that some classroom practices designed to increase performance on classroom tasks may, for children who have the most intrinsic interest in the activity, actually decrease the probability that they will exhibit continuing motivation. Therefore, educators must be careful in assessing these motivational traits in a regular classroom setting. Maehr's approach offers some promising ways to approach the assessment problem.

Creativity

Creativity is the ability to look at problems in new and unusual ways, to generate a large number of ideas, to challenge the existing ways of doing things (in school or in a field of study), and to be speculative, playful with ideas, and willing to take risks. Included in this cluster of characteristics are such traits as "originality of thinking and freshness of approaches," ingenuity, and "ability to set aside established conventions and procedures when appropriate" (Renzulli, 1978, p. 184). As with motivational traits, however, caution must be exercised in assessing creativity in students. Creative performance on a test of divergent thinking may have little or no relation to creativity in a person's life work. Educators may be able to observe some characteristics in children that would lead them to believe these children have the potential to become creative adults, but the persistence required to return to an idea again and again and the creativity necessary to generate relevant solutions to a pressing problem day after day may be something entirely different.

Achieving Success

Renzulli seems to be right about the importance of the interaction of these three traits in the achievement of eminence. Again and again, research on successful adults supports the conclusion that high ability alone does not predict an individual's success in a career. What educators must all remember, however, is, first, that most of this research was done on adults and, second, that the purpose was to identify the characteristics of those who had achieved success in a socially recognized manner. In Terman's (1959) study, for example, the "gifted" sample, identified by IQ tests, was divided into groups according to degree of success in life accomplishments. Terman then attempted to determine the characteristics on which the most and least successful groups differed most widely. He found that the groups differed most in their motivational traits and their self-concept or confidence in themselves. Maker, Redden, Tonelson, and Howell (1978) also identified the same pattern of traits in successful adults with disabilities. From this research, as with other research on successful adults, determining whether these characteristics were the result of the individuals' success or whether the characteristics were actually the antecedents of success is impossible. If these motivational characteristics were indeed the antecedents or causes of success, then educators would be justified in selecting students for participation in programs for the gifted based on their motivation. However, if these traits actually were results of the individuals' success, children should be chosen on other characteristics, and motivation should be developed through an interesting, exciting program and through successful experiences. Renzulli (1988) believes that the goals of social contribution and self-fulfillment are highly interactive. Creative work usually leads to feelings of self-fulfillment, self-efficacy, and the development of a positive self-concept; in turn, these feelings contribute to greater levels of creative productivity. "The process is best represented figurally by an upward spiral" (p. 20).

Gagne (1985) is critical of Renzulli's inclusion of creativity, stating that the selection of fields of study (architecture, arts, sciences) and the types of eminence researched biases the conclusions. Gagne believes that "creativity may be a major determinant of exceptional performance in certain fields of endeavor, but not in all" (p. 106). He would consider creativity an ability domain.

The achievement of success in a socially recognized manner also is an important aspect of many of these studies. What about those individuals who have achieved success by becoming self-actualized individuals, but who have not become eminent or recognized for superior accomplishments? If this kind of success is important, should those individuals be studied to determine their characteristics and children be sought who showed these traits early in life? All these questions must be considered in implementing the *Triad* model, because Renzulli has designed the approach to be used with individuals who have the three interacting clusters of traits—creativity, task commitment, and high ability—not those who have only one or two of the clusters.

In response to critics (e.g., Webb, Meckstroth, & Tolan, 1982) who argue that the *Enrichment Triad Model* excludes gifted underachievers who lack task commitment, Renzulli (1985) notes that the talent pool includes all students who have high scores on traditional tests of intelligence and achievement. Also, he argues that creative behaviors can be developed and that intense interest in a topic or project can be stimulated through exciting, involving enrichment activities. Newell (1989) provides interesting, valid recommendations for implementing the *Triad* model with underachievers. Educators who plan to implement the model must question whether they have the resources and skills to help potentially gifted children develop task commitment as well as creativity and intelligence.

In the implementation of the *Triad* model, many students are identified as potential producers. Whenever these students have projects they would like to complete, they can "revolve in" to the special program and receive assistance in the development of their investigations. When the project is completed, if they have another idea, they can remain in the special program; if they do not have an investigation or project in mind, they "revolve out" of the program until they are ready for another Type III investigation. This approach to selection recognizes that many children have the ability to be producers and that not all are sufficiently motivated to be high-level producers all the time. The RDIM is seen as an important adjunct to the curriculum framework of the *Triad* and is explained in more depth in Renzulli, Reis, and Smith (1981).

ELEMENTS/PARTS

Dimensions, Thinking Levels, or Steps

The *Enrichment Triad* has three types of enrichment: (a) Type I, General Exploratory Activities; (b) Type II, Group Training Activities; and (c) Type III, Individual and Small Group Investigations of Real Problems. The first two types of enrichment activities are considered appropriate for all learners; however, they also are important in the overall enrichment of gifted and talented students for two main reasons. First, Types I and II enrichment include strategies for expanding student interests and developing thinking and feeling processes that are necessary elements in any enrichment program. Second, these two types represent the logical input and support systems essential for the type of enrichment most appropriate for gifted students: individual or small-group investigations and productions.

In Type I enrichment, the teacher (or school team) plans general exploratory experiences on new and exciting topics, fields of knowledge, or ideas not included in the regular curriculum to "invite" students to greater involvement with areas of study. Students have opportunities to explore a variety of content and, perhaps, discover an area of fascination that may lead to a Type III activity. Type I enrichment also helps teachers decide what types of activities should be selected for Type II. Although much exploratory freedom is needed, students should be aware from the beginning that they are expected to have a purpose when exploring and that eventually they will be conducting further study in one of the areas of interest to them. An important point to remember in relation to Type I is that general exploratory activity is a cyclical and ongoing process, and even if students are involved in a specific project, they should be given continuous opportunities to keep generating new interests.

Type II enrichment activities are strategic and consist of activities, methods, materials, and instruction designed to develop higher level thinking processes, affective behavior and processes related to personal/social development, and specific research methodology and reference skills. These processes often are scheduled on a regular basis but also may be taught when a specific need is identified during Type III investigations. Thinking and feeling processes have been the focus of many programs for the gifted in the past since research shows that certain thinking and feeling processes provide students with skills and abilities that are applicable or transferable to new learning situations and other content areas. These skills or processes are useful in the changing world, where knowledge is expanding continuously. Thus students are prepared to face new problem-solving situations.

Attention should be given to ensure that these processes are used only as necessary tools to facilitate investigations. If not used as tools, they will become ends, rather than means. Process should go hand in hand with the content, as both are important. Even if thinking and feeling processes cannot be defended as being exclusively appropriate for the gifted, they can be defended as an essential part of a total enrichment model for the following reasons: (a) they provide an opportunity for gifted students to reach the levels of thinking and feeling that their natural abilities allow; (b) they have the potential for introducing students to more advanced kinds of study and inquiry; and (c) they provide the gifted student, who is characterized by a wide range of interests, with the skills and abilities to solve problems in a variety of areas and new situations.

Type III enrichment, individual or small group investigations, is the major focus of the *Triad* model for gifted students and the most appropriate activity for developing gifted behaviors. According to Renzulli, about half the time students spend in enrichment activities should be devoted to Type III experiences. In Type III enrichment, the students (or an individual) become actual investigators of real problems or topics and use the kinds of methods (even if less sophisticated) a professional in the area would use. Students also may do actual work with a professional mentor or create products for evaluation by professional standards. The main characteristics of Type III activities include the following.

- The student takes an active part in formulating both the problem and the methods by which the problem will be attacked.

- No routine method of solution or recognized answer exists, although appropriate investigative techniques upon which to draw and criteria by which a product can be judged often are available.

- The area of investigation is of sincere interest to an individual or small group, rather than being a teacher-determined topic or activity.

- Students use raw data rather than the conclusions reached by others as their information in reaching conclusions and making generalizations.

- The student engages with a producer's rather than a consumer's attitude and, in so doing, takes the necessary steps to communicate results in a professionally appropriate manner.

- A tangible product often is presented to a real (rather than a contrived) audience but, according to Renzulli (1988), "products are not the major goal of a Triad-based program" (p. 20).

MODIFICATION OF THE BASIC CURRICULUM

In his model, Renzulli provides for some modifications in all aspects of the curriculum—content, process, environment, and product—to make it more appropriate for the gifted. The major modifications directly suggested by the model are in the areas of product and learning environment. An important note, however, is that the model provides a framework for integrating a variety of content and process changes that are appropriate for the gifted. Renzulli suggests that thinking and feeling processes be developed that will enable students to be effective problem solvers. However, he does not specify in the *Triad* model which thinking and feeling processes should be developed and how they should be developed.

Content Modifications

Content is modified in that the students learn not only facts about an area but also the methods of inquiry within that discipline. The student also is exposed to a wide variety of topics within a discipline before selecting what to investigate. Content is modified based on the student's interests. Students are encouraged and allowed to select topics of interest to them. Teachers assess student interests continually and attempt to provide experience that will build on these student interests.

Process Modifications

Renzulli emphasizes the role of process as a means, not an end. The teacher chooses different processes all the time, according to the students' interests and needs, in order to equip them with the tools and skills to do an independent investigation.

The major process modification directly suggested by the *Triad* model is freedom of choice. In all the areas—content, process, product, and learning environment—students should be allowed the freedom to choose activities that are of interest. Either individually or in small groups, students should select the topic or area of study, decide on the methods and tools needed to carry out the study, and develop a product directed toward an appropriate audience of their choice. Students also should be able to conduct the study in any appropriate environment inside or outside the school. Freedom of choice is encouraged in the three types of enrichment activities, although to different degrees. In Type I exploratory activities, the students often choose among options created by the teacher. (The students, of course, played a part in determining the original options since the teacher assessed their interests.) In Type II activities, the students perhaps have less choice, although the kind of investigations in which they are engaged will influence the Type II activities provided. With Type III investigations, students have complete freedom to choose topics, methods, products, and environments.

Higher level thinking is a process modification somewhat indirectly suggested by Renzulli's model. Although he does not specify how this should be done, he emphasizes the need for development of problem-solving skills in gifted students or of operations that help the student deal more effectively with content. These operations or processes include critical thinking, reflective thinking, inquiry, divergent thinking, and productive thinking. Renzulli specifically mentions the *Taxonomies of Educational Objectives* and Guilford's *Structure of Intellect* model as approaches that can be used in implementing this aspect of the *Triad*.

A second process modification somewhat indirectly suggested by the *Triad* approach is open-endedness. Renzulli emphasizes as a criterion for selecting Type II activities that these experiences have the power to elicit advanced levels of thinking from gifted students. Also, the divergent production section of Guilford's model can be a useful framework for developing and classifying creativity training exercises for use with gifted students. This model encourages open-endedness by expecting and encouraging a variety of responses for each question or activity.

Discovery learning is another process modification that is suggested by the *Triad* model. Although the *Triad* approach does not provide for the use of guided discovery, discovery learning is certainly an aspect of Type III investigations. Since students are expected to use the techniques of real inquirers in making their own investigations, they are practicing discovery learning in a real-world context. However, the *Triad* model does not provide teachers with strategies for developing activities that will facilitate discovery learning or the use of inductive reasoning, important components of this curricular modification.

A final process modification made by the *Enrichment Triad* is variety. Teachers are encouraged to use a wide range of methods, including field trips, observation of real professionals at work, simulation games, learning centers, lectures, and any other methods that can be devised. Another aspect of variety is that a wide range of thinking and feeling processes are developed through Type II activities. This necessitates the use of many different methods.

Product Modifications

Product modifications in all areas are inherent in the Triad model. Renzulli (1985) believes that the success of most Type III projects is a "sense of audience" that students develop as they work on investigative and creative projects. This sense of audience also contributes to both task commitment and concern for excellence. His emphasis on creative productivity has made more impact in this area than any other theorist or practitioner involved in education of the gifted. In the early development of the model, he suggested that no investigation was a true Type III activity unless a tangible product was presented to a real audience. Ten years after the introduction of the model, however, Renzulli (1988) stated that products are not the major goal of the program. Instead, the product affords a means to bring together the complex cognitive, affective, and conative skills students learn to apply to planning, organization, resource use, and time management in a more naturalistic manner. "Products are viewed as 'the assembly plants of the mind,' . . . the catalysts and vehicles upon which a wide variety of advanced level processes are developed, applied, and made meaningful in a learning situation that was purposefully designed to be the antithesis of prescribed, presented learning" (Renzulli, 1988, p. 20). A product is designed to solve a real problem of interest to the student, employ methods appropriate to the field of study, and use raw data to generate unique conclusions. An important aspect of the process is that students are not acting as consumers of information but as producers of it. The students are not just emulating professionals, they are actually becoming professionals.

To provide guidelines for the teacher in implementing Type III activities and thus making the product modifications appropriate for gifted students, Renzulli and Reis (1985) provide suggested strategies for identifying and focusing student interests (for example, interest development and identification, the Interest-A-Lyzer, and interest refinement and focusing), finding appropriate outlets for student products, providing students with methodological assistance, and developing a "laboratory environment." Suggestions include reference books and materials, along with methods and strategies.

Learning Environment Modifications

Renzulli also makes numerous suggestions for developing environments appropriate for gifted students. He advocates a student-centered atmosphere in which independence is encouraged, few restrictions are present, complexity is essential, and high mobility is a must. In the learning environment appropriate for implementing the *Triad*, the teacher's major goal is to identify, focus, and facilitate student interests and ideas. In fact, student interests guide the selection of both content and process activities developed by the teacher.

In this atmosphere, the teacher cannot possibly be an information giver, except when asked by the students. Although the teacher may direct certain activities, at least half will be completely determined by the students since half their time (according to the model) should be spent in Type III investigations. Students certainly must be permitted to be independent in other than academic settings since many of them will be involved in small-group activities in which they are conducting studies. They should be allowed and encouraged to solve their own disputes when they arise, and they should assist the teacher in planning and implementing Type I and II activities that interest them.

The environment dimension of openness requires that few, if any, restrictions affect the students' participation. They should be encouraged to develop new ideas, produce different products, and use different investigative techniques. The physical environment must permit new people, exploratory discussions, and freedom to change directions when necessary. Complexity in the learning environment is encouraged by Renzulli in his suggestion that specialized equipment, varied reference materials, and sophisticated materials should be available. This includes both books and nonbook reference materials. To enable the teacher to develop a true laboratory environment, a variety of types of work space also must be present. This includes tables, study carrels, soft areas for discussions, easels for painting, and computer hardware and software.

The *Triad* approach also requires an environment that permits high mobility. Students must be permitted to conduct their investigations in any environment that facilitates the process. Renzulli's ideas that are most related to this dimension of the environment are found under the heading "developing a laboratory environment." In a laboratory environment, students are engaged actively in gathering some form of relevant information that is to be used in the development of a particular product. Examples given by Renzulli are (a) a street corner and classroom where children recorded the number of automobiles that failed to stop, then analyzed the data for a presentation to the commissioner of public safety; and (b) the school cafeteria and science laboratory where students collected leftover food and unused napkins in an antiwaste campaign. In these cases, the students could not have conducted investigations on their problem of concern if they had been confined to a classroom in a school. Thus, an environment permitting movement freely is an essential aspect of implementing Type III investigations.

Examples of Teaching Activities/Strategies

Type I Enrichment Activities

Three procedures the teacher can use to allow the student to explore a diversity of areas are interest centers, visitations or field trips, and resource persons or guest speakers. Interest centers should include a wide range of topics or areas of study, material that is stimulating for further research, and information related to methods of investigation in the field. A good example of provoking and stimulating material would be the completed investigations and products of other students. These should be included in interest centers.

Visitations should be to places where dynamic people are actively engaged in problem solving and the pursuit of knowledge. Instead of just looking at equipment and the environment, gifted learners should have an "escalated experience." This type of experience provides opportunities to look into and become involved with what is on display, being presented, or being produced. For example, students should have opportunities to interact with artists, curators, engineers, and other professionals by seeing them at work and by actually taking part in some of their activities. When inviting a guest speaker, teachers must choose persons who are actively engaged in contributing to the advancement of art or knowledge in their respective fields or areas of endeavor. Some examples are local historians, poets, dancers, architects, photographers, and scientists.

The major role of the teacher in Type I enrichment is to develop interests and identify areas for further study; the teacher also must assist students to analyze their own interests. A planned strategy for helping students examine their present and potential interests could be based on an instrument called the Interest-A-Lyzer (Renzulli, 1977, pp. 75–82). This instrument consists of a series of hypothetical situations in which the student is asked to respond to open-ended questions. Looking at the responses, consistencies are analyzed and general patterns of interest are detected. Teachers using the instrument should make the children familiar with the content of the items, and they may modify the contents or add their own ideas, especially when dealing with young children or children who are culturally different.

Another aspect of the teacher's role is to expose students constantly to new areas for creative expression. For example, when recruiting community resource persons as guest speakers, teachers should choose persons who are involved in types of professions and activities that are different from those with which the students are familiar. A community survey would be good for this purpose as well as for identifying persons who might be willing to follow up an exposure activity and become involved with groups of students. A survey could even identify individuals who would be willing to become mentors. A sample form for surveying community resources is the *Community Talent Miner* (Renzulli, 1977, pp. 82–86).

Interest development centers, field trips, and resource persons are organized approaches to Type I. However, students also should be given informal opportunities to examine topics for possible study. For example, they should be encouraged to browse in libraries or bookstores, encouraged to read how-to books, and provided opportunities for unstructured group discussion.

Type II Enrichment Activities

Any model that provides valuable systems for organizing thinking and feeling processes and factors that are essential for human learning can be used effectively as a Type II activity. Some examples of these would be Bloom's *Taxonomy of Educational Objectives,* Krathwohl's *Taxonomy of Affective Behaviors,* Guilford's *Structure of Intellect,* Parnes's *Creative Problem Solving,* Hilda Taba's *Teaching Strategies,* and Taylor's *Multiple Talent Model.* An important aspect of Type II is to select activities according to student interests whenever possible and integrate the thinking processes with substantive content.

The development of thinking and feeling processes necessary for Type III investigations is the ultimate goal of Type II activities. Students must acquire the process skills and abilities that will enable them to solve problems in a variety of areas. The following are given by Renzulli (1977) as examples of process skills:

Brainstorming	Comparison	Elaboration
Observation	Categorization	Hypothesizing
Classification	Synthesis	Awareness
Interpretation	Fluency	Appreciation
Analysis	Flexibility	Value Clarification
Evaluation	Originality	Commitment (p. 25)

Other Type II activities for talent pool students include (a) advanced reference and research skills; (b) inquiry processes such as research design and collection and interpretation of data; (c) planning, forecasting, and decision making; (d) specialized process training (e.g., laser photography); (e) minicourses in methods of the specific discipline (e.g., oral history techniques);

and (f) advanced computer programming or graphics production and specific technical skills needed for projects.

Type III Enrichment Activities

In Type III enrichment, the teacher's role is to be a manager in the learning process and to know when and how to enter into this process. The teacher thus has the following major responsibilities when managing Type III:

- identifying and focusing student interests
- finding appropriate outlets for student products
- providing students with methodological assistance
- developing a laboratory environment

Successful Type III enrichment activities depend on the interaction of these four basic responsibilities.

General interests must be refined and focused to enable students to identify a real and solvable problem. At this time, the teacher must make certain that students apply the proper investigative strategies so that they do not report instead of investigate. The teacher also must be careful not to rush students through the process or impose a problem on them; teachers should allow students to make their own decisions. Teachers must find appropriate outlets for student products, since one of the major characteristics of a real problem (as opposed to a training exercise or simulation) is that the producer is attempting to inform, entertain, or influence a relatively specific but real audience. This need to have an impact is one of the reasons why creative and productive persons are highly product oriented; they always have an audience in mind. Since real-world audiences frequently are grouped together by topical interests, teachers can look for them as potential audiences for the creative work of their students. Some examples of audiences are historical societies, science clubs, dramatic groups, and persons interested in preserving a certain species of wildlife or promoting a particular social action. Another potential outlet consists of children's magazines that include the work of young people. Following are some specific examples of possible outlets and products in Type III:

- writing a journal article
- making a conference presentation
- issuing a statement to legislators
- producing a television program

- publishing a book

- writing a play

- developing a new theory

- developing a lattice

- writing a brochure

- writing a computer program

One final concern that must be mentioned is the quality of products. Teachers should make their students aware that the creative/productive process goes beyond just generating ideas and that they must work hard to refine each product before it is considered final. Students should avoid circulating or presenting products that have not been revised, edited, and polished.

Reis and Schack (1993) provide a very helpful step-by-step process for teachers to assist students in developing qualitatively differentiated products:

1. Assess, find, or create student interests.

2. Conduct an interview to determine the strength of the interest.

3. Help students find a question or questions to research.

4. Develop a written plan.

5. Help students locate multiple resources and continue working on the topic.

6. Provide methodological assistance.

7. Help students decide which questions to answer.

8. Provide managerial assistance.

9. Identify final products and audiences.

10. Offer encouragement, praise, and critical assistance.

11. Escalate the process.

12. Evaluate.

The third responsibility of the teacher in Type III enrichment is guiding student application of the tools of inquiry, that is, the methodological techniques that are necessary to solve a problem. The teacher should help students locate books or mentors that offer step-by-step guidance in methodological activities in a specific area. Students also must learn about the existence, nature, and function of different types of reference materials.

These include bibliographies, on-line data bases, dictionaries, glossaries, indexes, atlases, reviews, abstracts, periodicals, surveys, almanacs, anthologies, nonbook reference materials (art prints, videotapes, filmstrips, charts, maps, or slides), and computer programs. Teaching effectively about the use of reference materials involves developing a systematic plan so that students are continuously learning where and how information is stored. One important activity for the teacher is analyzing the difficulty level of the methodological reference according to the reading and conceptual levels of the student, and serving as a translator whenever a particular concept is beyond the student's level of comprehension.

Also important to the implementation of Type III enrichment is the development of a "laboratory environment" where the students inquire or investigate. A laboratory is not necessarily a physical place. It is the environment—the psychological one—the mood and atmosphere, and a series of investigative activities that can happen anywhere. What determines the presence of a laboratory environment is whether students gather, manipulate, and use raw data or existing information to produce something that is new and unique. Some examples of laboratories could be street corners, a grove of trees, an audiovisual viewing room, a town hall, and a public library.

A good strategy for teachers to use to get investigative activities started is a Management Plan (Renzulli, 1977, p. 71; Renzulli & Reis, 1985, p. 439). This document, a somewhat simplified version of a proposal, provides a format for planning a project. It requires students to think ahead about the purpose of the investigation, the questions to be answered by it, the format of the product, where and to whom the product will be presented, the methodological resources to be used, and the criteria to be used in evaluating the product.

Learning Styles

Important to all three types of enrichment is respect for the individual learning style of each student, along with the general learning style preferences of gifted students. Stewart (1981) and others (Dempsey, 1975; Gallagher, Aschner, & Jenne, 1967; Hunt, 1975; Lundy, 1978; McLachlan & Hunt, 1973; Wasson, 1980) have found that gifted students as a group differ from nongifted students in their preferences for certain types of learning activities. They rank independent study, simulations, and discussion higher than average students, and they prefer low-structure over high-structure classes. They tend to prefer learning alone rather than with others (Cross, 1982; Griggs & Price, 1980; Kreitner, 1981; Price, Dunn, Dunn, & Griggs, 1981). However, gifted students also differ widely in their preferences for certain types of experiences. To provide valuable information about individual preferences, teachers can ask children to respond to questionnaires such as (a) *The Learning Styles Inventory* (Renzulli & Smith, 1978), which assesses children's preferences for certain instructional techniques (for example, lecture, discussion, projects, independent study, programmed instruction, recitation and drill, peer teaching, simulated environments, and teaching games), and (b) *The Learning Style Inventory* (Dunn, Dunn, & Price, 1975), which classifies 18 elements of learning into the categories of environmental, emotional, sociological, and physical elements.

A number of studies show that academic achievement increases when students are taught with respect for their individual learning styles (Cafferty, 1980; Krimsky, 1982; Pizzo, 1982; Tannenbaum, 1982; Trautman, 1979; Virostko, 1983; Wheeler, 1980). Instruction must then be designed to enable all students to learn in their preferred ways as much as possible.

Using the Triad Model

As a concrete example of the *Triad* model in use, the following specific examples are given. The activities are all organized around the following abstract generalization: *Every society has had rules, written or unwritten, by which social control over the people's conduct is maintained.*

Possible Type I Activities

- Observe a city council meeting and conduct interviews afterward with selected officers and members.

- Observe a legislative session.

- Schedule a lecture by a state or local legislator.

- Set up learning centers with copies of constitutions of various countries, books about constitutional issues, newspaper articles about constitutional and legal issues, and books about sociological analysis (that is, how to study societies and their means of social control).

- Schedule a lecture by a sociologist describing his or her work in investigating methods of social control.

- Have students read biographies of famous historians, sociologists, anthropologists, and statespersons.

- Show a film about Margaret Mead and her work.

- Schedule a lecture by a historian about the historical development of codes and how he or she has studied their development.

- Schedule a lecture by a cultural anthropologist about what kinds of things he or she does (for example, types of projects, how they are applied, and methods used).

Possible Type II Activities

- Have a Kohlberg discussion of a moral dilemma that involves an issue in which someone must break a law to save a life.

- Have several Taba discussions using the interpretation of data strategy to examine stories about various societies and their laws.

- Have a Parnes *Creative Problem Solving* activity in which the problem is in the area of how to study a society or how to settle a problem involving the breaking of a rule.

- Play the simulation game *Shipwreck* in which students create a society.

- Use Krathwohl's *Taxonomy* as a guide for making observations of students while engaged in this activity (that is, observe the level of development of their values related to social control).

- Have students devise a constitution for a hypothetical country.

- Have students lobby in the state legislature, city council, or board of education.

- Analyze the methods used by the different historians, anthropologists, and sociologists, including those eminent individuals studied and the individuals who have been guest lecturers or who have been observed.

- Study methods used by cultural anthropologists. (For example, show students how to use observation forms to decide who is in a position of authority based on how others react to this person.)

- Compare the characteristics of current state legislators and famous statespersons.

- Study the use of sociograms, that is, what information comes from them and how a person develops one.

- Develop a plan for creating and operating a school council that develops and enforces rules for the school population.

- Have the students present the plan to school officials and get permission to establish the school council.

- Have students practice their forecasting ability by attempting to predict how different societies in certain periods of history reacted to the imposition of certain laws or codes of conduct. Afterward, read a history text or view a film to check the accuracy of their predictions.

- Using Williams's Visualization strategy, plan an activity in which the students examine certain laws and social codes from the following perspectives: (a) law enforcement officers, (b) lawmakers, (c) prisoners, and (d) the general public.

- Using Krathwohl's *Taxonomy* as a guide, plan a discussion of differing values of investigators and how these can influence their choice of strategies for conducting investigations.

Examples of Type III Activities

- A group of students decided to investigate the law-making process in the city of Albuquerque. They interviewed the city council and made systematic, naturalistic observations of the council in action. Their final report to the city council was of great interest to parents, teachers, and the council itself.

- One student decided she would like to compare the Mexican and American societies' processes of developing and implementing rules to govern society. The student proposed that she would read about the two societies. The teacher, however, encouraged the student to read but also to design and send a questionnaire to Mexican and American lawmakers and to compile the results of this survey. The report then was submitted to a professional journal.

- A group of students interested in school rules conducted a survey of all classrooms asking for opinions on (a) the rules most needed and (b) the rules most often broken. The survey resulted in the development of a proposed discipline policy for the school that was presented to the principal of the school and the executive board of the parent-teacher association (PTA).

- In this project on school rules, the teacher was concerned at first about whether the students would be able to complete the project because many of those in the group were new to the program and had not had experience in directing their own investigations. In her observations of the working of the group, she used Treffinger's model to assess the levels of self-direction of the students. She was happy to discover that several students possessed many skills at the highest levels. She worked on an individual basis with some of the students who were causing the group some problems in an attempt to develop the skills they were lacking.

- One student was interested in studying the penal systems in various societies, but she was having difficulty figuring out exactly what to study and how. The teacher suggested that the student use the CPS process to help her select a topic and develop her investigation.

- One student was having a great deal of difficulty developing criteria for evaluating his product, a research report to be submitted to a professional journal. He wanted to evaluate the paper himself, have it judged by several others, and revise it before submitting it for publication. The teacher suggested that he consider Bloom's *Taxonomy* and Guilford's product categories for the evaluation or that he use them to get ideas for criteria. (Students had previously learned these as classification systems.)

- One student decided to do a research project on the amount of eye contact between people in a shopping center as a way to investigate some of the unwritten rules governing actions. The paper was submitted to an anthropology journal.

An important note is that only "possible" activities of each type are included. The teacher should survey the interests of the students and observe their participation in various activities to identify areas of interest and need. These interests and needs determine the learning experiences provided by the teacher or developed by the students. Interests can influence learning activities in a variety of ways. One way would be to use student interests to select the generalizations around which the activities are organized. Another would be to assess or determine student interests within the framework of a series of abstract, complex generalizations that are used as organizers. The first kind of influence might be most important in determining the Type I activities to be provided, while the second may be most appropriate for generating Type II experiences.

In the "possible" activities, various process models have been combined with the Triad to show how they can be used to generate Type II activities. An attempt has been made to illustrate how other recommended curricular modifications could be incorporated into the basic framework.

Table 6.1 provides a summary of teacher and student activities and roles for each type of enrichment in the *Triad* model.

MODIFYING THE APPROACH

Renzulli's *Enrichment Triad* is in many ways a framework for providing curricular modifications in all areas that are appropriate for gifted students. All of the content and process modifications suggested by Maker (1982) can be incorporated easily into a program that uses the *Triad* as a framework.

TABLE 6.1.   Summary of Teacher and Student Roles and Activities in the Renzulli Enrichment Triad Model

Step, Type, or Level of Thinking	Student		Teacher	
	Role	Sample Activities	Role	Sample Activities
Type I: General exploratory activities	Active participant Observer	Work in learning centers. Go on field trips. Explore new ideas. Interact with practicing professionals. Take an active part in activities of professionals.	Planner Organizer Interest stimulator	Plan experiences to expose students to new fields of inquiry and the methods used in those fields. Plan continuous experiences to put learners in contact with topics or areas of study in which they may develop a sincere interest. Encourage students to visit the library. Develop interest centers. Arrange for visitations, field trips, and guest speakers. Choose *active* professionals as speakers. Provide (or encourage) informal opportunities for exploration.
Type II: Group training exercises	Active participant Thinker	Play simulation games. Answer thought-provoking questions. Do thinking skill activities. Identify interests. Identify thinking process needs. Discuss ideas and methods.	Trainer Facilitator Discussion leader	Plan group and individual activities that will develop thinking and feeling processes. Select thinking and feeling processes that can be used in a variety of investigations. Plan process experiences to meet both individual and group needs. Plan activities to develop higher level thinking skills. Plan activities to develop divergent as well as convergent thinking skills. Plan activities designed to develop affective and organizational skills.

(continues)

TABLE 6.1.   *Continued*

Step, Type, or Level of Thinking	Student		Teacher	
	Role	Sample Activities	Role	Sample Activities
Type III: Individual and small-group investigation of real problems	Problem finder	Identify a problem of real concern (interest).	Manager	Develop a supportive learning environment.
	Data gatherer	Develop a management plan.	Resource	Assist students to identify and focus personal interests.
	Problem solver	Conduct an investigation of a real problem.		Help students develop a management plan.
	Producer	Work individually or with a small group.		Identify mentors.
	Inquirer	Develop a product that is new and unique.		Identify appropriate outlets or audiences for student products.
		Identify a real audience for the product.		Provide students with methodological assistance.
				Wait for students to make their own decisions.
				Assist in locating information.
				Encourage students to go beyond the school environment to locate and collect data.
				Assist students in revising and "polishing" their work.

The model itself makes suggestions in all product areas and in almost all environment dimensions. The changes suggested are designed to illustrate how the *Triad* approach can be implemented more effectively to achieve the purposes of a comprehensive program for gifted students.

Content Changes

Renzulli's suggestions for content changes fall mainly into the areas of variety and methods of inquiry. He does not recommend abstractness, complexity, organization for learning value, or the study of people in the sense that these have been recommended by Maker (1982). However, as shown in the examples of activities, modifications can be made easily. Type I and II activities have been organized around an abstract, complex generalization rather than some other framework, such as type of activity. Students were encouraged to explore a variety of concepts related to this idea. Many different types of experiences were provided. Each experience was chosen carefully to illustrate key concepts and to expose students to a variety of methods, a variety of disciplines, different "scientists" and different theories, and both present and past problems and ideas related to the generalization.

In addition, the sample activities show how a person might integrate the study of eminent or famous people. Type I activities include exposure to biographies and autobiographies of famous individuals who made significant contributions in this area along with a film about Margaret Mead and her work. Type II activities include an analysis of the methods used by present investigators, comparing them with those employed by the eminent individuals studied and comparing the characteristics of present lawmakers with statespersons of the past.

Process Changes

The *Triad* model by itself does not directly suggest process changes in all the areas recommended for the gifted. However, the design of Type II enrichment encourages teachers to incorporate many process models into their teaching and suggests that the selection of such activities be based on the interests and needs of the students. Renzulli (1977) and Renzulli and Reis (1985) do suggest process modifications that should be made in the areas of higher levels of thinking, open-endedness, and discovery. Numerous guidelines are given for providing freedom of choice and for the use of a variety of methods.

In the sample activities, several process models have been used to design activities and to show how various process models often used in programs for the gifted can be combined with Renzulli's approach to provide a more comprehensive curriculum. With these additions, all the process modifications are made by the example.

Higher Levels of Thinking

Skills in the use rather than acquisition of information are developed through the following Type II activities: (a) the Kohlberg discussion of a moral dilemma involving breaking a law, (b) the Taba discussions of societies and their laws, (c) the Parnes activity involving how to solve a problem over the breaking of a law, (d) the Taylor activity in which students develop a plan for a student council government, (e) the Taylor activity in which students predict reactions to certain laws and then check the accuracy of their predictions, and (f) the Krathwohl-based discussion of values and their influence on methods used by those engaged in research.

Open-endedness

Many of the activities included as both Types I and II are designed to be open-ended and to stimulate the interests of the students in further pursuit of the problems or topics encountered. Some of the more interesting ones include observation and interviews with the city council, playing the *Shipwreck* simulation, and devising a constitution for a hypothetical country. By using the Taba *Strategies* for several discussions and the Kohlberg discussion, and by carefully designing questions, teachers can ensure that open-endedness in all its forms is a significant aspect of all Type II experiences.

Discovery

Discovery learning is a definite aspect of all Type III activities, as students are acting as real inquirers and are producing rather than consuming information. Guided discovery, supervised or practiced, in the inquiry process has been incorporated through the use of Taba's interpretation of data strategy, which leads students through a process of examining data, inferring causes or effects, developing supportable conclusions, and generalizing to new situations. If the Krathwohl discussion of values is conducted as recommended in Chapter 3 for use with the gifted, guided discovery also would be a part of that activity. The Taylor forecasting activity in which the students predict and then check the accuracy of predictions also would involve discovery learning.

Evidence of Reasoning

This process modification can be incorporated easily into all discussions and activities without making major changes in the discussions. It would not be appropriate at certain steps or stages of steps in the Parnes process, however, as discussed in Chapter 5. Some models (the Taba *Strategies* and the Kohlberg discussion) already include the asking of questions to elicit explanations of reasoning. Chapters on the various models describe how this process change can be accomplished with each of the approaches.

Group Interaction

Structured group interaction is accomplished through the simulation game *Shipwreck*. Group participation can be observed by a small group of students, or the entire activity can be taped for later viewing by everyone. Analysis of group participation can include assessment of the roles assumed by individuals and their effectiveness in carrying out these roles. Analysis also can include an attempt to identify individual values and the level of development of those values by using Krathwohl's *Taxonomy* as a guide for observation. The group may want to spend some time brainstorming procedures for more effective participation, or students may wish to discuss values and their effect on various interactions between people.

Pacing

Pacing, as a process modification, is particularly important during Type I and Type II activities when new material or ideas are presented to the students. Guest speakers should be reminded that these are gifted students and that they can absorb material quickly. They should be prepared to answer in-depth questions from students about their work and use terminology appropriate to their field of inquiry.

Learning Environment Changes

One learning environment dimension not modified directly by the *Triad* model is acceptance versus judging. This dimension is important as a support for developing student products that truly belong to the students rather than to the teacher. The teacher must encourage (and assist) students to develop criteria for evaluation, implement the project, make their own mistakes and analyze the effects of mistakes, and redesign, revise, or improve products as needed. An effective way to develop an environment appropriate for gifted students who are engaged in Type III activities is to follow the suggestions made by Parnes in CPS. In so doing, the teacher will encourage elaboration and clarification prior to evaluation and encourage students to implement self-evaluation techniques that acknowledge the strengths of an idea or product and consider ways to minimize the limitations.

Although Renzulli does not address the group participation aspect of Type III activities, a few more suggestions about the independence dimension need to be made. Renzulli suggests that Type III investigations can be made by individuals or small groups of students. He does not address the question of how the teacher should handle difficulties that may arise during the course of these groups working together. To implement the learning environment modification that gifted students must develop—independence in both academic and nonacademic areas—students should be encouraged to develop their own group-management procedures. They also should develop their own solutions to problems. If students have learned CPS or the Taba resolution of conflict strategy, either is a natural process for them to use to develop a working plan and solve interpersonal problems.

Summary

The *Triad* model lends itself well to developing a program that is comprehensive in providing curricular modifications that are appropriate for the gifted. By integrating several process models and by organizing Type I and II activities around abstract, complex ideas, the content and process modifications not suggested by the *Triad* approach can be implemented.

DEVELOPMENT

Over a period of several years, Renzulli has been involved with programs for the gifted, both as a consultant in program development and as an evaluator. Based on these experiences and a growing concern for comprehensiveness and defensibility, he developed the *Triad* model. His approach was first to draw upon actual practices in enrichment programs and second to base the model on what is known about giftedness rather than the "romantic notions" that seem to abound in popular circles. His reviews of research on characteristics of individuals who are eminent and successful in their adult lives revealed the three well-defined clusters of characteristics: above-average intelligence, creativity, and task commitment. Since these three clusters of traits must interact to manifest themselves, an individual must have some type of real problem to investigate. Renzulli incorporated the research of Roe (1952) along with the ideas of Ward (1961) and Phenix (1964) in the development of his model: (a) Roe's classic study (1952) of 64 eminent scientists in which she concluded that the most important factor in the final decisions of these persons to become scientists was the sheer joy of discovery; (b) Ward's fundamental principles (1961) underlying differential education for the gifted, that superior students should become acquainted with the basic methods of inquiry within the various fields of knowledge; and (c) Phenix's (1964) conclusion that learning methods of inquiry is valuable because they are modes of active investigation. Renzulli also adopted Bruner's (1960) conclusion that young children are able to engage in critical inquiry.

RESEARCH ON EFFECTIVENESS

Much research was incorporated into the formulation of the *Enrichment Triad Model,* and numerous studies of its effectiveness have been published. For example, Reis and Renzulli (1982) compared the effectiveness of the model with 1,162 elementary school students from 11 districts. Students who scored at or above the 95th percentile were placed in Group A; Group B included those students who scored 10 to 15 percentile points lower. Double-blind rating of products on eight specific and several general characteristics of quality revealed no significant differences between the two groups. Schack (1986) and Starko (1988) found that children who participated in the program showed greater creative productivity and improved self-efficacy. Roberts, Ingram, and Harris (1992) compared performance on the *Ross Test of Higher Cognitive Processes* (Ross & Ross, 1976) by gifted and average students at a treatment school who participated in Types I and II activities with comparable students at a nontreatment school. In the pretest, no significant differences were found in the two schools. On the posttest, gifted students at the treatment school scored significantly higher ($p < .02$) than gifted students at the nontreatment school and higher ($p < .01$) than average students at the treatment school. Although gifted students at the nontreatment school scored higher than average students at the treatment school, when pretest scores were subtracted from posttest scores, the average gain significantly ($p < .05$) favored average-ability students.

Studies have shown that isolated aspects of Renzulli's model are effective. For example, a good Type II activity would be teaching students to use the Parnes CPS process. Several studies verify its validity. (See Chapter 5.) Another well-documented part of the *Triad* is the "independent study" aspect of its approach, which is present to a great degree in Type III activities. Studies show these procedures to be highly effective when used in programs for the gifted (Renzulli & Gable, 1976). Renzulli and Reis (1985) addressed key questions of organization and implementation in the design of the *Schoolwide Enrichment Model* (SEM). In this model, almost all students and teachers participate in various Type I and Type II activities, while members of the talent pool generally work on advanced thinking and methodological processes as well as design and implement Type III projects. Olenchak and Renzulli (1989) found that the use of the SEM resulted in more positive attitudes of students and teachers, numerous creative products whose quality was higher than usual, and increases in student-centered enrichment activities. Olenchak (1990) found that students enrolled in SEM schools had significantly more positive attitudes toward learning than comparable students in schools that did not employ SEM. Factors contributing to more positive attitudes included curriculum compacting, opportunities to study in areas of interest, greater understanding of the purpose of the program, and fewer people who felt the program was restricted to a select few. Several important questions still remain unanswered. What are the effects on student growth in areas other than creative production and thinking skills? What are some adequate measures of task commitment at early ages? Do those who show task commitment in school turn out to be task-committed adults? Do those who do not show task commitment in school turn out to be task-committed adults?

JUDGMENTS

Advantages

The most important advantage of the *Triad* is that it was designed specifically for use in programs for the gifted, and, as such, is based on research about characteristics of the gifted who achieve. A related advantage is that it takes into account that programs for the gifted must be related to the regular curriculum, and they must build on or expand on the basic competencies taught to all children. With the *Triad,* the relationship between the gifted and regular programs must be considered. Because it was designed specifically for use with the gifted, the *Triad* model directly addresses the issue of and need for a qualitatively differentiated educational program for the gifted. Renzulli provides specific guidelines for making some modifications of all aspects of the curriculum—content, process, product, and learning environment—and he provides a framework for integrating others easily, thus making it more appropriate for the gifted. Other models may modify one or two aspects of the curriculum but not provide as comprehensive an approach or framework as does Renzulli's.

Another advantage of the *Triad* is that it provides an overall program framework, including guidelines for program philosophy, definition of giftedness, identification of the gifted, teaching activities, and strategies for program evaluation. A number of program alternatives and curricular approaches shown to be effective with the gifted can be integrated easily into the *Triad* model, making a defensible and effective approach. Also, the *Triad* model is simple enough for parents, administrators, and students to understand without excessive educational rhetoric. Other advantages include the following: (a) it respects the interests and learning styles of gifted students; (b) it is based on and incorporated into a real-life environment; and (c) by providing a philosophy addressing which students should be served by a gifted program, it also provides guidelines for counseling out students who may not benefit from the program.

For teachers, students, and others involved in use of the model, many excellent materials are available. They are practical, affordable, and easily accessible. Many have been developed and field-tested in *Triad* or *School-wide Enrichment* programs. In addition, the SEM provides numerous examples of materials and strategies for managing the program.

Disadvantages

The most obvious disadvantage of the *Triad* model is that educators have sometimes adopted the model without seriously considering the philosophical approach necessary for its implementation. Too often, the framework has been adopted, and existing curricula have been incorporated into the framework, but few educators have made the philosophical and programmatic commitments that will make the model effective. Perhaps the expansion of the *Triad* into the *Schoolwide Enrichment Model,* with the attendant staff development and involvement of all school personnel may foster the necessary commitment. The philosophy is apparently hidden to some but is clear to others. The *Triad* model emphasizes the selection of those children who show the most potential to succeed (according to society's definition of success) rather than, for example, children who (a) show an educational need for services based on their intellectual deviation from the average or (b) need for a differentiated program because of their unique learning styles. This philosophy may be radically different from the school's, parent's, or teacher's beliefs. Seldom are these differences even recognized, and even less often are they reconciled.

Another disadvantage is that most of the research upon which the three-ring conception of giftedness is based was done with adults. One cannot determine whether these characteristics were the causes or results of success. This disadvantage has serious consequences, particularly in the selection of children from certain subgroups of the population. What about children from disadvantaged backgrounds who have never been exposed to an area of study or a task to which they can become committed? What do educators do about children from different cultural backgrounds whose cultural definition of success is not the same as a white, Anglo-Saxon, Protestant one? The gifted underachievers who are potential dropouts and who will most likely not demonstrate high levels of task commitment may not be identified for the talent pool program. If they are identified, they may be counseled out because they do not develop a Type III project soon enough. The motivation and persistence necessary to follow through on real-life activities may take years to develop, and indeed these characteristics may be the most important goals of education for these children. By developing continuing motivation while children are in school, educators may (a) prevent them from dropping out of school or (b) help them develop the skills that will enable them to become productive members of society.

Some of the more practical disadvantages of the *Triad* model include difficulty in assessing task commitment and creativity, the fact that teachers are not trained to implement a model such as this (that is, they are not scholars or methodologists in scholarly fields; they are trained to teach content rather than guide investigations), and the fact that the model is deceptively simple. At first glance, the philosophy seems clear and the implementation easy. However, many have realized after only a short time that the skills required are complex, and the practical problems are many and varied. Teachers must have a variety of resources available. They must know how to use these resources, and they must have time to help children locate them. Even though Renzulli and Reis (1985) have provided numerous management tools, provided examples of plans for Type III activities, suggested possible sources for Type I enrichment, and identified a multitude of commercially produced materials for possible Type II enrichment activities, the logistics of managing the total process can be daunting to all but the most committed teachers.

CONCLUSION

Although the *Triad* model does have its drawbacks, with careful consideration of its philosophical base, along with its specific strategies and how these aspects fit into a unique situation, teachers can implement it appropriately. Such a program also can have benefits for the overall program at the school, increasing the student-centered opportunities and developing more favorable attitudes toward talent development in all students. With the benefit of longitudinal studies of the model's effectiveness, educators may be able to develop qualitatively different programs for gifted students that are defensible to anyone who would question their existence.

RESOURCES

Background Information

Renzulli, J. S., & Reis, S. M. (1985). *The schoolwide enrichment model: A comprehensive plan for educational excellence.* Mansfield Center, CT: Creative Learning Press. This is a massive (522-page) book that includes the theoretical and philosophical foundations of the *Enrichment Triad Model* and a rationale for involving an entire school in some *Triad* activities. It offers numerous suggestions and guidelines for the implementation of the model. Much of the information contained in the *Enrichment Triad Model* and the *Revolving Door Identification Model,* including tools such as the Interest-A-Lyzer and the *Learning Styles Inventory,* has been incorporated into one comprehensive resource for implementors of SEM (or *Triad*). Contents include an introduction to the use of the model to stimulate school-wide excellence, a three-chapter section on the development and philosophy of the *Triad/Revolving Door* models, organizational components, and roles and responsibilities of the program coordinator. Subsequent chapters deal with assessing student strengths, the process of curriculum compacting, and procedures for planning, implementing, and evaluating Type I, Type II, and Type III activities. Specific teacher training activities, management forms, suggested resources, and examples of activities are incorporated into the chapters on each type of enrichment. Also available: *The schoolwide enrichment model: A videotape training program for teachers and administrators.* Mansfield Center, CT: Creative Learning Press. Nine 25–30 minute videotapes featuring Dr. Renzulli and Dr. Reis can be used in faculty meetings or in-service programs to develop the understandings needed to implement the model. Each videotape is based on a chapter from the book listed above.

Reis, S. M., & Renzulli, J. S. (1985). *The secondary triad model: A practical plan for implementing gifted programs at the junior and senior high levels.* Mansfield Center, CT: Creative Learning Press. This book adapts the model to the requirements of secondary school programs. Programming alternatives, guidelines for developing an interdisciplinary team, sample class descriptions, and suggestions for implementing a mentoring program for Type III enrichment are featured in a volume that includes numerous management forms and documents.

Burns, F. D. (1993). Independent study: Panacea or palliative? In C. J. Maker & D. Orzechowski-Harland (Eds.). *Critical issues in gifted education: Vol. III. Programs for the gifted in regular classrooms* (pp. 381–399). Austin, TX: PRO-ED. Burns, an experienced teacher and coordinator in programs for gifted students, discusses three models recommended for use in independent study programs (Betts, Renzulli, and Treffinger). She contrasts them and discusses how they can be combined.

Friedman, R. C. J., & Gallagher, T. (1993). Reaction to "independent study." In C. J. Maker & D. Orzechowski-Harland (Eds.). *Critical issues in gifted education: Vol. III. Programs for the gifted in regular classrooms* (pp. 400–412). Austin, TX: PRO-ED. In a reaction to Burns' chapter from a different perspective, the authors provide additional insights into the use of the three models.

Nash, W. R., Haensly, P. A., Scobee-Rodgers, V. J., & Wright, N. L. (1993). Mentoring: Extending learning for gifted students. In C. J. Maker & D. Orzechowski-Harland (Eds.). *Critical issues in gifted education: Vol. III. Programs for the gifted in regular classrooms* (pp. 313–330). Austin, TX:

PRO-ED. The authors explore the historical bases of mentoring relationships and identify the functions of such relationships in enhancing creativity, shaping careers, role-modeling, and shaping personal growth. Necessary elements of school-based mentorship programs and examples of mentoring programs also are discussed.

Reis, S. M., & Schack, G. D. (1993). Differentiating products for the gifted and talented: The encouragement of independent learning. In C. J. Maker & D. Orzechowski-Harland (Eds.). *Critical issues in gifted education: Vol. III. Programs for the gifted in regular classrooms* (pp. 161–186). Austin, TX: PRO-ED. The authors discuss 12 steps that classroom teachers can use to guide gifted students in the design and development of qualitatively different products. They also identify potential outlets for student products and include a few selected references on research methodology, science and social science topics, and invention.

Seghini, J. B. (1993). An expanded view of internships. In C. J. Maker & D. Orzechowski-Harland (Eds.). *Critical issues in gifted education: Vol. III. Programs for the gifted in regular classrooms* (pp. 374–380). Austin, TX: PRO-ED. Seghini, a veteran educator, notes that counseling for educational needs and planning is a critical issue for gifted students. She briefly reviews some models and concludes that the *Enrichment Triad Model* is an excellent program for the development of social, emotional, and organizational skills necessary to succeed in an internship or mentoring relationship.

Instructional Materials and Ideas

Allen, J. (1992). Meeting the needs of Australian rural gifted children: The use of curriculum enrichment projects (CEPPS) for primary schools in western Australia. *Gifted Education International, 8*(1), 23–31. In this article, the author describes the development of materials that can be used with gifted students to initiate and guide independent learning. The materials, framework for development, and examples are provided. The reference list contains sources for these materials.

Bunker, B., Pearlson, H., & Schultz, J. (1975). *The student's guide to conducting social science research.* New York: Human Sciences Press. This volume provides a nine-step approach to research including explanations of research design, hypothesis testing, surveys, observation, and experiments. Recommended by Reis and Schack, the book also includes ready-to-use activities for data collection.

Burns, D. E. (1990). *Pathways to investigative skills: Instructional lessons for guiding students from problem finding to final product.* Mansfield Center, CT: Creative Learning Press. This resource book consists of 10 step-by-step lessons focused on interest finding, problem finding, topic webbing, topic focusing, and creative problem solving, and is designed to teach students how to initiate a Type III investigation. Slides and a script for a show provide examples of Type III projects students have done. Classroom posters, planning sheets, a parent pamphlet, and masters for worksheets are included.

Henderson, K. (1986). *Market guide for young writers.* Sandusky, MI: Savage. Recommended by Reis and Schack, this book is designed to help young people get their work published. Lists of publications and contests open to young writers are featured.

Kramer, S. (1987). *How to think like a scientist.* New York: Crowell. In an easy-to-read (grades 2 through 5) introduction to the scientific method, the author gives examples of the steps in the scientific method: asking a question, collecting data/information, forming a hypothesis, testing the hypothesis, and reporting the results.

The best storehouse of ideas for teachers is other teachers, yet finding published materials is often difficult. Creative Learning Press has published *The Triad Prototype Series,* edited by Linda Smith, which now includes a number of units based on the *Enrichment Triad Model.* Each unit has been field-tested in classrooms by its author, includes a complete management plan, and lists numerous sources of information about its subject. Titles in this series include:

Storytelling: A Triad in the Arts

Lights! Camera! Action!: Film Animation in the Classroom

Classroom Computers: A Triad of Creative Applications

Lunchroom Waste: A Study of "How Much" and "How Come"

Entomology: Investigative Activities for Could-be Bug Buggs

Genealogy: Your Past Revisited

Cartoon Art: An Adventure in Creativity

Gaming It Up with Shakespeare

Digging Through Archaeology

Victorian Housekeeping: A Combined Study of Restoration and Photography

The Creative Learning Press catalog (P.O. Box 320, Mansfield Center, CT 06250) features more than 200 books either specifically written for use with the *Enrichment Triad Model* or selected for compatibility with the model. Almost every student will be able to find one or more great ideas for Type III activities, including idea books, methodological or how-to books, inquiry processes, and statistical methods. Teachers also can choose from numerous resources for Type II thinking processes, research and data-collection skills, and creative activities.

Chapter 7

Shlomo and Yael Sharan: Group Investigations

C ooperative learning is a controversial issue among educators of the gifted. Although the benefits of collaboration and the importance of group interaction are widely recognized, many educators, parents, and students feel that the gifted are exploited in most models of cooperative learning (Feldhusen & Moon, 1992; Mills & Durden, 1993; Robinson, 1991). The asymmetrical relationships built into peer tutoring approaches have negative consequences for both tutors and tutees (Foot, Morgan, & Shute, 1990).

One significant exception is a model developed in Israel. *Group Investigations,* a student-centered approach to cooperative learning, is based on John Dewey's (1938, 1943/1902) philosophy that active experience, inquiry in a social setting, and reflective thinking are the tools of intellectual development. The *Group Investigations* model also derives theoretical support from research in cognitive development, social learning theory, and group processes. In this view, learning is conceptualized as a dynamic, reciprocal process embedded in social, cultural, physical, and psychological environments. The ways people communicate and construct meaning, the kinds of knowledge valued, and individual access to knowledge all depend on social interaction and cultural context (Heath, 1983; Newman, Griffin, & Cole, 1989; Rogoff, 1990; Vygotsky, 1978).

Group Investigations is designed to incorporate students' interests, abilities, and past experiences in the planning of small-group activities. In this model, peer collaboration and student choice of projects is emphasized. Students form groups on the basis of friendship or interest in a topic/project, or to meet agreed-upon classroom goals (e.g., learning to value cultural diversity). They may belong to several different groups during a school term and have the freedom to leave one group to join another in the early stages of an investigation. Students are active in planning and evaluating their learning experiences as well as in the performance of learning tasks, experiences that promote self-efficacy and individual responsibility. Learning and cooperation are viewed as inherently satisfying. Mutually beneficial activities are emphasized, self-efficacy promoted, and students' unique abilities and learning goals are respected (Sharan & Sharan, 1976).

Major goals of the *Group Investigations* model are to nurture democratic participation, develop students' skills in differential social roles, differentiate work assignments so that students need not duplicate each other's work, help students develop social skills that enable group members to work cohesively, and deal effectively with differences or conflict. The model has a strong process orientation and aims to help students develop both cognitive and cooperative interaction abilities. *Group Investigations* is an ambitious and complex approach to cooperative learning that may not be appropriate for all subjects or all students (Sharan et al., 1984). However, the emphasis on complex content, student choice and planning, and its process-oriented structure makes *Group Investigations* an excellent collaborative-learning model for gifted students.

ASSUMPTIONS UNDERLYING THE MODEL

The *Group Investigations* model is based on the belief that cooperation and communication among students are keys to achieving the more important goals of learning and teaching. Students learn concepts and strategies best and enjoy learning more when they are engaged directly in activities in a social context. The goal of *Group Investigations* is to create a 'group of groups' and transform the class into an active, inquiring community of learners.

Several assumptions about social relationships are intrinsic to this model. Friendship and mutual respect grow out of constructive cooperation in which goals and tasks are interdependent. Learning is best facilitated in small groups where members hold a personal attraction for each other and the tasks of the group are compatible with an individual's own values, goals, and interests. Finally, working together on mutually satisfying tasks can help students learn to value classmates from diverse racial or ethnic groups and break down cultural stereotypes.

About Learning

Learning is a natural process of social inquiry. Satisfying curiosity about the world, gaining a measure of control over one's several environments, and growing in the ability to make sense of perceptual data are as natural to a child as breathing. In classrooms, learning is most likely to occur when:

- children have a role in planning and implementing learning tasks;
- competition and performance anxiety are reduced;
- communication and cooperation are encouraged;
- learning tasks are relevant to the individuals involved; and
- self-evaluation and reflective thinking are part of every project.

Learning and cooperation, interdependent primary goals of *Group Investigations,* are intrinsically rewarding. As a result, competition for extrinsic rewards is unnecessary.

About Teaching

The *Group Investigations* model fundamentally changes the relationship between teachers and students. The teacher is neither the main dispenser of knowledge nor the sole judge of products. Instead, the teacher's role is to act as a guide and advisor to help students investigate issues and solve problems. A teacher's role might be compared to Vygotsky's (1978) conception of a more skilled partner in thinking and problem solving. Initially, the teacher provides considerable structure and support in selection and design of learning activities. As students become more skilled in the use of inquiry processes and develop effective social interaction skills, the teacher gradually withdraws from the leading role and transfers many planning, decision-making, and group-maintenance responsibilities to students. This nondirective approach to teaching-learning is crucial to the development of self-directed, collaborative learners.

In the Deweyian tradition, a teacher must be an active inquirer and a reflective thinker. Examining experiences, beliefs, new information, and changing purposes is a critical factor in personal growth and thoughtful collaboration with others.

About Characteristics and Teaching of the Gifted

The *Group Investigations* model, like many excellent teaching-learning models, was not developed for gifted students. Instead, the intent of the developers was to reform educational practice for all students through a variety of small-group learning methods. *Group Investigations* is a more elaborate model that also was designed to improve relationships between racial and ethnic groups in integrated schools. Sharan and Sharan (1976) emphasize the importance of interest in a topic or friendship, rather than ability, in creating groups. Several researchers, however, have emphasized the importance of collaboration with peers (Damon, 1984; Doise & Mugny, 1984). Children of similar abilities, working together, make greater gains in achievement in conceptual development than do children in whole class instruction or in peer tutoring situations (Phelps & Damon, 1989). Peer cooperation is essentially a dialogue between equals and incorporates many features of critical thinking—verification of ideas, clarity of communication, strategic planning, and contemplation of new patterns of thought (Damon, 1984). Students learn from each other because they are matched closely in knowledge and/or ability, no authority relationship exists between or among them, and they pool their efforts to work out a solution to a problem or understand a concept.

ELEMENTS/PARTS

Four broad dimensions are essential in the *Group Investigations* approach. First, topics for investigation must be broad and general so that a number of related subtopics can be identified. Second, subtopics must be sufficiently challenging that a meaningful subdivision of labor and interdependence among group members is possible. Third, frequent communication within and between groups is essential as students plan, coordinate, collect information, analyze data, and integrate their work with that of other students and groups. Finally, the teacher must create a learning environment that stimulates interaction, search, and communication while maintaining an indirect, facilitative style of leadership.

Organization of the Classroom into a "Group of Groups"

Students organize into ad hoc groups with three to six members and investigate different aspects of a general topic, theme, or issue. The length of time scheduled for an investigation depends on the complexity of the topic, the maturation level of students, and the format(s) selected for sharing results. As students work on different aspects of the topic, a steering committee composed of representatives from each group may be necessary to coordinate between-group planning and decision making. At other times, informal discussions are sufficient to maintain contact and exchange information with other groups.

Facilitating effective social relationships among group members, a complex and constantly evolving process, is essential to the achievement of group goals. In collaborative groups, learners provide academic and psychological support, encouragement, and constructive feedback to each other. Together, they monitor progress toward group goals. If students have little experience working in groups, teachers should not begin collaborative inquiry with *Group Investigations*. Sharan and Sharan (1976) suggest a range of small-group activities (e.g., discussion skills, communication games, creative problem solving) to help students acquire the experience necessary to regulate their own learning and work cooperatively with peers. Teachers also can conduct a series of small-group seminars in which students observe and practice effective behaviors for discussion, goal setting, planning, decision making, and conflict resolution.

Multifaceted Tasks

Topics for investigation must be sufficiently complex that a single student cannot complete the investigation alone. Learning tasks that do not require coordination of viewpoints, mutual exchange of views, or interdependence among group members are not appropriate. Topics for *Group Investigations* are best organized as problems or questions that can be explored from several perspectives and have a variety of possible solutions, for example, "Acts of civil disobedience are a result of institutional abuse of power." The use of abstract generalizations would ensure that problems or questions are appropriate.

Multilateral Communication and Active Learning Processes

In *Group Investigations,* students must engage in a variety of communicative processes. Reading, summarizing, efficiently using reference materials, and collecting data are even more important than in traditional instruction because each student does a different part of the investigation. In the social context of the group, students plan together and decide what they will study, who is responsible for each part of the work, and how they will integrate their data. Students collect data from a variety of sources; therefore, strategies for interviewing, research design, analysis and organization of data, and procedures for evaluation must be negotiated among group members or demonstrated by a mentor. Integration of the varied data collected by individual group members into a coherent whole for presentation also requires listening, reflecting on and elaborating another's ideas, clarifying statements, and choosing the final format.

Teacher Behavior: Guiding and Communicating with Groups

For students to develop the autonomy necessary to carry out group investigations, teacher leadership must be indirect. Important teacher behaviors include:

- facilitating research,

- consulting with a group or an individual about a specific aspect of a topic or process,

- asking questions or suggesting ideas to help a group clarify a problem,

- demonstrating a skill (e.g., polling methods) when a group requests assistance, or

- helping groups coordinate their activities.

In addition, the teacher and students organize the classroom environment to facilitate communication, mobility, and access to information sources. One major purpose of *Group Investigations* is to build a community of learners in which academic work is coordinated, shared, and purposeful.

When a classroom is structured to promote choice, active planning, and decision making by students in a relaxed social atmosphere, the teacher's role changes from active direction of student learning to facilitation and guidance of multivariate group activities. Relinquishing control does not mean that the teacher abandons students to their own devices once groups are organized. In this model, the teacher assumes the responsibility of overall planning and selection of materials, structuring the learning environment, and teaching processes that help students organize a learning team. Students need guidance, but the adoption of a nondirective role by the teacher is prerequisite for changing learning from passive acceptance of information to an active decision-making and responsibility-sharing role. For many teachers, the most difficult task may be to recognize the necessity of freeing students to investigate problems or work out solutions in their own way and at their pace.

MODIFICATION OF THE BASIC CURRICULUM

In the *Group Investigations* model, social inquiry in small groups, multilateral communication and cooperation, and active exploration of ideas and objects are emphasized. This approach dramatically changes curriculum and instructional practice. The traditional notion that information can be transmitted from a teacher (or other expert source), received by students, and evaluated through objective tests is totally rejected. Cooperative learning can be implemented only to the extent that traditional whole-class teaching is supplanted, not just altered (Sharan, 1990).

Content Modifications

General topics, broad concepts, themes, or persistent issues are the content of *Group Investigations*. This approach to learning through collaboration requires that content be complex, multifaceted, and abstract. Methods of inquiry, particularly the scientific method, are integral, and variety is assured through the investigation of different subtopics by each small group.

Process Modifications

As a model of social inquiry, *Group Investigations* emphasizes higher level thought, open-ended questions, experimentation and discovery, group interaction, and reflective thinking. Students select their own topics and cooperatively plan investigations. Appropriate pacing and evidence of reasoning are an integral part of the group inquiry process.

Product Modifications

All students in a group collaborate on a single product but work individually on one or more facets of the product. A wide variety of products are possible and data are transformed into a form suitable for presentations to an audience of peers and, on occasion, invited guests. Student products are designed to share information with classmates and are an integral part of the learning experience of an entire class. Student products are evaluated by a jury of peers and by the members of the group. If tests are given, questions are open-ended with a range of possible answers.

Learning Environment Modifications

The learning environment is modified by the teacher and students to support autonomy, mobility, group communication, and a wide variety of learning activities. During investigations, students must be free to leave the classroom to conduct research in other settings. As students work in groups, the environment is learner centered and interactive. Students work independently on varied complex tasks and participate in both self-evaluation and evaluation of group activities. With the wide variety of activities and complex, challenging tasks for gifted students, the modification of the psychological environment is assured. One recommendation is that teachers should be sure that the physical environment is designed to support active inquiry and includes a rich assortment of varied equipment and materials.

IMPLEMENTING THE MODEL

The *Group Investigations* approach to collaborative inquiry learning can be adapted by teachers so that projects are appropriate for the abilities and backgrounds of students, the subjects studied, and the constraints of time and space in the classroom/school. Guidelines for implementation are organized into six stages: (a) identifying a topic and organizing research groups, (b) planning the learning tasks, (c) carrying out the investigation, (d) preparing a final product, (e) presenting the final product, and (f) self-evaluation individually and in small groups.

Identifying a Topic and Organizing Research Groups

The teacher designates a general subject or a broad theme based on curricular goals or persistent issues (for example, social implications of technological development, problems of poverty and overpopulation, interdependence of all living things) important to students' educational growth. Teachers may arrange a joint experience and/or set aside a period of time for exploration. For example, reading, viewing a film, listening to records or tapes, watching a videotape, going on a field trip, or listening to a guest speaker exposes students to a topic in advance. Alternatively, teachers may trust that students have a wealth of concepts and experience to help them make initial decisions about preference of topics to investigate. One typical way to organize a topic for investigation is to brainstorm possible subtopics then categorize related ideas into research topics. A Taba concept development strategy would be an excellent process to use for this purpose. Another excellent organizational tool is a web (Short & Pierce, 1990) or matrix of subtopics as shown in Figure 7.1. The teacher and students all make suggestions during this idea-finding stage. Then students choose a subtopic for in-

Figure 7.1. Web of possible causes.

vestigation and join two or three other students with the same interest to explore and classify possible components of the subtopic and develop categories with potential for investigation. This step should not be rushed; students need time to explore and categorize ideas, assess the possibilities for investigation of a subtopic, and work out group arrangements. At this stage, three types of goals, instructional, organizational, and social, are considered.

Instructional

- Students form an overall view of the topic and its research possibilities.

- Students propose topics that pique their interest; this may not be the same topics that teachers normally suggest.

- Students classify suggestions into categories and subcategories.

- Students focus on subtopics crucial to understanding rather than on peripheral features.

Organizational

- Students join a group to study the topic of their choice. Some adjustments may be necessary to form groups no smaller than three and no larger than six members. Reducing the size of a group larger than six is more critical than increasing the size of a smaller group.

- Students may change their minds about a topic during the early stages and leave one group to join another.

- Students decide on ways for the groups to maintain contact and exchange ideas or coordinate activities during the course of the investigation.

- Students organize the furniture and other resources in the classroom to meet their needs.

Social

- Groups discuss ideas to set goals and identify subtopics that suit each member best.

- Groups divide investigation tasks and establish work patterns that will encourage mutual support and cooperation among members.

- Groups are composed of students of both sexes and include students with different abilities and ethnic backgrounds whenever possible.

- Groups should exist for the life of an investigation, not for an extended period of time. Students should work with different partners when new groups are formed to avoid cliques and to encourage social interaction.

During this organizational stage, teachers help students work through problems or difficulties encountered in stating problems and planning and organizing the project. The Parnes *Creative Problem Solving* strategy is a useful tool to assist students in designing an investigation project. Time spent preparing and troubleshooting at this stage will pay off in smoother operations and more effective learning in later stages.

Planning the Learning Task

Each group must formulate a researchable problem about the topic they choose to investigate. Once the problem is defined, students set goals, identify sources of information, set up procedures to follow, and create a plan of action. In addition, each group must decide what parts of the investigation are best done by individual members and what parts require collaborative action. Three questions guide the planning stage of *Group Investigations*:

- What shall we study? (Teachers may need to remind students that tasks for investigation are problems that can be considered in a variety of ways. Information can be obtained through a variety of sources, and there are a range of ideas, opinions, analyses, or solutions to the topic being studied.)

- How do we study it? (Identify subtopics for each group member, possible resources, procedures, members' responsibilities, group participation, etc.)

- For what purpose or goal do we study it? (How will we make sense of the information we collect? How will it be shared/presented? How will we apply the knowledge we acquire?)

Advocates of learning through a social inquiry process, such as *Group Investigations,* assume that a serious effort to answer these three questions will stimulate personal involvement by students. When students use inquiry processes, they actively generate ideas and construct knowledge—a process comparable to the work of practitioners in a discipline or craft.

As part of the planning process, specific areas in the classroom may be designated for special purposes. A seminar center where students can consult the teacher for special help, support, or feedback on an idea, or to get together with others to communicate about work in progress is essential. A center to house the master work schedule, resources, and materials needed for group work provides easy access to information sources and facilitates autonomy and mobility. Learning stations can be set up for viewing and listening to media, holding group discussions, conducting interviews, making graphics, and facilitating other activities needed by students during an investigation cycle. Other learning stations can be set up to provide specific kinds of information or experiences all students need. In addition, each group should have a portable container to keep their materials together.

Carrying Out the Investigation

During this stage, students implement their plans. They collect, analyze, and evaluate their data, draw conclusions, and coordinate their information with each other. This is typically the longest part of the study. It often takes longer than the teacher and students originally planned but should not be cut short as long as students are working productively.

When students are inexperienced, the teacher may have to intervene more frequently to steer students in a more productive direction and help students overcome their insecurity and obtain needed resources, such as videotape equipment or permission to travel away from school to do an interview. Teachers also may need to demonstrate specific skills to one or more students. At times, the teacher may stop group work to help all students learn better discussion behaviors or processes to resolve conflict among group members. Cooperative and cognitive skills taught in the context of small-group collaboration are more likely to be learned and used in subsequent activities.

Collaborative learning involves multiple skills and information-management processes. Students collect data from a variety of sources, communicate with each other, discuss the implications of their data in terms of group goals, clarify ideas, and negotiate meaning. Thinking is more complex and students are involved more directly when they work in small groups to understand a concept or accomplish a mutually agreed-upon goal.

Preparing a Final Product

Once data have been gathered and analyzed, members of a group must determine how to present the information to others. This is primarily an organizational task, but it also includes processes of abstracting the essential meaning of the data, putting component parts into perspective so that others can gain an overall view of the topic, and planning a presentation that will communicate effectively and also appeal to their audience.

At this stage, between-group planning must take place. What will each group present and how will it be presented? A steering committee may receive reports on each group's work, process requests for materials, create a time schedule for presentations, and make sure each group's presentation is realistic and interesting. Coordinating activities on a classwide basis requires cooperation to select and organize the overall format for presentation fairly and may require compromise on differences of opinion. Presentation formats may be jointly agreed upon, such as the mid-nineteenth century fair or exposition in the example on page 218. At other times small groups may prefer to present, for example, a seminar, a television documentary, a simulation game, or a debate.

The teacher should highlight some key ideas for students to consider during the design and preparation of their presentations.

- Emphasize main ideas, supporting evidence, and conclusions of the investigation.

- Identify the sources of data and other information.

- Include all members of the group in the presentation.

- Involve classmates as much as possible in the presentation. This may include giving them roles to perform or activities to do.

- Allow time for questions.

- Set and observe time limits.

- Make sure to request in advance all materials or equipment needed.

As students prepare to present the essence of what they have learned about their topic to an audience, they act as investigators, planners, decision makers, designers, and teachers. Rather than simply receiving and responding to transmitted information, students are creating and generating new knowledge for a socially valuable purpose.

Presenting the Final Product

Presentations are made to the entire class and, often, to invited guests. If the presentation format were an exhibition, for example, each group might set up its display in a different part of the room or at various sites in the school or community. Groups take turns as viewers and presenters; it is critical that all students in the class participate as an audience for other groups so they can integrate all subtopics into the general concept or theme.

Each group must communicate its ideas clearly to others and presentation roles may be unfamiliar to them. The teacher or a mentor may spend time with groups to demonstrate specific skills or help with technical details prior to a presentation. Some general suggestions for varied types of presentations follow.

- Speak clearly and expressively when addressing an audience but avoid lecturing.

- Practice the content of a speech and use notes only for reminders.

- Use a blackboard, chart, overhead projector, or other device to illustrate important concepts when giving an oral presentation.

- Use learning stations where classmates and visitors can do tasks or conduct experiments you set up to help them learn concepts or interact with your data.

- Dramatize an event or relationship that illustrates an important concept or issue from your investigation.

- Illustrate written reports/books with pictures, drawings, graphs, tables, or other visual devices that help to explain the data or illustrate the information.

- Conduct formal debates or panel discussions in front of your audience.

- Design a quiz program or a role-playing simulation to involve your audience. (You must figure out a way to get the necessary information to your audience in advance.)

- Make a videotape, slide show, or other audiovisual presentation and set up a viewing/listening station.

- Publish a newspaper or magazine to share your information with a wider audience.

- Create a simulation of a historic event or a possible future scenario.

- Conduct a trial to represent the laws and customs of a given civilization.

- Build a model in as much detail as possible. Label the essential features of the model and explain its function.

- Participate in an industrial fair. Showcase your model and compete for investors.

Making a presentation to share the results of group investigations is a powerful intellectual and emotional experience. Students not only demonstrate the knowledge they acquired during the investigation, they also demonstrate their ability to plan, organize, coordinate, and produce a presentation that allows others to share that knowledge.

Evaluation

Group Investigations exposes students to constant evaluation by their peers and teachers throughout the entire study. Ideas, time spent on task, grasp of the subject, and dependability are highly visible. Interaction with peers in discussions, planning, decision making, and analysis and organization of data can be observed to assess communicative behaviors, social skills, and higher level thinking. During a group investigation, teachers may interview individual students formally or have frequent conversations with them to assess their academic growth. Teachers also can write brief observations of a student's cognitive, affective, or social behaviors on self-stick notes or labels, date them, and place the notes in student portfolios at the end of the day.

If formal tests are necessary, Sharan and Sharan suggest that each group prepare open-ended questions about the most important points of their presentation. The steering committee and the teacher work together to review questions and select two from each group for the test. If there were six groups, for example, each student would respond to 12 questions covering all aspects of the study. Students would get all the questions and have some time (1 or 2 weeks) to think about the questions before writing responses. This gives all students time to review the topics and think about the ideas from the presentations. They can question members of other groups to clarify some data or conclusions from their investigation.

Group members become a committee of experts on their topic. Each group receives the written answers to their two questions and evaluates the answers of their classmates. They can see how well their classmates understood the information presented about the topic and learn what other students thought about the ideas. Once questions have been evaluated, they are returned to the writers. Students can again discuss answers or evaluations with members of each research group. This multilateral communication and interaction is a powerful spur to intellectual development. Although this form of evaluation may be too complex for novice investigators, it is recommended for students with more experience in collaborative learning.

One form of evaluation with definite value for every student is self-analysis. At the beginning of an investigation, each student selects one or more cognitive and social goals. At regular intervals, the teacher schedules time for students to review their goals, reflect on their progress, and write a brief report for personal use. Groups map out the different steps they followed in their work, analyze factors that contributed to progress or complemented the work of other students, and make recommendations for future investigations. Using personal progress and group reports, students can reflect on their experiences, contributions to the group, and how other students contributed to their learning. This reconstructive evaluation helps students develop a broad and critical view of their own study procedures, achievement, and interactions with others. Reflection on practice is an excellent way to help students improve their ability to plan future investigations. A summary of teacher and student roles in each component of *Group Investigations* is given in Table 7.1.

Examples of Activities

Example 1: An Elementary Interdisciplinary Study

In an elementary classroom, students recently completed a study of seasons. The teacher wanted to extend the concept of "cycles" or phenomena that occur in patterned ways.

First, all students did a productive thinking activity to list many, varied, and unusual phenomena that occur or operate in cycles. Items on the list were discussed and arranged into the following categories: life, weather, economy, sports competition, holidays, reproduction, elections, mechanical devices, fashions in clothing, migration, and water.

Next, after exploring possible resources and thinking about the topic, May, Sally, Roland, and Bryan chose the topic of cycles in the economy and formed an interest group. They elected May to be their group leader and Bryan to serve on the coordinating committee. They also set up procedures to follow during the investigation and elected Sally to prepare and post a weekly schedule. Roland then led the group in a decision-making process to decide which specific aspects of the economy would be studied. The group made a list of many, varied alternatives then asked the following questions about each alternative:

1. Will there be enough information available on this aspect of the economy?

2. Will studying this aspect of the economy help us learn more about cycles?

3. What other aspects of the economy could be integrated with this one?

4. Will this aspect contribute interest to our presentation?

After some reflection, May chose to investigate seasonal retail sales, Roland chose the causes and effects of consumer confidence, Sally chose to investigate the causes and effects of depressions, and Bryan chose to investigate the causes and effects of discovery and exploitation of a scarce resource (e.g., oil).

TABLE 7.1. Summary of Teacher and Student Roles and Activities in the Group Investigations Model

Step, Type, or Level of Thinking	Student		Teacher	
	Role	Sample Activities	Role	Sample Activities
Building discussion skills	Active participant	Speak concisely for 15 seconds. Listen reflectively; wait 3 seconds before responding. Reflect/summarize previous speaker's ideas before adding one's own. Wait until all group members have spoken before speaking for second time. Take a turn serving as an observer to note how well group members do on a specific skill. Report results of observations in a constructive manner.	Resource Facilitator	Plan and implement experiences to assist students in the development of discussion skills. Plan and implement training experiences for student observers. Model active listening and concise speaking behaviors.
Reflect on group process	Active participant Reflective thinker Evaluator	Use a Taba interpretation of data strategy to evaluate/reflect on group interaction: (a) identify specific behaviors that occurred during interaction, (b) analyze causes/effects of the behaviors, and (c) generalize how skills used in this session can be used in another context.	Resource Facilitator Planner	Plan and implement a small-group interaction activity, such as reaching consensus using *The Untitled Story* strategy (Graves & Graves, 1990). Review the steps and guidelines for an interpretation of data strategy. Have students meet their small groups to reflect on their group interactions and construct generalizations about behaviors.

(continues)

TABLE 7.1.   *Continued*

Step, Type, or Level of Thinking	Student		Teacher	
	Role	Sample Activities	Role	Sample Activities
Students determine subtopics, organize research groups.	Active participant Classifier Evaluator Decision maker	Use a Taylor decision making strategy to (a) generate a list of many, varied subtopics of the main topic; (b) generate criteria for evaluating alternatives; (c) reach consensus on several subtopics for investigation; and (d) generate support for the selection. Select a subtopic on the basis of interest. Form a group with two to five others who are interested in the same subtopic.	Planner Facilitator Resource	Plan and implement activities to assist students in the understanding of the main topic and stimulate interest in further investigations. Provide many, varied resources pertinent to the topic. Facilitate a discussion of possible subtopics. Assist students in generation of criteria for decision making. Allow students time to consider possible topics for investigation.
Groups plan investigation.	Active participant Decision maker Planner	Use a Williams strategy of search process to identify what group members know about the subtopic and what they want to learn, and to identify possible resources. Use a Taylor planning strategy to set goals for the investigation, identify resources needed, and list steps and responsibilities for the investigation.	Facilitator Resource	Circulate among groups to observe interaction, identify needs. Facilitate group thinking and organizational strategy discussions. Review specific skills as needed. Respond to student questions. Ask key questions to stimulate or redirect students' thinking.

(continues)

TABLE 7.1. *Continued*

Step, Type, or Level of Thinking	Student		Teacher	
	Role	Sample Activities	Role	Sample Activities
Group members conduct research.	Active participant Researcher Inquirer	Identify useful resources both in and out of classroom. Read. Observe. Take notes. Organize and interpret information. Identify sources of data. Discuss data, coordinate activities with group members; integrate findings.	Facilitator Resource	Provide resources and a possible format to assist students in data collection. Arrange for students to use resources outside the classroom for the collection of data. Respond to requests for information or help with thinking and/or search strategies.
Groups plan presentation.	Active participant Idea finder Planner	Appoint a member to the class steering committee. Identify the main idea in the group's integrated findings (What is the main outcome of the research?) Identify a presentation format that will present ideas clearly, stimulate interest, and involve all group members. Use the Creative Problem Solving strategy to plan and organize the presentation. Obtain equipment and materials required for the presentation.	Facilitator Planner Resource	Coordinate group presentation plans. Convene steering committee meetings periodically for joint planning, scheduling, and coordinating requests for special materials. Assist the committee and/or groups as needed to arrange for facilities/materials; clarify ideas. Ensure that all group members are involved in planning and presenting.

(continues)

TABLE 7.1. *Continued*

Step, Type, or Level of Thinking	Student		Teacher	
	Role	**Sample Activities**	**Role**	**Sample Activities**
Group presentation	Active participant Presenter Listener Evaluator	Present results of investigation in an interesting, well-organized manner. Respond to questions. Facilitate interactive experiences for other class members. Constructively evaluate others' work; reflect on appeal, clarity, and relevance of the presentation. Observe and select good ideas/techniques for future presentations.	Coordinator Resource Audience	Post presentation schedule. Review guidelines for audience participation and etiquette. Provide a brief evaluation form or set of questions for consideration. Sit back and enjoy the presentations. Facilitate evaluation discussions after each presentation.
Students and teacher evaluate their projects.	Active participant Reflective thinker	As a group, prepare two open-ended questions about the main ideas of your findings. Answer questions from class members. As a small group, evaluate classmates' responses to your test questions. As a group, evaluate your own interactions and presentation. Individually evaluate own participation and growth. Contribute thoughtfully to "wrap up" discussion and evaluation of the project. Record ideas for new investigations.	Facilitator Resource Evaluator	Review and compile test questions. Present list of questions to all students for study. Provide criteria and facilitate evaluation of test questions by small groups. Guide discussion to integrate and "wrap up" the group investigations.

The students then used *creative problem solving* to do fact finding, select their problem statement and their proposed presentation project, and identify the roles and responsibilities of each member of the group. They also set time schedules for group meetings to coordinate their joint investigation. For the next 3 weeks, students read, observed, and interviewed members of their community to learn more about their topics. In group meetings, they explored the application of the law of supply and demand to their specific subject and chose to design a "boom and bust" simulation for their presentation. During the fourth week, they wrote a scenario, created various roles for participants, and designed materials to be used in the simulation. At the same time, they prepared comparison charts to summarize their new knowledge at the end of the simulation activity.

While this group was exploring economic cycles, other groups investigated other subtopics from the list generated by the class. The coordinating committee met with the teacher periodically during the investigation to plan schedules and review plans so that presentations would go smoothly. Since the economy group planned an interactive simulation, the coordinating committee scheduled the presentation near the end of the day so the classroom could be rearranged to provide space for the activity.

After the group facilitated the "boom and bust" simulation, Roland led a discussion of feelings participants had experienced during the activity. After the discussion, he summarized the feelings that had been expressed and linked them to the main ideas discovered in the investigation and summarized in the comparison charts.

In the final step of the group investigation, the four group members jointly evaluated the strengths and limitations of their project, assessed their own contributions to its success (or limitations), and summarized what they had learned and what they still wanted to know. All other groups followed a similar procedure.

Example 2: Outline for a Secondary Interdisciplinary Unit

Broad Theme: Westward Expansion

Generalization: *Many apparently unrelated social, economic, political, and personal factors led to westward expansion in the United States and, in turn, were affected by the westward movement.*

Goal: Students will make connections between historical, scientific, economic, literary, cultural, and religious movements of the first half of the nineteenth century and infer their influence(s) on the exploration and settlement of western North America.

Presentation Format: A mid-nineteenth century fair or exposition

Figure 7.1 on page 206 illustrates a web of causes/factors leading to westward expansion in the United States that high school students generated after an introduction to the theme and an opportunity to examine several sources of information (e.g., texts, novels, biographies, newspapers, videotapes, realia, etc.). (An alternative generative process is the Taba interpretation of data strategy; see Chapter 8.)

Following the web discussion, students reflect on the subjects and then sign up for a group based on their interest(s). Group size is capped at six; if all the slots in a subtopic have been taken, a student may choose to work on another area of interest or, in rare instances, propose an independent project in the area of interest. In small groups, students use a fact-finding strategy (see Chapter 5, Parnes) to assess prior knowledge of group members, forecast additional information they want to discover, and make a plan to guide the investigation. The Taylor *Multiple Talent Model* includes four steps for planning: (a) a clear statement of purpose and/or questions to guide the investigation, (b) a list of resources and materials needed, (c) a sequence of steps needed to reach the goal, and (d) a list of possible problems and at least one alternative way to solve or bypass each problem. The next step is to discuss the plan with the teacher (or a mentor), show how the small-group goal is related to the theme goals, and reach consensus on the plan.

A group investigating the abolitionist movement, for example, might plan to have each of four students select a leading abolitionist and study her or his life using biographies, fiction, the abolitionist's own writing, and contemporary views. Students then prepare to participate in a symposium as the abolitionist. One person would focus on abolitionism as a social reform movement, using history and fiction to gain a broader view of the topic, then moderate the symposium.

Students each pursue an individual study with an interdependent goal. In group meetings, students discuss progress toward the goal, share information they discover, make decisions, and plan the presentation. In private, each student reads, reflects, and writes a position paper for the symposium that incorporates the language and ideas of the abolitionist she or he chose to study. The time plan for this group includes more time for reading and writing than would the work of a group who chose, for example, to build a model of a textile mill to demonstrate the economic connections between cotton growers in the South and milling towns in New England. Members of the mill group also would do research to learn about textile mills in New England but probably would spend more time designing and constructing the model. In each case, tasks and goals are interdependent.

MODIFYING THE APPROACH

The *Group Investigations* model incorporates most of the content, process, product, and learning environment modifications recommended for gifted students. Care should be taken to select abstract and/or complex topics, themes, or persistent issues that challenge the thinking of gifted students and pique their interest. The authors of the model have recommended process changes comparable to those recommended by Maker (1982) and Renzulli and Reis (1985). However, teachers must look at other models to find guidelines for developing complex thinking processes. The levels of analysis, synthesis, and evaluation in Bloom's *Cognitive Taxonomy* are essential for this approach. In addition, Parnes' *Creative Problem Solving*, Taylor's *Multiple Talent* approach, and Taba's *Teaching Strategies* are excellent models to help students organize their investigations, make sense of their data, resolve conflicts, and communicate more effectively.

Product and learning environment changes recommended for *Group Investigations* are essentially the same as those recommended for gifted students. In programs for the gifted, greater emphasis is placed on submitting products to appropriate audiences such as magazines, newspapers, community groups, government representatives, or other decision makers in addition to making presentations to other students.

DEVELOPMENT

Sharan and Sharan (1976) based their small-group learning models on the theories of John Dewey, with his emphasis on the importance of experience and the interdependence of members of a community, and those of Jean Piaget, who theorized that a child actively constructs meaning through interaction with objects and others in the environment.

Dewey (1902/1943) advocated changes in instructional practice and classroom organization to respond to children's natural learning abilities and recommended changes that allow students to communicate with others, actively observe, research, experiment, discover information, and reflect on real experiences. He strongly believed that democratic principles must be taught and experienced in classrooms designed to support active communication (Dewey, 1916/1944) if students were to be prepared to function effectively in democratic societies. He also pointed out that the words *communication* and *community* have common linguistic roots and that learning to communicate effectively requires participation in a variety of social interaction experiences.

Piaget (1952/1963) hypothesized that development is an ongoing process of assimilation of sensory data, accommodation (modifying existing cognitive structures when data no longer fit), the experience of disequilibrium when new ideas and old structures are in conflict, and integration (revising or transforming cognitive structures that are no longer useful in explaining natural or social phenomena). Like Dewey, Piaget believed that peer interaction facilitates development. He argued that cognitive conflict among peers helps learners see a concept from different perspectives and, thus, construct more adequate representations.

Social learning and group contact theories also are important to this model. Following school integration, many educators, concerned about wide disparities in achievement between students from dominant social groups and those from lower socioeconomic or ethnic minority groups, designed a number of approaches to reform educational practice.

Several cooperative learning programs have been developed and tested in classrooms in the United States and other countries over the past 15 years. Model developers claim many and varied benefits for cooperative learning (e.g., improved achievement for all students, improved social skills, and improved peer relations). However, cooperative learning models differ radically in structure and philosophy (Kagan, 1985). Phelps and Damon (1989) identify three approaches:

1. peer tutoring in which an "expert" student teaches a "novice" to master objectives determined by teacher or text,

2. cooperative learning teams in which children work jointly on the same problem or separately on individual components of the same problem, and

3. peer collaboration in which relative novices work together to complete tasks or solve problems none of them could do alone.

In collaborative learning, peer relationships are more symmetrical; cognitive development and knowledge or skill needed to solve problems is more equivalent than in the highly structured forms of peer tutoring or cooperative learning. The peer tutoring approach to cooperative learning is an integral part of several methods developed by Robert Slavin (1983). His *Student Teams Academic Divisions* model is used in this chapter as an exemplar of peer tutoring. An example of the second approach is the original *Jigsaw* model developed by Aronson, Blaney, Stephan, Sikes, and Snapp (1978). *Group Investigations* (Sharan & Sharan, 1992) is an outstanding example of the third approach. Theories from sociology and group dynamics also have been incorporated to create a model that still maintains the philosophical and theoretical approach of the Sharans' small-group teaching methods.

RESEARCH ON EFFECTIVENESS

Numerous studies on cooperative learning in small groups with students in almost all grades have been conducted over the past 20 years (see Johnson,

Johnson, & Maruyama, 1983, for a meta-analysis of these studies). In an early study of small-group teaching methods with elementary school children, grades 2 through 6, Sharan, Hertz-Lazarowitz, and Ackerman (1980) compared the achievement of children working cooperatively in small groups with that of peers in traditional whole-class instruction. Students working in small groups scored significantly higher on questions that required higher level thinking or creativity. Scores on lower level questions did not differ significantly. Behavior patterns established through cooperative learning experiences were found to transfer and operate in contexts and situations other than those found in classrooms (Hertz-Lazarowitz, Sharan, & Steinberg, 1980).

In a large-scale investigation, Sharan et al. (1984) studied the effects of participation in either of two different models of cooperative learning— *Group Investigations* (GI) and *Student-Teams Academic Divisions* (STAD) (Slavin, 1980)—or traditional whole-class instruction (WC) on academic achievement and interethnic relations of junior high school students. In general, the achievement of students in either of the cooperative learning classes was superior to that of students in whole-class instruction. Students in STAD and WC classes had slightly higher scores on low-level test questions; students in GI classes had significantly higher scores on questions that required more complex thinking. These findings were consistent across all ability levels and in all ethnic groups. However, a finding that the most advanced students, previously ability grouped in English classes, made smaller achievement gains than had been expected is disturbing to advocates for gifted children. The authors suggest this result may have been due to the abolition of ability grouping during the study, but they have no data to confirm or deny that inference. The authors report some methodological problems with the research in literature classes but conclude that trends suggest that the GI method is better for developing higher level thinking than it is for helping students acquire specific information.

In general, students who participated in GI classrooms were most cooperative, those in the STAD classrooms somewhat less so, and those in WC classrooms were most competitive. The GI method clearly was superior in promoting cross-ethnic cooperation. The distinction between the two methods of cooperative learning appears to hinge on the ways peer relationships are structured by the method. In STAD, academically successful pupils help less successful pupils, usually of a lower socioeconomic or ethnic group, to master subject matter assigned by the teacher. The status of students in a STAD group basically is the same as that in the classroom or the society as a whole.

The key to the superiority of the *Group Investigations* model in improving social relationships is in the design of the group task and the structure of peer interactions. Each group member performs a different task, mutual assistance is required to meet group goals, and all members of the group are equally important to the success of the project. Peers are potential sources of ideas and information. Subjects for investigations and plans of operation for each group differ, so less social comparison and competitive behavior is present than when all members of the class have the same task to do.

Sharan and Shachar (1988) compared language and achievement of eighth-grade students using the *Group Investigations* methods with students in whole-class instruction in ethnically mixed geography and history classes. They used pretest and posttest measures of achievement and videotaped discussions of 27 groups of students (3 groups of six students selected randomly from each of nine classrooms). Data about students' interethnic cooperation and verbal and intellectual behaviors were extracted from the videotapes and analyzed by two judges. Students from the GI classes showed a very superior level of academic achievement on questions requiring both low-level and high-level answers, greater interethnic cooperation, and greater equality in the frequency of speech acts by members of the two ethnic groups. The data obtained from group discussions correlated highly with the results of achievement tests indicating that small-group study leads to significantly higher performance on tests of academic achievement. Other significant findings were that ethnic minority students in the GI classes showed greater language proficiency and used more complex thinking strategies than did ethnic minority students in traditional whole-class instruction.

Research using the *Group Investigations* approach with gifted students would be valuable but, at this time, few studies have been reported in the literature. In those few, limited information is available about prior achievement of participants (Robinson, 1991), cooperative learning groups are compared to control groups in traditional classrooms, and basic skills outcomes are the usual measures of achievement. "In other words, cooperative learning in heterogeneous classrooms has not been compared with educational treatments of choice for academically talented students" (Robinson, 1991, p. 5). Based on our own observations and from research in cognitive psychology (Damon, 1984; Phelps & Damon, 1989), we believe collaborative learning can be a powerful method for stimulating cognitive development and improving social relationships among gifted students as long as they have opportunities to work with peers.

JUDGMENTS

Group Investigations is an excellent model for collaborative learning in classrooms for the gifted. When gifted students lack the opportunity to attend homogeneously grouped classes, this model also can be used to structure small-group learning activities that offer greater opportunities for gifted students.

Advantages

Most of the curriculum modifications recommended for gifted students are integrated into the *Group Investigations* approach. Students have freedom of choice and opportunities to engage in complex and functional thinking, investigate real problems and issues, interact with peers, and create a variety of products for real audiences. Students have many opportunities to learn social interaction skills, deepen their conceptual understanding, and express their creativity. Students participate in inquiry in the same ways that professionals in a field would do. Thus, their activities and products are authentic and functional. Student participants in *Group Investigations* report satisfaction with this approach and consistently show greater achievement on tests of higher level thinking or creativity. In addition, students report a wider circle of friends and greater appreciation of the talents of others.

Group Investigations differs from other models of cooperative learning in several essential ways. Students select topics of interest and plan investigations rather than performing a teacher-prescribed task in a group setting. Complex and functional thinking skills are integrated with interesting and challenging content. Finally, students are evaluated by their own individual products and on group projects. The emphasis is on self-evaluation of real products and contributions to group success rather than scores on basic skills tests. Based on an extensive analysis of the research on cooperative learning, Robinson (1991) makes five recommendations for the use of cooperative learning with gifted students:

1. Cooperative learning in the heterogeneous classroom should not be substituted for specialized programs and services for academically talented students.

2. If a school is committed to cooperative learning, models which encourage access to materials beyond grade level are preferable for academically talented students.

3. If a school is committed to cooperative learning, models which permit flexible pacing are preferable for academically talented students.

4. If a school is committed to cooperative learning, student achievement disparities within the group should not be too severe.

5. Academically talented students should be provided with opportunities for autonomy and individual pursuits during the school day. (pp. 7–8)

With the exception of Recommendation One, *Group Investigations* meets these standards and can be used effectively in programs for gifted students.

Disadvantages

Because of its complexity, *Group Investigations* may not be appropriate for young gifted students. Some experiences in group processes, conflict resolution, planning, decision making, and organizational skills are prerequisite to participation in this approach to collaborative inquiry. Unless students have mutual respect and a disposition to work together to meet group goals, interdependence can be a problem when one or more students fail to perform their responsibilities. Problems can be solved by careful planning and formulation of research questions, but teachers and students must be prepared to deal with uncooperative individuals.

Availability of resources and mentors may be a problem in many schools. This approach to learning requires a variety of information sources and the ability to move freely from the classroom to other sites. School rules or transportation problems may interfere with freedom of access to needed information. In some cases parents may be able to assist, but this again requires careful coordination and scheduling.

One factor that may concern some teachers and parents is that *Group Investigations* discourages competition for grades and does not focus on acquisition of specific information. All students do not study the same content, and some students may not do as well on achievement tests; research results are mixed on this point. To avoid criticism for lack of rigor, teachers must be prepared to document student progress with portfolios, examples of sophisticated products, examples of professional behavior, and results of assessment using measures other than traditional standardized tests.

CONCLUSION

Collaborating with peers in social inquiry is recognized by many cognitive psychologists and educators as the most effective means of intellectual and social development. *Group Investigations* is an excellent model for this purpose, but it does require careful organization, planning, and multilateral coordination in the classroom, school, and community. Although gifted students can learn to make many of the arrangements necessary for access to information, cooperation from parents, school officials, and community mentors still is necessary for the success of a complex inquiry project. A relatively simple investigation can be completed in as little as 2 weeks. Investigations of more complex concepts, themes, or issues may involve students for several weeks.

A key to the success of collaborative learning is the competence and preparation of teachers. With this model, teachers can create conditions that are more conducive to learning, that motivate students to learn and achieve at higher levels, and that foster more positive social relationships. These are primary goals of differentiated education for gifted students as well. The *Group Investigations* model, although embedded in the paradigm of cooperative learning, includes most of the recommendations for differentiated curriculum for the gifted. Students develop research skills, focus on open-ended tasks, create new ideas or construct products that challenge existing ideas, and participate in functional, socially viable projects. The multitude of possibilities for content, process, and product modifications and the opportunities for mutually reinforcing experiences make this model of collaborative learning an important addition to teaching-learning methods for the gifted.

RESOURCES

Background Information

Robinson, A. (1991). *Cooperative learning and the academically talented student: Executive summary*. Storrs, CT: National Research Center on the Gifted and Talented. The author examines the research base on cooperative learning, compares models, and summarizes the advantages and disadvantages of various models. She spotlights the weaknesses in cooperative learning research related to academically talented students. She concludes that if a school is committed to cooperative learning, a model that permits flexible pacing and student choice in topics of study and group membership (i.e., *Group Investigations*) is preferable for gifted and talented students.

Sharan, S. (Ed.). (1990). *Cooperative learning: Theory and research*. New York: Praeger. This volume contains a well-developed presentation of the *Group Investigations* model and discussions of a variety of models of cooperative learning. *Co-op Co-op*, a model developed by Spencer Kagan, with some of the same philosophical foundations, is less complex and may be used as an introduction to collaborative learning with younger students.

Sharan, S., Hare, P., Webb, C. D., & Hertz-Lazarowitz, R. (Eds.). (1980). *Cooperation in education*. Provo, UT: Brigham Young University Press. The proceedings of one of the first international conferences on cooperative learning, this volume is an excellent resource for comparison of the theoretical assumptions and procedures of several cooperative learning models.

Sharan, S., & Sharan, Y. (1976). *Small group teaching*. Englewood Cliffs, NJ: Educational Technology Publications. A superb collection of activities for helping students to develop interpersonal and organizational skills needed to work as productive members of a small group, this book lays the groundwork for the structure of the *Group Investigations* model.

Sharan, Y., & Sharan, S. (1992). *Expanding cooperative learning through Group Investigations.* New York: Teachers College Press. Clearly and concisely, the Sharans describe the six steps of the model, provide examples of student activities, and identify resources needed to implement the model in the classroom.

Slavin, R., Sharan, S., Kagan, S., Hertz-Lazarowitz, R., Webb, C., & Schmuck, R. (Eds.). (1985). *Learning to cooperate, cooperating to learn.* New York: Plenum Press. Another volume of proceedings from an international conference on cooperative learning, this book includes articles by the authors of various models of cooperative learning plus extensive charts comparing the models and summarizing the research that had been done up to that time.

Instructional Materials and Resources

Booth, D., & Thornley-Hall, C. (1992). *Classroom talk: Speaking and listening activities from classroom-based teacher research.* Portsmouth, NH: Heinemann. This practical, hands-on reference includes topics such as peer leaders in discussion groups, interactive talk as a classroom model, relating talk to text, the role of talk in drama, and peer conferencing. The 17 essays in the book are written by teachers and filled with examples and illustrations. Although the emphasis is on heterogeneous classrooms, most of the group-interaction activities can be applied effectively in classrooms for gifted and talented students.

Dalton, J. (1992). *Adventures in thinking: Creative thinking and cooperative learning talk in small groups.* Portsmouth, NH: Heinemann. A compendium of practical ideas and oral activities designed to develop strategies for creative and critical thinking, skills of cooperative talk, small-group interaction, small-group management, and evaluation. The author also includes ideas for integrating theme studies with small-group learning.

Fleisher, P. (1993). *Changing our world: A handbook for young activists.* Tucson, AZ: Zephyr Press. From his experience as a teacher and social activist, the author has prepared a step-by-step guide for young people interested in social justice issues. Suggestions for developing effective leadership skills and historical information about activists also are included.

Kagan, S. (1989). *Cooperative learning: Resources for teachers.* San Juan Capistrano, CA: Resources for Teachers. Recommended by the Sharans, this book includes a variety of ways to organize group work in any content area.

Kunz, C. (n.d.). *Brainstrains: Creative problem-solving and logical thinking.* Victoria, Australia: Down Under Books. The author combines fiction with facts about the lives of eminent individuals to pose problems that promote creative mathematical problem solving and logical thinking. Grades 3 through 8.

Moy, M. (n.d.). *Animal addresses: Mapping and world knowledge.* Victoria, Australia: Down Under Books. The author uses provocative questions to encourage students to learn more about animal habitats in 10 different areas of the world. Reproducible worksheets and maps are included.

Scott, J. (n.d.). *Teach thinking strategies.* Victoria, Australia: Down Under Books. Based on Bloom's *Taxonomy of Cognitive Objectives,* this book contains ideas for teaching higher level thinking skills for students in grades 7 through 12. Photocopyable resource pages are designed to help students reflect on and write about their thinking strategies.

Short, K., & Burke, C. (1991). *Creating curriculum: Teachers and students as a community of learners.* Portsmouth, NH: Heinemann. Both theoretical and practical, this short book is full of ideas for developing integrated curriculum and integrating the inquiry method into small-group work. One strong emphasis is theme-based learning with a variety of "authentic" books, rather than a basal text.

Short, K., & Pierce, K. (Eds.). (1990). *Talking about books: Creating literate communities.* Portsmouth, NH: Heinemann. Most of the chapters in this attractive book are written by teachers who use literature-based theme studies and small-group discussions in their classrooms. Examples of classroom (small-group) projects, student work, and organization strategies are included.

The *W.E.B.,* published quarterly by The Ohio State University. *Wonderfully Exciting Books* is both a superb review of books and a source of ideas for organizing integrated units for group investigations or literature discussion. An idea web on a complex theme is featured in every issue, and a complete bibliography of all web resources is provided.

Chapter 8

Hilda Taba: Teaching Strategies Program

The *Hilda Taba Teaching Strategies* are structured, generic methods in which the teacher leads students through a series of sequential intellectual tasks by asking them open-ended but focused questions. Four strategies have been developed: (a) concept development, (b) interpretation of data, (c) application of generalizations, and (d) resolution of conflict (also called interpretation of feelings, attitudes, and values). The four strategies, although not designed to be hierarchical or sequential, can be used sequentially since they build on each other. Within each strategy, however, the questions have a definite sequence, with a theoretical and practical justification for the order. A close associate of John Dewey, Taba incorporated many of his ideas along with the research and writing of Piaget, Bruner, and Vygotsky in developing her approaches to teaching and curriculum development. Although her strategies are of a generic nature and are appropriate for use in any content area, because of her social studies curriculum (Ellis & Durkin, 1972) Taba's methods are viewed by some as social studies techniques. However, as can be seen by examining the theoretical and empirical bases for the strategies, they are techniques for developing thinking skills, or, in Piaget's terms, methods for arranging the environment so that maximum cognitive growth can occur.

On a personal note, the first author's involvement with the *Hilda Taba Teaching Strategies* has been interesting and rewarding. After the first series of training in their use, her reaction was similar to an "Aha!" experience. Another immediate reaction was that these strategies, particularly the second, interpretation of data, were close to what she had always attempted to do in her teaching, although her methods always were lacking in some way. Taba had perfected these methods and even had data to show they were effective! Further, the methods Taba developed for training teachers were the best she had encountered: demonstrations and modeling, analysis of the demonstrations, step-by-step planning, team planning and team tryouts, and finally, classroom tryouts, taping, and self-analysis. Both the teaching strategies and the teacher-training process have had a profound, positive effect on her teaching.

ASSUMPTIONS UNDERLYING THE MODEL

In developing the teaching strategies, Taba rejected the following assumptions commonly made about children's thinking because they tend to retard progress in developing thinking skills:

- An individual must accumulate a great deal of factual knowledge before thinking about this knowledge.

- Thinking skills are developed only through "intellectually demanding" subjects (for example, physical sciences, math, and foreign languages).

- Abstract thinking is an ability that can be developed only in bright or gifted children.

- Manipulation of the environment will not improve or cause growth in thinking skills since cognitive growth is locked into a predetermined developmental time sequence.

These ideas were rejected and more positive alternatives proposed because of the results of Taba's three research projects (Taba, 1964, 1966; Wallen, Durkin, Fraenkel, McNaughton, & Sawin, 1969).

About Learning

Probably the most basic idea underlying the Taba *Strategies* is acceptance of Piaget's (1963) assumptions about cognitive development: the sequence, how it occurs, and the type of thinking exhibited at each developmental stage. Although discussing all of Piaget's ideas in this chapter is impossible, a few of the general principles will be presented briefly since they are necessary to understanding the teaching strategies.

Sequence

First, cognitive development occurs in an invariant sequence. Children begin at the sensorimotor stage and progress sequentially, without skipping any stages, through preoperational to concrete operations. Finally, they achieve formal operations at about age 11. Change, or cognitive growth, occurs through children's interaction with the environment and their attempts to construct their own reality or organize their world. As children interact with the environment and attempt to interpret it using increasingly sophisticated ways of thinking, the phenomenon of disequilibrium occurs; they experience discomfort because they begin to recognize previously unnoticed inconsistencies. When this happens, they attempt to consolidate and integrate various schemes for interpreting what is seen to achieve equilibrium (and be "comfortable") again.

Assimilation and Accommodation

The concepts of assimilation and accommodation are related closely to equilibrium and disequilibrium and are crucial to understanding "pacing" in the Taba program. A somewhat simplistic but effective way of explaining the two ideas begins with the conception of a person's mind as a filing system with file folders representing categories (for example, dogs, furniture, books). When new information comes in, it needs to be filed somewhere in the system. The individual doing the filing essentially has the following three choices: (a) fit the information as it is into one of the existing categories; (b) change the information in some way so that it fits into the existing system; or (c) change the system in some way so that it can handle the new information. This change can be a small one, such as adding a new category, or it can be more extensive through redefining a whole series of categories or even reorganizing the whole system.

In this example, filing the information as it is represents a form of assimilation. Changing the information is another form of assimilation, which occurs when the item does not fit but there is no desire to change the system. Accommodation is represented by some change in the system, from limited (making a new category) to extensive (revising the entire structure). The changed system that results from an extensive revision is a more sophisticated one. Thus it is with cognitive growth. Individuals experience disequilibrium when they recognize inadequacies in their existing organization of reality, so they make changes that improve that organization. They now experience equilibrium again. Intellectual growth, then, can be seen as a progression of assimilation, attempted assimilations that will not work, necessary accommodations, and then new assimilations at a higher order.

Developmental Trends

As children progress through the stages of cognitive development, they become increasingly able to use more formal systems of logic and to rely on symbols of meaning. A second trend is away from egocentrism or an egoistic view of the world toward the ability to differentiate the self from the rest of the world. A third related trend in development is toward internalization and "interiorization." Actions become less overt and more internal. In this movement, individuals go through distinct stages. The thought processes of previous stages are incorporated into the thinking at higher levels, but at each higher level, the processes are qualitatively different from those at lower stages. As children mature, they develop cognitively at their own rate, with movement through the stages determined by the interaction of both internal and external factors.

Facilitating Cognitive Growth

The one aspect of Piaget's theory that is not accepted by Taba is in the area of environmental influences on cognitive growth. Although Piaget recognizes the importance of a child's interaction with the environment as the growth processes occur, he believes that deliberate manipulation of the environment to enhance development or to quicken its rate is a futile exercise. In other words, educators can do nothing to hasten or improve the quality of a child's cognitive development. They must simply wait for these natural changes to occur. Experiences that provide for horizontal elaboration (for example, enrichment within stages) can be helpful, according to Piaget, but vertical elaboration (for example, enrichment at different levels) is neither helpful nor desirable.

On this point Taba disagrees. Her basic assumption is that the environment is extremely important; it can and should be manipulated so that maximum horizontal and vertical elaboration occurs. In other words, she agrees with the sequence identified by Piaget but disagrees with his deterministic assumptions about how growth occurs.

One of the most important ideas underlying the Taba program is that thinking involves an *active* transaction between an individual and the information with which he or she is working. This idea has numerous implications for the learning process. It means, for one thing, that children do not develop their thinking skills by memorizing the products of adults' thinking. Children develop these skills by manipulating ideas, examining them critically, and trying to combine them in new ways. Data become meaningful only when individuals perform certain mental operations on those data. Even if children reach exactly the same conclusions as an adult after reviewing certain materials, the process of manipulating the information is necessary and valuable. This is not to say that children should not read the conclusions of others. They certainly should, but they also should be encouraged to reach their own conclusions and to examine the data of others critically to see if they would draw the same conclusions.

A second assumption relates content and process. Although Taba believes that thinking skills can be developed through any subject matter (that is, not just through the so-called intellectually demanding subjects), process cannot be separated from content. The "richness" and "significance" of the content with which children work will affect the quality of their thinking, as will the processes used and the initial assistance given in developing these processes. Because of this belief, every lesson has both a content and a process purpose that are interrelated and can be accomplished by the particular strategy. Selection of content that is rich and significant enough to be appropriate for developing thinking skills then becomes an important aspect of learning the teaching strategies, as does the organization of that content.

Another relationship between content and process centers around Taba's ideas about "thought systems" in each content area. Although the precise nature of the relationships between content areas and the processes used by scholars in those areas is unclear, Taba hypothesizes both generic processes of inquiry cutting across all types of content and specific processes of conceptualization in each area. For example, all areas deal with such processes as inferring cause–effect relationships. However, in the social sciences multiple causation and probabilistic reasoning are much more important than in the physical sciences, where phenomena are more easily predicted. In short, the nature of the content and the thought systems in each content area will determine in part the most important thinking skills to be practiced by the students.

About Teaching

Unfortunately, not all teaching results in learning. Since teaching is a complex process requiring an infinite number of decisions that must meet many criteria, each objective of teaching will require a different analysis and different teaching strategies.

The Importance of Specific Strategies

Productive teaching involves "developing strategies that are focused sharply on a specific target while at the same time integrating these specific strategies into an overall strategy that accommodates the generic requirements of multiple objectives" (Taba, 1966, p. 42). In other words, many thinking skills can be taught, and particular methods can be used for developing different thinking skills. Before teachers can be successful in developing thinking skills, they must have a clear idea of how these thinking skills are manifested and what methods can be used to develop them. One specific effect of this idea on Taba's methods is that each teaching strategy and each step in each strategy has particular "overt" and "covert" objectives. In other words, she has pinpointed the behavioral (overt) manifestations of the underlying (covert) thinking processes.

Related to the development of thinking skills and following from her agreement with Piaget's sequence of cognitive development is Taba's (1964) assumption about the sequencing of learning experiences. If educators assume a sequential order in the development of thought processes, learning experiences also should be sequenced so that each step develops skills that are prerequisites for the next step. This sequence would apply to the day-to-day learning experiences provided for children as well as to those experiences spanning one school year or a series of years.

Teacher Questions

A crucial factor in developing thinking skills and the sequencing of learning experiences is appropriate questioning by the teacher. Important aspects of teacher questions are *open-endedness,* allowing for and encouraging responses at different levels of abstraction, sophistication, and depth and from different perspectives; *pacing,* which matches student capacity for mastering the skills at each step; and *sequencing and patterning.* Sequencing and patterning are particularly important in that the "impact of teaching does not lie only in the frequency of single acts" (Taba, 1966, p. 43) but also in the ways these single acts (questions) are combined into sequences and patterns.

Rotating Learning Experiences

Also following from an assumption about how development occurs is Taba's (1966) belief in the value of "rotating" learning experiences that require assimilation and accommodation. Putting this idea into practice suggests alternating experiences in which children absorb information with those experiences that challenge their current mental schemes for organizing the information. Primitive or inadequate schemes can be challenged by having children consider examples or information that is "dissonant with their current schema" (p. 23) so that they are required to revise their present conceptualization. The teacher's task is not to correct the student or to point out these inconsistencies but to present or otherwise arrange the situation so that students encounter the dissonant information in activities with potential for causing change. Students must manipulate data themselves. To be successful, however, this process of rotating experiences must "offer a challenge that is sufficiently beyond the student's present schema to induce accommodation, and yet not so far removed that the student cannot make the leap" (p. 23). This underlying idea of rotation and challenge is related closely to Taba's concept of "pacing," which is discussed later.

Organization of Content

Since content is an important aspect of the learning process and sets limits on the kind of learning and on the teaching strategies that can be used, it must be organized to develop thinking skills. Suggested organizational schemes are those advocated by Bruner (1960), Ward (1961), and Taba (1962). Basic concepts and ideas provide the underlying system of organization rather than chronology or type of information.

About Characteristics and Teaching of the Gifted

Taba's (Institute for Staff Development, 1971a) assumption that "All school children are capable of thinking at abstract levels, although the quality of individual thinking differs markedly" (p. 148) resulted from her research showing a low positive relationship between IQ and performance on the tests and other measures of the effect of the teaching strategies. When growth was measured, results showed that students with low IQs gained as much as did those with high IQs. In the teaching strategies, pacing is important. With learners who may not learn as quickly, new material is not presented as rapidly, and sufficient opportunities are provided for concrete operations before transitions are made to abstract operations with symbolic content. With faster learners, pacing is different. In short, the same basic intellectual tasks can be used with gifted and nongifted children and can be effective in developing their abstract-thinking capabilities. However, the pacing of assimilation and accommodation activities and the frequency of the rotation between them must be different.

No statements are made by Taba about the most effective grouping of students to achieve appropriate pacing for all students. Taba assumes that, at least during some parts of the day, children need to be grouped according to learning rate. However, in many of the classrooms in which the teaching strategies were tested, many discussions involved the whole class rather than small groups within it. Perhaps the reason few differences were found between gifted and other learners in Taba's research is that gifted children were always in groups with all ranges of ability. Thus, appropriate pacing for their needs may have been difficult.

Those who implement Taba's approach in programs for the gifted emphasize that although the strategies can be used with all children (and should be used part of the time with groups consisting of varied ability levels), having gifted children grouped with other gifted children part of the time is essential for maximum cognitive growth to occur. A theoretical justification for this idea comes from Piaget's (Piaget & Inhelder, 1969) statements about the importance of peer interaction in fostering cognitive growth. Since Taba accepts Piaget's assumptions about how cognitive development occurs and since the teaching strategies are designed to foster development along the lines suggested by Piaget, his ideas form an implicit assumption, even though Taba did not make it explicit.

In discussing the importance of peer interaction, Piaget emphasizes that children learn from each other. They learn both content (for example, specific facts or pieces of information) and reasoning processes (for example, logic or ways of handling information). An important way in which cognitive growth occurs is through exposure to higher levels of reasoning. However, these higher levels must be only slightly higher than the child's present level of reasoning in order for the child to incorporate this reasoning into his or her repertoire. In addition, this "learning from others" is beneficial only when the child is ready, which usually means when the child is in some transitional stage of development. Extending this idea to the use of the Taba *Strategies* with gifted children, then, suggests that they need to be grouped with their gifted peers at least part of the time. One or 2 gifted children in a heterogeneous fourth-grade classroom will not learn as much from each other as will 9 or 10 gifted children drawn from all the fourth-grade classrooms in a school. A further extension of the idea suggests the value of multi-age grouping of gifted students.

Since Piaget's theory of cognitive development forms a theoretical basis for the Taba *Strategies,* his possible conception of giftedness needs to be considered. Although Piaget makes no direct references to giftedness, educators and psychologists often have interpreted his ideas without a full understanding of them. Most psychometric (measurement) conceptions of giftedness emphasize the importance of rate of development: a child who talks earlier, reads earlier, thinks abstractly at an early age, and does tasks normally accomplished only by older peers is considered more intelligent. Often, this same idea is carried over into interpretations of giftedness in Piaget's developmental scheme: Those who progress through the stages more quickly will be (and are) more intelligent.

This perception of intellectual development ignores a concept important in Piaget's theory: horizontal elaboration. According to this idea, an individual who passes through all the periods of development more rapidly may not be as capable intellectually as a person who has passed through the periods more slowly. The individual who has moved more slowly and has interacted with a variety of resources will have more time to develop cognitive structures at each stage, and thus the individual will have a better base for the next higher stage because of the interaction with a greater variety of content. Although Taba does not address this Piagetian concept directly, it seems to be an underlying idea that influences her perception of giftedness.

Summary of Assumptions

The major ideas underlying the Taba *Strategies* can be summarized as relying heavily on Piaget's developmental theory, including the sequence of development, the major stages, and the importance of interaction with the environment. Her major disagreement with his theory, however, forms the basic rationale for the Taba *Teaching Strategies* program: Thinking skills can be taught. If educators are familiar with the various thinking skills and their behavioral manifestations, and if they use precise teaching strategies designed to enhance these skills in students, teachers can arrange the environment so that maximum cognitive growth occurs.

ELEMENTS/PARTS

Four separate but related teaching strategies make up the Taba model: concept development, interpretation of data, application of generalizations, and resolution of conflict. Each has specific cognitive tasks and a rationale for placement in the sequence.

Concept Development

This strategy deals with the organization and reorganization of information, and with the labeling of categories (Institute for Staff Development, 1971a). The name *concept development* indicates the planned end result, the derivation of fundamental ideas or major concepts from broad categories of data that are related in some way. Students classify data and support their classifications. Concepts are formed, clarified, and extended as students respond to questions that require them to enumerate items, notice similarities and differences that form a basis for grouping items, label groups in different ways, regroup items in different ways, and give reasons for all groupings. In all cases, students must perform these operations for themselves; teachers must be able to ask major focusing questions at the appropriate time and recognize when to employ other tactics to extend, clarify, refocus, or support a discussion that will foster the conceptual development of the students.

Rationale for the Concept Development Task

Concept development is considered the basic form of cognition on which all other processes depend. Closely related to assimilation and accommodation, the process allows each student to clarify ideas (through expressing personal thoughts) and extend concepts (through building on ideas and thoughts expressed by others). Concept development enables students to participate at their own levels but also provides a model to which they can aspire. For example, one student may group items on the basis of descriptive attributes (for example, color, shape), while another may make abstract groupings (for example, fruit, animals). Still another may be at an even higher level, adding or multiplying classes (for example, putting things together that are either wood or blue, or putting things together that are both wood and blue).

From a content standpoint, the task assists students and teachers in organizing data or information to be studied into units that are meaningful to the students and that can facilitate further investigation. When used in this way, the task also helps teachers assess the breadth and depth of the students' concepts so they can plan individual and group experiences that will expand students' concepts. In general, the strategy helps students develop (a) greater openness and flexibility in thinking and (b) better processes for developing and organizing data.

Rationale for the Steps

Each step in the concept development strategy has a rationale for inclusion and a rationale for its placement in the sequence. The first step, *listing*, involves the process of differentiating relevant from irrelevant information, an important skill upon which all other skills will be built. Each student can make a useful contribution, and each can learn from the contributions of others.

At the second step, *grouping*, students become involved in the cognitive task of noticing common attributes and putting items together on the basis of these commonalities. They not only make their own groupings but also see the different groups made by other students. This promotes identification of multiple attributes and stimulates openness and flexibility in thinking (for example, seeing many sides of an issue). Making certain that the reasons for groupings are clear to all students is important to (a) help students clarify their reasoning to themselves and others and (b) enable students to build on others' ideas by adding to a group made by someone else.

Labeling, the third step, is an abstracting or synthesizing process in that a student must find a word or a phrase to express the relationship or commonality among diverse items. The more accurate and inclusive a person's labels are, the more efficient that person is in handling a variety of information. When a teacher consistently asks for variety in labels, students improve in vocabulary development and creativity. When teachers judge the appropriateness of labels, evaluation is taking place, so all children must understand why a label is appropriate or inappropriate.

The fourth step, *subsuming*, provides another opportunity to see different relationships and new attributes of the items. Perhaps more important, however, is that this step helps students see hierarchies in the relationships. When deciding what labels can fit under other labels, they begin to analyze the inclusiveness of each label.

At the fifth step, all the previous steps are recycled. This not only accomplishes the same purposes already mentioned but also promotes openness and flexibility in thinking because it emphasizes that one can always find fresh ways to look at the same data.

Interpretation of Data

As the name implies, this strategy deals with gathering information and making inferences about it (Institute for Staff Development, 1971b). Based on class discussions, students derive conclusions and form generalizations about similar situations or events. Through processing information, students make inferences about cause–effect relationships and defend the statements they make. A critical element of the interpretation of data strategy is that students have meanings for their interpretations and that they recognize the significance of these data in relation to other events in the past, present, or future. Teachers must help students recognize the tentativeness and probabilistic nature of conclusions and generalizations, and they must help students reach these conclusions on their own. They also must be able to guide a discussion by using appropriate questioning techniques.

Rationale for the Interpretation of Data Strategy

This "discovery" or "inquiry" technique provides a sequential method for helping children use the observable data in their own experience as a starting point for developing their own conclusions and generalizations. In this strategy, students process the data in their own way and also have the opportunity to observe how others process the same information. Although it is appropriate for a variety of types of data (for example, scientific, literary, symbolic, or quantitative), the particular type of data will call for greater precision (for example, scientific and quantitative data) or more "reading between the lines" (for example, literary or symbolic data).

Rationale for the Steps

At the first step, listing, the same purposes are served as in the concept development task. Students have the benefit of their collective observations, and they must decide what is relevant and what is not. Sometimes the data may need to be transformed even at this initial step into similarities, trends, or sequences.

At the second step, inferring causes and effects, students apply their own reasoning, experience, and knowledge to the data to arrive at and give support for their inferences. By listening to different interpretations that often are equally justifiable, students learn to attend to and seek out the basis for differing ideas. Providing support for inferences helps students clarify their reasons and develop the habit of justifying their ideas.

The process of making inferences is carried further in the third step, inferring prior causes or subsequent effects. At this step, the fact that cause–effect relationships are usually complex and interrelated rather than simple and linear is emphasized. The fact that many influences are far removed from the immediate data or situation also is stressed. The development of new inferences based on supported inferences encourages students to probe deeply into the phenomena that influence their lives, rather than looking only at surface conditions.

In the fourth step, students are required to reach conclusions. Even though they may not have all the information they would like, they must make the soundest conclusion possible and support it.

Generalizing, the fifth step, is an efficiency-building technique similar to labeling. Doing this task gives students practice in transferring knowledge gained in one situation to other situations where it might apply. In its most extreme form (for example, stereotyping), overgeneralization can be dangerous, since an individual is using knowledge about too few cases to infer about too many cases. Students rarely practice this essential skill to become more accurate and more tentative in their generalizing. At this step, students reach their own generalizations, justify them, have the opportunity to review critically the general statements developed by others, and also have their own generalizations examined critically.

Application of Generalizations

In this strategy the major objective is to help students apply previously learned generalizations and facts to other situations (Institute for Staff Development, 1971c). Students use these generalizations to explain unfamiliar events and to make predictions about what will happen in hypothetical or proposed situations. For example, if students are asked, "What will happen if our country continues to pollute our streams and lakes?" they must apply previous knowledge about the causes of pollution and the conditions present now in the water supply and knowledge of the previous effects of pollution on lives and environments. In this strategy students develop the ability to make predictions about things that will happen in the future and are enabled to apply what they have learned. The real test of a concept or generalization comes when it is applied in a real-life situation. As in all other strategies, students must support all predictions and inferences made. After discussing various predictions, reasons, and conditions, each student is asked to make judgments about the events that are most likely to happen based on the discussion and what they already knew. The teacher must use the appropriate questioning strategies that will lead children through the intellectual tasks identified.

Rationale for the Application of Generalizations Strategy

In this strategy, students apply previously learned facts, principles, or processes in new situations to explain new phenomena or to predict consequences from known conditions. This process is an important vehicle for transfer of knowledge, enabling students to get more "mileage" out of their direct experiences. The application of generalizations strategy allows for and encourages divergent thinking in making predictions. However, students also are required to establish both the parameters of data and logical relationships by which to judge the validity of predictions. These established parameters also are judged on their completeness; students must generate the chain of causal links that will connect the conditions and the predictions.

Rationale for the Steps

At step one, *predictions,* students are encouraged to use their creativity in brainstorming the possible results of some hypothetical situation. It requires the logical proposition of "If _____, then _____." They then are asked to explain the reason(s) for making a particular prediction. Explaining the relationship they see between the situation and a stated prediction gives students practice in clarifying their own thinking and expressing their thoughts distinctly; listening to the predictions and thinking of others helps them to extend and deepen their own understanding. This is also the part of the process from which the strategy gets its name. Students verbalize and explain the particular abstract principles, facts, or processes they are applying to the new situation.

The second step, *inferring conditions,* brings the discussion to a reality base by requiring that students build a logical, justifiable chain of relationships. This process strengthens and expands the students' understanding of multiple causality as they understand that no consequence directly follows from a given situation and that many other factors also must be present.

The next step, *inferring consequences and conditions,* is essentially a recycling of the first two steps and, as such, serves the same purposes. However, additional purposes also are served in that each time the processes are recycled, the predictions and conditions are extended further from the original situation and are therefore more complex and probabilistic in nature.

At the fourth step, *conclusions,* the same purposes are served as in step four in the interpretation of data strategy. Students are required to consider all the predictions, conditions, and reasons that were discussed and make a judgment on their own about which conditions they think are likely to prevail and lead to a particular prediction coming true.

Examining a generalization, the fifth step, strengthens students' abilities to form their own general statements and to look critically at others' statements that may be too general, inaccurate, and unqualified.

Resolution of Conflict

This strategy, often called interpretation of feelings, attitudes, and values, leads students through a process helpful in resolving conflict situations (Institute for Staff Development, 1971d). Resolution of conflict is an extension of all the other strategies, with human behavior as the data to be interpreted. The primary purpose is to help students deal more rationally and effectively with situations encountered in life by giving them practice in exploring the feelings, attitudes, and values behind people's behavior. Students are encouraged to take the viewpoints of all individuals involved in a conflict situation and discuss their possible motives, feelings, and reasons for feelings before talking about what each individual can do to resolve the conflict situation. They are asked to generate a variety of alternatives for action by each person and then to analyze these alternatives in relation to their general consequences and effects on all the other people involved in the situation. Based on the discussion, students evaluate the alternatives and make individual judgments about the most appropriate action that should be taken. After explaining their judgment and considering its possible long-range consequences, students are asked to consider a similar situation experienced by a member of their own group. The same process is followed with this situation, from exploration of reasons for behavior through evaluation of alternatives. Finally, on the basis of this discussion and prior experiences, students are asked to form a generalization about how people usually handle conflict situations of the type discussed. As in the other strategies, the teacher's role includes asking the appropriate questions that will elicit information, inferences, and conclusions from students.

Rationale for the Resolution of Conflict Strategy

This strategy, as an extension or combination of two previous strategies, serves the same purposes as those tasks. However, the subject matter being interpreted and the principles being applied are particularly subjective: human behavior and emotions are the target areas. This strategy gives students practice in assuming the viewpoints of others, an ability that, according to Kohlberg (1971) and Selman (1971), is a necessary prerequisite for advanced moral reasoning to occur.

Rationale for the Steps

At the first step, *listing,* the same purposes are served as in the other strategies. Students learn to differentiate relevant from irrelevant data. The step also builds the idea that a person must understand the facts and know what actually happened in a situation before taking any action.

In the second step, *inferring reasons and feelings,* the same purposes are served as in the inference steps of other strategies. Additionally, this is the major aspect of perspective taking. Students must learn to examine the possible motivations and feelings of all people involved in conflict situations before making judgments about their actions or suggesting alternatives.

Generating alternatives and examining their consequences is an important skill for everyone and one that seldom is practiced. People often act (or react) immediately and do not think about the results of their actions, especially in emotionally charged situations. Through this strategy, students learn to realize that effective decision making and conflict resolution require careful consideration of all contributing factors and the likely consequences of each alternative course of action.

At the next step, *evaluation,* students are asked to decide the most appropriate action. This involves much the same processes as at the conclusion step in the other strategies since students must think carefully about the discussion and interpret it in their own way.

In the next phase of the discussion, steps five through eight, students are asked to apply the same processes of listing facts, inferring reasons and feelings, generating alternatives and consequences, and evaluating alternatives in a situation in their own lives or in the life of one of their peers. This heightens the transfer effect and provides additional emphasis on the validity of these processes in handling the day-to-day situations these students may encounter.

At the last step, *generalizing,* students are asked to form an abstract statement about how people usually handle such situations. The same purposes are served as in the previous strategies.

Supporting Behaviors

Although the particular steps in each strategy are different, certain teacher behaviors are necessary at all steps of a discussion. For example, teachers always must ask questions that are both open-ended and focused. Except for the listing step, they always must ask students to provide evidence or reasoning to support inferences unless support has been provided when the student gives an answer. Certain kinds of supporting behaviors also are necessary for particular types of steps. For example, every strategy begins with a listing of information that is relevant to the focus of the discussion. During this step, the teacher should encourage variety and ask questions that require students to clarify the meanings of words they use and provide specific data or facts rather than inferences.

General Behaviors

At all steps of Taba discussions, the teacher must encourage participation by all students and ask open-ended questions that will permit and encourage a variety of answers. Teachers must follow the appropriate sequence of steps and must avoid negative acts such as (a) giving opinions or value judgments about student ideas; (b) rejecting, ignoring, or cutting off a student response; (c) doing the task students are supposed to do; and (d) editing or changing a student's idea.

Other general supporting behaviors are accomplished through the appropriate four types of questioning techniques:

Questions Calling for Variety. These are questions to encourage students to come up with completely different responses from those already given.

- What else might happen?
- What are some completely different ways these items can be put together?
- What are some other causes for that?
- What else could we call that group?
- What are some completely different things she could do?

Questions Calling for Clarification or Extension. These are questions to encourage students to explain the meaning of statements or words, provide specific examples, or elaborate on an idea to extend its meaning.

- What do you mean by freedom?
- How is your idea different from Sally's?
- Please give me some examples of "transportation vehicles."
- Please explain more about that idea.
- What do you mean when you say _____?

Questions Calling for Reasons or Support for Ideas. These questions are used at all steps of discussions except when listing. They encourage students to explain or cite reasons for the inferences, conclusions, or generalizations they have made. Since asking for reasons or support is often threatening to students, questions should be clearly expressed and carefully used. They are used often, so the teacher must be able to vary the questions to avoid being repetitious.

- What are your reasons for grouping these items together?
- In what way are these items alike?

- Why do you think these items go together?
- How are these items alike?
- What is your basis for grouping these items together?
- What are you thinking that makes you say that?
- Tell us how you know that.
- What leads you to believe that?
- How do you know that _____ causes _____?
- How do you know that _____ results in _____?
- What makes you believe that _____ would be an effect of _____?
- What are your reasons for thinking that is true of all people?
- What from our discussion led you to that conclusion?

Focusing Questions. These are the initial questions that focus students on the task at a particular step. They should be worded carefully to be both open-ended and clear in their focus. If students stray from the topic or focus, the initial question needs to be restated to bring them back on task. Focusing questions also may need to be reworded to avoid monotony. Following are some examples of different focusing questions for particular purposes.

Grouping

- Which items could you put together because they are alike in some way?
- Which things would you group together because they are alike?
- Which items go together because they are alike?
- Which items would you put together in groups?

Causes and Prior Causes

- What has promoted _____?
- What are some factors contributing to _____?
- What helped _____ to come about?
- What do you think prevented _____?
- How did _____ happen?

Effects and Subsequent Effects

- What has happened because _____?
- What resulted after_____?
- What were the results of _____?
- What have been some of the consequences of _____?
- What do you think happened as a result of _____?

Supporting Behaviors for Specific Steps or Types of Tasks

As shown in Table 8.1, similarities exist among the types of tasks, important behaviors, teacher and student roles, and activities in the four Taba *Teaching Strategies*.

When getting the data, the teacher's main task, other than general support behaviors (for example, encouraging variety, clarification), is to make certain that students stick to the data rather than make inferences. If students begin to give inferences, the teacher should ask questions such as "What did you see (hear, read) that led you to believe that? Please give me an example of that from the story. What did her mother do that made you think that?" In the concept development task, students must give specific examples rather than categories. Otherwise, no items are available for grouping at the later steps.

Organizing data is a task that requires teachers to pay careful attention to possible structure of the data in order to facilitate the discussion. One way to keep things moving (with all but young children) is to put common numbers beside each item to indicate which group(s) it is in rather than rewriting lists. If this is done at the labeling step, the number can be written on the board in a separate place with the labels beside them. For example:

3, 1 item	3 item	1 - LABEL	2 - LABEL	3 - LABEL
2 item	1 item	LABEL	LABEL	LABEL
2 item	2 item	LABEL	LABEL	LABEL
3 item	1 item			

The first item is in two groups, 3 and 1. At the subsuming step, the task is easier since additional numbers are written beside the items when they are added to a group. With younger children, however, this system would be confusing. Writing the items on mountable tagboard strips facilitates classification and grouping as items can be moved close together. When an item is classified in more than one group, a duplicate strip can be made quickly and placed with the second group so that items and labels can be kept together. If groups are rewritten, space for writing labels above each group should be provided.

TABLE 8.1. General Supporting Behaviors in Taba's Teaching Strategies

Task	Teacher Role	Strategy	Student Role
Gathering information	Ask focusing questions. Request clarification. Seek variety. Make sure only data is given.	All	List relevant items. Clarify as necessary. Identify facts.
Organizing data	Ask focusing questions. Request reasons and support. Request clarification. Refocus students as needed.	All	Organize data (e.g., grouping, labeling, subsuming). Identify relationships. Give reasons/support.
Making inferences	Ask focusing questions. Ask for reasons and/or support. Ask for clarification. Refocus. Broaden patterns of thinking; seek variety.	All	Explain relationships. Justify inferences. Infer causes/effects. Identify conditions. Infer consequences. Actively listen. Subsume labels.
Generating alternatives	Ask focusing questions. Ask for reasons and/or support. Ask for clarification. Refocus.	All	Generate alternatives. Provide reasons/support. Consider consequences of varied actions. Actively listen.
Making conclusions	Ask focusing questions. Seek variety. Ask for clarification.	All	Conclude about causes/effects. Conclude about predictions. Evaluate alternatives. Support conclusions.
Making generalizations	Ask focusing question. Ask for clarification. Broaden patterns of thinking. Seek variety.	All but concept development	Form generalizations based on data, inferences, predictions. Evaluate generalizations.

Encouraging the whole group to participate is another important aspect of discussions that center around organization of data. For example, the teacher should encourage adding to the groups that have been formed based on the reasons the groups were initially made. Also, the whole group should be involved in recalling the reasons why groups were formed and in considering the appropriateness of labels. This should not be carried to the point of taking a vote, however.

To subsume is to classify into a larger category or under a more general principle. The subsuming task often is difficult for children to understand. They may need an example and, if so, the teacher should provide only one or two. If students have put items in two different groups at step two, this is a good example to point out. Sometimes young children will tend to combine groups or combine labels rather than subsume them. The teacher should respond to their combining by saying, "Yes, these labels do go together, but which one goes under the other?" or "Yes, these groups are alike, but which items from one of the groups could go under one of the labels we already have?" When items are moved at this step, they are not removed from the first group. They are added to other groups. Taking them out of the first group to put them in the second may reinforce the idea that they cannot belong in two places. This action would be detrimental to the idea that things can be classified on the basis of multiple attributes.

The task of making conclusions often is difficult for students, and they may tend to summarize the discussion. Conclusions must show evidence of synthesis and personal reflection rather than summarize or simply recount what was said. The statement should carry a personal conviction. To this end, the teacher should accept students' summaries but push them for a conclusion (for example, "Yes, that's what we said. Now, what do you think about what we said?").

Generalizing also is a difficult task for children. It requires careful thought, so they should be given time to think about and write their ideas before sharing them orally. Often, telling students to write a complete sentence will help. More important, however, is the teacher's focusing question. The question must be narrow enough to give students an idea of what the teacher wants. For example, after an interpretation of data discussion about the effects of differences between types of solvents, if a teacher asks, "What can you say generally about solvents?" anything they say is a shot in the dark. The question must relate to the focus of the discussion. In this example, since the students have been discussing effects (for example, what happens because there are differences between these solvents), the generalization question must focus them on effects. A more appropriate question would be the following: "What can you say generally about what happens when we use different kinds of solvents?" If the discussion were about causes, an appropriate question would be as follows: "What general statement could you make about why we use different kinds of solvents? Write a sentence about why you think there are differences in the types of solvents we use for chemical processes."

The Importance of Planning

When implementing the Taba *Strategies,* detailed planning is important if the objectives of each strategy are to be achieved. When learning the strategies and trying out a completely new approach or a complex idea, the teacher should develop a detailed plan that includes the following: (a) the content and process purposes of the strategy as a whole (including a sample generalization for all strategies except concept development), (b) the prediscussion procedures, (c) the objectives at each step that are specific to this lesson, (d) focusing questions for each step, (e) support procedures for each step, and (f) a "cognitive map" of possible student responses to the focusing questions at each step.

The sequence of the planning process is as follows:

- Identify the overall content and process purposes, developing a planning generalization when appropriate.

- Identify the prediscussion procedures and necessary materials.

- Develop the actual discussion plan for each step in a particular order. First, write the objective specific to that lesson, then write a focusing question for that step. Next, consider the focusing question, and write some possible student responses to the question on the cognitive map. Based on this tryout of the question, rewrite it to improve clarity if necessary, write the question asking for reasons or support, and write some support procedures that will be necessary for achieving the desired objective at that step.

By following this sequence in detail, teachers can increase the likelihood of a thoughtful and successful discussion.

After the strategies are learned and when a familiar topic is the focus, a shorter and simpler process is followed using a short form. With the short form, teachers plan only a focusing question for each step and develop a sample cognitive map.

Summary of Steps and Activities

Learning how to use the *Hilda Taba Teaching Strategies* program is not simple. The strategies are complicated, and differences between an appropriate and an inappropriate teacher question or behavior that can throw a whole discussion off track often are subtle. Although comprehensive, this description of the strategies would not enable a person to use them effectively. Demonstrations, practice followed by critiques from experienced leaders, classroom tryouts, and self-analysis are necessary components in the learning process. Many teachers feel years of practice have been necessary for them to perfect their techniques. However, they also attest to the effectiveness of the strategies when implemented appropriately. Table 8.2 presents a summary of student and teacher roles and activities in each type of task in the *Hilda Taba Teaching Strategies*.

MODIFICATION OF THE BASIC CURRICULUM

The Taba model suggests modifications of the regular curriculum that are appropriate for the gifted in process, content, product, and learning environment. Although primarily a process approach, Taba's (1962, 1964) comprehensive approach to curriculum development and implementation provides for many changes that are important in programs for gifted students. Content modifications suggested by the approach are in abstractness, complexity, organization for learning value, and methods of inquiry. Process changes are an emphasis on higher levels of thinking; open-endedness; use of discovery, requiring students to verbalize their reasoning or evidence; group interaction; and pacing. One product modification, transformation, is suggested. Four learning environment changes are suggested: learner centered, independence, openness, and acceptance.

Content Modifications

A good example of the content changes suggested by Taba and Bruner is the social studies curriculum (Ellis & Durkin, 1972) developed and field-tested during the same time period as the teaching strategies. Since Taba assumed an interactive relationship between content organization and quality and the processes taught, naturally, Taba would test these at the same time. The best way to explain how the Taba model suggests content changes is to provide examples from this curriculum. In the social studies curriculum, three levels of knowledge serve different organizational functions.

Key Concepts

The most abstract knowledge level is key concepts. These are words that represent highly generalized abstractions that were selected because of their power to synthesize and organize large numbers of specific facts and ideas. These words are developed in a more abstract and complex way at each higher

TABLE 8.2. Summary of Teacher and Student Roles and Activities in the Taba Teaching Strategies Program

Step, Type, or Level of Thinking	Student		Teacher	
	Role	Sample Activities	Role	Sample Activities
Getting the data	Observer Active participant Listener	Notice what happened. Recall events or knowledge from past experience. Generate ideas.	Presenter Questioner Facilitator Active listener	Present a situation, provide information to read, or initiate some other "intake" experience. Ask focusing questions to get students to recall specific facts/data from past experience or the intake experience. Ask for clarification when needed. Ask refocusing questions when needed. Strive for a variety of specific facts/data.
Organizing data	Active participant Listener	Group like items together. Provide labels for groups. Subsume items under labels. Subsume labels under labels. Explain reasons for grouping, labeling, and subsuming. Listen to the ideas and reasons of others. Think of different ideas.	Questioner Active listener Facilitator	Ask questions that invite students to group, label, subsume, and recycle. Ask for clarification when needed. Seek variety. Ask refocusing questions as needed. Ask for support or reasoning for all answers given. Encourage student-to-student interaction.

(continues)

TABLE 8.2. *Continued*

Step, Type, or Level of Thinking	Student		Teacher	
	Role	Sample Activities	Role	Sample Activities
Making inferences	Active participant Listener	Make inferences about causes and prior causes of data. Make inferences about effects and subsequent effects of data. Explain reasoning behind inferences made. Make predictions about a hypothetical situation. Infer conditions necessary to make a prediction come true. Infer consequences of predictions. Listen to the ideas and reasoning of others. Think of different ideas.	Questioner Active listener Facilitator	Ask questions that stimulate students to make inferences and focus on the task. Ask for clarification when necessary. Ask for support or reasoning for all answers given. Ask refocusing questions when necessary. Seek variety.
Generating alternatives	Active participant Listener	Develop alternative courses of action for each individual involved in a conflict situation. Think of new ideas. Listen to ideas of others.	Questioner Active listener Facilitator	Ask questions to focus students on the task. Divide class into pairs or small groups. Ask for clarification when needed. Seek variety.

(*continues*)

TABLE 8.2. *Continued*

Step, Type, or Level of Thinking	Student		Teacher	
	Role	Sample Activities	Role	Sample Activities
Drawing conclusions	Synthesizer Listener Active participant	Evaluate alternatives for action. Think about the discussion and reach a conclusion about the most likely outcome. Explain reasons for conclusions. Reach a conclusion about important causes or effects. Listen actively to the ideas of others; react thoughtfully to them.	Questioner Active listener Facilitator	Ask questions to focus students on the task. Ask for clarification when needed. Ask refocusing questions when needed. Accept summaries, but ask for interpretations and conclusions. Encourage student-to-student interaction.
Making generalizations	Synthesizer Generalizer Active participant	Make general, abstract statements about causes, effects, or human behaviors. Examine the general statements made by others; thoughtfully react to them. Explain reasons for general statements or evaluations of statements of others. Write generalizations in complete sentences.	Questioner Active listener Facilitator	Ask questions that focus or refocus students on task. Ask for clarification, extension, and elaboration when necessary. Encourage student-to-student interaction. Wait for students to think. Present a generalization for students to examine in the application of generalizations strategy.

grade level and form threads running throughout the program. Some examples of key concepts are causality, conflict, cultural change, differences, institutions, interdependence, and modification. In an overview of the Taba program, generalizations pertaining to each key concept illustrate the meaning or use of that key concept. For example, the explanation of interdependence is the following:

All persons and groups of persons depend on other persons and groups in important ways. These effects on others are often indirect and not apparent.

The solution of important human problems requires human beings to engage in joint effort. The more complex the society is, the more cooperation is required.

Cooperation often requires compromise and postponement of immediate satisfactions. (pp. T4, T5)

Main, Organizing, and Contributing Ideas

The second level of knowledge consists first of main ideas, which serve as the answer to the question of what the students will need to remember after they forget specific facts. Each year's work centers around several main ideas, which may be treated as a hierarchy reappearing at several grade levels. The *main idea* expresses a relationship that applies both to the content being studied and to parallel examples of human behavior in other settings. Some examples of main ideas related to interdependence are the following:

Main Idea 1:
Interaction between people and their physical environment influences the ways in which they meet their needs.

Main Idea 3:
The way people choose to live and the knowledge they have influence the use they make of their environment (p. T31).

Main idea 1 is developed at grades 3, 6, and 7. In addition to the key concept of interdependence, this main idea also involves the concepts of modification, power, and tradition. Main idea 3 is developed at grades 1, 2, and 3. It involves the key concepts of differences, modification, and tradition, in addition to the concept of interdependence.

The *organizing idea* is an example of the main idea as it pertains to the particular content being studied in each unit. It is stated in a way that enables students to understand and use it. *Contributing ideas* represent generalizations that illustrate further dimensions of the main idea. Examples of organizing and contributing ideas that relate to the main ideas listed earlier are the following:

Main Idea 1:
Interaction between people and their physical environment influences the way in which they meet their needs.

Organizing Idea:
The Bedouin modify their behavior and their environment in order to make a living (p. T31).

Contributing Ideas:
Herders living in a desert area may be able to meet their needs by modifying their behavior (p. T33).

Herders in a desert area may be able to make a living by modifying their environment (p. T34).

The seasons influence the way in which herders of the desert meet their needs (p. T34).

Main Idea 3:
The way people choose to live and the knowledge they have influence the use they make of their environment.

Organizing Idea:
The Yoruba people combine their skills as farmers and craftsmen. Their organization allows them to live in a city and yet farm some distance from home (p. T31).

Contributing Ideas:
The products of an agricultural group allow its producers to meet many of their needs (p. T83).

A specialized society requires a means of exchange (p. T83).

A specialized society fosters interdependence among its people (p. T83).

Content Samples

The lowest level of knowledge, specific facts or content samples, provides the means for illustrating, explaining, and developing the main ideas as well as the organizing and contributing ideas. They are in the form of an in-depth study of human behavior and are selected because they demonstrate the main idea. They are sufficient in depth, richness, and breadth to provide the opportunity for students to develop their own generalizations, which approximate the main and organizing ideas. Some examples of specific content samples used to develop the main, organizing, and contributing ideas given earlier are the following:

Main Idea 1:
The Bedouin
    move regularly in order to get food and water.
    herd animals adapted to the desert environment.
    use animals for transportation.

The Bedouin
    plant some crops to feed their animals.
    get water from wells.
    store grain and food for winter use.
    use animals to meet need for food, clothing, and shelter (p. T34).

Main Idea 3:
    The Yoruba farmer meets many of his needs
        by using mixed-crop farming to feed his family.
        by using his cocoa crop to get cash to buy clothes, tools, etc.
    The Yoruba use the marketplace
        as a place for the exchange of goods.
        as a place for earning a living.
    The Yoruba craftsmen exchange services.
        Blacksmith makes hoes for farmers.
        Leatherworker makes drum pieces for the drummer (p. T83).

In these examples, the abstract key concepts and generalizations are used as the organizing framework for the content presented to students. These concepts and generalizations also are complex in that they include several traditional content areas and integrate methods of study or "thought systems" into the study of a particular discipline.

Process and Product Modifications

Process modifications appropriate for the gifted are integral parts of the Taba *Strategies*. Higher levels of thinking are developed through the sequential tasks (spurred by teacher questions) in each of the strategies and by each strategy as a whole. The four basic strategies are arranged hierarchically. Open-endedness is a necessary ingredient since all teacher questions are required to be open-ended and since the focusing and extending questions also are provocative. Having students verbalize their reasoning and support for inferences is also an integral, required aspect of the Taba *Strategies*. Taba provides many suggestions for appropriate pacing in discussions, and she supplies specific techniques for facilitating interaction between students in a group.

In the Taba model direct product modifications are made only in the area of transformation. Emphasis is placed on student participation in analysis of content, and students are encouraged to organize, interpret, and evaluate the information they receive, then develop their own conclusions and generalizations about it. Because of this active involvement, if the teacher is using the strategies appropriately, the products developed will be transformations. During this process, students also learn skills in appropriate evaluation of their own products and the products of others. They are encouraged to critique and react to others' logic and products.

Learning Environment Modifications

Correct and frequent implementation of the Taba *Strategies* ensures that the learning environment will be learner centered. Since the strategies are discussion techniques, if they are used frequently, the teacher will conduct few lectures. Also, with the major focus placed on student ideas, the teacher is not the central figure in discussions. Most of the general support behaviors discussed earlier would ensure a learner-centered classroom, for example, asking open-ended questions, asking questions calling for variety, avoiding opinions or value judgments, encouraging student reaction/response to student ideas, and waiting for students.

Independence is fostered through the strategies by emphasis on student ideas. Students are encouraged to explain and justify their ideas, and teachers are discouraged from expressing their opinions of the ideas and from editing or changing the ideas when recording them. Specific skills involved in interpersonal independence also are taught through the fourth strategy, resolution of conflict. In this strategy, students generate alternatives, predict consequences, evaluate alternatives, and suggest ways of applying what they have learned to personal situations. Thus, this technique develops specific ways for students to manage their own playground and classroom behavior, an essential element in the development of independence.

An open environment is developed through appropriate implementation of the Taba *Strategies*. No restrictions are placed on the types of answers that can be given, and the teacher does not suggest in any way that the students conform to an ideal. In fact, teachers encourage and push for divergent ideas through their methods of questioning. No restrictions are placed on the kind of generalization(s) that can be developed and stated as a result of a discussion.

Acceptance rather than judgment is another integral aspect of the Taba *Strategies*. Teachers are cautioned against providing an opinion or value judgment of a student idea. They are to accept all ideas and encourage the students to look at their own statements by asking questions of clarification, extension, and support. Student ideas are not even edited or changed when they are written on the blackboard. Teacher questions are designed to develop understanding of, clarification of, and support for student ideas rather than criticism of them. Such questions have the effect of encouraging through examination of ideas, which usually results in a consideration of both their positive and negative aspects, rather than only the negative.

Examples of Teaching Activities

To provide a specific example of the teaching strategies and to illustrate the relationship between process and content, a series of four lessons will be described. They would be used to develop the key concepts and main ideas given as examples in the previous section.

Concept Development

The first lesson, concept development, is designed to clarify and extend the key concept of interdependence. It could be used also at the beginning of the year or at the beginning of a unit in which the concept is introduced. It could be used also at the end of the year as a way to get students to integrate all their knowledge related to the concept. Students would be drawing from the specific content of several units (for example, from information about both the Bedouin of the Negev and the Yoruba of Ife). When used at the beginning of the year, the discussion serves a diagnostic function for teachers, and when used at the end, it can serve as an evaluative one. Following are the focusing question(s) for each step in the lesson:

Step 1. Listing

What are some specific ways the people we have studied depend on each other or on other people or tribes?

Step 2. Grouping

(a)   Which of these ways of depending on each other would you group together because they are alike?

(b)   Why would you group those together?

Step 3. Labeling

(a)   Based on the reasons why we put these ways of depending together, what would be a good label for this group?

(b)   Why is _____ a good label?

Step 4. Subsuming

(a)   Which of these ways of depending that is already under one label also could go under another label?

(b)   What are your reasons for putting _____ under _____?

Step 5. Recycling

(a)   Now, look back at our original list of ways people depend on each other. Which of these ways could be put together in completely different groups?

(b)   What are your reasons for putting those together?

(c–f) Ask the initial focusing questions for steps three and four about these new groupings.

Interpretation of Data

The second lesson, interpretation of data, involves students in analyzing specific data related to the lives of the Bedouin. The planning generalization is main idea 1. (See Table 8.3.) Since this main idea also is developed in the unit about the Yoruba, a similar lesson could be used with that specific data. At step five in the lesson, students are expected to state a generalization that goes beyond their specific knowledge of either of the groups studied. This generalization may be similar to the main idea developed.

In this lesson, the focus is on causes for the Bedouin lifestyle. A similar lesson could be planned focusing on effects relating either to the Bedouin or Yoruba. In this detailed plan, the lesson has both a content and process purpose, and objectives, focusing questions, and support procedures are developed for each step in the discussion. A major part of this planning process is the development of the cognitive map, a listing of the possible responses students might make to the focusing questions. The cognitive map helps teachers see where the discussion could go and helps them develop support procedures necessary to keep the discussion moving. This includes the possible data (step one), possible causes (steps two and three), possible conclusions (step four), and possible generalizations (step five). When conducting the lesson, however, teachers must remember that the cognitive map is developed only for planning purposes, and they should not attempt to elicit answers from students that are written on the cognitive map.

To develop the concept of interdependence further, interpretation of data discussions could be held that focus on the ways the Bedouin and Yoruba depend on their own people and on others. For example, (a) within each extended family, each person has duties that contribute to the whole group; (b) the Bedouin travel to the market to purchase imported goods; and (c) in hard times, the Bedouin graze their herds on Israeli lands. These examples of interdependence are listed as data, and the discussion can focus on either causes of this interdependence or effects of it. Several discussions of different people can take place.

Application of Generalizations

The next discussion, application of generalizations, follows interpretation of data by asking students to predict what kind of lifestyle might be developed by a group of people in some futuristic society. When presenting a hypothetical situation, the teacher describes the physical environment of another planet

TABLE 8.3. Sample Discussion Plan for Interpretation of Data Lesson

Discussion Purposes	
Content: To draw warranted conclusions about the following relationships: People and their physical environment + The ways people meet their needs *Process:* To make and support cause-and-effect inferences, to draw warranted conclusions, and to generalize from specific instances to other such instances.	**Topic:** The Bedouin of the Negev **Level:** Intermediate **Prediscussion Procedures:** Arrange students in a semicircle. Have chalkboard/chalk or butcher paper and markers available. **Materials:** Library resources on the Bedouin people.

Behavioral Objectives	*Focusing Questions*	*Support Procedures*
Step One—Data: Students will enumerate what they know or have read about the ways the Bedouin people meet their basic needs for survival.	What are some things you know about the Bedouin people? What are some things you have learned about the ways Bedouin people meet their basic needs for food and shelter?	Encourage students to list data about the lifestyle, food, shelter, and habits of the Bedouin people. Seek a variety of observations. Focus on facts rather than inferences.
Step Two—Causes (a) Students will state inferences about the causes for the ways Bedouin people meet their basic needs. (b) Students will cite evidence or reasoning to support their inferences.	(a1) What are some possible causes for (e.g., the Bedouin people moving from place to place)? (b1) Why would that (e.g., dry climate) cause them to move around? (a2) What causes (e.g., children learning mainly from their parents)? (b2) Why would moving from place to place cause (e.g., children learning mainly from their parents)?	Choose data to follow up that provides the most promise of eliciting causes relating to the environment and people. Seek a variety of causes for each item of data. Ask for support for inferences immediately after inferences are given. The basic question when seeking support is "Why does (cause) cause (data)?"

(continues)

TABLE 8.3. *Continued*

Behavioral Objectives	Focusing Questions	Support Procedures
Step Three—Prior Causes (a) Students will state inferences about the prior causes of selected causes given at Step Two. (b) Students will cite evidence or reasoning to support their inferences.	(a1) Why do you think (e.g., the pastures are picked over by summer)? (b1) Why do you think (e.g., winter rains would cause pastures to be picked over by spring)? (a2) What are some of the causes of (e.g., each man having several wives)? (b2) Why would (e.g., needing a large family cause men to have several wives)?	Step Three can be repeated many times. Depth of thought is developed through asking for prior causes of the prior causes. Choose causes and prior causes that will elicit answers relating the environment to the people. Ask for a variety of prior causes for each selected cause. Seek support for all inferences. The basic question is "Why does (prior cause) cause (cause)?" Step 3 answer Step 2 answer
Step Four—Conclusions (a) Students will state conclusions about the causes for the Bedouin lifestyle. (b) Students will cite evidence or reasons for their conclusions.	(a) Thinking back over our discussion, what would you say are the most important causes for the Bedouin people meeting their basic needs in the ways that they do? (b) Why do you think (e.g., the climate) is an important cause for the Bedouin lifestyle?	Encourage each child to reach her/his own conclusions. Encourage a variety of conclusions. Ask for clarification of ideas when needed. Encourage synthesis of inferences about causes rather than summaries. Conclude about *causes*.
Step Five—Generalizations (a) Students will generalize about the causes for the ways most people meet their basic needs. (b) Students will cite support for their statements.	(a) What would you say generally about what causes all people everywhere to live the way they do? (b) Why do you think (e.g., the characteristics of people and their environment) determine the ways people meet their basic needs?	Allow time for students to jot down some ideas before asking for responses. Ask students to write a complete sentence or statement. Encourage each student to write a statement. Ask for clarification when needed. Encourage students to consider information about other peoples they have studied.

(continues)

TABLE 8.3. *Continued*

Planning Generalization: Interaction between people and their physical environment influences the ways they meet their basic needs.	

Cognitive Map

Possible Prior Causes and Causes		*Possible Data*
Winters are cold. There are no rains in spring. Most have large herds. Rains come in winter. They store their heavy tents in the summer. They stay in one place in the winter. A large family is needed to care for animals. Some social life is needed. Each man has several wives. The land supports very few people. They must constantly look for food and water. They are not technologically advanced.	They must continually move to find grass. There is little rain. The desert is dry and doesn't support much grass. Pastures are picked over by summer. Winters are cold and rainy. They live in heavy tents in the winter. Most of the year, they are moving. They seldom see each other except in winter. Often, the religious month comes in winter time. Children are needed to help with crops and animals. Families live together. Families move around. There are few towns and cities. Meeting basic needs takes most of their time.	The Bedouins live in tents. Barley crops are planted in the fall. The Bedouins move from place to place except in winter. The whole family helps with the harvest. Winter is a social time. Baby animals are born in the winter. They seldom go to the marketplace to buy goods. Children learn mainly from their parents. Money is made from selling animals.

Possible Conclusions
The climate of the desert causes the people to live the way they do.
The Bedouin have to live in tents and move around because they must follow the grass with their herds.
The Bedouins live together in tents because they are in a lonely desert and must have some time and opportunities to socialize.
The major causes of the Bedouin's nomadic lifestyle are the climate, the terrain, and the traditions of the people.

Possible Generalizations
People everywhere develop ways to meet their needs for survival that depend on the environment in which they live.
The inherited traits, traditions, and religion of a people and the characteristics of the environment in which they live determine the ways in which food, shelter, and needed clothing are obtained and the type of food, shelter, and clothing that are needed.

and provides a description of the habits, traditions, and values of the people who have landed on the planet. The students are asked to predict what will happen to the people. Following are sample discussion questions at each step of application of generalizations:

Step 1. Predictions

(a) What do you think these people will be like after 30 years?

(b) Why would you predict that they will, e.g., develop highly industrial-ized cities?

Step 2. Conditions

(a) What other things will have to happen or be true in order for, e.g., these people to develop highly industrialized cities?

(b) What are your reasons for believing that, e.g., technology on the rest of the planet would have to be very advanced?

Step 3. Consequences and Conditions (Recycle 1 and 2)

(a) Suppose that all you said was necessary did occur and the people did, e.g., develop highly industrialized cities. What would happen as a re-sult of that?

(b) Why do you think, e.g., that these people would become the rulers of the planet?

(c) Under what conditions, e.g., would these people become rulers or take control of the planet?

(d) Why would it be necessary, e.g., for the other people to be living in scattered small cities?

This step can be continued or recycled as many times as necessary to focus students on a variety of possible, opposite predictions.

Step 4. Conclusions

(a) From all we've said, what would you conclude is likely to be the lifestyle of these people in 30 years?

(b) Why have you decided, e.g., they will become an industrialized nation?

Step 5. Generalizations

(a) Considering our discussion of what might happen to these people, what changes or additions, if any, would you make in the following statement: "All persons and groups of persons depend on other persons and groups in important ways"?

(b) Why would you, e.g., change it to read "depend on other persons, groups, and the environment"?

In this discussion, the two main ideas presented earlier are used as the planning subgeneralizations that students are expected to apply in making their predictions. At step five, they are asked to go beyond these subgeneralizations and examine an even bigger or more abstract idea, a "description" of the key concept of interdependence.

Resolution of Conflict

After the interpretation of data and application of generalizations discussions, or at any other point in a unit, the discussions can focus on the people, their feelings, their attitudes, and their values. One way to do this is through a resolution of conflict lesson involving conflict between new and old ways of life. For example, students read a story about a Bedouin son who is a member of a large family of uncles, aunts, and cousins. His father is considered the head of the family. The son wants to use his money earned from selling cattle to buy a jeep, and eventually he wants to go to school in town. The son tries to convince his father of the usefulness of a jeep to their family and tribe, but his father does not want to listen. Following are the focusing questions that would be asked in such a discussion.

Step 1. Listing

• What happened in the story?

• What did the son do/say?

• What did the father do/say?

Step 2. Reasons and Feelings

(a) Why do you think, e.g., the son wanted to buy the jeep?

(b) How did the boy's father feel about, e.g., the son wanting to buy the jeep?

(c) Why do you think the father felt, e.g., threatened?

Step 3. Alternatives and Consequences

(a) What are some things the son could do to resolve the conflict?

(b)   If the son, e.g., goes ahead and buys the jeep even though his father disapproves, what do you think will be the consequences?

(c)   Why do you think, e.g., the father will disown the boy?

Step 4. Solutions and Long-Range Consequences

(a)   Looking over the possible solutions we have listed, what do you think is the best thing the boy can do?

(b)   Why would, e.g., saving his money be the best thing for the boy to do?

(c)   What do you think would be some of the long-term effects of, e.g., the boy saving his money?

(d)   What leads you to believe that, e.g., the father will eventually allow the son to go to college if he saves the money now rather than spending it on the jeep?

Step 5. Listing—Similar Situation

• Thinking about this story, what are some similar situations you have experienced or know about in which a conflict occurs between new and old ways of life?

• What happened?

• What were the new and old ways?

• What did you (or the other person) do?

Step 6. Feelings

(a)   How did you feel about, e.g., your parents wanting you to go to a private school?

(b)   Why do you think you felt, e.g., upset?

or

(a)   How do you think your parents felt about, e.g., you wanting to go to an integrated public school when they offered to pay private tuition?

(b)   Why do you think they felt, e.g., hurt?

Step 7. Evaluation

(a)   What were your reasons for choosing, e.g., the public school?

(b)   Thinking back on the situation, how would you evaluate your decision?

(c)   Why do you think, e.g., you did the right thing?

Step 8. Alternatives and Consequences

(a)   In what ways might you have handled the situation differently?

(b)   What do you think would have been the consequences of, e.g., dropping out of school completely?

(c)   Why do you think, e.g., your parents would have realized that you were right?

Step 9. Generalizations

(a)   Thinking back over the situations we have discussed in which there is a conflict between old and new ways of life, what could you say generally about the way people handle situations like that?

(b)   What did we say or what do you know that would lead you to believe that, e.g., young people usually choose new ways?

A lesson similar to this could also be planned in which the conflict is between two Bedouin tribes or between the Bedouin and people living in Beersheba or one of the other marketplaces. Other lessons could involve a conflict between the Bedouin and the Yoruba, two groups that had been studied recently. These lessons integrate knowledge from several content units and can be used before, during, and/or after the units. If used before, they may enhance interest in the upcoming units of study and serve a diagnostic function. When used during a unit, they could serve as another way to apply the information learned. When used after a unit they could serve as a vehicle for integrating knowledge gained from the two content units.

MODIFYING THE APPROACH

Content Changes

Although the Taba model makes many of the content, process, and learning environment changes recommended for the gifted, the approach will be more appropriate for use with gifted children if certain additions are made. For example, the two content changes not made by the model are variety and the study of people. The study of people can be integrated easily by using the Taba *Strategies* as methods to study the lives of productive, eminent people.

Interpretation of data can be used to make inferences about the causes for the characteristics of eminent people or to make inferences about the effects these characteristics had on their products or their careers. Application of generalizations can be used to predict what would have happened to a famous or eminent individual if that person lived today or in a different period of time. Resolution of conflict can be used to examine conflicts in the lives of the individuals, either inner, personal conflicts or conflicts between individuals. The students can then discuss similar situations in their own lives.

A second content change, variety, can be accomplished in a way that is similar to the modification of Bruner's approach described in Chapter 4. Using this worksheet (see Exhibit 8.1), the teacher can write the key concept at the top. The main idea becomes the generalization. Instead of listing the concepts involved in the generalization, the teacher can list the contributing ideas. Organizing ideas and content samples that pertain to the main idea are then listed as data, either data taught in the regular curriculum or data that need to be taught in the special program. Exhibit 8.1 provides an example using the ideas presented earlier in this section.

In this example, in the regular curriculum, students learn about farmers and herders in this country. To further develop the concept of interdependence in the special program, they would learn about the Bedouin and the Yoruba as other examples of how people must depend on each other and how the environment influences their lives. By analyzing the content taught in the regular program according to key concepts and ideas, educators retain the organization, and what is taught in the special curriculum is different from the regular curriculum.

Process Changes

Only two process modifications need to be incorporated into the Taba model: freedom of choice and variety. To ensure freedom of choice of topics, one teacher of the gifted (Maker, 1982) allows the students to choose general topic areas for discussion several weeks in advance. She then selects the planning generalizations and reading materials and plans a Taba discussion on the topics chosen. Other ways of integrating freedom of choice would be the following: (a) in the *application of generalizations* strategy, students could choose one or more of the predictions given at the first step and develop reasons, conditions, and consequences for it; (b) in the *resolution of conflict* strategy, students could choose conflict situations to discuss, they could select alternatives to develop, and they could write about similar situations of their own choice; (c) in the *concept development* strategy, they could choose either the concepts to be discussed or the data to be used at the listing step; and (d) *interpretation of data* could involve interpreting (discussing) the data chosen by students.

EXHIBIT 8.1.   Sample Worksheet for Overall Curriculum Design—Building Content Plans upon the Regular Curriculum

---

Key Concept: Interdependence

Main Idea #1: Interaction between people and their physical environment influences the ways in which they meet their needs.

Contributing Ideas:

(a) People living in a desert area may be able to meet their needs by modifying their behavior.

(b) People living in a desert area may be able to make a living through modification of their environment.

(c) The seasons influence the way in which nomadic people living in a desert meet their needs.

(d) The products of an agricultural group allow its producers to meet many of their needs.

(e) A specialized society requires a medium of exchange.

(f) A specialized society fosters interdependence among its people.

Organizing Ideas and Content Samples Regular Program	Organizing Ideas and Content Samples Special Program

Farmers in the western United States modify their environment and their behavior to meet their needs (CI #b). Farmers
 	
  irrigate their crops.
  build very few fences.
  use large ranches rather than small farms.
  organize cooperative groups to supply water to all.
Farmers of the United States sell their crops to provide money for needed goods and services (CI #f). Farmers buy
 	
  specialized equipment for harvesting.
  materials for building homes.
  veterinary services.
  repair services for equipment.
  fuel for equipment.
	The Bedouin people modify their behavior and their environment in order to meet basic needs for survival (CI #b)
	
	The Bedouin
	
	  move regularly to get food and water.
	  use animals for transportation.
	  herd animals adapted to the desert environment.
	  plant some crops to feed animals.
	  store grain and food for winter.
	The Yoruba craftsmen exchange services (CI #f).
	
	  The blacksmith makes hoes for farmers.
	  The leatherworker makes drum pieces for the drummer.

Another way to incorporate freedom of choice would be to allow students to choose areas of study, investigate them independently, and then organize discussions so that all students "pool" their knowledge and findings. These are processes used in both the *Group Investigations* model (see Chapter 7) and the *Autonomous Learner Model* (see Chapter 2). For example, in the social studies unit, each student or group of students could select the people of interest to them. Using the basic plans for the lessons presented as examples, each student or group would list data at step one that pertained to the group of people they were studying. After the first step, all students should be encouraged to make inferences about all data, not just the information they reported. In this way, students not only have freedom to study topics of interest to them, but they also learn a variety of information from other students.

Variety in methods is integrated through alternating different methods with the basic discussion strategy. The first step, getting the information, is a part of each strategy. Students can get the information they need to participate in a discussion in many different ways, such as playing a simulation game, reading an article, listening to a tape, participating in a role-playing incident, listening to a lecture, watching a film, watching a television program, or making observations. The first author once conducted a lesson on prejudice in which the students' task was to observe and record evidence of prejudice through taking pictures, taping conversations, or making notes on things they had heard or seen. These observations were then used as a basis for concept development, interpretation of data, and resolution of conflict discussions.

Other variations can be made by having the same intellectual tasks done by the students but in small-group or individual settings. One example is making the concept development task into a game. The students are given a variety of cards with either pictures or words pertaining to a certain concept. They are to make as many different groupings as possible, provide at least three labels for each group, and indicate which items go under different labels. The teacher can discuss the groupings with students individually and ask their reasons for groups, labels, and subsuming, or the teacher can have a small group of students share their groups, labels, reasons, subsuming, and regroupings. Another easy way to vary any of the strategies is to alternate small- and large-group activities and to integrate individual activities. With the application of generalizations strategy, for instance, students can work in small groups to develop their predictions. The groups then share these predictions and discuss reasons. Resolution of conflict lends itself to small-group or individual work when the task is to generate alternatives. Students also could develop a "similar situation" in this strategy through a writing assignment.

The easiest way to vary the Taba *Strategies* is to alternate between small and large groups or to vary the groupings. Since interaction with at least a small group is important, any individual work would need to be shared in a discussion setting.

Product Changes

Since the Taba model makes direct changes only in one area (transformation), the Taba *Strategies* should be used differently to provide product modifications. One of the most important ways to use the strategies would be to teach students the steps involved in each strategy. This can be done by having "debriefing" sessions after the discussions to show students the steps (intellectual tasks) and questions asked by the teacher at each step. After participating in several discussions, the students will learn the processes and will be able to use them in their individual investigations and product development.

As an important aspect of this process, the teacher should show students how the different strategies can be helpful to them in their product development. The concept development strategy is useful at the beginning of a project to organize questions about a topic. The first author often has used this strategy with graduate students as a way to help them develop thesis or dissertation topics. The graduate students first list or brainstorm all the questions they have about a topic, then they group, label, subsume, and regroup these questions. Often this exercise helps them to clarify what they want to investigate and to select the major questions and minor subquestions.

Concept development also is useful as a process for organizing a final product. For articles, chapters, and even longer pieces, the process can be used in the following way: (a) list all the important information that needs to be included, as specifically as possible; (b) group the similar items together; (c) develop titles for the groups; (d) subsume items; (e) examine each category to see whether all the essential information has been included; and (f) try another regrouping of all the information in an attempt to find a better organization. The titles for the groups become subheadings, and the items within each category are then combined and explained to form the text.

The concept development strategy also can be used in research to analyze the content of responses to open-ended questions. All of the responses to a particular question can be listed, preferably one response to a note card. These cards can then be sorted by one person into piles containing similar items. After the groups have been completed, titles can be given, and then the subsuming task is attempted. A second person can then take the titles of the groups along with a description of the groups and attempt to classify the items into the groupings established by the first individual. The degree to which they classify items into the same groups is the index of agreement. If the index of agreement is high, the groupings remain the same, perhaps with minor changes, but if their agreement is low, completely new groupings may need to be made.

The interpretation of data strategy is useful as a technique for developing discussions and conclusions after an experiment has been conducted. The data collected in the experiment comprise the information used at step one. The investigator or writer then follows through the process by developing inferences about either causes or effects of the data or both causes and effects. Prior causes and subsequent effects also are listed, as are conclusions and generalizations. These inferences, conclusions, and generalizations then are used as the basis of discussion of and conclusions about the research. Use of this strategy before actually beginning the task of writing can make the writing easier and can ensure that many different aspects of the experiment will be considered rather than just the most obvious.

Application of generalizations is a useful process for developing products that involve making predictions or forecasting future events. As such, it is an extremely useful tool in developing hypotheses to guide experimental research. In addition to the development of hypotheses, the strategy can be used to predict how audiences might react to a certain product. Each individual could use the process when developing a product, or the teacher could lead group discussions to assist each student in the development of products acceptable to different audiences.

When students are involved in group investigations or development of products, conflicts are bound to arise. The resolution of conflict strategy is an excellent process for solving these problems. It also can be used to develop fictional stories involving some kind of conflict between people.

In summary, the Taba *Strategies* can provide useful processes for students and teachers in the development of products that address real problems, are directed toward real audiences, and are evaluated realistically.

Learning Environment Changes

The only two learning environment modifications not made by the Taba strategies are complexity and high mobility. These changes certainly are necessary if students are to develop professional products of the caliber expected of the gifted. Students need a variety of complex references and equipment for their use, or they need ready access to these items. Movement in and out of the classroom is necessary for access to supplies and environments not in the classroom. Flexible grouping arrangements also are necessary so that interaction with gifted peers can occur during discussions.

Summary

Although the Taba *Strategies* make many of the content, process, and learning environment changes recommended for the gifted, certain modifications and additions still need to be made if Taba's approach is to be used as a comprehensive curriculum for the gifted. It can be combined easily with Renzulli's model, with Bruner's approach, and with *Self-Directed Learning,* the *Autonomous Learner Model,* and *Group Investigations.*

DEVELOPMENT

Two aspects of Taba's approach discussed in this chapter—the specific teaching strategies and the social studies curriculum—were developed along separate but related lines. The *Hilda Taba Teaching Strategies* program (Institute for Staff Development, 1971a, 1971b, 1971c, 1971d) resulted from the refinement of the teaching strategies and teacher training program used in three studies of the effectiveness of teaching strategies in the development of children's thinking (Taba, 1964, 1966; Wallen et al., 1969). The *Taba Program in Social Science* (Ellis & Durkin, 1972) was developed concurrently but was more complete before the studies of children's thinking were completed than were the strategies. In the research projects, as in Taba's theoretical orientation, content and process were somewhat separate entities but played complementary roles. For instance, in the research projects, Taba's (1964) overall objective was "to examine the development of thought under the optimum training conditions" (p. 27). These optimum conditions included the following: (a) a curriculum designed to develop thinking skills, (b) teaching strategies focused specifically on the mastery of certain thinking skills, and (c) an adequate time span for a developmental sequence in training.

Development of the social studies curriculum that was ultimately published by Addison-Wesley (Ellis & Durkin, 1972) actually was begun much earlier, with Taba's involvement in the development of a social studies curriculum for Contra Costa County, California. Development of the teaching strategies program began with the first research project in 1964. Hilda Taba's untimely death in 1967 left much of her work incomplete. However, several of her associates completed the different projects: Norman Wallen and his associates at San Francisco State College completed the research project in 1969; Lyle and Sydelle Ehrenberg, with the help of other associates of Taba, completed the teacher-training and teaching strategies program and founded the Institute for Staff Development to provide this training nationwide; and Kim Ellis and Mary Durkin were primarily responsible for the completion of the curriculum in social science.

In the research projects, which provided the setting for development of the strategies and refinement of the curriculum, emphasis was on how thought could be developed best in elementary school children. The first study (Taba, 1964) was exploratory, serving as a setting for the development of the methodological tools (for example, methods of categorizing thought processes, methods of coding classroom interaction, and criterion measures [tests] necessary for studying the development of thought). During the course of this study, teaching strategies became the most important variable being studied. Thus, throughout the first study and subsequent ones, the following three dimensions of classroom interaction were studied: (a) behavior of the teachers, (b) behavior of the students, and (c) the content or product of the interaction. While the first study was concentrated only on the effects of strategies of trained teachers (in 20 classrooms from grades 2 through 6), in the second study (Taba, 1966) the classrooms of trained teachers were compared with classrooms of untrained teachers. The final study involved the training of leaders around the country who in turn provided training for teachers. Thus, the strategies were revised and refined through a long process of trial and error, assessment of effectiveness, and input from numerous classroom teachers with different teaching styles and skills.

RESEARCH ON EFFECTIVENESS

To assess the effectiveness of the teaching strategies (Taba, 1964), two kinds of instruments were devised and used in conjunction with the *Sequential Tests of Educational Progress* (STEP) (Educational Testing Service) social studies achievement test. The first was an objective test, *The Social Studies Inference Test* (Taba, 1964), in which students are presented with a series of stories followed by a list of statements (inferences) about the story. Students read the story and the statements and decide whether each statement is probably true or probably false, or whether a person cannot tell from the story if the statements are true or false. Scores are provided on the dimensions of *inference* (that is, the students select correct inferences), *caution* (that is, students are overly cautious and select the "cannot tell" alternative much more often than necessary), *overgeneralization* (that is, students make inferences that are not warranted by selecting an inference when they should choose the "cannot tell" alternative), and *discrimination* (that is, students can discriminate between the items given in the test problem).

The second measure developed for assessing the effectiveness of the teaching strategies was a system for coding and analyzing classroom interaction using tapes of discussions held during the year. The system of coding included scoring each "thought unit" (that is, remark or series of remarks expressing a complete idea) by three different sets of codings. The first coding was a *designation* of the sources, whether it came from the teacher or student, and whether the person was seeking or giving information. The second coding was *function* and included two large groups, managerial or content-free (for example, agreement, approval, disagreement, disapproval, management, reiteration), and content-related (for example, focusing, refocusing, change of focus, deviation from focus, controlling thought, extending thought on the same level, and lifting thought to a higher level). The third type of coding identified the *level of thought*. The same system was used for both teacher and student behavior, and a different system was developed for each cognitive strategy: grouping and labeling, interpreting and making inferences, and predicting consequences. Within each strategy, the specific tasks were ordered from low to high levels whenever possible. A procedure also was developed for relating the levels of thought across cognitive tasks.

To analyze interaction patterns, several measures were obtained for each child, each classroom, each grade level, and across all classrooms and grade levels including the following: amount of participation, interaction between teaching strategies and thought levels, frequency of success of extending and lifting functions, amount and effect of other teacher functions, and amount of thinking at three levels across the three types of strategies. Children also were classified as high or low participators. Finally, these aspects of children's participation in the discussions were compared with their performance on *The Social Studies Inference Test* and with the other variables assessed (that is, IQ scores, mental age, social studies achievement, reading achievement, and socioeconomic status of the family).

Effectiveness with All Children

Taba's research was conducted in classrooms of heterogeneously grouped children of wide ranges of ability. Some of the general conclusions of the studies that have implications for the teaching of all children, briefly listed, are the following:

- Formal operational thinking appears much earlier than Piaget assumes but follows the sequence he identifies. Steady growth occurs in formal thinking from grades 2 through 6, with this type of thinking occurring in about one sixth of all thought units in grade 6 (Taba, 1964).

- The most marked influence on cognitive performance of the children was the teaching strategies. Of these strategies, two variables were of particular importance: teacher questions and the sequencing or patterning of teacher acts. Teachers got what they requested most of the time. If they asked for thinking at a low level, the children generally responded on a low level. When teachers asked for thinking at a high level, the children generally responded at that level. However, the level of thinking of students was affected not only by the single teacher question preceding it but also by the whole pattern of teacher behavior prior to the student's response (Taba, 1964).

- The teacher function of reiteration (for example, the habit of re-stating or repeating what children have said) is used abundantly by teachers and constitutes almost half of all teacher functions (46%) but has little impact on the course of discussion (Taba, 1964).

- The students in experimental groups performed better on the tests and in discussions than did students in the control groups (Taba, 1966).

- The trained teachers had a greater success rate in getting students to respond at the higher levels than did the untrained teachers, even though the trained teachers sought more high-level thinking (Taba, 1966).

- Teacher training is more effective when directed toward specific strategies rather than overall improvement in teaching (Taba, 1964).

Effectiveness with Gifted

One of the most surprising findings of the first study (1964) was the generally low relationship between the level of thinking and traditional variables that influence thought (that is, IQ, achievement, reading comprehension, and economic status). When growth was measured, the relationships were almost nonexistent. To explain this phenomenon and justify the use of the strategies with homogeneous groups of gifted children at least part of the time, it is necessary to explain further the results of the research relating to the patterns of teacher functions—particularly extending and lifting—and the pacing of these functions in the total discussion. An important aspect of the use of the Taba *Strategies* is to pace the discussion and rotate assimilation and accommodation activities so that all children can participate. For this reason, the discussion must remain at the lowest level until an adequate basis is found for moving as a group to the next highest level. This is the time when the teacher functions of extending and lifting are significant. A discussion begins at the lowest level with a process such as listing. Teachers then must keep the discussion at this level by extending (that is, asking for additional ideas, examples, new ideas, or explanations of ideas given). When they feel the group has an adequate basis at this level, they ask a question that "lifts" the level of thought required (for example, moving from listing to grouping in the concept development strategy or moving from listing to inferences about causes or effects in the interpretation of data strategy). If teachers remain too long at a low level, the discussion may never reach the higher levels. On the other hand, if they attempt to move students too quickly from the lower to higher levels, often the children are unable to make the leap requested, so they return to the lower level. To illustrate these points, the four class discussion patterns presented by Taba (1964, p. 129) are shown in Figure 8.1.

In pattern A, the teacher attempts to raise the level of thinking early in the discussion and continues to attempt to lift it without providing an adequate basis at the lower levels. The children are unable to maintain these levels and keep returning to the lowest level. Pattern B represents an effective discussion in which the teacher remains at the lower levels long enough to accumulate a large amount of information before moving the children to higher levels. The teacher is generally effective in keeping the discussion moving upward. In pattern C, the teacher constantly attempts to move the discussion too high and too quickly without much basis at the lower levels or any steps in between. The result is that the children repeatedly return to the information level. Pattern D represents still another ineffective strategy. The teacher is constantly changing the focus of the discussion, which results in the children being unable to accumulate enough information about any focus to be able to move to higher levels and remain there.

These results indicate that when gifted children are grouped with other gifted children, discussions can be paced much more rapidly. Not as much time must be concentrated on the lower levels before moving upward. Perhaps interaction pattern B could be modified as demonstrated in Figure 8.2 (Taba, 1964).

The authors' and other teachers' experiences verify the validity of this idea. Perhaps the most significant reason for the fact that low IQ children's growth in cognitive skills was as great as that of high IQ children was that most discussions had to be paced so that all children could move upward together. This increases the boredom and decreases the challenge of the tasks for gifted children.

Two recent dissertations (Schiever, 1986; Brooks, 1988) reported positive results of the Taba *Strategies* with gifted students. Schiever (1986) compared the cognitive growth effects on students in six groups: two service delivery systems (gifted students in either self-contained or once-weekly programs) and three curriculum models: *Creative Problem Solving* (Parnes, 1981), *Hilda Taba Teaching Strategies* (Institute for Staff Development, 1971a, 1971b, 1971c, 1971d), and regular curriculum and instruction. Using the *SEA Tests*, Form X and Form Y (Callahan, Covert, Aylesworth, & Vanco, 1981) in a pre–post design, Schiever found a significant model by treatment interaction (p < .0001), significant differences between daily treatment and control groups and between the Taba self-contained and one-day-per-week service delivery models. Brooks also used the *SEA Test* and the *Sentence Completion Test* (Hunt, Butler, Noy, & Rosser, 1978) as measures to assess growth in conceptual complexity and cognitive maturation among 97 seventh-grade gifted students in self-contained classes in an existing school

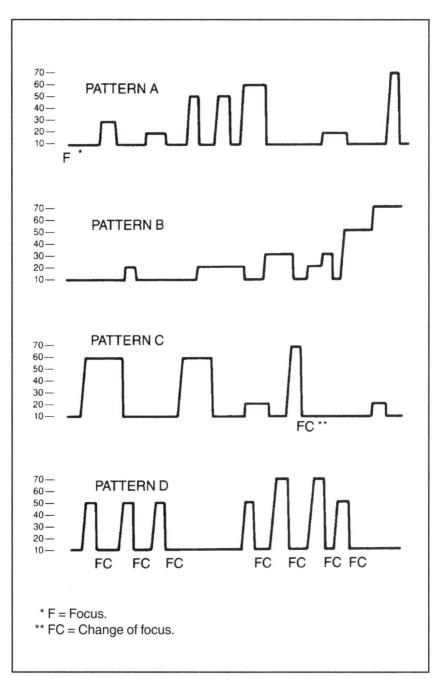

Figure 8.1. Class discussion patterns. From *Thinking in Elementary School Children* by H. Taba, 1964, San Francisco: San Francisco State College. Reprinted with permission.

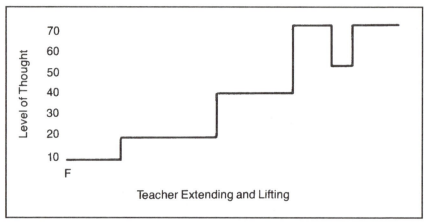

Figure 8.2. Modification of interaction pattern B.

program. A quasi-experimental, pretest–posttest, nonequivalent control group design was selected for the natural setting. Two of four social studies classes for the gifted were designated as experimental groups; the remaining two served as control groups. The same teacher taught all classes. After 12 weeks, the mean gain for students in the experimental classes on the *SEA Test* was 2.636; the control classes averaged a mean loss of –0.98 ($F = 6.82$; $p = .0105$). No significant differences were found on the *Sentence Completion Test*. The results provide support for the effectiveness of the Taba strategies with gifted students; additional comparative studies still are needed.

JUDGMENTS

Advantages

The *Hilda Taba Teaching Strategies* program has many advantages recommending its use in programs for the gifted. Perhaps the most obvious is its strong research base that shows the effectiveness of the strategies in developing higher levels of thinking in children. This research not only provides general information about its effectiveness but has resulted in the development of specific strategies and clear methods for applying them to achieve the desired objectives. An excellent teacher-training program and specific procedures for teacher self-evaluation, for analysis of classroom interaction, and for student evaluation also have been developed during the course of the research. A curriculum organized to facilitate the development of thinking and designed for use with the strategies also has been developed.

Another advantage of the teaching strategies is their generalizability or transferability. Once learned, many aspects of the strategies can be incorporated into a total approach that goes beyond the use of specific strategies. For example, asking open-ended but focused questions is an extremely important skill for use with gifted children, as are the appropriate pacing of discussions and the asking of questions that require children to verbalize their reasons. After learning the Taba *Strategies,* teachers find that these skills become internalized. Also, this approach can be combined easily with others used in programs for the gifted. Since Taba's ideas about the organization of content are almost identical to Bruner's, the combination of Bruner-based curricula with the Taba *Strategies* is an easy one. This combination can enhance the effectiveness of both approaches since few curricula have been developed (in social science) built around Taba's approach, but numerous ones are based on Bruner's ideas. Also, the Taba *Strategies* fill a definite "process" need not addressed in depth by Bruner. Furthermore, they provide a nice addition to Renzulli's *Enrichment Triad,* Treffinger's model for *Self-Directed Learning,* Sharan and Sharan's *Group Investigations,* and Betts's *Autonomous Learner.* The *Teaching Strategies* also can be combined with moral or emotional development models such as Kohlberg (1966) and Dabrowski and Piechowski (1977) as the interdisciplinary concepts[1] recommended in the Taba social studies curriculum are both affective and cognitive.

Another advantage is the comprehensiveness of the approach if both the curriculum and teaching strategies are used. This would provide almost all of the content, process, and psychological learning environment modifications advocated for gifted children. It provides one of the product changes and sets the stage for others to be made. The relationships of content and process are made explicitly clear when combined in the Taba model.

A final advantage is that research demonstrates its effectiveness with gifted and other students in a variety of settings.

Disadvantages

Since the Taba *Strategies* are complicated and require the learning of subtle teacher behaviors, they are difficult for many teachers to learn. For some a complete change in style is required and may take a long time to internalize. In the authors' teacher-training program, for example, at least one 3-hour semester course is necessary for teaching the strategies. To learn the strategies adequately during this semester teachers must practice them, tape their discussions, analyze their own performance, and then receive evaluations of their performance. Some even feel a need for extended practice in a supervised practicum setting in which discussions are videotaped and later analyzed, or the discussion is observed and then discussed.

---

1. Causality, conflict, cooperation, cultural change, differences, interdependence, modification, power, societal control, tradition, and values.

One problem with the training and later use of the Taba *Strategies* is that the training manuals (one for each of the four strategies), which in the past could be purchased by trained leaders for use in teaching teachers, are now out of print and few trained seminar leaders are available to conduct staff development sessions. However, Schiever (1991) has developed *A Comprehensive Approach to Teaching Thinking*, which includes an overview of the Taba strategies, clear explanations of each strategy, extensive examples, and complete lesson plans adapted from the Institute for Staff Development training manuals.

As with the manuals, other information regarding the strategies and their use is extremely difficult to find. The research reports are out of print, and only one is available through an information service. For these reasons, the research is difficult to replicate and the information difficult to disseminate.

CONCLUSION

The advantages of Taba's approach far outweigh its disadvantages. In the years since publication of this book in its original form, use of the Taba *Strategies* has spread widely. We anticipate that this trend will continue.

RESOURCES

Background Information

Schiever, S. W. (1991). *A comprehensive approach to teaching thinking*. Boston: Allyn & Bacon. This book is that rare combination of scholarship—both theoretical and practical. The *Hilda Taba Teaching Strategies* are adapted from the original materials prepared by Taba and her associates, with each of the four strategies explained clearly and illustrated with effective examples. In addition, the author extends the concept of the spiral curriculum, traces its connection to developmental theory and complex thinking skills, and provides guidelines for curriculum development and conduct of classroom discussions.

The following materials are out of print and difficult to locate. However, they are included to provide information for those who may wish to search in academic libraries or curriculum archives for more information than is found in books currently in print.

Institute for Staff Development. (1971). *Hilda Taba teaching strategies program: Unit I, Unit II, Unit III,* and *Unit IV.* Miami: Author. The *Hilda Taba Teaching Strategies* program, based on Taba's work in the 1960s, was developed for classroom teachers who are interested in utilizing her approaches to education. There are a total of eight volumes, four each for the secondary and elementary levels. The Taba program has four major strategies; therefore, for each of the two levels, a volume was published for each strategy. The individual volumes contain objectives, planning materials, tryout plans and ideas, and skill-refinement activities centered on the particular strategy. Also included are materials for the teacher, such as self-evaluation forms for discussion leading, background reading material, and a reference list and glossary. Finally, an individual is able to evaluate the effectiveness of the unit. The lack of a clear and detailed introduction describing the basic philosophy of the *Hilda Taba Teaching Strategies* is the one major oversight in the materials.

Ellis, K., & Durkin, M. C. (1972). *Teacher's guide for people in communities* (The Taba program in social studies). Menlo Park, CA: Addison-Wesley. A social studies curriculum has been developed based on the theories of Hilda Taba. *Teacher's Guide for People in Communities* is one book in the series. This particular text is for use in elementary schools. It is well illustrated, and the subject matter is interesting and unusual. The book is divided into two parts: an extensive teacher's edition and the actual text used by students. The teacher's guide discusses the objectives, content, learning activities, and teaching strategies of the program. The chapters in the text then are analyzed for these components to aid the teacher in instruction. Units in the text center around different cultures in the world. Each chapter in a unit has a central "main idea," similar to an objective, that is used to emphasize the key concepts of the Taba philosophy. These main ideas are continually reintroduced throughout the series. The curriculum is spiraling in content and encompasses both the affective and cognitive domains.

Instructional Material

Udall, A. J., & Daniels, M. A. (1991). *Creating the thoughtful classroom: Strategies to promote student thinking.* Tucson, AZ: Zephyr Press. Classroom tested and classroom ready, this is a guide that teachers can use to help develop students' thinking skills in grades 3 through 12. Methods of assessment also are included.

Chapter 9

Calvin Taylor: Multiple Talent Approach

alvin Taylor's *Multiple Talent Model* is one of the more versatile approaches for helping students, from kindergarten to graduate school, develop creativity and complex thinking processes. Teachers can use a single talent for a 5-minute thinking exercise, design a lesson to teach a specific thinking process, or combine several talents to promote development of many, varied information-processing skills. The model also is sufficiently flexible that teachers can integrate functional thinking processes with complex content in any curriculum area. The *Multiple Talent Model* also can be used effectively with a management system, such as the *Schoolwide Enrichment Model* (Renzulli & Reis, 1985), or as a framework for designing independent studies (Nielson, 1984).

Taylor, a pioneer researcher in the field of creativity, startled the educational world in 1967 with a theory that nearly all children, if evaluated for achievement in several different talent areas, would be gifted in some way. His presentations and articles included such catch phrases as "Nearly all students are talented: Let's reach them" (1968c), "Potentially all kids are gifted" (1968a), and "Educated followers don't succeed" (1968b). Readers who looked beyond the catch phrases, however, found that Taylor's theory was based solidly in research in three fields: primary mental ability factors, creativity, and world-of-work skills. His definitions of *gifted* and *talented* differ from those of many of his contemporaries. One common distinction made is that *gifted* refers to intellectual abilities while *talented* refers to the so-called nonintellectual or less general abilities in visual or performing arts, creativity, leadership, and mechanical or psychomotor skills. From another viewpoint giftedness is defined as superior ability in many domains, and talent is equated with high ability in one domain. Gagne (1985) defines giftedness as "competence which is distinctly above average in one or more domains of ability" (p. 128) and talent as "performance which is distinctly above average in one or more fields of human performance" (p. 108). Taylor's distinction is a matter of degree. He refers to the gifted as those persons who are at the top in any identified talent area and the talented as those who are between the average and the gifted in any talent[1] area. Taylor argues that if educators would recognize and develop a wide range of abilities, rather than focusing narrowly on academic talent, a much greater percentage of students would be above average in at least one talent area.

> If we limit ourselves merely to one talent, only 50% of the students will have a chance to be above average (the median). However, if we consider two talents, the percent above average in at least one of the two talents will be in the high 60's; for three talents, in the 70's; for four talents in the low 80's, etc. Across several talents, nearly 90% will be above average in at least one talent area; and almost all others will be nearly average in at least one of the talent areas. Therefore, almost all students are above average. From the same evidence, about one-third of the students will be highly gifted in at least one of the multiple-talent areas. (Taylor, 1968c, p. 2)

The *Multiple Talent* approach arose out of Taylor's research in three main areas: primary mental ability factors, creativity, and functional thinking abilities needed for success in the world of work. From that research, Taylor extracted clusters of thinking skills, or talents, commonly needed in the world of work; "creativity, foresight, planning, decision-making abilities, communication skills, and executive and human relations skills are examples" (Taylor, 1967, p. 23). This approach, with its emphasis on functional thinking processes integrated with curricular content, has validity both as a philosophical basis for the education of all children and as a framework for curriculum planning within a program for the gifted. The model is flexible and supports development of varied talents and abilities for learners of all ages. For this reason, the *Multiple Talent Model* is included as an appropriate approach for the education of the gifted.

ASSUMPTIONS UNDERLYING THE MODEL

About Teaching

Assumptions about teaching that are central to the *Multiple Talent Model* are that (a) talents can be taught, (b) teachers should be talent developers as well as dispensers of knowledge, and (c) teachers must provide many opportunities for student interaction in a variety of talent development activities.

---

1. Taylor uses the word *talent* to designate a functional thinking process and the word *talented* to describe a degree of achievement in a talent area.

Taylor argues that educators focus too narrowly on academic talents to the neglect of creative talents. "Our approach is to provide students with opportunities to develop and increase their creativity, innovation, and risk-taking attributes" (Taylor, 1986b, p. 307). He stresses the importance of recognizing and developing many different areas of talent in schools, rather than the narrow range of academic abilities that usually are the focus of traditional education (Taylor, 1968a). By broadening the base of talents used in classrooms, educators can develop more of the whole person, increase individual capabilities, and strengthen the self-esteem and self-efficacy of students. Teachers who function effectively as talent developers need a repertoire of thinking skills and creativity skills. Inquiry, active listening, restating, generalizing, encouraging curiosity and questioning, treating students as thinkers rather than knowledge absorbers, and encouraging student creativity all are necessary for the development of high-level talents (Taylor, 1978).

If educators accept these assumptions about the nature of talent and its presence in many, different individuals, certain instructional changes must occur. Teachers can develop open-ended activities that will allow the expression and development of several different talents, or they can plan activities deliberately to develop a particular talent. Certain kinds of activities, especially in the self-expression area, are open-ended enough that children can use a wide variety of talents to achieve the desired goals. Other activities require different approaches for each type of talent. Just as students may be better at one talent than another, teachers may be better at developing a particular type of talent and should be allowed to specialize (Taylor, 1968b). However, some means should be devised to ensure that students have frequent opportunities to use each type of talent. To make the *Multiple Talent* approach successful, students must experience the learning and thinking processes of a talent (or talents) while "simultaneously acquiring a variety of subject matter content in a total educational program," a "double-barreled curriculum" (Taylor, 1978, p. 100) that stimulates growth in both knowledge and talent.

An interesting statement Taylor makes is that "too many school activities are not relevant and too many relevant activities are not in school programs" (Stevenson et al., 1971, p. 9). Reflecting back on our own educational experiences, we concur that virtually every "real-world" skill we learned came from our participation in extracurricular activities. In out-of-school settings, such as clubs, athletics, music, drama, and publications, students gain valuable leadership and group interaction skills. They learn how to plan events, how to handle difficult people, and how to carry a project through from initial idea to final evaluation. Why could these activities not be a regular part of the educational program? Students whose parents are unable or unwilling to take them to meetings or allow them to stay after school or those who are not elected to club or student body offices have little opportunity to gain these leadership and interpersonal skills so valuable in the world outside the classroom.

About Learning

The most significant assumption Taylor (1967) makes about learning is that children will learn more or grow more in knowledge, as well as talent, if the *Multiple Talent* approach is used. This assumption is supported by two related ideas. First, children will acquire more knowledge because they will be using more than one way to acquire it. Second, since the focus is on talent development integrated with academic content, knowledge is a by-product or the means to an end rather than an end in itself. An underlying assumption is that turning the major focus away from knowledge itself enhances learning. Active involvement with content and process plus interaction with peers are powerful stimuli to creativity and intellectual development.

A second assumption is that the adult potential of many students is enhanced greatly because they have opportunities to begin to use some functional talents (e.g., planning, decision making) that otherwise might have gone undeveloped until adulthood. Taylor (1967) states, "In my model, processes are emphasized so that they will also be available for later use. Thus my model capitalizes on possible transfer effects from both content and processes" (p. 29). Subject knowledge is a means to developing talents, and the acquisition of knowledge is a meaningful by-product of active student engagement in relevant processes. Taylor (1986a) further avers that the *Multiple Talent* approach increases synchronization between school experiences and career/life activities.

> Having both talents and knowledge together as a double curricula overcomes both ignorance of knowledge and ignorance of effective functioning. The double curricula also stretches students' minds by working them at a wider range and depth of knowledge and by activating more total brain power potentials through thinking ways of learning knowledge. (p. 260)

About Giftedness and Talent

The multiple nature of giftedness and talent, controversial when Taylor's theory was first proposed, has since been posited by other scholars (Gardner, 1983; Sternberg, 1990; Sternberg & Davidson, 1986). The belief that individuals can be gifted in one area of intelligence and be average or below average in another area was controversial when Taylor first proposed the idea but now is accepted more widely. Taylor's *Multiple Talent* approach is based on the beliefs that (a) each person has talents in a variety of areas; (b) each person is likely to be gifted in only a few talent areas; (c) potentially, all children can be above average in at least one talent area; and (d) almost all learners will benefit from talent-focused instruction.

Taylor assumes that giftedness is specific to a talent area. An individual will demonstrate strengths in one or more talents but is unlikely to excel in all the different areas. To illustrate this point, Taylor uses the now well-known "Talent Totem Poles," which show the placement of seven elementary school children[2] in order of ability in each of six areas. As can be seen from Figure 9.1, the seven children are at different levels on the totem pole; no one child is consistently at the top or consistently at the bottom. Although a pattern of differential achievement is common, this is not always the case. A few children excel at nearly everything they do while others are consistently near the bottom in most talents. Very seldom, however, is one student in a classroom always in the top (or bottom) position on every talent totem pole.

Taylor posits that all individuals, especially children of school age, have far more talents than they use. When teachers recognize and help learners develop these varied talents, many more students will be able to excel in at least one talent area. More students will feel good about themselves and will become more self-directed as they experience and display their unique talent profiles; fewer students will drop out of school. Conversely, some individuals who always have been at the top academically will experience the uncomfortable feeling of being closer to the bottom in some talent area, thus gaining a more realistic picture of themselves in relation to other people (Taylor, 1968b).

ELEMENTS/PARTS

Talent Areas

In the theoretical approach to multiple talent development, Taylor (1986a) includes several talent areas. For the first public school implementation, *Project Implode* (Stevenson et al., 1971) at Bella Vista Elementary School in Utah's Jordan District, a decision was made to focus on six talents: academic, productive thinking, communication, forecasting, decision making, and planning. Creative/productive thinking is integral to all nonacademic talents in the *Multiple Talent* approach. Thus, productive thinking, with its stress on production of many, varied, and original ideas, is taught first. The other talents can be taught in any order and all five functional thinking talents can be integrated into any content area.

---

2. The original illustration used seven hypothetical children. Later, Lloyd (1984) prepared totem poles for actual children in her classroom; the placements of seven representative children from that class are now shown on the Talent Totem Pole.

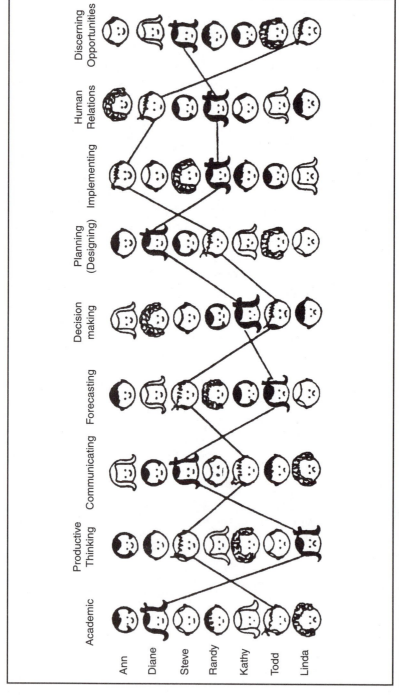

Figure 9.1. Multiple Talent Totem Poles—1984 extended version. © Calvin W. Taylor. Reprinted by permission.

Several demonstration projects based on Taylor's *Multiple Talent* theory were developed and positively evaluated during the 1970s (Taylor, 1986a), including *Project Implode* and *Project Seagull* in Utah, *Talents Unlimited* in Alabama, *Project Impact* (Nielsen & Clark, 1978; Norris, Nielsen, Clark, & Coe, 1978) in Iowa, and *Project Reach* (Juntune, 1979) in Minnesota. Definitions of each talent and guidelines for recognizing and developing them are based primarily on the first, *Project Implode* (Lloyd, Seghini, & Stevenson, 1974; Stevenson et al., 1971), and the most widely disseminated, *Talents Unlimited* (Schlichter, 1986).

Academic Talent

Traditionally, academic excellence is focused on learning and returning "the library of the past" (Taylor, Allington, & Lloyd, 1990). Because academic talent, demonstrated through tests of knowledge and comprehension, is emphasized so strongly in schools, the *Multiple Talent* approach does not include guidelines for its development. Instead, Taylor stresses that knowledge must be learned in a sufficiently full form that it can be efficiently retrieved, worked on, added to, and transformed for appropriate applications. Information that is received by a student and returned on a test seldom is stored in long-term memory. However, information that is "churned" through multiple sites in the brain is more likely to be associated with, compared to, and contrasted with previous knowledge. The purposeful transformation of information for functional applications stimulates stronger connections with past experience and is more apt to be memorable. Taylor argues that teachers and learners should cultivate both knowledge and talents—not one without the other (Taylor, 1978). The goal is to convert knowledge into a purposeful tool or resource, through creative processing, for the acquisition and production of new knowledge in the future.

Productive Thinking

Productive thinking, which includes divergent, convergent, and evaluative components, is defined as the ability to go beyond the obvious, to put seemingly unrelated pieces of information or ideas together to construct new solutions, new ways of expression, and new groups or classifications, and to create original ideas or products. Productive thinking talent includes four components: fluency, flexibility, originality, and elaboration. Fluency is the ability to produce many ideas or solutions although not all may be of the highest quality; the emphasis is on quantity rather than quality of ideas. Flexibility is the ability to generate a variety of ideas or solutions. A thinker who is flexible will consider an object/event/problem from many points of view and express ideas of many, different kinds even though not all of the ideas may prove useful.

Originality is the ability to generate unique ideas or solutions and to consider problems from an unusual point of view. An original thinker consistently connects ideas not previously considered together and solves problems in new and unusual ways. Elaboration is the ability to improve on a basic idea by adding details or variations to make the idea more interesting and complete.

Productive thinking talent is developed best through activities that encourage the generation of ideas without a specific product or solution in mind. The major emphases in this talent are originality and creativity—helping learners to stretch their minds, to look beyond the obvious, to see something in a new way, and to consider many possibilities. This talent also may include elements of convergent and/or evaluative thinking: classifying or grouping responses, using criteria (e.g., suitability, workability) to choose a problem solution or idea for further development, and providing rational support for choices. However, these activities take place only after many, varied, and unusual responses have been generated. An underlying assumption is that creative/productive thinking helps people to adjust to a rapidly changing world, prepares them to find better problem solutions to meet their own and group needs, and teaches them to respect their own values and goals.

The teacher or group leader sets the stage for productive thinking by

1. structuring the classroom in such a way that students are prepared for interaction, reviewing student talent behaviors, stating ground rules, presenting the problem/topic to consider, and stating whether responses are to be "real world" or in the realm of fantasy;

2. encouraging students to ask many questions about a topic or problem and then allowing students time for thinking and listing some ideas;

3. encouraging students to share many, varied, and unusual responses and accepting all responses;

4. helping students shift categories when they seem to be in a rut by asking questions (e.g., What other kinds of _____ can you share? What are some ideas/solutions that are different from the ones we have listed?);

5. encouraging originality by questions (e.g., What can you think of that is different from anything we've listed?) or statements (e.g., Try to think of something no one else will think of);

6. encouraging elaboration by inviting students to add details or extensions to make ideas/solutions more complete or more interesting; and

7. having students select their best or most original idea(s) and encouraging unusual and effective ways to summarize, present products, or implement solutions.

Products generated through Productive Thinking may be a single response (e.g., a design, transformation, illustration), a list of many responses, a presentation, or an implementation activity.

Communications Talent

The ability to communicate is basic to social interaction and learning. As Gardner (1983) states, an individual "could not hope to proceed with any efficacy in the world without considerable command of the tetrad of phonology, syntax, semantics, and pragmatics" (p. 77). The four core operations of language Gardner discusses are comparable to Taylor's three developmental facets of the communications talent.

GARDNER	TAYLOR
Sensitivity to the meaning of words	Word fluency
Sensitivity to the order among words	Associational fluency
Sensitivity to sounds, rhythms, inflections, and meters of words	Word fluency and associational fluency
Sensitivity to the different functions of language	Expressional fluency

The purpose of communications talent development is to help students not only to use verbal and nonverbal language to share their thoughts, ideas, and feelings but also to develop richness of expression, clarity, and completeness of ideas (Schlichter, 1986). Activities in the communications talent are designed to help learners develop fluent, flexible, associative, elaborative thinking and to describe significant ideas, objects, events, and relationships with clarity, sensitivity, imagination, and creativity. The reciprocal nature of communication is emphasized. Verbal and nonverbal means of expressing thoughts or feelings and the powers to express, respond, interact, question, and create are developed. Because it is aligned so closely with language development, the communications talent can be integrated easily into many, varied classroom activities.

In the *Talents Unlimited* model (Schlichter et al., 1974), the communications talent includes six skills: (a) producing many, different words that fit a given category or describe something; (b) producing many, different words to describe feelings; (c) using words together to make comparisons among objects/ideas/events and to show relationships or associations (e.g., simile, metaphor, analogy); (d) demonstrating the capacity to understand another's feelings by sharing similar thoughts or experiences; (e) organizing and weaving a network of ideas to create a linguistic product such as a story, poem, essay, or report; and (f) interpreting the actions and words of others and using nonverbal forms of communication to express ideas, feelings, and needs. The first two skills differ from productive thinking in that the emphasis is on single, descriptive words rather than on production of original ideas or problem solutions; the third emphasizes associative/analogical thinking and figurative language. While all six skills have affective aspects, the fourth is almost purely affective in that a person demonstrates empathic understanding of the feelings of others. The fifth skill, creating a network of ideas, is product oriented and the most influenced by formal rules or patterns of composition. The sixth skill, often product oriented as well, is nonverbal and involves varied kinds of visual representation or psychomotor activities.

In addition to its central role in academic disciplines, the communications talent is essential for group interaction and conflict resolution. A breakdown in communication often precedes stress between individuals or groups. Teachers should plan activities to help students understand the complexity of human interaction, including the barriers that may inhibit communication (e.g., cultural mores, age, language variants or dialects, personal and national goals or values). Once learners are aware of this complexity, they can learn strategies and develop attitudes that lead to better understanding of themselves and others.

Renzulli et al. (1976) focus on two areas of communication talent, expressiveness and precision, that can be used to infer giftedness. Expressiveness in communication is demonstrated when an individual

1. uses her/his voice expressively to convey or enhance meaning;

2. conveys information nonverbally through gestures, facial expressions, and "body language";

3. is an interesting storyteller; or

4. uses colorful and imaginative figures of speech such as puns and analogies.

Precision in communication is demonstrated when an individual

1. speaks and writes directly and to the point;

2. modifies and adjusts expression of ideas for maximum reception;

3. is able to revise and edit in a way that is concise yet retains essential ideas;

4. explains things precisely and clearly;

5. uses descriptive words to add color, emotion, and beauty;

6. expresses thoughts and needs clearly and concisely;

7. can find varied ways of expressing ideas so others will understand;

8. can describe things in a few very appropriate words;

9. is able to express fine shades of meaning by use of a large stock of synonyms;

10. is able to express ideas in a variety of alternate ways; and

11. knows and can use many words closely related in meaning.

A gifted communicator also is empathic and recognizes commonalities between his [or her] and others' experiences and relates his [or her] own thoughts and ideas to others' experiences (Shartzer, 1972).

When characteristics of high competence in communication can be observed or identified, they also can be developed. Teachers should plan activities to enhance latent communication talent in each of the above characteristics and also should strive for a balance between assignments for products that must be precise and those that are expressive.

Forecasting Talent

Forecasting talent is the ability to evaluate cause and effect sequences and then, based on evaluation results, to decide what is most likely to happen. Forecasting ability includes three components: conceptual foresight, penetration, and social awareness. Conceptual foresight is the ability to see patterns or chains of events and their causes and effects. Penetration implies a searching mind and the ability to go beyond that which is obvious or superficial, to see clearly all aspects of a situation, to predict how the situation or conditions might change, and to understand how such changes might affect a prediction. Social awareness is skill in predicting how other people will react and how their reactions will affect future events. It includes the ability to foresee whether change will impose unpleasant or unacceptable conditions upon others and whether change will cause a positive or negative effect on people. The forecasting talent helps students think ahead, foresee possible problems in a plan, adjust behaviors as conditions change, consider possible consequences of a decision or act, recognize when additional information or resources are needed, and infer connections between the known and the possible. One definite plus of including forecasting activities in the curriculum is that students become more aware of the effects of their actions on others and the environment.

Eberle (1974) suggests that individuals who demonstrate forecasting talent

1. anticipate effects or outcomes;

2. evaluate (and recognize) past knowledge and experience;

3. view situations objectively, consider human reactions, and display empathy;

4. are attuned to their own feelings and hunches;

5. are not overly concerned about being "right";

6. are socially aware;

7. are sensitive to actions that would affect a situation or other people; and

8. clearly perceive connections between cause and effect.

Other characteristics of talented forecasters include remembering the causes and effects of past events, recognizing what information is known and what is still to be discovered, and anticipating how situations and conditions may change (Shartzer, 1972).

Activities planned to develop each of these characteristics should be an integral part of the curriculum. In addition to inferential cause–effect thinking, students also may engage in speculative thinking (e.g., What would happen if _____?), project what their lives might be like if they lived in a particular era or in a different part of the world, or describe themselves in some future situation. Schlichter (1985) points out that forecasting deals with predicting many, varied causes or predicting many, varied effects that might occur. Not all questions or activity descriptions that use words such as *if, could be, might,* or *future* call for forecasting talent. Other types of "predicting" activities that do not fit with this definition of forecasting include statements like the following: (a) Predict who will win the 100-yard dash; (b) Predict how many times you can jump rope without missing; (c) Predict how many tiles are on the floor of our classroom; or (d) Predict which sunflower plant will grow the tallest. Predictions like these may involve estimating or hypothesizing, but the goal is to come closest to one right answer rather than seeking many, varied causes or effects.

To develop forecasting talent, teachers should present a hypothetical situation and encourage children to think of (a) many, varied effects/consequences/happenings that might occur if that situation were true or (b) many, varied causes that might have contributed to that situation. Ask children to keep an open mind and to explore all possibilities. If the teacher then wants students to select the most likely causes/effects, the forecasting activity can be combined with academic research or a decision-making activity. Teachers also should (a) plan forecasting activities that have real meaning in the lives of students, (b) model forecasting behaviors, (c) help students to compare forecasted outcomes with real outcomes and determine conditions that may have differentially affected the outcome, (d) assess goals in terms of their impact on both individuals and systems, and (e) communicate to students that they are capable of improving their forecasting abilities. Forecasting activities help students gain an awareness of their own values, goals, priorities, and needs as well as develop a sense of responsibility toward others. Related thinking process activities, especially for older students, include two of Hilda Taba's *Teaching Strategies*: interpretation of data and application of generalizations (see Chapter 8).

Decision-Making Talent

Decision making may be one of the most essential talents that an individual can develop. The ability to evaluate data clearly and accurately, generate several alternative solutions to a problem or dilemma, consider each solution in terms of relevant criteria, and select the best alternative for implementation is needed in all aspects of life. Decision making involves experimental evaluation, logical evaluation, and thoughtful judgment. In experimental evaluation, an individual looks at possible solutions from a variety of points of view then examines all possible limitations, constraints, and conditions that affect the implementation of a decision. In logical evaluation, one lists the main goals and actions that relate to a problem, selects the best possible alternatives, and ranks each possible solution (or alternative) in relation to established logical criteria, goals, and steps necessary to implement the decision. Then the individual forecasts what the end results might be if given conditions exist. Judgment follows logical evaluation of the information available. One considers conditions, preferences, and values related to the situation, then a decision is made on the best means to meet individual or group goals. When communicating a judgment, one provides reasons that justify the decision based on goals and ethical considerations.

In the *Talents Unlimited* model, the decision-making process has four steps:

1. generating many, varied alternatives, although all may not be of the best quality;

2. identifying relevant criteria for evaluating alternatives;

3. assessing the value of each alternative in relation to each criterion;

4. selecting the best solution then supporting the selection through the use of reasoning related to evaluation criteria.

Emphasis also is placed on helping learners develop the ability to generate clear, pertinent, and useful evaluation criteria. For many learners, developing relevant criteria is a difficult and frustrating task. Teachers can help by suggesting one or two criteria then asking students in small groups to generate two or three more. Criteria should be framed as questions and have only one element. Avoid questions such as "Is this dress attractive and durable?" Some criteria questions can be answered yes or no; other questions can be quantified, such as "What percentage of my income will this purchase require?" Attention to this step of the decision-making process leads to more valid, supportable decisions.

Students who demonstrate ability in decision making can

1. describe a problem clearly;

2. seek additional information if necessary to understand the problem or situation;

3. select relevant criteria related to the problem, values, goals, and needs of those who are involved in the situation and will be affected by the decision;

4. make a judgment that identifies the best possible decision, then support the decision with evidence of logical reasoning and social responsibility.

Some characteristic behaviors of talented decision makers (Eberle, 1974) are that the individual remains emotionally detached from the problem, considers more than one course of action, poses penetrating questions and collects essential data, uses data to support her [his] decision, and is willing to make and defend a decision. Shartzer (1972) adds that a talented decision maker is willing to discuss a situation and listen to advice and also is willing to evaluate decisions and changes when needs arise or new evidence is presented.

Teachers who promote the development of decision-making ability provide numerous opportunities for students to make decisions that directly affect classroom activities and plans. Teachers demonstrate the steps in the decision-making process and plan activities that allow students to practice those steps. They also establish a classroom climate in which students have many opportunities to make choices. In addition, teachers should

1. respect student decisions, evaluate them in relation to the child and the situation, and refrain from imposing own personal values in assessing student choices;

2. plan opportunities for student interaction in group decision making;

3. involve class members in major decisions related to classroom rules, procedures, and projects;

4. schedule frequent cooperative evaluation discussions of the observed effects of making a specific decision;

5. set up procedures that support frequent self-evaluation of products or progress toward goals; and

6. relate decision-making activities to world-of-work problems, social issues, and real problems/situations whenever possible.

Planning Talent

Planning is a complex process with elements found in all of the other thinking talents. Planning often is preceded by decision making and requires clarity in communication; organizational skills; awareness of goals, priorities, and possible problems; and the ability to develop detailed lists of resources and step-by-step (often parallel) sequences of activities. The ability to plan effectively is an intellectual process that involves goal setting, organization, elaboration, sensitivity to people and problems, and frequent decisions. Elaboration is the ability to identify the purpose, process, and product of a proposed activity, develop detailed sequences explaining what is to be done, and project resources and time required to complete the activity. Sensitivity to people and problems is the ability to predict how outside conditions or personal factors may affect the implementation of the plan. A talented planner can identify conditions that cannot be changed, relationships among human and nonhuman factors in the environment, and the possible consequences of specific acts. Organization includes the allocation of money, coordination of human and material resources, allocation of time, and arrangement of space necessary to accomplish the task. In addition, a planner conducts ongoing evaluation to detect potential problems and adapts the plan to solve or minimize them. A person with organizational talent considers economy and efficiency along with the most effective application of individual competencies and interests.

Some characteristics teachers might observe in good planners, according to Renzulli et al. (1976), include skill at strategy games in which a player must anticipate several moves ahead, organization in her or his own work habits, ability to prioritize when organizing activities or setting goals, and awareness of space, time, material, and personnel limitations that must be considered when implementing a plan. A talented planner often makes schematic representations of parallel sequences of steps to facilitate coordination and evaluation of multiple activities and to pinpoint where trouble may occur. She or he also can see alternative ways to arrange time, materials, and personnel to accomplish the task.

Planning ability is developmental; before students can make complex plans, they must have numerous opportunities to make and execute simple plans. Teachers can help students improve their planning talent by

1. identifying and modeling the steps in the process,

2. discussing and evaluating sample plans,

3. providing some structural tools (forms, charts) to aid in planning,

4. giving students the opportunity to implement a plan even if it is flawed, and

5. following implementation with evaluation of the plan(s) and reflection on the planning process.

Having students make a plan and act according to the plan is crucial to the development of planning talent. "The right to fail with honor is just as important as the right to succeed with praise" (Lloyd et al., 1974, p. 55). As often as possible, plans should relate to real-life situations and be incorporated into curriculum design so that the students simultaneously develop mastery of content as well as planning talent. Students should be involved in planning and evaluating regularly scheduled activities, special events, presentations, group projects, and extracurricular activities. Writing computer programs involves careful planning of very specific steps and, frequently, a number of alternate paths. Writing a "choose-your-own-story" book or designing a game also are excellent activities to develop planning ability. The teacher must recognize the importance of setting up situations or experiences that will enable students to hone their planning talent and also recognize the importance of the planning process in all walks of life.

Implementing the Multiple Talent Approach

The purpose of this section is to suggest ways that the Taylor model can be used within a program for the gifted as a way to develop functional talents in gifted students. Even though the model was developed as a total educational approach for all children and is an excellent one to use in regular classrooms, the focus of this section is on its use within a special program. An appropriate beginning to the implementation of the model is to design learning experiences in each talent area to teach the steps and expected behaviors in each talent and to get all students involved in each talent experience. During this stage of implementation, teachers can observe students to note areas of talent strength and areas of talent that have not been developed as well. As both teacher and students have more experiences, teachers can begin to note their own strengths and weaknesses as talent developers and can team with others to provide a total talent approach whenever necessary. As children gain more skill in the use of all the talents, they can be encouraged to choose from a variety of activities in talent areas. However, according to the model, they should participate in activities designed to develop all talent areas; therefore, early specialization should not be an option.

The characteristics of gifted individuals listed earlier in each talent area can be used both as indicators of talent and as guides for developing the specific talent. When students are observed participating in talent activities, their patterns of strength and weakness within a talent area can be developed into an individual talent profile and used to plan a talent development program. At no time, however, should a teacher expect a student to focus only on remediating weaknesses. Each student is a unique person with individual talents and differing rates of growth and development in the talent areas. One of the basic assumptions in the *Multiple Talent Model* is that no one person is expected to be gifted in every talent. Another assumption is that most human enterprises require cooperation and interaction among individuals who can bring different strengths and talents to the collaboration. Social interaction is a critical component of talent development. Taylor also stresses the importance of serious playfulness and posits that laughter and learning often go hand in hand. The purpose of talent development activities is serious, but the activities themselves should be fun and/or engaging. Through social interaction, small-group interdependence, and communication in *Multiple Talent* activities, gifted students have many opportunities to develop cognitive, creative, and social skills in a functional, nonthreatening environment. For guidance in designing activities in each of the talent areas and integrating talents into the curriculum, consult the resources listed at the end of this chapter.

MODIFICATION OF THE BASIC CURRICULUM

The major curricular modifications suggested by Taylor's model are in process, that is, stressing the use rather than acquisition of information. However, the model does suggest certain content and product modifications depending on the talent areas being developed. By concentrating on ideas and skills not usually learned in school, the Taylor model introduces variety into the curriculum. It teaches some of the methods of inquiry, or at least some generic aspects of methodology, through its concentration on world-of-work abilities. Most scientists, for example, must be able to plan their experiments or studies carefully to avoid wasting valuable time or resources. They must plan several years in advance and write detailed proposals to secure funding. They must be able to communicate their results effectively. Even greater skills in planning and decision making are necessary if a person is directing or coordinating a large research project. Indeed, the most appropriate use of Taylor's model in a program for gifted students would be in combination with the development of skills of inquiry. As students learn the more scholarly aspects of methodology, they also could be learning the more practical side.

The Taylor model strongly suggests the use rather than acquisition of information through all talent areas. The entire philosophy of the model centers around having students who are active rather than passive, who do rather than listen. In the assumptions about the student talent area of planning, for example, students are involved in making plans for their own activities and for hypothetical ones. Communication talent involves developing ways to express ideas so that others can understand them. Other talents also develop ways of using information more effectively.

In addition to stressing the use rather than acquisition of information, the *Multiple Talent* approach suggests open-endedness, a form of discovery learning, some freedom of choice, and variety. Open-endedness and freedom of choice are somewhat related in this instance; in certain types of activities, students are encouraged to accomplish a particular purpose through whatever means or whatever talent area the student chooses. Many "right" answers are possible since students select and apply criteria for evaluation, develop and implement their own plans, and communicate in their own way. Usually numerous right or effective ways can be found for handling day-to-day situations.

Taylor's model also suggests the use of forms of discovery learning in certain talent areas. In most of the activities, students develop a plan, make predictions, or develop some procedure. The teacher then asks questions that require students to perform some step or process. Different answers or reactions are then discussed in a group situation. In effect, the teacher is leading them through a process of discovering effective ways of personally doing something successfully.

Product modifications would occur in most instances. Since activities are designed as practical, relevant, world-of-work experiences, the problems would be real and the evaluation appropriate. In most cases, the audience would be real or simulated, and the final product would be a transformation rather than summary of existing information. However, these last two product modifications are not explicitly stated by or generated from the model. They would be present most, but not all, of the time.

Taylor also suggests the following learning environment modifications recommended for the gifted: learner-centeredness, independence, openness, and acceptance. Some of these ideas are not fully developed in his model, but the basic ideas are present. With regard to learner-centeredness, the philosophy of the model requires that emphasis be placed on student ideas, questions, and problems. Because learning activities must be realistic, with an orientation toward the world of work, students are not required to listen to teachers lecture or talk but are expected to produce ideas and products. No specific indication is given for the type of interaction pattern Taylor would encourage in discussions, but since the activities are open-ended and divergence is encouraged, the pattern probably would be learner centered.

Encouraging student independence in nonacademic activities is an important aspect of Taylor's approach, particularly in the talent areas of planning, decision making, and forecasting. With regard to planning, having students plan their own group and individual activities in the class is emphasized. They should develop plans for parties, field trips, management functions, and academic activities. Decision making involves examining their own decisions to determine their effectiveness, while forecasting involves attempting to predict how others would react to something. These predictions and decisions relate to day-to-day interaction with other students as well as to more theoretical or academic content.

Openness (divergence) and acceptance also are significant aspects of Taylor's approach, particularly in developing creative talent. Taylor suggests an environment similar to that recommended by Parnes, with emphasis on quantity rather than quality in the idea-production stage, with deferred judgment, and considering the potential of all ideas. Both students and teachers are encouraged to generate ideas without specifically looking for a solution. Divergence is encouraged in behavior and ideas through the recognition and development of a variety of talents.

Examples of Teaching Activities

The following sample activities will be two types suggested by Taylor. The first is a series of separate learning experiences in each talent area. Although they are built around a theme to enhance the learning of methods of inquiry, they are separate and should involve all children. In other words, all students should participate in every activity to gain experience in each talent area. The second is a series of learning activities that are open-ended enough to allow students to choose their areas of self-expression.

The following series of activities is designed to develop this methodological generalization: *The growth of knowledge in science occurs through questioning, observation, experimentation, manipulation of materials, observation of results, and revision of original theories.*

Creative Talent

In Step 1, students are asked to consider the following problem: "You are a scientist who has been curious about the long- and short-range effects of volcanic ash on the health of residents of the area surrounding a volcano that periodically erupts. What are all the ways you can find out the answer(s) to this dilemma?" In Step 2, in small groups, the students discuss the problem and list some ideas. After working in a small group for a while, they report these ideas to the large group and list as many additional ideas as possible. In Step 3, the students select one or two of the wildest ideas and figure out ways to make them practical. These revised or refined ideas are discussed with the small group. In Step 4, students put these ideas in the back of their minds for a while and return to them again the next day. In Step 5, in a large group, the students see how many new ideas can be added to the list. In Steps 6 and 7, back in the small groups, they select their group's most original and best solutions. The most original may not be the best. Finally, in Step 8, the small groups begin working on a way to carry out their best solution.

Decision-Making Talent

From the previous activity, the students discuss in the same small group how they decided on the best solution. What criteria did they use? What different criteria or standards were used by each person in the group? How did the group make the final decision? Without looking back at the solutions, they discuss what criteria should be used to evaluate each possible solution to select the best. Out of all these criteria, those that are most important and those that do not overlap are chosen. In the large group, all of the alternative solutions are discussed and 10 of the best alternatives chosen. In small groups or individually, the students apply the selected criteria to each of the 10 alternatives and assign a rating of 1 to 3 for each alternative on each criterion. This will yield a total score for each solution.

After this small-group and individual work, students reconvene for a large-group discussion. In this discussion, the teacher's purpose is to stimulate their thinking in new ways about each of the alternatives. The teacher then takes each solution the students have chosen and some from the original list that show promise but were not selected and asks the students the following series of questions about each alternative:

- What would be some of the consequences of this alternative being implemented?
- How would it affect people?
- How would it help in answering the first question?
- What are some of its limitations?

Based on this discussion and without reviewing the initial ratings, each student decides on the best solution and defends that solution. Now, individuals compare their new conclusion with the total scores derived from the systematic rating of each solution.

The teacher then asks the following questions:

- How do your selections compare?

- Why do you think they are similar or different?

- Of the two methods of evaluation or decision making, which do you prefer?

- Why?

- What are the advantages and disadvantages of each method?

Planning Talent

Since students have carefully considered several alternatives and have tentatively decided upon a solution, they can now develop this idea into a definite plan of action. Each student has selected a "best" solution. Individually or in small groups according to the solution they have selected, students plan an actual experiment to find out the answer to their question. The only limitation is that it must be something they actually can carry out; it must be realistic. Students are free to work on their own to develop these plans, and they bring them to class in 2 or 3 days.

When the plans are developed, the teacher works with students in groups of 10 to 15 individuals. Each small group is asked to share its plan. After hearing each proposed plan, the teacher asks the following series of questions:

- What are the elements of a good plan for a scientific experiment?

- List the specific kinds of details that must be included in a good plan.

- Which of these elements would you group together because they are all alike?

- Why would you group them together?

- What would be some good labels for the groups?

- Why would that be a good label?

- Which items already in one group could also go into another?

After this, the items are again regrouped and labeled. Students think about this discussion and their plans and develop, individually or in small groups, an outline for developing plans for scientific experiments. The following day these outlines are shared. The teacher looks at each outline carefully to see that all necessary elements are included. If so, the outlines are made available for future use by the class. If important elements are left out, the teacher asks questions to stimulate students' thinking about what would happen if certain types of elements were left out.

Each individual or small group can then examine its plan based on the discussions and make any needed revisions or additions. After this, the teacher works with the individuals or groups on each plan. He or she considers each one carefully and asks the following series of questions when appropriate:

- What are some problems that could occur?

- How will each of these problems be handled?

- What are some outside forces that might affect the plan?

- How will the plan be modified if _____ happens?

- What is your sequence of steps?

- How can this plan be made more efficient?

- What is each person's responsibility?

The students are now ready to refine the plans one last time and carry them out. The teacher helps secure materials, facilities, and access to equipment. When each individual or group has completed its experiment, the teacher again discusses with them the effectiveness of their plans and how they could be improved the next time. The teacher can ask such questions as the following:

- What was good about your plan?

- What would you do differently next time?

- What were some unanticipated problems or situations?

- How did you handle them?

- How could you have solved these problems through more effective planning?

- How could the process have been made more effective or efficient?

Communication Talent

Now that the students have completed experiments to answer a scientific question, they are ready to consider how to communicate their results in the best way to other interested individuals. As a large group, students consider what they would like to communicate. Questions to stimulate their thinking include the following:

• What were some interesting results?

• What were some surprising results?

• What results had theoretical significance?

• What results had practical significance?

Next, they are asked to think about with whom they would like to share these results. Some questions would be the following:

• What individuals or groups would profit from knowing what you found?

• What groups or individuals are investigating similar questions?

• Whose job would be made easier by knowing the results of your experiment?

• Who would be curious about your results?

After considering what and to whom, they are now ready to think about how these results should be communicated to each identified audience. Each small group or individual is asked to name one person or group with whom they wish to share their results. The large group then considers each of these audiences (one audience at a time) and answers the following questions:

• What results would you share with this audience?

• What are all the ways you could communicate these results? (Brainstorm and list all the possible ways.)

• How do you think this audience would judge your presentation of results (that is, what would they be looking for)?

• With this in mind, which of the ways you have listed would you choose for sharing your results?

The various small groups work together and decide with whom to share their results, and they develop a way to do so. If they decide on a multimedia presentation, they develop this. If a paper seems to be the best method, they write a paper. During this time, the teacher works with individuals and groups. When each is ready, they try out the "communication" on the large group of classmates. This group acts as a simulated audience and points out areas needing clarification or elaboration. The whole group then brainstorms possible ways of improving the communication. It is then revised if necessary and presented to the real audience. Students should ask for an evaluation if it is not automatically provided. The teacher should discuss these evaluations with the students and help them develop better means of communication for the next time. Follow-up activities could include discussing how scientific communication differs from other communication and what the elements of a good scientific report are. Individual words could be chosen and a list of synonyms developed as alternative ways of saying the same thing (word fluency).

Forecasting Talent

In the next activity, students are asked to extend their thinking about the present activity and to predict what might happen in a new situation based on what happened in the previous experiment: "Suppose that the volcano continues to erupt at least twice a month with about the same force as in the past. What do you think the health of the local residents will be like in 5 years?" After allowing the students to think for a few minutes, the teacher should ask the following questions in the order listed:

Step 1. What do you think might happen to the local residents? (List all predictions, stopping the flow only to seek clarification of unclear ideas.)

Step 2. Why do you think this might happen (that is, what were some of the results of your experiment that led you to believe that might happen)? (Ask for reasons for all predictions.)

Step 3. What other conditions would be necessary, both before and during this time, to make this prediction come true? Why would that be necessary? (Ask for conditions and reasons for as many of the predictions as possible.)

Step 4. Suppose all the conditions you listed as necessary did happen and this prediction (select a few medium-range predictions from the list) did come true. What would happen then? Follow the same procedures as in Step 3 with each of the new predictions.

Step 5. Based on this discussion and what you already know, what would you conclude would be most likely to happen to the health of the local residents in 5 years? How did you reach this conclusion? Why did you conclude that would be the most likely result?

During this discussion, the teacher should be an active listener, noticing the types of conditions and consequences listed by students. He or she should make certain the students consider the human element (social awareness), patterns or chains of cause–effect relationships (conceptual foresight), and possible changes that might occur that would affect the predictions (penetration).

MODIFYING THE APPROACH

Content Changes

Taylor's model directly suggests only two content modifications appropriate for the gifted. For this reason, the teaching examples presented incorporate content changes not recommended by a "pure" use of the approach.

The previous example has a high degree of coordination between activities to develop each talent. In fact, they even have a logical sequence. According to Taylor's model, this sequencing and coordination is not necessary. However, to achieve the element of organization for learning value, coordination is desirable. A second element not included by Taylor is having a complex generalization serve as an organizer and as a more abstract idea to provide a long-range focus, thus making the approach more appropriate for use with gifted students. In this case, the generalization used is a methodological one, concerned with the scientific method. It is abstract and complex, contains a variety of concepts, and is appropriate for many disciplines or fields of study. This example illustrates how the practical side of research can be integrated with the theoretical one.

Another content modification that can be integrated easily was not illustrated by the example, that is, the study of eminent or famous people. To continue with the same example, the study of people can be developed through each talent area by studying the life of a famous individual who has conducted research related to volcanic eruptions. This study could include those persons who have looked at sociological effects, effects on health, or geological aspects of volcanic action. Students could examine a selected person's research methods, methods for making decisions, research plans and implementation, communication of results, and accuracy of hypotheses or predictions. They could compare these methods with their own and discuss the differences and similarities along with the possible reasons for these likenesses and differences.

Process Changes

Although Taylor's approach uses many elements of a discovery method, the example has a stronger emphasis on discovery than is recommended by

Taylor. Every talent is developed through a process using elements of discovery. For example, in the planning activity, a didactic (or deductive) approach would have been to discuss the elements of a good plan and even give the students a sample plan before having them make any plans of their own. Children would carry out their own plans and then develop ideas for more effective planning as a result of discovering their own mistakes.

Other aspects of the examples are developed from Taylor's model with some elements of Taba's approach added to enhance or make the questioning of students more systematic. (See Chapter 8.) In the first example, Taylor's suggested eight-step process is followed closely as students list ideas, discuss and refine, incubate, list additional ideas, select the most original idea, select the best idea, and begin to work on the implementation of an idea. The decision-making example follows nicely from the previous activity since the students were involved in some decision making. In this example, students use two means of making decisions; one is a structured, logical approach (that is, logical evaluation), and the other is a less structured, more open-ended approach (that is, experimental evaluation). Students then make their final decisions based on both kinds of evaluation. These two kinds of processes are discussed by Taylor. However, having students compare the two processes and discuss their strengths and weaknesses also is important and is not a part of Taylor's guidelines.

The planning talent example follows easily from the decision-making activity. Once a decision is made, some sort of plan (either brief or detailed) needs to be developed for implementing the decision. In this example, the subskills listed by Taylor are included, as is the Taba concept development strategy. The students are asked to develop detailed plans and to refine these plans (elaboration); to anticipate possible problems and plan ways to handle them (sensitivity to problems); to include their strategies for overall organization and to include sequential steps (organization); and to develop, through a discussion of the elements of a good plan, an outline for planning future experiments (Taba concept development). The skills of alternate planning, replanning, diversified planning, unplanning, and flexible planning are developed as the students develop, revise, discuss, refine, carry out, and then evaluate their own plans. They also discuss how the situation affects planning procedures.

The communication example also follows directly from the previous activity. Although this example concentrates on verbal communication rather than nonverbal, it includes development of expressional fluency (for example, deciding what results to communicate, practicing, receiving criticism); associational fluency (for example, deciding how to communicate with various audiences, practicing for simulated audiences, role-playing audiences); and word fluency (for example, developing lists of synonyms). Other aspects include the elements of real audiences and appropriate evaluation and product modifications necessary for gifted students.

The flow is logical from this to the forecasting example. Students use previous experience to predict what might happen in a new situation. The Taba strategy, application of generalizations, provides an appropriate sequence of questions. The teacher needs to be alert to what students are saying so that they consider all types of influences in making their predictions.

The addition of elements of Taba's *Strategies* not only provides sequence and structure to the Taylor model but also develops the process modification of having students express their reasoning or provide support for their ideas. This combination of strategies ensures that group interaction will occur and provides guidelines for the teacher that can assist in appropriate pacing for different groups of students.

The process modification, freedom of choice, is suggested by Taylor in his recommendation that open-ended activities be developed that will allow for the expression of a variety of talents. Students are encouraged to choose their method of expression. This idea could be carried further. The teacher could encourage the students to choose from a variety of activities or from a variety of content areas. Treffinger's model also could be used in conjunction with this approach as a way to structure the process and assist the teacher and students in moving from teacher-directed activities to entirely student-directed ones.

Following are activities that are open-ended enough to allow the expression of a variety of talents:

- *Activity 1*: Develop, design, or figure out a way to express your appreciation to your mother for everything she has done for you. This can be done individually or in a small group. *Talents*: productive thinking, planning, decision making, communication

- *Activity 2*: Develop an image of the future and share it with an individual or a group. It can be as elaborate or simple as you wish it to be. *Talents*: planning, productive thinking, decision making, communication, forecasting

- *Activity 3:* Create your ideal environment and share it with someone who can help to make your actual environment more ideal. Design it as a way to convince the person to make some needed changes. *Talents*: productive thinking, planning, forecasting, decision making, communication

Table 9.1 provides additional activities.

A final process change that must be made is structured group interaction in which students practice and analyze their own performance as leaders and/or participants in group activities. This change is integrated easily by having the group activities videotaped or audiotaped and then viewing or

TABLE 9.1.   Summary of Teacher and Student Roles and Activities in the Taylor Multiple Talent Approach

Step, Type, or Level of Thinking	Student		Teacher	
	Role	Sample Activities	Role	Sample Activities
Creative talent	Creator Problem solver	Invent a game. Create new uses for familiar objects. Create an object of art that expresses some emotion. Create a useful object by recycling junk.	Stimulator Questioner Resource	Ask questions that lead students through the process of listing, refining, incubation, choosing, and implementing. Develop provocative and/or interesting situations in which students can engage in creative activity.
Productive thinking talent	Active participant Idea generator	Generate many, varied, unusual ideas in response to a question/stimulus. Add to (elaborate on) ideas. Seek unique ideas. Classify ideas/items.	Stimulator Questioner Resource	Ask questions that will lead students to offer many, varied, original ideas. Ask for clarification when needed. List ideas on chalkboard or ask students to generate lists in small groups. Seek variety and originality. Ask questions that lead to classification of ideas.
Forecasting talent	Active participant Idea generator Forecaster	Predict possible effects of a phenomenon or act. Predict possible causes of a phenomenon or act. Predict what might happen if . . . (e.g., there were no gravity). Predict what might happen in the future (e.g., 50 years from now). Give reasons for predictions. Generate a hypothesis. Predict what might happen in an unfinished story.	Stimulator Questioner Resource	Ask questions that assist students in establishing cause and/or effect relationships. Ask questions to stimulate students to use past experiences to predict future events. Develop hypothetical (e.g., What if . . .) situations that enable students to make predictions. Ask questions that will encourage students to notice (1) how conditions change and can affect predictions, (2) how people affect and are affected by events, and (3) how their behavior affects others.

(continues)

TABLE 9.1. *Continued*

Step, Type, or Level of Thinking	Student		Teacher	
	Role	**Sample Activities**	**Role**	**Sample Activities**
Decision-making talent	Active participant Idea generator Decision maker	Make personal choices (e.g., decide what to take on a 2-week trip when you are allowed only one small suitcase). Make value choices (e.g., decide on the characteristics of your ideal person). Make social action choices (e.g., decide what to do about an unjust law). Make life choices (e.g., decide what courses to take in secondary school or college). Make evaluative choices (e.g., select a group of people to include on a planning committee). Contribute to group choices (e.g., decide on a destination for an adventure trip).	Stimulator Questioner Resource	Develop activities in which students must make criteria-based decisions. Pose questions that encourage (or require) students to consider a variety of alternatives, develop criteria for evaluation, relate decisions to goals, consider the effects of their decisions on themselves and others, and use both logic, values, and intuition to reach an effective decision. Ask questions that encourage (or require) students to support and/or defend their decisions. Encourage students to implement their decisions whenever possible. Ask questions that will help students evaluate the results/effects of implementing a decision.

(*continues*)

TABLE 9.1. *Continued*

Step, Type, or Level of Thinking	Student		Teacher	
	Role	Sample Activities	Role	Sample Activities
Planning talent	Active participant Idea generator	Develop personal plans (e.g., goals, resources needed, sequence of activities, and a time line for completing a project). Plan an activity with a group (e.g., a party for the class). Implement plan exactly as prepared. Evaluate the results/consequences of the plan. Draw a blueprint for a new school or other building for young people. Plan a presentation for the results of a group investigation. Plan an in-depth study on a topic of interest. Give directions to a person who is blind. Develop a code or set of universal symbols.	Stimulator Questioner Resource	Plan and implement activities that will help students develop their planning talent. Ask questions that require students to elaborate on their plans, become more sensitive to problems, design alternatives for solving possible problems, develop step-by-step procedures, and use resources wisely. Provide opportunities and support for students in the design of efficient and effective organizational plans. Plan activities in which students write "how-to" plans. Provide opportunities for students to plan real events. Assist students to implement and evaluate their plans. Involve students in making classroom activity plans.

(continues)

TABLE 9.1. *Continued*

Step, Type, or Level of Thinking	Student		Teacher	
	Role	Sample Activities	Role	Sample Activities
Communication talent	Active participant Idea generator Communicator	Generate a list of many, varied words that describe a specified object, event, person, or place. Generate many, varied words that describe feelings. Develop several ways to express a specific feeling—both verbally and nonverbally. Generate similes, metaphors, analogies, and other figurative language to help others understand a relationship or idea. Convey a message to others without using words. Communicate with an audience without using gestures or other body language. Create a "network of ideas" (e.g., essay, letter, story, report) to express your thoughts or share information. Use words or actions to convey to another person that you understand how they feel. Write about an event from the perspective of several different participants. Use "universal symbols" to convey a message to those who speak other languages.	Stimulator Questioner Resource	Provide activities in which students can develop their communication talents with real or simulated audiences. Create situations in which students analyze the effectiveness of a communication and identify successful practices for use in their own writing. Provide numerous opportunities for small-group study and interaction. Provide opportunities for students to practice both verbal and nonverbal communication. Ask questions that encourage students to relate their own experiences to others, select words with clear meanings, seek alternative ways of expressing ideas, develop a large vocabulary, and examine the effects of their words on the feelings/thoughts of others. Set up role plays or simulations in which clear, sensitive, and effective communication can be practiced. Provide opportunities for students to create a variety of communications (e.g., drama, writing, speeches, debate, poetry, choral reading, letter writing). Identify appropriate audiences for student communication products.

listening to the tapes. The previous activities that would easily lend themselves to taping would be the productive thinking exercise, decision making, planning, and forecasting. The lists of characteristics of individuals with each type of talent can be used as observation tools or as a structure for tape analysis. Other behaviors related to group participation or leadership also could be used for the observations.

Product and Environment Changes

Although the teaching example presented earlier incorporates all the product modifications recommended for the gifted, Taylor does not suggest all these changes. He does recommend that problems and questions be relevant, which would imply that the problems are real. However, the students do not necessarily select the problem they will investigate. No suggestions are made pertaining to "real" audiences, but consideration of the audience is a definite aspect of communication talent. Evaluation and transformation are definite aspects of Taylor's approach.

In the example, students are actively engaged in developing products that address problems real to them, that are directed toward real audiences, that involve appropriate audiences, and that are transformations rather than summaries of existing information. Within the problem area of erupting volcanoes, students may choose a topic or an aspect of the investigation. During activities related to communication talent, they consider audiences who would be interested in their product and develop ways of communicating more effectively with those audiences. Decision-making talent activities develop in students the skills involved in evaluating their own products more effectively. The thinking skill, evaluative thinking, which is involved in many of Taylor's talent areas, helps develop the ability to assess individual products effectively.

The learning environment changes of complexity and high mobility, although not addressed by Taylor, are essential if a person is to use the model in the ways suggested by the example. To develop these high-level products and conduct research, students need access to sophisticated materials and equipment, and they must have the freedom of movement that will allow them access to a variety of learning environments.

Summary

The Taylor model can provide a useful structure for a program for the gifted when modified in certain ways or combined with other models. The teaching example presented in this chapter has shown how it could be combined with the Taba *Strategies*. It also could be used effectively in conjunction with Bruner's approach or combined with Renzulli's *Triad* or Treffinger's *Self-Directed Learning Model.*

DEVELOPMENT

The *Multiple Talent* approach arose out of Taylor's research in three main areas: primary mental ability factors, creativity, and functional thinking abilities needed for success in the world of work. Taylor participated in the factor analysis studies that L. L. Thurstone used to identify mental ability factors and show that intelligence involves multiple dimensions or specific talents. Taylor (1947) contributed two new factors—ideational fluency and expressional fluency (verbal versatility)—to the more than 20 primary mental abilities that Thurstone (1935, 1947) and his associates had identified by that time (Taylor, 1978). This body of research was separate from J. P. Guilford's (1959) development of the *Structure of Intellect* theory but not incompatible. Taylor considered Thurstone's and Guilford's models of intelligence too complex for practical use in education (Taylor, 1967). From his own research on scientific talent (sponsored by the National Science Foundation) and communications talents (sponsored by the United States Air Force), Taylor extracted clusters of thinking skills, or talents, commonly needed in the world of work. Based on this research, Taylor proposes that classroom instructional practices be reformed to integrate these functional thinking processes, or talents, into the curriculum. Additional stimulation and research support comes from the work of Taylor, Ellison, and others (Ellison, James, & Fox, 1970; Ellison, James, Fox, & Taylor, 1971; Ellison, Callner, Fox, & Taylor, 1973; Ellison, Abe, Fox, Coray, & Taylor, 1976; Ellison, Nelson, Fox, & Abe, 1978) through the Institute for Behavioral Research in Creativity. IBRIC has been involved in both basic and applied research in creativity, the relationship of behavioral characteristics and biographical information to creative productivity, and career development. *Igniting Creative Potential* (Stevenson et al., 1971), *Igniting Creative Potential II* (Lloyd, Seghini, & Stevenson, 1974), and numerous theme units published by Utah's Jordan School District demonstrate the effective integration of Taylor's approach into all curriculum areas. All activities have been used successfully by regular classroom teachers and teachers of the gifted in a variety of situations.

Talents Unlimited, the nationally validated project, is a three-faceted multiple talent development model that includes staff development services, development of materials to facilitate the integration of talent processes into the curriculum, and the enhancement of student performance in all six talent areas (Schlichter, 1981). The model was developed and implemented initially with 37 teachers of grades 1 to 6 in diverse schools in Mobile County, Alabama. After 3 years of implementation, McLean and Chissom (1980) found significant differences (p < .05) favoring the experimental classrooms in fluency, flexibility, originality, and elaboration. Students in experimental classes also showed significant gains (p < .05) from pretest to posttest on 14 of 35 subparts of the *Stanford Achievement Test* (1989), compared to gains in only 3 subparts for control group students. Experimental research from a sampling of more than 200 adopting sites in all areas of the United States, summarized by McLean and Chissom (1980), also showed significant gains for children in *Talents Unlimited* classes. The project was validated by the U.S. Office of Education as an exemplary program and designated an adoptable program through the National Diffusion Network (NDN). *Talents Unlimited* (Schlichter, 1981), adopted by school districts in 49 states and many countries, holds the record as the most adopted NDN project. The simple, direct "Teacher Talk" used to teach and reinforce steps in each of the talent areas is particularly appealing. The *Multiple Talent* approach also is the basis of two national programs for young inventors: *Invent America* (Canedo, 1987; United States Patent Model Foundation, n.d.) and *Project XL* (Canedo, 1988).

In the initial implementation projects, based on *Multiple Talent* theory, Taylor and his colleagues chose to focus on six talents: academic, productive thinking, communication, forecasting, decision making, and planning. About 10 years later, the featured talents were expanded to include human relations, implementation, and discerning opportunities (Taylor, 1986b). However, activities are not yet available in these three areas.

Originally designed and validated for schoolwide implementation, the *Multiple Talent Model* frequently has been adapted for use in programs for the gifted. Taylor likens programs for the gifted with laboratories for research and development (Taylor, 1986b). In such programs, ". . . there may have been more serious attempts to do new things and to improve education-in-practice than in any other movement in recent years or perhaps in any other period in educational history" (Taylor, 1986b, p. 257). Although Cattell and his associates (Cattell & Butcher, 1968) question the low correlations between giftedness in different talent areas, as shown in Thurstone's (1934) *The Vectors of Mind* and Guilford's (1967) *Structure of Intellect,* on the basis of the method used for factor analysis and assert that the overwhelming evidence of research on the relationships between human abilities shows a high correlation, more recent research supports a theory of multiple talents. For example, Gardner (1983) asserts that at least seven separate intelligences can be supported. Giftedness in one intelligence is not necessarily associated with giftedness in others.

JUDGMENTS

Advantages

The most important advantage of Taylor's model is its relevance to real-world activities through a practical grouping of talents and abilities. It can provide a much-needed dimension to programs for the gifted by its new ways of looking at students. By using the model, the intellectually gifted students in a program will be viewed not only in terms of their academic strengths and weaknesses but also in terms of their nonacademic abilities. These more practical skills then can be included in school experiences and in extracurricular activities. A wider range of learning should occur, thus developing more well-rounded students.

A multidimensional view of giftedness has humanistic appeal to most people and can aid in gaining initial public support for a program for the gifted. Often a narrow definition of giftedness as academic ability promotes the feeling that gifted programs are elitist and that educators are taking the best students to make them better. A different view of giftedness that emphasizes nonacademic abilities and allows more children to be considered talented does not stimulate as much public resistance. Educators could develop a definition of giftedness and a program plan that states that outstanding children in each of five or six talent areas would be served in a program for the gifted. Specific provisions for each of the talent areas could be developed gradually (that is, a talent area could be added every year or every other year) to avoid a massive initial program that may be unmanageable. Of course this is not really the way Taylor intends his model to be used. He emphasizes that talent development should be a part of the total educational approach and not solely the responsibility of a special program. However, the two approaches—a special program for the top children and regular classroom programs emphasizing multiple talents—are not incompatible. In fact, they could complement each other well. At one demonstration site, for example, the *Talents Unlimited* model is integrated with the *Schoolwide Enrichment Model* (Renzulli & Reis, 1985) as an effective approach to comprehensive programming for gifted students and as a tool for educational reform.

As a total educational approach, the *Multiple Talent Model* has numerous advantages. It provides a positive way of looking at children, a practical approach to education, and a promising way to reach all children. In special education programs for the disabled, for example, the *Multiple Talent* approach provides a much-needed positive side. Indeed, it is an approach that has been advocated by the first author (Maker, 1979). Since programs for students who are disabled are designed to provide remediation for weak areas and since special educators are well-trained in identifying and developing weaknesses, they often overlook a child's talents or strengths. These strong areas, in addition to having potential as career areas, can serve as avenues for developing strengths. Evidence from research shows that emphasis on the development of certain kinds of strengths can improve weak areas (Maker, 1979).

In a practical sense Taylor's model is easy to implement in a classroom since the talents are skill areas that adults (teachers) must use frequently. Many classroom-tested idea books are available. Expensive materials are not necessary; most of the activities can be implemented with the materials usually present in a classroom. They just need to be used with a different focus.

As a way to make curricular modifications appropriate for the gifted, Taylor's model is helpful in the content, process, and product areas. In addition to the changes directly suggested by the model (for example, different content, methods of inquiry, and use rather than acquisition of information), several other changes are incorporated easily into the model (for example, discovery learning, real audiences, and real problems).

Extensive research on the *Talents Unlimited* model shows the effectiveness of Taylor's model on student achievement and creativity. Although the question of differential impact on gifted students is not addressed in this research, the model clearly is effective in a variety of programs.

Disadvantages

On the negative side, using all of Taylor's ideas as the basis for a categorically funded special education program could jeopardize the funding for such a program. One simply cannot justify a special education program that could potentially serve 30% to 50% of the students in a school. Since Taylor suggests that one third of the students will be "highly gifted" in some area and 90% will be above average, if a program served only the highly gifted and the gifted, and if Taylor is correct in his percentages, it probably would serve at least 50% of the students.

Although the talent areas do reflect a different emphasis, they are not mutually exclusive or well defined. For example, the proposed step-by-step sequence for development of talent in productive thinking includes two steps that relate to decision making (for example, choosing the best solution or the most original solution) and one step that relates to planning (for example, implementing the solution). Even though "choosing the best solution" is the whole act of decision making, Taylor does not suggest that appropriate decision-making activities be incorporated when developing the productive thinking talent. This encourages an unrealistic situation: using an appropriate process for making decisions when decision-making talent is the instructional focus but using an inappropriate one when productive thinking is the instructional focus. In this case, the step-by-step procedure (that is, the talent development guideline) does not go well with the definition and subskills of fluency, flexibility, and originality. Choosing the best solution and implementing the solution are not steps in developing these three skills. Several other examples of category overlap can be found.

In addition, certain subskills within talent areas overlap or are ill-defined. For example, in the talent area of decision making, two subskills, experimental evaluation and logical evaluation, would be almost the same if a person used only the definition given instead of developing individual ideas about the two types. Both types involve carefully considering a variety of alternatives and then choosing the best of these. The only difference is that in logical evaluation a person goes through the process more systematically by writing down each alternative, evaluating each, and then choosing the best from the list. In the *Talents Unlimited* model, this confusion between evaluative components of productive thinking talent and decision-making talent has been removed. Productive thinking talent is focused on divergent thinking skills of fluency, flexibility, originality, and elaboration. Evaluative and convergent thinking processes are included in decision-making talent activities. With so much overlap between talent areas, developing learning activities "pure" enough to develop a particular talent or observations to identify talented children is difficult.

CONCLUSION

Although Calvin Taylor's *Multiple Talent* approach in its entirety may not be appropriate for categorically funded programs for the gifted because of its philosophy that most children are talented in some way, adaptations of the model can enhance a program. It provides a new way of looking at students and can serve as a model for making education more relevant to the real-life needs of adults. Gifted students, who may be skilled academically, may need help in developing some of the practical skills addressed by this model. Taylor's approach encourages the development of thinking skills and the acquisition of knowledge at the same time as the development of practical talent areas.

RESOURCES

Background Information

McLean, J. E., & Chisson, B. S. (1980). *Talented Unlimited program: Summary of research findings for 1979–80.* Mobile, AL: Mobile County Public Schools. (ERIC Document Reproduction Service No. ED 198-660)

Reynolds, L. R. (1978). A history of the multiple talents approach to education (Doctoral dissertation, University of Utah, 1978). *Dissertation Abstracts International, 39,* 787A.

Schlichter, C. L. (1986). Applying the multiple talent approach in mainstream and gifted programs. In J. S. Renzulli (Ed.), *Systems and models for developing programs for the gifted and talented* (pp. 352–389). Mansfield Center, CT: Creative Learning Press.

Taylor, C. W. (1967). Questioning and creating: A model for curriculum reform. *Journal of Creative Behavior, 1*(1), 22–23.

Taylor, C. W., Ghiselin, B., & Yagi, K. (1967). *Exploratory research on communication abilities and creative abilities* (Final report). Research sponsored by the Air Force Office of Scientific Research Directorate of Information Sciences Office of Aerospace Research, U.S. Air Force under Grant AF-AFOSR-144-63.

Resources and Materials

Lloyd, B. C., Seghini, J. B., & Stevenson, G. M. (1974). *Igniting creative potential II.* Sandy, UT: Jordan School District. A second volume of teacher-tested activities in all of the multiple talent areas. Teacher behavior checklists and guidelines for the development of specific talents are integrated with many, varied examples of activities to use with students. Very few of the activities are "dated" and the book retains its usefulness in classrooms today.

Stevenson, G., Seghini, J. B., Timothy, K., Brown, K., Lloyd, B. C., Zimmerman, M. A., Maxfield, S., & Buchanan, J. (1981/1971). *Project implode.* Sandy, UT: Jordan School District. Project Implode is based on the research findings of C. W. Taylor and his colleagues and was written by teachers for teachers. Participants in the project believe individuals are capable of thinking in more creative, productive ways than they normally do and that they do not use all their creative capacities. The basic goal of the book is to recommend materials and strategies that can be used in all content areas to develop creative thinking in all six multiple talent areas: productive thinking, planning, communication, forecasting, decision making, and academic pursuits. The book features separate chapters on all categories except academic talent and includes a section on divergent production, convergent production, and evaluation. Each chapter provides theoretical background, curriculum construction guidelines, and examples of activities designed to develop the talent discussed in the chapter.

Discovering space: A partnership in exploration. (1990). Provo, UT: Brigham Young University Public School Partnership Gifted and Talented Education Committee. A valuable resource for a yearlong, K–12 theme study of space exploration collaboratively written by university scholars and teachers of the gifted, the book contains initial lessons on key concepts, procedures, and possible products; both print and nonprint resources are identified for each module. Many of the modules integrate activities in several talent areas with complex content.

Both Implode books and the BYU-Public School Partnership books are available from

> Jordan School District
> 9361 South 300 East
> Sandy, UT 84070

Materials and staff development based on the *Multiple Talent* approach are available through

> Talents Unlimited
> 1107 Arlington Street
> Mobile, AL 36605

> Talents Unlimited to the Secondary Power
> P.O. Box 1997
> Tuscaloosa, AL 35486-1997

Resources for inventive thinking include:

> Invent America
> 1505 Powhatan Street
> Alexandria, VA 22314

> Project XL
> Public Service Center
> Patent and Trademark Office
> Washington, DC 20231

Chapter 10

Donald J. Treffinger: Self-Directed Learning

An important priority in education of the gifted is to help children develop independent learning skills so they can become self-directed learners. This self-regulation may be particularly important in areas that do not have formal programs for gifted children. Often educators assume that because children are gifted, when they are free to work on their own they automatically will become self-directed learners. However, independent learning requires some specific skills and attitudes, and even gifted children probably do not possess skills that will enable them to conduct their own research and make plans for their own learning until they have had some guided experience in the process. Children who always have been told what to learn, how to learn it, when and where to learn, and whether their learning or products are satisfactory cannot be expected to take over these responsibilities and handle them well. Students need some training in certain prerequisite skills before they take on the challenge of learning on their own. The *Self-Directed Learning Model* provides a structure in which students gradually develop the skills necessary to become self-directed learners. It is a model for moving both teacher and student toward an environment in which self-directed learning can occur through a sequential development of management, organizational, and research skills. In this setting, gifted students become more involved in designing and conducting their own learning; motivation is increased as students are able to investigate topics of interest to them.

ASSUMPTIONS UNDERLYING THE MODEL

Self-directed learning is neither random nor disorganized (Treffinger, 1975). Successful independent study requires careful organization and thoughtful planning by both student and teacher. The learner's movements in the class-room and to other research sites must be purposeful activity directed toward the attainment of specific goals. Self-directed learning also must have a structure that works for the benefit of students rather than one that inhibits or restricts their learning. Also, students involved in self-directed learning should have many opportunities to work with other students as well as time to work alone. As students become better managers, or more self-directed, they have greater freedom to pace their own learning, select the content and outcomes of independent studies, and participate in the evaluation of their products and experiences. Both student and teacher assess the progress of the learner and identify evidence of progress, areas of concern, and evidence of accomplishment as a step toward identifying new goals and learning ob-jectives for the next independent study. Three of the models in this volume emphasize independent research as an essential skill for students but do not provide clear guidelines for development of the necessary skills. Treffinger's model helps to fill that gap.

About Teaching

A central idea underlying the model is that teaching involves the follow-ing basic factors that can be used to analyze any instructional event or se-quence: (a) identification of goals and objectives, (b) assessment of entering behavior, (c) identification and implementation of instructional procedures, and (d) assessment of performance. In most classrooms, all these factors are completely under the direction and control of the teacher. To foster self-directed learning, the teacher can provide systematic experiences that in-volve varying degrees of self-direction in each of these four areas. For exam-ple, in identifying goals and objectives under a teacher-directed model, the teacher decides what will be learned. In the first step toward self-direction, the teacher provides choices or options for the students. In the second step, the teacher involves the students in creating the options. At the third step, or *Self-Directed Learning,* the learner controls the choices, and the teacher simply provides the resources and materials.

Movement toward self-directed learning must involve all four aspects of the instructional process, that is, identification of goals and objectives, as-sessment of entering behavior, identification and implementation of instruc-tional procedures, and assessment of performance. If students have deter-mined their own areas of study, the teacher should not be the only source of assessment of existing level of development or knowledge. Also, if students have determined their own methods of study, practice time, and activities, the teacher should not completely control the evaluation and subsequent assignment of grades. Most students also need to be moved sequentially from teacher direction to teacher options with student choice, then to options created by both student and teacher, and finally to options and choices determined by students. The teacher's role undergoes a dramatic change, from the person who makes the decisions to the one who advises, assists, and provides resources for the learning options selected by students.

About Learning

Treffinger makes two assumptions about learning. First, children will learn better if involved in their own learning. Second, they will be more motivated to learn if they are directing their learning in areas of their own choice. These assumptions are closely related to Bruner's (1960) ideas about discovery learning. When children are active rather than passive participants in the learning process, they learn more, remember it longer, and develop more self-confidence in their ability to figure things out on their own. This also contributes to greater motivation for learning.

About Characteristics and Teaching of the Gifted

Although the *Self-Directed Learning Model* was not developed exclusively for use with gifted children, Treffinger planned it to enhance certain unique characteristics associated with giftedness: independence of thought and judgment, persistence, and the ability to initiate one's own work. The model also is designed to capitalize on curiosity about problems and issues, ability to think abstractly and to make inferences and generalize, and the drive to understand something that is unknown or puzzling. Because of these traits, self-directed learning for gifted children is not selfish or trivial. By using the natural desires of gifted students to learn about or investigate "adult" problems and important issues, teachers can make certain that students are involved in studying content areas that are important in their overall development.

A related reason for considering self-directed learning as a priority in the education of gifted students is that it enables educators to accomplish other goals that often are discussed but seldom accomplished, such as applying what is learned in school to other day-to-day challenges. In addition, the skills involved in directing individual learning in school are similar to (if not exactly the same as) the skills involved in lifelong learning and scholarly inquiry. The ability to organize resources to meet goals, manage time effectively, and direct one's own studies may be the most important outcome of using this model.

ELEMENTS/PARTS

Levels

Within each of the four instructional areas (identifying goals and objectives, assessing entering behavior, implementing instruction, and evaluating performance), Treffinger identifies four levels, or movement from teacher direction to self-direction. In the first step toward self-direction, the teacher creates options from which the students choose. In the second step, the students are involved in creating the choices. Table 10.1 contains specific descriptions of each of the levels within the four areas of instruction.

Implementing the Approach

When implementing Treffinger's model and moving students toward self-directed learning, teachers must first assess how much self-direction they have been allowing each student. Are all plans always made by the teacher? Are learners now allowed to suggest areas of study? Are students' choices limited to rate and pace rather than the more important areas of content and sequence of activities? Who conducts the evaluations? How much direction is the teacher willing to share?

After reflecting on his or her own performance, a teacher also must carefully assess each student to determine level of self-direction in each of the four areas. An assumption that most students are still at the teacher-directed level may be safe in heterogeneously grouped classes, but gifted children often are able to identify areas of interest for independent study. Making a choice would place the student at level two of self-direction in identifying goals and objectives. Few children, however, have had much experience in evaluating their own performance, so a student who can identify goals and objectives still may be unable to identify appropriate criteria for evaluating the quality of his or her own work. Teachers may make an estimate of the level of self-direction attained by a student in each of the four areas, or the teacher and student may cooperatively determine the level attained in each of the four areas. The teacher also can use more formal assessment procedures, such as tests of research and study skills. The most common form of assessment is a self-report in which students are asked to rate themselves on a series of characteristics necessary for self-directed learning.

Learning style inventories also determine student preferences in areas relating to independent learning. For example, the *Learning Style Inventory* (Dunn, Dunn, & Price, 1975) contains items that are related to student emotional characteristics, such as motivation, persistence, responsibility, and the need for either structure or flexibility. Another instrument, the *Learning Styles Inventory* (Renzulli & Smith, 1978) is designed to determine (among

TABLE 10.1. Treffinger's Model for Self-Directed Learning

Decisions To Be Made	Teacher Directed	Levels of Self-Direction		
		Self-Directed—Level 1	Self-Directed—Level 2	Self-Directed—Level 3
Goals and objectives	Teacher prescribes for total class or individuals.	Teacher provides choices or options for students.	Teacher involves learner in creating options.	Learner controls choices; teacher provides resources and materials.
Assessment of entry behaviors	Teacher tests, then makes specific prescription.	Teacher diagnoses, then provides several options.	Teacher and learner hold diagnostic conference; tests employed individually if needed.	Learner controls diagnosis, consults teacher for assistance when unclear about some need.
Instructional procedures	Teacher presents content, provides exercises and activities, arranges and supervises practice.	Teacher provides options for student to employ independently at her or his own pace.	Teacher provides resources and options, uses contracts that involve learner in scope, sequence, and pace decisions.	Learner defines project and activities, identifies resources needed, and makes scope, sequence, and pace decisions.
Assessment of performance	Teacher implements evaluation procedures, chooses instruments, and gives grades.	Teacher relates evaluation to objectives and gives student opportunity to react or respond.	Peer partners used to provide feedback; teacher and learner conferences used for evaluation.	Learner does self-evaluation.

Note. Adapted from "Teaching for Self-Directed Learning: A Priority for the Gifted and Talented" by D. J. Treffinger, 1975, *The Gifted Child Quarterly, 19,* pp. 46–49. Adapted with permission.

other areas) student preferences that are related to projects (for example, working on a project with other students with little help from the teacher or working with other students on a project the teacher suggests) and independent study (for example, planning a project individuals will work on by themselves or working individually to collect information on a topic chosen by the student).

Although self-reports are valuable sources of information about students' perceptions of their own abilities and preferences, additional procedures are necessary to supplement this information. Students can be placed in simulated situations where characteristics related to self-direction are observed by the teacher; peer evaluations can be used; and teacher or parent ratings can be obtained.

To facilitate the assessment of student self-directedness as it relates to each of the dimensions of instruction identified by Treffinger, a checklist similar to the one shown in Exhibit 10.1 could be devised. In this checklist, items have been adapted from various instruments and from reports of research on the characteristics of self-directed learning. They have been categorized according to the areas and levels of Treffinger's model. The same checklist used to assess the entry level of each child in each area also could be used as a guide in planning activities designed to facilitate a student's movement toward higher levels of self-direction and to evaluate progress. If a student already is a self-directed learner, he or she should be assisted at that level and not be required to progress through the lower levels with other students.

In addition to assessing each child's independence skills with respect to Treffinger's levels, the teacher can identify certain characteristics of successful, independent learners, assess a child's level of development on each of them, and use them as independent learning goals. A useful list of competencies is given by Atwood (1974):

II. Investigation and organization
  A. Investigation
    1. Recognize and understand a variety of investigatory techniques and why they are used
      a) Conduct observations
      b) Conduct surveys
      c) Conduct multi-media research
      d) Conduct interviews
      e) Conduct experiments
      f) Participate in simulations
    2. Know what sources are available and appropriate for investigation
      a) Recognize and use a variety of media as sources of data and ideas

(outline continues on page 333)

EXHIBIT 10.1.   Sample Checklist for Rating the Independent Learning Characteristics of Students

Area	Self-Directed Level 1	Self-Directed Level 2	Self-Directed Level 3
Identification of goals and objectives	(a) Given several choices of topics/areas of study, can choose one of interest. (b) Likes to select learning activities from a small number of choices. (c) Asks questions about topics being studied. (d) Establishes priorities when given a small number of choices. (e) Is good at games of strategy when anticipating only one move ahead. (f) When some consequences or effects are listed, can predict additional ones.	(a) Given a general subject area and examples of topic areas within the subject, can identify additional questions or topics to study. (b) Given a general subject area, can identify several topic areas to study or several interest areas. (c) Sometimes asks questions about new topics. (d) Establishes priorities when provided with choices. (e) Is good at games of strategy when anticipating a few moves ahead. (f) Sometimes foresees consequences or effects of actions.	(a) Without being given a subject or topic area, can identify a variety of topics or problems of interest. (b) Likes to develop own learning options. (c) Constantly asking questions about new topics. (d) Develops own priorities from unlimited or undefined choices. (e) Is good at games of strategy when anticipating many moves ahead. (f) Always foresees consequences or effects of actions.

(continues)

EXHIBIT 10.1. *Continued*

Area	Self-Directed Level 1	Self-Directed Level 2	Self-Directed Level 3
Assessment of entering behaviors	(a) Given several options of areas of need, can select area of greatest need. (b) Given a list of prerequisite skills necessary to accomplish a goal, can understand why these are necessary. (c) Can accept and understand the teacher's assessment of skill development in identified areas. (d) Given a list of details that may be necessary to accomplish a goal, can select those that are important.	(a) Given several examples of areas of need, can suggest additional areas to be assessed. (b) Can identify, with the help of a teacher, prerequisite skills necessary to accomplish a certain task or project. (c) Can contribute to a discussion of own level of skill development in identified areas. (d) Can take into account most of the details necessary to accomplish a task.	(a) Can identify prerequisite skills necessary to accomplish a task or project. (b) Can match own assessment of entering skills with assessment on standardized or teacher-designed assessment measures. (c) Can identify areas of personal need not already identified by teacher. (d) Can take into account almost all the details necessary to accomplish a task.

(continues)

EXHIBIT 10.1. *Continued*

Area	Self-Directed Level 1	Self-Directed Level 2	Self-Directed Level 3
Identification and implementation of instructional procedures	(a) Chooses learning center activities that have sequential task cards.	(a) Chooses learning center activities with many suggested options.	(a) Chooses learning centers with materials but no specific suggestions for activities.
	(b) Can stick with a self-identified project for 1 or 2 weeks without losing interest.	(b) Chooses learning centers with open-ended activities.	(b) Develops own learning centers.
	(c) Can stick with a self-identified topic or project if the teacher gives continual reinforcement and reminders.	(c) Can stick with a self-identified project for a month without losing interest.	(c) Can stick with a self-identified topic or project (for an indefinite period of time) until it is completed without losing interest.
	(d) Given examples of several sources of information, can select the most appropriate.	(d) Can stick with a self-identified topic if a contract has specified the objectives, procedures, and due date.	(d) Can use the card catalog and other means to identify all possible sources of information on a topic.
	(e) Given options for information or resources, can determine which ones are necessary and/or desirable for accomplishing a task.	(e) Can identify several sources of information on a topic.	(e) Can select the most effective and efficient sources of information on a topic.
	(f) Given a set of steps that may be necessary to accomplish a task, can select all that are necessary and develop a realistic sequence.	(f) Given some options for information or resources, can generate additional ones necessary and/or desirable.	(f) Can determine, without assistance, what information or resources are necessary to accomplish a task.
	(g) Given alternative methods for accomplishing a task, can select the most important, effective, and/or interesting.	(g) Can break an activity down into general component steps, but needs assistance in identifying smaller components and in sequencing steps.	(g) Can arrange a complex activity into sensible, sequential steps.
	(h) Allots time necessary to execute steps if constantly reminded or has deadlines for intermediate steps.	(h) Given examples of alternative methods for doing a task, can generate additional methods.	(h) Can identify various alternative methods to accomplish a goal.
		(i) Allots time to execute most steps in a process effectively, but must do some things hurriedly at the end.	(i) Effectively allots time to execute all steps in a process.

(continues)

EXHIBIT 10.1. *Continued*

Area	Self-Directed Level 1	Self-Directed Level 2	Self-Directed Level 3
Assessment of performance	(a) Needs daily feedback from teacher on progress toward goals on teacher-identified criteria.	(a) Needs intermittent feedback from teacher on progress toward goals.	(a) Can determine criteria for evaluation of progress with occasional requests for teacher advice.
	(b) Can react or respond to teacher evaluation of progress (agree or disagree).	(b) Can suggest additional criteria for evaluation of performance when given examples by the teacher.	(b) Can closely match self-evaluation with evaluations made by others.
	(c) Can realistically react (or respond) to teacher-determined areas of strength and weakness in own products.	(c) Can discuss progress toward goals with a teacher.	(c) Can pinpoint general and specific areas of strength and weakness in own products.
	(d) Given criteria that would be used by different audiences to evaluate products, can understand why those criteria would be important.	(d) Can pinpoint some general areas of strength and weakness in own product.	(d) Can determine criteria that would be used by various audiences to evaluate a product.
		(e) Given a list of possible criteria for evaluation of a product by various audiences, can select criteria that are important.	

       b) Give examples of specific sources for a variety of data
  3. Know why and how sources are organized
       a) Understand why sources are organized
       b) Recognize and understand the parallel between media and the places media (sources) are stored
       c) Recognize and understand various patterns of organization
       d) Understand the concept of cross-referencing

B. Organization
  1. Understand why data are organized
       a) Recognize organization techniques that facilitate understanding (of data)
       b) Recognize organization techniques that facilitate future reference
       c) Recognize organization techniques that communicate data and ideas
  2. Know how to select data for organization
       a) Identify relevant and irrelevant material
       b) Identify topics and themes
       c) Identify sequences
       d) Identify main ideas and details
  3. Organize data in a variety of ways
       a) Use classification patterns and techniques
       b) Use sequential patterns and techniques
       c) Use symbolic patterns and techniques

III. Analysis and evaluation
A. Analysis
  1. Understand why and how to pull data apart
       a) Distinguish between main idea and supportive details
       b) Distinguish between fact, fiction and opinion
       c) Recognize cause and effect relationships
       d) Recognize trends and patterns
  2. Know how to interpret individual findings
       a) Make comparisons and analogies
       b) Draw conclusions
       c) Make inferences
       d) Weigh possibilities
       e) Make predictions
B. Evaluation
  1. Understand how to assess data from a variety of viewpoints
       a) Verify data
       b) Recognize forms of bias
       c) Determine adequacy of data

2. Understand how to assess a variety of interpretations of the same data
    a) Compare interpretations with previous knowledge
    b) Compare interpretations with other data (Atwood, 1974)

Examples

After each student's present level of self-direction is identified, the next step is to design activities to enhance skills at the present level and move students gradually to the higher ones. The following examples present three students from the same classroom who are at different levels of self-direction. For the sake of simplicity, each student is characterized as being at the same level in all four areas of instruction. However, in a real situation, one learner might be at a different level in each of the areas.

Self-Directed, Level 1

Amy is a newly identified gifted 9-year-old student who has been in traditional classrooms in which little, if any, self-directedness is allowed. As a somewhat typical gifted student, she has shown signs of an independent nature and prefers to work on her own to a certain extent.

During her first few weeks in the program, Mr. Jenkins, her special teacher, observed her closely during free choice time. He noticed that she enjoyed having a small number of learning center activities from which to choose but that she preferred centers that provided sequential task cards to follow. She was unable to develop her own learning activities at the open-ended centers and would frequently ask Mr. Jenkins to suggest some things for her to do. After these observations, he began to work with Amy to increase her skills in independent learning. The first challenge was having her make choices from a wide variety of activities and encouraging her to begin to identify some new learning center activities. He also decided, at the same time, to have Amy work for longer periods of time on activities they identified together. In the first 2-day plan for learning center time, Amy was given a list of six possible experiments that could be done at a learning center of her choice (science). She was to complete four of the experiments and write her observations. At the end of the 2 days, Amy and Mr. Jenkins were to have a conference to discuss the experiments, Amy's progress, and any problems she might have had.

After the first day, Amy was having trouble with the task. She kept coming back to the teacher to ask where to get materials, about specific steps in her experiments, and for advice about which experiment she should try next. Mr. Jenkins thought he should help her plan more carefully at the beginning so that she would know in advance what to do. He then sat down with Amy and developed a 2-day "contract" (see Exhibit 10.2). Together they reviewed the choices and decided which experiments and activities Amy would do. They decided on a time to meet again and both signed the contract. At the end of the 2 days, Amy proudly came back to talk with Mr. Jenkins about her successful experience. She was happy to have been able to work on her own. They discussed the results of her activities and any problems she had in working on her own. Together they identified some possible solutions to the problems and decided to develop a contract for a longer period of time.

EXHIBIT 10.2.   Amy's Learning Contract

I, __*Amy L.*__, agree to do the following experiments or activities at the science learning center. I will work on my own as much as possible until I am finished. I will find my own materials and will work hard.

__X__   Look at an onion skin under the microscope. Draw a picture of how it looks.

__X__   Mix a solution of iodine and water and put it on an onion skin. Look at the onion skin under the microscope and draw a picture of how it looks.

_____   Do the taste test on all mystery powders and write what happened.

_____   Do the smell test on all mystery powders and write what happened.

__X__   Make a clay boat that will float. Draw a picture of it and write how long it floated.

__X__   Make a clay boat that will float and carry at least 5 marbles without sinking. Draw a picture of the boat and write how long it floated and how many marbles it held.

I will finish this contract on __*Tuesday*__ and will talk about my experiments or activities with my teacher.

Signed,

_____
Student

_____
Teacher

Self-Directed, Level 2

Tom, an 11-year-old, also a newly identified gifted student, has recently moved to the school from a nontraditional setting where he has been encouraged during the past year to assume more responsibility for his own learning. He now is able to identify problems to investigate within a topic area and to develop, with his teacher, alternative ways for solving the problems.

As Mr. Jenkins and Tom began to talk about possible learning activities for him, Mr. Jenkins found that Tom had never researched a topic and written a review using more than a couple of standard references. After he asked Tom a few questions about the card catalog, Mr. Jenkins suggested that before Tom began to look for references on his topic, he should learn how to use the card catalog to locate sources in the school and public libraries. Tom agreed and suggested further that he learn about other reference sources since his topic, "terrorism," had been the subject of recent newspaper and magazine articles. Tom thought this new information would be valuable. Based on this need that Tom identified, Mr. Jenkins decided to give Tom and a few other students a short test to see how much they already knew about references. Mr. Jenkins then planned a short minicourse to teach what they did not know.

During the minicourse, Tom did some preliminary checking on possible sources of information about terrorism, so he felt ready to discuss his investigation and develop a plan for it. He and Mr. Jenkins then scheduled a long conference to develop a learning contract. The contract they developed was more open-ended than Amy's but had the structure and clarity Tom needed in order to continue on his own. (See Exhibit 10.3.) While they were discussing the research and how Tom would use different references, Mr. Jenkins was pleased with the detail and sequencing of Tom's plans. Tom had even made telephone calls to a local university requesting suggestions for individuals who might be interviewed on the topic. A tentative plan was developed, along with an estimated time schedule for completion. They both agreed that in a few weeks they would get together again, and by that time they would be able to set a more definite date of completion.

The only problem Tom seemed to have was in figuring out what criteria to use in evaluating his project. His work had always been graded by someone else, so he had assumed this would still be true. When Mr. Jenkins asked, "What standards shall we use in judging the quality of your work?" Tom just looked blank and asked, "What standards shall we use?" "Yes," said Mr. Jenkins. "It is important that these standards be decided upon ahead of time so you will know what to work toward." Clearly, Tom needed help in developing this part of his contract. Mr. Jenkins then suggested that Tom look through some research reports done by other students and write

EXHIBIT 10.3.   Tom's Learning Contract

Title and Description of Project: I plan to research the topic of terrorism and present my findings to the class. At the same time that I am learning about the topic, I also will learn how to use a lot of different references.

Proposed Areas of Exploration:

(1) *History of terrorism*

(2) *Countries where terrorists have been or now are active*

(3) *Possible causes of terrorism*

(4) *Possible effects of terrorism*

Sources of Information for Each Area:

Area   Source(s)

(1) *Newspaper and magazine articles, books*

(2) *Newspaper and magazine articles, books, TV news*

(3) *Articles, books, interviews, TV news*

(4) *Articles, books, interviews, TV news*

Steps To Be Accomplished (in order of completion):

(1) *Use card catalog in school library to locate books.*

(2) *Use other references (e.g.,* Reader's Guide*) in school library to identify articles.*

(3) *Review sources from school to determine whether additional ones are needed.*

(4) *Locate additional sources (if any) suggested by these resources.*

(5) *If necessary, use card catalog and other references to locate resources in other libraries (public and university).*

(6) *Locate someone to interview. Make calls to the university, local historical society, etc., to attempt to find a subject.*

(7) *Develop questions for interview based on readings.*

(8) *Check questions with Mr. Jenkins and review interview procedures.*

(9) *Organize information and make outline. Go over outline with Mr. Jenkins.*

Description of Product:

The product will be a written research report with seven sections. The sections are: (1) What is terrorism? (2) History, (3) Facts about terrorism, (4) Some causes and effects, (5) One person's encounter with terrorism, (6) Some solutions, and (7) A list of references.

(continues)

EXHIBIT 10.3.   *Continued*

Evaluation of Product:

Method	Person	Criteria
checklist	*self*	*completeness, accuracy, interest, use of references, organization*
checklist	*Mr. J.*	*same as above*
checklist	*Marcy*	*same as above*

Conferences:

Day	Date	Time	Comment
Tues	*4/18*	*8:30*	_____
Thurs	*4/20*	*9:00*	_____
Tues	*4/25*	*8:30*	_____
_____	_____	_____	_____

Expected Date of Completion: _____

Signatures:

_____
Student

_____
Teacher

Notes: _____

_____

_____

what he thought was good about them, what he thought was bad about them, and what things he thought would separate the good ones from the bad ones. After this process and after thinking seriously about his own project, Tom talked again with Mr. Jenkins about the criteria and methods for evaluation. Two days later, they met again, discussed the other research reports, and together decided how Tom's project would be evaluated.

Self-Directed, Level 3

Marcy, the third student, is a 13-year-old who has been in Mr. Jenkins' program for 3 years and in other special programs since she was 7. She always has been an independent person and has developed skills in managing her own time. This allows her to work for several months on a project with minimal involvement of her teacher. Since she has been working with Mr. Jenkins for 3 years, she understands how much self-directedness is allowed and encouraged in his program. Marcy is a curious girl and always has ideas for a million projects or investigations. Her biggest problem is being able to narrow down a topic so that it is manageable in a reasonable length of time. Since Marcy recognizes this as a problem, she always comes to Mr. Jenkins for help when beginning a new project. They usually spend several days discussing a general topic area, with Mr. Jenkins asking questions about Marcy's interests until they can identify a reasonable project or investigation. Since she is a realistic planner, Marcy realizes she cannot do everything related to a topic and wants to concentrate on the most important or most interesting aspects.

This time, Marcy became interested in color theory (Lüscher, 1969) or the area of psychology that is concerned with the prediction of personality characteristics based on people's preferences for certain colors. As a result of their first conversation, Mr. Jenkins found out that she wanted to know how the color tests are done, something about the underlying theory, how this theory differs from other personality theories, and what psychologists think about the validity of this popularized idea. She also wanted to try out the tests on some people so that predictions made as a result of the test could be compared to her knowledge of the individual's personality characteristics.

To help Marcy choose what to study and to help her develop some skills in narrowing a topic, Mr. Jenkins decided to use some *Creative Problem Solving* strategies in the problem-finding step. (See Chapter 5.) After explaining to her what he'd like to try and getting her enthusiastic approval for the idea, Mr. Jenkins asked Marcy to begin at the fact-finding step. She would develop a brief chart of things she already knew, things she needed to find out, and the sources for unknown information. The purpose of this activity was to find out more about the topic so she would have a better idea of its magnitude. She also might identify some areas of particular interest at the same time.

The next activity Mr. Jenkins asked Marcy to do was to brainstorm and list as many open-ended, creative questions (problem finding) as she could about color theory. Over a period of a few days, she wrote on note cards all the questions she might possibly ask about the topic. Armed with her half-inch stack of cards, Marcy came back to Mr. Jenkins for her next conference. Together they spread out the cards and read through the questions. Mr. Jenkins asked Marcy to begin grouping together (Taba's concept development strategy) the questions that seemed similar. They worked on the task for quite a while, grouping and regrouping the questions until they were satisfied with the categories.

The categories they developed were the following: (a) theoretical development (What other theories led to this one? From what "branch" or "school" of psychology was it generated? When did it begin?); (b) theoretical validity (What do practicing psychologists and university professors think of the theory? What research has been done to test the accuracy of predictions? What would happen if it were given to friends whose personality is known?); and (c) the test itself (Exactly how does a person conduct the color test? Why is it done that way? How are predictions made from it? How long does it take?). Mr. Jenkins then asked Marcy which she thought would be more interesting or more beneficial: selecting the one most important question out of each category (resulting in an overview of the theory) or selecting one category and asking the questions within only that category (resulting in an in-depth study of some aspect of the theory). After much talk and several days of thinking, Marcy decided that her main interest was in the validity of the theory but that she would need to answer a few of the questions from other categories, and she would certainly need to learn how to do the test so she could try it on some known individuals.

Marcy now had to design her investigation and get started on the project. Using the major questions as a guide, she developed a brief outline of the steps she would take. (See Exhibit 10.4.) The whole project would be completed by the end of the semester and presented to the class.

Later, Marcy might decide to present her project elsewhere, but at the moment she is planning only a class presentation. Since she is a good planner, Marcy is expected to ask for assistance only when needed and to tell Mr.

EXHIBIT 10.4. Marcy's Tentative Outline

Name:	*Marcy G.*
Topic:	*Color Theory*
Questions:	*What are the important parts of the theory?* *How was it developed?* *What do psychologists think of it?* *What research has been done on it?* *How does one do the test?* *What would happen if the test were given to friends?*
Sources:	*Lüscher's book, psychology department teachers at university and high school, reviews of the book*
Materials Needed:	*Construction paper, paint*
Possible Evaluation:	*Interest to class, interest to psychologists, a reasonable number of sources*
Progress Notes:	

Jenkins when she needs resources or materials. Her outline of steps is filed in her folder, where she also keeps brief notes about her progress. Mr. Jenkins will check the folder periodically if they do not have a chance to talk about her progress.

All Levels

As a way to keep in touch with his students and to provide a setting for them to learn from each other's successes and mistakes, Mr. Jenkins holds Monday morning meetings or process seminars developed to support students involved in long-term independent study programs.

These seminars serve a dual function. One purpose is to provide a setting in which students can discuss the subject matter of their investigations and projects, getting assistance from other students and learning about several content areas. A second, perhaps more important, purpose is to provide a structured time for students to discuss the processes they are using, the problems they are having, and the solutions they are finding. They can discuss their progress toward becoming self-directed learners, and they can learn from each other's progress. An interesting thing that Mr. Jenkins has learned as a result of these seminars is that his students seem to learn more about becoming independent from each other in these group settings than they learn directly from him. Perhaps this happens because they can observe others who are at different stages or levels in the ability to direct their own learning.

In the seminars, students must talk about something every week; they must give a progress report, bring up a problem, or tell about a particularly successful or interesting experience related to their investigation. In addition to free discussions, seminars often have special topics that relate to the development of self-directed learning. Some of the more recent topics discussed by Mr. Jenkins's class are the following:

- What is self-directed learning?
- How do you know when you have learned something?
- What things do you want to learn about? How do you decide what is most important to learn?
- What is the role of the teacher in the whole process of developing self-directedness in students? What things does your teacher do well? What else would you like him or her to do that he or she does not already do?
- What is motivation? What things decrease your motivation? What part do other people play in your motivation?

Expanding the Model

As can be seen from these three examples, the most extensive of the four aspects of the instructional process is that of implementing instruction. This involves making decisions about types of activities, sequencing, pace, where the learning will take place, and the final result or product of learning. To assist students in moving through the levels of self-directed learning and to assist teachers in their task, Treffinger's (1978) model must be expanded in this one aspect so that the steps or stages can be broken into smaller units. (See Table 10.2.) In this expanded version, implementing instruction has been divided into the three areas of process, product, and learning environment, since all these are decisions that must be made about every learning activity. To show how the expanded model might work and to provide a summary of the previous example, the three students—Amy, Tom, and Marcy—and their topics are used to illustrate the levels.

MODIFICATION OF THE BASIC CURRICULUM

Content and Process

The major modifications made by Treffinger's model are in process. However, it does provide for the content modification of variety since students at higher levels are allowed to make their own choices about the content to be studied. In the lower levels, for example, students are encouraged to choose from options and add to the options; at the highest level, they are encouraged to choose their own content areas. Since gifted students are interested in big ideas, real problems, and adult topics, they often will choose content that is different from the subjects usually taught. The model also helps to develop methods of inquiry by providing the structure for students to develop methods and plans for conducting their own learning activities. Thus, students not only learn how to use the methods of scholars in a particular field, but they also learn how to develop these methods and carry them out on their own.

In the process area, as students move toward self-direction, the modifications of open-endedness, discovery, freedom of choice, and variety in methods become more pronounced. As students begin to assume more of the responsibility for their own learning and the project is entirely under the control of the student, the learning becomes more open-ended. The teacher, at this level, serves only as an advisor. As students are encouraged to draw their own conclusions from data they have collected, the element of discovery is present as well. At the higher levels of self-direction, students have more freedom to choose their methods, topics, products, and evaluation standards.

TABLE 10.2. An Expanded Model for Self-Directed Learning

Decisions To Be Made	Levels of Self-Direction		
	Level 1	Level 2	Level 3
Content	Amy chooses learning centers from a small number of choices. She sometimes asks Mr. Jenkins to help her decide what to do.	Tom and Mr. Jenkins discuss several possible topics. They both make several suggestions.	Marcy knows she would like to learn about color theory. She wants to learn how to do the Lüscher test and try it out on friends.
Assessment of entering skills and need	Mr. Jenkins observes Amy, then gives her several options for activities to work on.	Mr. Jenkins asks Tom several questions and discovers that Tom needs to work on his card catalog use skills. Tom then points out that he also will need to learn to use other reference sources. Tom takes a pretest on referencing followed by a minicourse.	Marcy recognizes that she has difficulty in narrowing a topic and asks Mr. Jenkins for assistance. He usually asks her several questions, but this time they decide to use two Creative Problem Solving steps for that purpose. Marcy's decision is to do an in-depth study rather than an overview of all aspects of color theory.
Process	Amy's learning center choices have sequential task cards to follow. Mr. Jenkins initiates a new plan in which he and Amy develop a list of experiments for her to do.	Tom and Mr. Jenkins cooperatively develop a learning contract that specifies the sequence Tom will follow including a literature review and interviews with experts. No date of completion is yet specified; Tom will follow a proposed schedule until he has a better idea of the magnitude of his task.	By herself, Marcy develops a tentative outline of steps to follow in her study.

(continues)

TABLE 10.2.   *Continued*

Decisions To Be Made	Levels of Self-Direction		
	Level 1	*Level 2*	*Level 3*
Product	The task cards in learning centers selected by Amy specify the product. Later, the cooperatively developed contract identifies the new product(s).	The learning contract specifies the product. Tom and Mr. Jenkins both suggest several options. The final decision is made by Tom with Mr. Jenkins' advice.	Marcy decides to present her results to the class in an audiovisual format. Later, if she is satisfied with the quality of the results, the report will be presented to an audience other than her class.
Learning environment	Amy chooses structured learning centers in the classroom. She works on her experiments mainly at the science learning center but can gather needed materials from other places.	Tom and Mr. Jenkins cooperatively make a decision to use references in a variety of locations: school library, public library, university library. Also, the environment for interviews will be determined by the interviewee.	Marcy will decide independently where to conduct her research and testing.
Evaluation	Mr. Jenkins and Amy discuss the results of her experiments and develop solutions to problems. Amy reacts to the evaluation and expresses additional thoughts on her progress.	As Tom has little experience in self-evaluation, he needs more direction from Mr. Jenkins in this step. Mr. Jenkins suggests Tom review other research and write down some possible criteria to assess quality. Mr. Jenkins also makes several more suggestions. Tom and Mr. Jenkins discuss the options and cooperatively evaluate the project.	Marcy will decide whether to share her results with others and uses criteria and procedures she has developed. These include a rating scale to be completed by her peers and her teacher following her presentation.

Product and Learning Environment

As with process, products and learning environments become more appropriate for gifted students as the teacher and student move toward self-direction. Students choose the form of their products when at the highest levels of self-direction. Thus, they are free to decide whether to address real problems and whether to direct their products toward real audiences. They also are free to decide how and by whom the product will be evaluated. Since the form and substance is their own choice, students can decide to develop only a summary of existing information rather than a transformation. The teacher's responsibility is not to require that students develop a particular type of product but rather to encourage them to go further with their ideas and produce a "professional-type" product. Certainly, every product cannot be a professional one. An additional responsibility of the teacher is helping students develop a belief in the importance of original, sophisticated products.

When gifted students participate (or learn) at the highest levels of self-direction, all of the learning environment modifications necessary for the gifted must be present. Treffinger's model addresses all these dimensions of the environment with the possible exception of complexity. Complexity is definitely necessary if students are to develop sophisticated products, but Treffinger does not make specific suggestions related to this dimension. The entire model provides a structure and specific suggestions for developing an environment in which self-directed learning can and will occur.

Certainly, the environment will be learner centered rather than teacher centered if students choose what to study, how to do their investigations, what products to develop, and the methods for evaluating learning. Since Treffinger's model is a comprehensive one, students are involved in all aspects of the instructional process, including the usual areas of involvement (choice of topic and methods) and some aspects of instruction in which students usually are not involved (setting goals and objectives, assessing entering behavior, and assessing performance). For this reason, independence is encouraged to a greater degree and the environment includes nonacademic and academic areas. The environment is open since the students choose what to learn, where, and how. The environment must be designed to permit and encourage a high degree of movement, as students are allowed to choose where and how they will study. To be completely free to choose in the instructional area, students must be allowed ready access to the school library, media services, and other learning options. This requires freedom of movement in and out of the classroom.

MODIFYING THE APPROACH

Treffinger's *Self-Directed Learning Model* was developed for a specific purpose: to provide a structure for moving students and teachers from a teacher-directed setting to an environment in which self-direction and independence can occur. It was not intended as a total approach to curriculum development for the gifted and is not advocated as such by its author. The *Self-Directed Learning Model* meets a need not adequately met by any other approach advocated for use in programs for gifted students and should be combined with other approaches when appropriate. The *Self-Directed Learning Model* can be integrated easily with any basic curriculum-development model and also is compatible with a comprehensive curriculum for the gifted, such as the *Enrichment Triad Model* or *Group Investigations,* when a model for the development of self-directed learning strategies is needed. The model also can be used by teachers in heterogeneously grouped classrooms to provide strategic assistance to the one or two children who need to have greater challenges and independence than are provided in regular classroom curriculum.

Content Changes

The major content modifications would involve developing or selecting abstract, complex generalizations around which the content is organized. To incorporate the other modifications, these generalizations should include those pertaining to creative, productive people and to the methods of inquiry within different fields of study. At the teacher-directed level, the teacher would select the generalizations and key concepts and the specific data used. At the second level, the teacher could provide options for the students in either or both of the following ways: (a) present the possible abstract ideas that could be studied and allow the students to choose or (b) select the generalizations and concepts as organizers but allow students to choose the specific data or area they will study. In the second option, the generalizations are used as the organizing scheme for creating the choices. When students and teachers are at the third level, both students and teachers can identify optional areas of study within a planning generalization, or the students could be allowed to create options that do not relate at all to the abstract idea(s) used by the teacher for planning purposes. The teacher's role at the highest level of self-direction can be that of a stimulator or a person who encourages students to pursue "big ideas" and abstract concepts rather than the collection of data or specific facts. The learner is in control, but the teacher is a guide and facilitator.

Process Changes

The *Self-Directed Learning Model* can be integrated easily with any of the process models to structure the options offered to students. If combined with Bloom, for example, at the teacher-directed level, the teacher would develop all learning activities and present them to the students. At the next level the teacher could create optional learning activities at each level of

Bloom's *Taxonomy* and allow the students to choose from activities at each level. If the students have learned the taxonomy, they can create optional activities when at the third level of self-direction. When students are at the highest level of self-direction, the teacher should not place any requirements on students related to the taxonomy but certainly should encourage students to work at the highest levels whenever possible. Treffinger's approach could be used in a similar manner with the other process models.

Another way to integrate this approach with others is to suggest that students use a particular process or model when choosing or developing options. Two examples of this idea are included in the sample activity described earlier. To assist Marcy in her study, Mr. Jenkins suggested that she use *Creative Problem Solving* in the initial stages. She also used Taba's concept development strategy as a way to organize her questions for the investigation.

The process modification of requiring students to express their reasoning can be integrated in a variety of ways. One way would be to ask students to explain why they have selected a particular option for goals, instructional procedures, or evaluation. Another would be to have them explain their self-evaluations. Of course, when teachers question students about what they have learned, concentration on reasoning also would be important.

When planning group-interaction experiences at the teacher-directed level, the teacher should choose. At the later levels of self-direction, however, the students could choose from several optional activities and ways of observing the group's interaction. At the highest levels, the students should be encouraged to develop their own learning experiences that would facilitate group interaction and the development of leadership abilities. They could set their own goals, assess their own skills, and then develop ways to learn and to evaluate their success.

Pacing of instruction and the presentation of new information are the responsibilities of the teacher at the teacher-directed level but become a shared responsibility at the second two levels. When students are self-directed, they are responsible for pacing their own activities.

Summary

Treffinger's *Self-Directed Learning Model* provides a structured way for teachers to develop experiences that will move their students and themselves toward student-directed learning. Rather than assuming that gifted students already possess the self-management skills that will enable them to be independent learners, the model provides a way to develop these skills gradually. In this process, both teacher and student roles change drastically as students assume more responsibility. (See Table 10.3.) The teacher moves from director to a provider of options, and then to a resource person or facilitator when needed by the student. On the other hand, the student moves from passive learner to a developer and chooser of options, and then to diagnostician, director of learning, and self-evaluator.

DEVELOPMENT

The model is a logical one and was developed by Treffinger as a way to facilitate the movement of students toward self-directed learning. It is considered a tentative plan or a set of hypotheses rather than a set of conclusions based on research. The plan was developed from research on the characteristics of students and from studies of programs designed to foster divergent thinking and creative problem solving. According to Treffinger (1975) many of the educational programs designed to stimulate creativity and develop positive attitudes are necessary but are not sufficient for establishing an appropriate learning environment for gifted students. By adding the elements suggested in his model, Treffinger feels that educators can effectively meet the learning needs of gifted children; they can make learning more joyful, more applicable to the day-to-day world, and more flexible for meeting children's unique needs.

In the past 15 years, Treffinger has focused his research and development efforts on *Creative Problem Solving* and other approaches to the development of creativity. As a result, no further development has taken place on his model of *Self-Directed Learning*. Despite that fact, the model is again featured in this volume because of its clarity and sequential approach to the development of self-regulated, independent learning. Goal setting, planning strategies to reach goals, and self-evaluation of progress and the quality of one's own work are essential to the success of learning, but few gifted children report using those strategies (Zimmerman & Martinez-Pons, 1990). Planning sequential activities to aid in the development of self-regulatory strategies may be especially important for gifted students identified as "underachieving," or not living up to their potential (Risemberg & Zimmerman, 1992).

RESEARCH ON EFFECTIVENESS

Although research on the characteristics of students and on effective programs for developing creativity and problem solving was incorporated into the development of this model, only one study has been done of its validity (Barton, 1976). In this study, Barton found that elementary students and their teachers in heterogeneous classrooms were able to move from a command style to one in which they assumed responsibility for carrying out much of their own learning. In addition, the students still learned as much academically as did a control class. All students, not just the gifted, increased in self-direction and independence. A frequent component of programs for the gifted is

TABLE 10.3.   Summary of Teacher and Student Roles and Activities in the Treffinger Self-Directed Learning Model

Step, Type, or Level of Thinking	Student		Teacher	
	Role	Sample Activities	Role	Sample Activities
Teacher directed	Passive complier	Learn what the teacher identifies as important. Participate in pretests of specific skills. Complete learning activities as specified by the teacher. Receive evaluation or assessment of progress.	Director	Decide on goals and objectives both for the class and for individual students. Use test results to make specific prescriptions for each child. Present content, provide exercises and activities, and arrange for practice of skills. Implement evaluation procedures, develop criteria for success, assign grades.
Self-directed, Level 1	Chooser	Choose goals or areas of study from those identified by the teacher. Choose areas of strength or weakness, as identified by the teacher, to work on. Choose learning activities. Do learning activities independently and at own pace. React to and discuss teacher evaluation of own progress.	Provider	Develop optimal goals or areas of study. Develop diagnostic procedures, share with students, provide optional areas to be worked on. Provide learning activities to be done independently by students. Evaluate each student in relation to objectives, share evaluation with students, provide an opportunity for students to respond or react.

(continues)

TABLE 10.3. *Continued*

Step, Type, or Level of Thinking	Student		Teacher	
	Role	**Sample Activities**	**Role**	**Sample Activities**
Self-directed, Level 2	Developer of options	Assist teacher in creating options or identifying areas of study.	Developer of options	Involve students in creating options or identifying areas of study.
		Discuss one's own areas of need with teacher, as well as interests, strengths, and weaknesses.		Have individual conferences with each student to cooperatively identify areas of need, strengths, weaknesses, and interests.
		Complete tests or other assessments identified with the teacher as necessary or desirable.		Employ individual tests, if necessary and if cooperatively identified by student and teacher.
		Assist teacher to identify learning options.		Provide resources, develop options with students, and assist in preparing learning contracts.
		Develop a learning contract by choosing from options cooperatively developed with the teacher.		Involve students in decisions about the scope of activities, the sequence of activities, and the student's rate of learning.
		Implement learning contract as developed with teacher.		Involve students in the development of methods and criteria for evaluation.
		Assist in identifying and developing methods and criteria for evaluation.		Develop student–teacher conferences for student evaluation.
		Participate in student–teacher conferences for evaluation of progress.		Use peer partners and other sources for product evaluation.
		Suggest new areas of study based on results of evaluation and own interests.		

(*continues*)

TABLE 10.3. *Continued*

Step, Type, or Level of Thinking	Student		Teacher	
	Role	*Sample Activities*	*Role*	*Sample Activities*
Self-directed, Level 3	Director of learning Diagnostician Evaluator of learning	Set own goals and objectives. Determine needs, strengths, weaknesses, and interests. Select and develop projects, learning activities, places to study, pace of learning. Consult the teacher when advice is needed. Develop criteria, methods, and responsibilities for evaluation of own performance. Use evaluation results to plan new goals and objectives or new learning activities.	Resource person Facilitator Advisor	Assist student in identification of goals and objectives. Provide resources and materials. Assist student to assess own levels of need or performance. Assist student in the development of learning activities when consulted. Assist student in self-evaluation or in using results of self-evaluation to plan new learning activities.

independent study. Independent study or completely self-directed learning is highly successful with gifted students (Renzulli & Gable, 1976). Zimmerman and Martinez-Pons (1990) conclude, from a review of research on self-regulatory strategies and metacognitive development, that activities designed to help gifted students learn self-regulatory strategies are an effective and productive way to help intellectually able students. Gifted students who have participated in these programs feel that independent study has a positive influence on the following: (a) their motivation and career (increases their excitement about learning, helps them make decisions about future careers, and allows them to choose content areas and depth of content); (b) their study habits and thinking processes (increases critical thinking and helps in organizing and focusing thoughts); and (c) the degree of challenge and opportunity for self-expression in school. In many cases, parents also are pleased with their children's progress in an independent learning program and list many of the same positive influences as do their children.

However, more research is needed to test the effectiveness of the levels in Treffinger's structured, developmental approach. Do students who begin at the lower levels actually develop skills needed for directing their own learning? Are the four levels in the appropriate sequence? Are they gradual enough, or are intermediate steps important? All these questions need to be answered before the model can be considered a successful approach. To enable teachers to apply the model more effectively, answers to questions about student characteristics and how they interact with the model are needed. For example, at what ages should educators begin to encourage self-direction in gifted children? What developmental differences can be identified at different ages? All these questions await further study.

JUDGMENTS

Advantages

The Treffinger model takes into account the unique present and probable future characteristics of gifted students and is designed to enhance their strengths. With a teacher who is excited about the approach and a learning environment flexible enough to allow the model to work, this approach should be successful.

Another advantage of this model is its potential for enhancing the success of some other approaches used in education of the gifted by complementing their weak areas. For example, a frequent difficulty encountered by students pursuing independent studies or investigations in the *Enrichment Triad Model, Group Investigations,* or the *Autonomous Learner Model,* is that they do not yet possess the skills in self-management and self-direction that will enable them to do in-depth investigation of real problems. Treffinger's *Self-Directed Learning Model* provides a step-by-step way to develop these needed skills. This approach is different from many "thinking," or information-processing, models used in education of the gifted because of its concentration on some of the more "practical" skills of inquiry: (a) managing time, (b) sequencing activities, and (c) identifying resources. Freedom of choice and development of independence, two recommended modifications seldom present in thinking process models, are stressed in *Self-Directed Learning*.

Finally, some preliminary, short-term research (Barton, 1976) does indicate that students can move toward more self-directed learning through experience in this model. In this model, students also continue to achieve academically at the expected level based on comparisons with students in a control group.

Disadvantages

The biggest disadvantage of this model is the lack of research on its effectiveness when used over a long period of time. If given a choice, will students still study subjects that provide the foundation for later learning? Use of the model clearly can provide a helpful and effective complement to other approaches, but it probably cannot stand alone as a total approach to education of gifted children. Too many unanswered questions and too many needed curricular modifications are not addressed in this model.

A final disadvantage is that the model requires a particular kind of teacher, that is, a person who is willing and able to move from a directive role to a facilitative role as the students become effective directors of their learning. Not all teachers are willing to make these changes, and not all parents are willing to see teachers give up the major responsibility for their children's learning. Parental pressure can create an additional negative factor for teachers who are not quite certain of their willingness to change roles. Maintaining a teacher-directed program for some children and helping others to move toward more independent learning is difficult; if a teacher is not committed to the principles of self-directed learning, he or she may choose to retreat to a more teacher-directed approach.

CONCLUSION

Although developed for a somewhat narrow purpose, the model fills a need not met by other approaches discussed in this book. It can (and should) be combined and integrated with other models to provide a comprehensive structure for curriculum development for the gifted. At the highest levels of self-direction, the teacher becomes a guide or facilitator who encourages the students to pursue abstract, complex ideas, to choose learning experiences that develop higher levels of thinking, and to develop products that are at a level of sophistication equal to their abilities.

Treffinger's *Self-Directed Learning Model* can provide a valuable complement to other approaches used in programs for gifted children. It is a practical developmental approach that builds on some of the more salient (and often troublesome) characteristics of gifted children, such as their stubbornness when told what to do, their curiosity about a wide range of topics, their constant questions, their nonconforming nature, and their tendency to direct the activities in which they are engaged. The model is not difficult to learn or understand but may be difficult to implement.

RESOURCES: INSTRUCTIONAL MATERIALS

Allen, J. (1992). Meeting the needs of Australian rural gifted children: The use of curriculum enrichment projects (CEPPS) for primary schools in western Australia. *Gifted Education International, 8*(1), 23–31. In this article, the author describes the development of materials that can be used with gifted students to initiate and guide independent learning. Materials (with sources), a framework for development, and examples are provided.

Burns, F. D. (1993). Independent study: Panacea or palliative? In C. J. Maker & D. Orzechowski-Harland (Eds.), *Critical issues in gifted education: Vol. III. Programs for the gifted in regular classrooms* (pp. 381–399). Austin, TX: PRO-ED. Burns, an experienced teacher and coordinator in programs for gifted students, discusses three models recommended for use in independent study programs (Betts, Renzulli, and Treffinger). She contrasts them and discusses how they can be combined.

Feldhusen, H. J. (1993). Individualized teaching of the gifted in regular classrooms. In C. J. Maker & D. Orzechowski-Harland (Eds.), *Critical issues in gifted education: Vol. III. Programs for the gifted in regular classrooms* (pp. 263–273). Austin, TX: PRO-ED. A veteran classroom teacher and advocate for gifted children, Feldhusen briefly outlines practices (e.g., cluster seating, learning centers and resource materials, student planning of daily activities, individualized learning of basic skills, independent study) necessary to provide individualization and differentiated education for gifted students in the regular classroom.

Friedman, R. C. J., & Gallagher, T. (1993). Reaction to "independent study." In C. J. Maker & D. Orzechowski-Harland (Eds.), *Critical issues in gifted education: Vol. III. Programs for the gifted in regular classrooms* (pp. 400–412).

Austin, TX: PRO-ED. In a reaction to Burns' chapter from a different perspective, the authors provide additional insights into the use of the three models.

Learning Packets Series. Tucson, AZ: Zephyr Press. More than two dozen stimulating topics, from "Early people" to "Futuristics," for self-directed learning provide interdisciplinary and integrative topics for independent study. Each packet contains a set of reproducible activities for research, critical and creative thinking activities, an art exploration component, learning center ideas, and a bibliography for two complete units (one K–3 and one 4–8). Topics include "The Columbus encounter: A multicultural view," "Archaeology," "Entomology," "Early Japan," "The Jade Garden: Ancient to modern China," "Paleontology: Dinosaurs and other fossils," and "Apprenticeship in creativity: Activities based on the art of Wassily Kandinsky." These are excellent resources for learning centers and for students in the earlier levels of self-regulated learning.

Nash, W. R., Haensly, P. A., Scobee-Rodgers, V. J., & Wright, N. L. (1993). Mentoring: Extending learning for gifted students. In C. J. Maker & D. Orzechowski-Harland (Eds.), *Critical issues in gifted education: Vol. III. Programs for the gifted in regular classrooms* (pp. 313–330). Austin, TX: PRO-ED. The authors explore the historical bases of mentoring relationships, identify the functions of such relationships in enhancing creativity, shaping careers, role-modeling, and shaping personal growth. Necessary elements of school-based mentorship programs and examples of mentoring programs also are discussed.

Oudheusden, S. (n.d.). *Go for it! A student's guide to independent projects.* Mansfield Center, CT: Creative Learning Press. This fun-to-read book has practical step-by-step explanations to help students develop the process skills of topic selection, research, organization, and presentation. A section, "Work Pages," contains reproducible forms to help students organize their thinking and their data to produce a quality product.

Chapter 11

Other Approaches

PART ONE
J. P. Guilford: The Structure of Intellect

J. P. Guilford's (1959, 1967) theory of the structure of human intelligence has no doubt had a greater influence on the field of education of the gifted than any other theory or model. Its influence has been felt in all areas of programming, including definition, philosophy, identification, and testing, as well as curriculum development and teaching strategies. Indeed, the theory is used as the basis of many programs for the gifted. Perhaps its most important influence has been in expanding the concept or definition of giftedness. Prior to Guilford's work, the concept of giftedness was almost synonymous with IQ, but after his ideas spread into the educational community, the multifaceted or multidimensional conception of giftedness began to form the basis for programs.

In addition to its influence on the operation of programs for the gifted, Guilford's model had a great deal of influence on several of the theorists and leaders in education of the gifted. For example, Parnes, Taylor, and Williams were all stimulated in some manner by the ideas in Guilford's theory. Taylor's and Williams's approaches were developed as educational counterparts to Guilford's psychological model. E. Paul Torrance (1974) drew heavily upon the work of Guilford in the development of the *Torrance Tests of Creative Thinking.*

A distinction must be made between the work of J. P. Guilford and the work of Mary N. Meeker. Guilford, a psychologist and theorist, spent most of his professional life conducting research on human abilities, their structure and function, and the various means of testing them. Using factor analytic statistical techniques, he attempted to identify or isolate the basic abilities that are a part of human intelligence. After several years of measuring and analyzing various tests of ability, Guilford developed a morphological model to describe what he had found through his research. After developing the model, he continued his attempts to isolate abilities predicted by the model but not yet identified by psychological tests.

Mary Meeker, an associate of Guilford's, became interested in the practical psychological and educational implications of the model. She developed extensive testing materials, test item "mapping" procedures for development of *Structure of Intellect* ability profiles using existing test data, workbooks for use with children, and computer programs for analyzing ability profiles, developing prescriptions, and for use in classrooms to develop students' abilities. She also has developed materials for training teachers and others to use the model. Meeker and others continue to compile data on the unique ability patterns of various cultural and clinical groups. One final distinction should be noted. When referring to the theoretical model, Guilford uses the abbreviation SI for the *Structure of Intellect,* while Meeker uses SOI to refer to her educational applications of the theoretical model. The same abbreviations will be used in this chapter.

Because of the extensive nature of this theory, the amount of research validating or attempting to validate it, and psychological literature written about it, this chapter can contain only an introduction to the model. It will provide a description of the basic principles of the theory and elements but will focus mainly on the uses of the SOI model for curriculum development in education of the gifted.

ELEMENTS/PARTS

The SI model (Guilford, 1959, 1967) depicts human intelligence as consisting of three "faces" or dimensions: (a) an *operation* is performed on a particular kind of (b) *content,* yielding a certain type of (c) *product.* Four types of information or content of thought can be identified: (a) figural, (b) semantic, (c) symbolic, and (d) behavioral. Five types of thinking processes or operations can be performed on this content: (a) cognition, (b) memory, (c) convergent production, (d) divergent production, and (e) evaluation. The result of operations on content is one of the six types of products: (a) units, (b) classes, (c) relations, (d) systems, (e) transformations, and (f) implications. The intersection of each of the three dimensions results in a unique ability or a component of intelligence. This means that at least 120 separate human abilities (4 × 5 × 6 = 120) can be identified.[1] As Guilford continued his factor analyses, however, he identified more than one ability in some of the "cells" in which only one had been predicted by the theory. Current predictions are that approximately 150 separate human abilities can be identified (Guilford, 1988).

Content

The first and most primitive type of content is *figural* (F). It includes concrete objects or forms that are perceived visually, auditory elements such as rhythms and simple sounds, and tactile or kinesthetic materials. Figural content has sensory character. *Symbolic* (S) information includes signs and other materials that represent something but have no meaning in and of themselves. These codes can be combined in many ways and include such items as letters, numbers, musical notation, and universal traffic signals. The third type of information, *semantic* (M), differs from figural and symbolic in that it has meaning. Usually these meanings are external. For example, the word *house* is semantic content, because it relates to an image in a person's mind. It is somewhat abstract in that one person's image of its meaning may be different from another's image. *Behavioral* (B) content is nonverbal information pertaining to human interactions. The actions, emotions, intentions, and moods of people are interpreted without the aid of verbal cues. Behavioral information includes body language and facial expressions that are evidence of some affective state. See Figure 11.1 for examples of each of these types of content.

Operations

The operations or thinking processes in Guilford's (1967) model are not hierarchical. They are simply different abilities. *Cognition* (C), the most basic of the operations, is recognition or perception of a stimulus. It is the

---

1. In Meeker's educational applications of Guilford's theory, each of these abilities is represented by a trigram symbol containing a letter from the content, process, and product dimensions. This letter is usually the first letter from each type within each dimension. For example, the ability involving the operation of Cognition, Figural content, and the product area of *Units* is referred to as CFU. The operation is listed first, the content second, and the product last. In this chapter, the same system of notation will be used. In the first explanation of abilities, the whole names will be listed. However, in subsequent references, only the trigrams will be used.

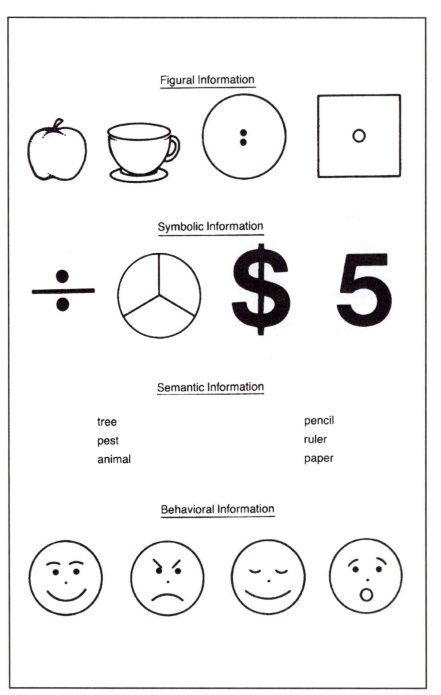

Figure 11.1. Examples of types of content in Guilford's Structure of Intellect Model.

immediate discovery of various forms of content. For example, in one of Guilford's (1977) tests called "disemboweled" words, the task is to recognize familiar words without their vowels:

p-ct-r-	(picture)
s-lf	(self)
c-l-br-t--n	(celebration)

This involves cognition of symbolic units (CSU). Another example of cognition is the familiar test item in which sets of items are given along with one item belonging to each of the sets. The task is to figure out which of the extra items belongs with each set. This involves cognition of figural classes (CFC).

The second operation is *memory* (M), or remembering any type of information. It includes ways of storing information and the ability to retrieve the information when needed. Most of the items testing memory require the individual to study some information and then reconstruct that information on a test page. In one test, Monogram Recall (Guilford, 1977), several different arrangements of three letters are given on the study page, such as

On the test page, only the three letters, C J M, are given and the task is to reconstruct the arrangements seen earlier. This item tests memory of figural systems (MFS).

Convergent production (N) is generating answers when a correct answer exists and when the solution requires more than just retrieval or recognition. The first component of the definition, the availability of a conventionally accepted best or correct answer, distinguishes convergent production from divergent production. The second component requires more than recall and distinguishes it from memory. In convergent production, new information is generated from given information. For example, a well-known item from the *Wechsler Intelligence Scales for Children--Revised* (WISC–R) (Wechsler, 1974) requires the person to put a series of pictures into their correct order. This Picture Arrangement Test taps the ability of convergent production of semantic systems (NMS). Another example involves convergent production of semantic relations (NMR) (Guilford, 1977, pp. 115–116):

What word is related to both words in each pair?
1. nonsense—bed
2. recline—deceive

3. hit—fruit drink
4. tiresome—drilling
5. sphere—dance
The answers are bunk, lie, punch, boring, and ball.

Divergent production (D) is generation of information when the emphasis is on variety, quantity, and quality rather than on a best or correct solution. In divergent production, more information usually is generated than was given initially. For example, an item measuring divergent production of semantic units (DMU) requires a person to generate titles for a story. In another item (testing divergent production of semantic systems [DMS]), the task is to generate several analogies from one given pair:

SLEEP is to BED as _____ is to _____.

SLEEP is to BED as _____ is to _____.

SLEEP is to BED as _____ is to _____.

SLEEP is to BED as _____ is to _____.

SLEEP is to BED as _____ is to _____.

Evaluation is decision making or making judgments about something. It requires decisions on the basis of known or understood standards. For example, in one item, a principle for a number series is given (for example, contains odd numbers and skips two numbers each time), and a group of number series, some of which follow the principle and some of which do not, also is given. The task is to decide which series follow the principle. This item tests evaluation of symbolic systems (ESS).

Products

The product dimension relates to organization of figural, symbolic, semantic, or behavioral content. The product dimension can be considered hierarchical or at least inclusive in that later products subsume earlier ones (for example, systems include relations, relations include classes, classes include units). *Units* (U) are the simplest forms of products. A unit is a single item, for example, one figure, one symbol, or one idea. *Classes* (C) are categories or classifications of items grouped together because they have certain properties in common. *Relations* (R) are connections between items of information or between classes of information. *Systems* (S), complex types of information, are composed of more than two interconnected units. Systems are organized or structured complexes of interrelated parts, such as melodies and rhythms (auditory), numbers in a series, sequences of events, or cartoon strips. *Transformations* (T) are modifications of existing information so that a new item is created. Some examples of transformations are rotation of an object, reading words spelled backwards, and substitutions of meaning of words, as in making puns. *Implications* (I) are predictions made from the given information. They include generalizations or expectations that are extended beyond what is given. The most common example of implications is in the semantic area in the form of prediction of future events based on past or present events or conditions. Figure 11.2 contains some examples of each type of product. In the examples, only two types of information are illustrated, figural and symbolic. Since this information is the most concrete, these items are simpler than items containing semantic or behavioral content. In addition, the items chosen were selected because of their simplicity so that the reader can quickly understand them. Many similar items can be designed that are more difficult.

According to Guilford (1972), teachers who wish to apply SI theory in their classrooms need not memorize each of the abilities and their descriptions. Knowledge of the 15 basic types of content, processes, and products and an understanding of how they can be combined is sufficient for the curriculum planner. Meeker, however, has recognized the need for developing a series of aids for the teacher including tests, computer analyses or profiles, workbooks, worksheets, computer software, and educational games.

Curriculum Planning Based on the SOI

The general approach advocated by Meeker (1969a) is an individualized one based on the analysis of a student's intellectual profile of strengths and weaknesses in the ability areas identified in the SI model. This profile can be developed through an analysis of existing psychological test data or through testing with instruments designed to assess abilities included in Guilford's model (e.g., *The SOI Learning Abilities Test* [Meeker, Meeker, & Roid, 1985]). When a profile has been developed, an individualized education plan is designed. Depending on the student, this prescription will be based on development of strengths, weaknesses, weaknesses through strengths, or a combination of strengths and weaknesses. Meeker's general guidelines for the gifted without disabilities focus on a balance between development of strengths and remediation of weak areas. Work on individual SOI prescriptions should result in significant gains if approximately 20 minutes is spent on the activity three times a week (Meeker, 1969a). Student gains in all abilities, especially the target areas, should be evaluated periodically by administering the pretests again or by administering any of Guilford's tasks used for identifying the ability.

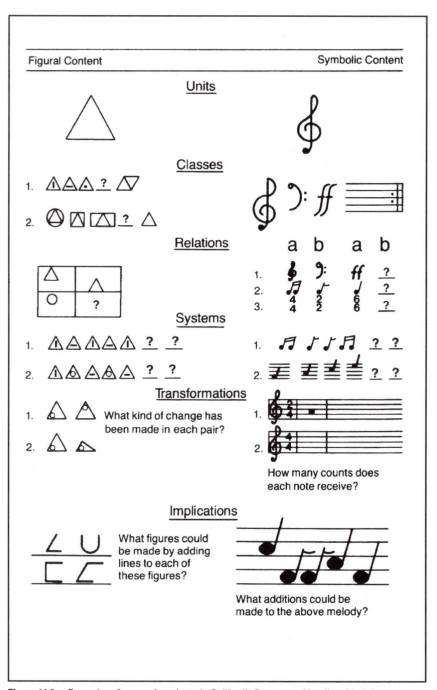

Figure 11.2. Examples of types of products in Guilford's Structure of Intellect Model.

MODIFICATIONS OF THE BASIC CURRICULUM

Content Modifications

The Guilford model with Meeker's applications contains guidelines for modifications of the basic curriculum in all four areas. One content change is recommended directly by the model, while two are suggested indirectly. The major content modification, which is a part of the SI model, is that of variety. *Structure of Intellect* theory points to the existence of four basic types of information, ranging from the most concrete, figural, to the most abstract, behavioral. These types of content assume equal importance in general but have differential importance based on individual needs. Indirectly, the theory provides a framework for viewing the abstractness of information in that the basic types of information range from concrete to abstract. However, it does not suggest any particular level of abstraction for gifted students. In fact, no overall suggestions are related to content except that the ability to deal with all types of content is important, and certain types of content may be important to people in certain kinds of occupations (or with certain kinds of talents). Complexity of content is suggested, somewhat indirectly, by the product dimension of the SI model. Products essentially are ways of organizing or combining types of content, and they range from simple units to the more complex classes, relations, systems, transformations, and implications. Since the theory states that content serves as the input, a process is performed on the content, and a product results, the implication is that the elements in the product dimension are always the output and never the input or stimulus. However, if the items used to identify abilities involving the product dimension are examined, the stimulus is often the same type as the product expected from the respondent. (See Figure 11.2.) For example, in the test of convergent production of symbolic systems (NSS), the input is a particular symbolic system. The task of the respondent is to produce two more items that belong in the system. Thus, both the input and output are systems.

Although Guilford and Meeker do not specifically recommend complexity of content for intellectually gifted individuals, the model provides a useful framework for viewing the complexity of content. Of all the product types, a system is the most complex organization of content. The next two product types, transformations and implications, can result from the initial input of a system. By organizing abstract content (that is, semantic or behavioral) into systems, transformations, and implications, content would be both complex and abstract.

Process Modifications

Process modifications also are suggested by the SI model. Although Guilford (1959, 1967) states that the processes of cognition, memory, convergent production, divergent production, and evaluation are not hierarchical, Meeker (1969a) believes that learning flows from cognition to all the other processes. In other words, information must first be recognized before it can be evaluated, new information can be produced from it, or it can be stored in memory for later retrieval. Thus at least one of the operations is a prerequisite to the others.

The same is true of memory. Even Guilford (1972, 1975) recognizes the role of memory in convergent and divergent production. He quotes creative individuals as saying that having a store of information on a particular topic ready for easy access is important to their creative production in that area. Thus, memory and cognition can be viewed as prerequisites or lower processes, and convergent production, divergent production, and evaluation as higher processes. In Bruner's (1960) terms, cognition and memory would be considered acquisition of information, while the other processes would be considered use of information. Taken together, these ideas lead to the conclusion that SI theory and the SOI applications of the theory do recommend or at least provide a framework for the process modification of "development of higher levels of thinking."

The process modifications of open-endedness and variety are more directly recommended by the model. Divergent production is by definition open-ended in that no "correct" answers are sought or intended. Emphasis on divergent production in programs for the gifted is recommended by both Guilford (1972, 1975) and Meeker (1969b). The principle of variety also is provided for by the SI theory because of the recommendation that educators provide training in all intellectual abilities. This recommendation at least ensures that a variety of thinking processes would be developed by using the model. Use of a variety of teaching methods, however, is a different matter. Even though teaching activities of all kinds can be designed for developing most of the SI abilities, because of the readily available SOI workbooks, worksheets, prescriptions in the form of workbooks, and computer software (Learn Smart, 1991), many individuals who use the model tend to overemphasize these methods of teaching.

Product and Learning Environment Modifications

Product modifications recommended by Guilford (1972) for the gifted and the creative are transformations and realistic evaluation, with particular emphasis on self-evaluation. Emphasis on transformation is recommended, as a result of interviews with creative producers who rated transformations higher in importance in their work than the process of divergent production.

Guilford suggests self-evaluation because of the resistance of creative individuals to criticism of their work by others.

None of the learning environment changes recommended for use with the gifted are directly addressed by Guilford or Meeker, although the idea of deferred judgment (an aspect of acceptance) is viewed as an important strategy by Guilford when dealing with divergent production abilities. He states that a person should not attempt to develop the ability of divergent production at the same time as evaluation because evaluation tends to inhibit divergent production.

JUDGMENTS

Advantages

One of the most important advantages of the SOI approach is its usefulness in diagnosing and developing appropriate programs for gifted students who are having problems learning. Identifying and planning for development of intellectual strengths and weaknesses is made easier with a model of intellectual abilities, such as the *Structure of Intellect*. Often, gifted students with learning problems have unusual discrepancies among separate abilities. These discrepancies are not identified by traditional means of testing since the child has developed strategies for compensating or masking the disabilities. A model such as the SOI offers a way to separate intellectual abilities into small definable units. Using the well-developed approaches of specific remediation combined with more general remediation of weaknesses through strengths, individualized education programs (IEPs) can be developed. Parents who wish to assist in their child's education can use the workbooks, activities, and computer software at home.

A second advantage is the ease of individualization when using the tests, computer analysis, workbooks, and computer software. All the materials and systems are readily available at a price most schools can afford. The development of IEPs is made simple by the availability of SOI tests and materials. In addition to its value in individualized curriculum planning, the SOI offers support to the teacher through career and vocational analysis based on individual intellectual profiles. The task of counseling students about career choices is easier because of this service.

Indirectly related to curriculum development but an important prerequisite, the SI model is useful in helping teachers, parents, children, psychologists, and others understand the multidimensional nature of giftedness and talent. Gifted children (because they are gifted) often are expected to be superior in everything they do. Educators and parents often are disappointed or feel the child is different if a few weak areas are identified. Use of a model such as the

SI helps to show graphically why children should not be expected to excel in everything and provides a framework for viewing talented children as individuals. Perhaps in the future, because of models such as this, educators will develop valid profiles of types of giftedness and talent based on particular clusters of intellectual abilities and will build individual programs for every child to develop the entire cluster of abilities necessary for the talent to be realized.

Disadvantages

Although the availability of tests and materials for remediation/development is considered a major advantage of Guilford's model, it also can be a disadvantage. Because of the ease in using a cookbook approach where specific cells are targeted and the workbooks and software are keyed to these cells, teachers may have a tendency to use only these types of tasks and ignore, for instance, the use of concrete, manipulative materials and real-life problems. Not as much creativity is required on the part of the teacher as with some other approaches, so not as much creativity is used. This is not the fault of the model, because many exciting non–paper-and-pencil tasks can be designed to develop the SI abilities. However, the availability of workbooks makes them easy to fall back on. Perhaps a related reason for using what has already been developed is a feeling of insecurity based on the lack of knowledge about various abilities and how they can be developed.

Another disadvantage is the lack of research on the validity and reliability of some of the procedures advocated. No research shows the effectiveness of the recommended specific versus general remediation strategy. Which approach is best to use with what children and under what circumstances is not clear. Although the approach is humanistically appealing, research results are not available to document whether the approach of combining strengths with weaknesses is more effective than concentrating directly on the weak areas or the strong ones. Other questions need to be addressed through comprehensive validity of the model for curriculum development.

The SI model does not provide a total framework for curriculum development, although it does provide for curricular modifications in several areas. It should be combined with a good content model so that the modifications relating to abstractness, complexity, and organization for learning value can be incorporated. As often used, the SOI approach contributes to a fragmentation of the content areas rather than the integration of ideas into abstract thought systems.

A big concern of critics is the validity of methods used to identify the SI factors. By using only orthogonal rotation in factor analysis, many feel that Guilford attempted to make reality fit his model rather than fitting his model to reality. Certain abilities seem to be prerequisites to others. For example, an ample and readily available memory store on a particular topic is a necessity in divergent production and often in convergent production. Cognition is an even more basic operation. In the product dimension, a hierarchy or at least a sequence of abilities can be identified with units being the simplest, and transformations and implications the most complex. Because of Guilford's use of marker tests in an attempt to identify pure abilities, he may actually be partialling out the variance caused by one of the prerequisites or underlying abilities. In other words, the basic problem is that his methods have limited his results and also the theory because of their restrictiveness.

CONCLUSION

J. P. Guilford's SI model can be used effectively in planning IEPs to develop the intellectual abilities of gifted students. Research has shown that the approaches designed by Meeker can be effective in enhancing specific abilities. These approaches also are practical and easy to implement. However, the SOI model is not recommended as a total framework for curriculum development in programs for the gifted. Perhaps the most important drawback in this respect would be the tendency toward fragmentation. The SOI approach needs to be combined with another model (for example, Bruner, Taba, or Renzulli) that would provide some of the important elements that are lacking.

RESOURCES: INSTRUCTIONAL MATERIALS AND ACTIVITIES

Gangi, J. M. (1990, January/February). Higher level thinking skills through drama. *G/C/T,* pp. 16–19. The author presents a potpourri of activities for children that develop both dramatic talents and thinking skills.

Key Technologies International. (1991). *Learn Smart: A systematic program of assessment and training tools and materials for the identification of individual learning styles and the improvement of basic and literacy skills, for remediation and enrichment.* San Diego, CA: Author. A computer-based assessment and training program based on the Guilford *Structure of Intellect.* The system consists of three components: (a) *Online SOI,* a computerized version of the SOI paper-and-pencil assessment measure that features computer-generated reports and prescriptive activities; (b) *Smart Mods,* SOI training tools and materials; and (c) *LOCAN,* computer-based literacy games for concrete/spatial learners.

Meeker, M., Meeker, R., & Roid, G. (1985). *Structure of the Intellect Learning Abilities Test (SOI-LA).* Los Angeles: Western Psychological Services.

PART TWO
Lawrence Kohlberg:
Discussions of Moral Dilemmas

The development of values, moral reasoning, ethical behavior, and virtuous action has been a concern of educators of all students. Educators of the gifted have been interested primarily in the development of values and assisting students to clarify their values through the processes advocated by individuals such as Raths (1963) and Raths, Harmin, and Simon (1966). Educators and parents often are concerned about developing ethical behavior in children and, in the past, they attempted to do so through such means as religious education, Boy Scouts, Girl Scouts, and other approaches emphasizing to children that the virtuous person is honest, loyal, reverent, just, and altruistic. If they acquire these virtues, children are told, they will be happy, well-respected, and fortunate.

In contrast to the attempts to develop ethical behavior is the approach of values clarification, the position that the school's and teacher's responsibility is not to indoctrinate children as to what values they should hold but to assist them in thinking seriously about what values they hold and what values they should hold. The teacher's role in the process is a nonjudgmental one and involves posing questions and planning activities that will lead children through the processes of choosing (for example, choosing freely, choosing from alternatives, choosing after thoughtful consideration of the consequences of each alternative), prizing (for example, prizing and cherishing oneself, affirming publicly), and acting (for example, acting upon choices, repeating the action in a pattern over time) (Raths et al., 1966). A fundamental idea behind this approach is that of "ethical relativity"; no universal ethical principles can be identified, because values and ethics are relative. As long as a person has followed the processes of choosing, prizing, and acting, all values developed are equally valid.

Kohlberg's (1966) theory of the development of moral reasoning and his approach to moral education is a response to the failure of indoctrination programs and disagreement with the idea of ethical relativity as a basis for values education (Kohlberg, 1971). In the late 1920s, a classic study of children's cheating and stealing by Hartshorne and May (1930) shocked the educational community by showing that indoctrination approaches were ineffective. Children who attend Sunday school, participate in Boy Scouts and Girl Scouts, and whose parents emphasize ethical behavior do not behave more ethically than children who do none of these things. Other results of this study, also confirmed by later research, are that (a) the world cannot be divided into honest and dishonest people since almost everyone cheats at some time; (b) if a person cheats in one situation, whether the person will cheat in other situations cannot be predicted (in other words, cheating seems to be situationally deter-mined); and (c) the moral values expressed by people have nothing to do with how they act; people who express extreme moral disapproval of cheating will cheat as much as those who do not verbally express disapproval of cheating.

Perhaps the values clarification approaches were formulated as a reac-tion to the ineffectiveness of indoctrination or as a 1960s reaction to adults' attempts to manipulate students through developing certain moral values advocated by the "educational establishment." However, Kohlberg rejected the most fundamental idea behind this approach, ethical relativity, on a philosophical basis. His key idea (Kohlberg, 1971), which in part is based on the writings of Kant (1929/1965) and the contemporary moral philoso-pher John Rawls (1971), is that, although different values relating to per-sonal choice (for example, what clothing to wear, the most appropriate way to spend time) are equally appropriate, different values relating to basic moral questions (for example, the sanctity of life, the equality of all people) are not equally appropriate. In other words, certain universal ethical princi-ples do exist. For example, even though an individual arrives at the decision that all blacks should be slaves because they are an inferior race through the seven-step process of values clarification, this conclusion is not as appropri-ate as the conclusion that slavery is wrong for everyone. A conclusion such as this would be based on such universal ethical principles as the worth of every person and the equality of every person relative to certain rights and freedoms. Such ethical principles as respect for the worth of all individuals, justice and liberty for all, and "inalienable rights" are embedded firmly in and necessary to a democratic way of life. As educators and individuals par-ticipating in a democracy, teachers can and should assist children in devel-oping moral reasoning that will consider these higher philosophical princi-ples in decisions involving basic moral questions.

Relative to this philosophical position, Kohlberg (1966) studied the de-velopment of moral reasoning by interviewing 50 boys over a period of time. He posed moral dilemmas to them and asked them to tell first what would be morally right for the individual to do and, second, why this action would be right. He found that children's reasoning about moral issues proceeds through certain stages in a sequential order and becomes more sophisticated at each stage. Subsequent to the research on these developmental stages, nu-merous individuals including Kohlberg, his colleagues, and his students have studied how this development can be facilitated. They have concluded that educators can encourage the development of higher levels of moral reasoning through methods emphasizing class discussion of moral dilemmas.

Although Kohlberg and his colleagues do not write specifically about gifted students, educators of the gifted have long been concerned about the moral and ethical development of bright students. If these children are to be-come future leaders, they should serve as models of the highest ethical behavior in addition to being models of intellectual/productive behavior. Many educators of the gifted have accepted the idea of ethical relativity and advocated the use of values clarification as the most effective means for dealing with moral/ethical principles in schools. Ward (1961), however, is convincing in his argument that intellectually superior individuals have a greater capacity than average individuals to develop consistency between their ethical ideals and their actual behavior. Many of the characteristics of the gifted (for example, their ability to foresee consequences of their own behavior, their ability to choose long-term benefits over short-range consequences, and their greater capacity to generalize learning from one situation to another) suggest that a concentration on moral reasoning and the development of an understanding of "universal ethical principles" would be an effective approach to the development of ethical behavior.

Ward (1961) suggests that the gifted be instructed in "the theoretical bases of ideal moral behavior and of personal and social adjustments" (p. 202). In further explanations of this idea, he suggests that gifted individuals should examine critically the historical development of societal philosophies and values, and that they should study the effects of these ideas on the development of societies. This examination also should include the analysis and classification of values with an emphasis on the individuals' development of their own "reasoned synthesis" of values. Such an approach differs from values clarification in that individuals have examined high ideals and considered their appropriateness rather than simply looking within themselves for these ideals. The approach is somewhat similar to values clarification in that individuals must go through a process of self-examination and develop personal conclusions.

Some of the new approaches such as "problem-based learning" (Gallagher, Stepien, & Rosenthal, 1992) are designed to give students practice in examining all aspects of a problem, including ethical and moral issues. Kohlberg's ideas can be incorporated easily into this strategy. Kohlberg's approach fits well with these ideas since the emphasis is on "reasoning," with the objective of ultimately reaching a level at which certain universal ethical principles or ideas guide behavior. An analysis of the philosophical and theoretical bases of the ethical principles being discussed should be added to Kohlberg's approach.

ELEMENTS/PARTS

Dimensions, Thinking Levels, or Steps

The most important aspect of Kohlberg's approach to the development of moral reasoning is the *Discussion of Moral Dilemmas*. Dilemmas are chosen or created on the basis of several criteria: (a) A central character must decide between alternative possibilities for action, (b) at least one moral issue is involved, and (c) society lends some support for any of several actions that could be taken by the protagonist. Dilemmas are presented to students, and a discussion follows. Moral discussions follow a six-step process and may be accomplished in several ways to avoid boredom with the process (Guidance Associates, 1976a).

Step One: Present the Dilemma

Moral dilemmas can be presented in several ways. Sound filmstrips are available, as are written materials. Students also can be asked to role-play conflict situations.

Step Two: Have Students Clarify the Facts of the Situation and Identify the Issues Involved

At this step, the teacher asks for information about what happened in the story. Students summarize the events, identify the principal characters, and describe the alternatives open to the protagonist. This part of the discussion will take a short period of time.

Step Three: Have Students Identify a Tentative Position on the Action the Central Character Should Take and State One or Two Reasons for That Position

At this step, students are asked to choose from the identified alternatives what the character should do and the major reason for their choice. This can be done in writing to ensure that students will think for themselves and develop a position. While students are writing, the teacher can walk around the room to get an idea of how the class is thinking. After each student has developed a written opinion, the teacher then asks for a show of hands on the various alternatives to get an idea of the differences or similarities that exist. This information also is used to guide in the organization of the next step.

Step Four: Divide the Class into Small Groups

In this setting children have the chance to share their reasons for the positions they have taken. Shy children and those who may feel threatened by the teacher's presence should find this setting more comfortable for sharing their ideas. Small-group discussions with four to six members should take approximately 10 to 15 minutes. To organize these small groups for maximum effectiveness and interaction among students, the teacher should divide them differently depending on how the class is split on the issue. If the class splits unevenly on the issue, students can be divided into groups that have taken the same position. They can discuss their reasons and decide on the two best reasons for the position. If the class splits evenly on the issue, students can be divided into groups with an approximately equal number that agree with each position. In groups, students discuss both positions and choose the best reasons for each. If the class agrees about one position, the students can be divided into groups based on the similarity of their reasons for supporting a position. Each group can then decide why the reason they prefer is the best one. In this situation, students also can be divided according to differences in reasons. The small groups then discuss their reasons and decide on the best two or three to support their decision.

During these small-group discussions, the teacher should move around the class to make certain that students understand the task and that they focus on reasons rather than argue about the facts or some aspect of the situation. While observing the groups, the teacher can get some ideas for opening the discussion in a large group.

Step Five: Reconvene the Class for a Full Class Discussion of the Dilemma

This part of the process should take the majority of class time. The class should be seated in a circle, with the teacher included, to encourage a maximum amount of student-to-student interaction. Although student interaction is the most important aspect of this discussion time, the teacher's role is crucial in encouraging interaction among students with different points of view, establishing an atmosphere where students feel free to express different ideas, and keeping the discussion focused on the reasons and positions rather than side issues or facts of the situation.

A full class discussion can be initiated in several ways: (a) having each group write its position and supporting reasons on the board, and then asking opposing groups to respond to each other; (b) asking for oral reports from each group, beginning with those who seemed to function well in the small group setting, and then asking for comments from those with opposing viewpoints after each report; or (c) opening the discussion to all, asking the general question, "What should the central character do? Why?" and keeping the discussion going with teacher questions when needed.

During this part of the discussion, teacher questions are crucial for keeping the conversation focused on reasons, encouraging shy students to participate, encouraging interaction among students who are reasoning at different stages, and encouraging students to think about reasons at stages higher than their own. Following are some examples of the types of questions teachers can ask at this step of the discussion.

- Perception-checking questions are asked to determine whether or not other students understand a statement that an individual has made: "Mary, will you tell me in your own words what Sheila said?"

- Interstudent-participation questions are designed to encourage one student to respond to the position of another student: "Mary, what do you think of what Charles said?"

- Clarifying questions are designed to help students make the meaning of their own statements clear: "What do you mean by justice?"

- Issue-related questions focus attention on one or more moral issues: "Is it ever all right to break a law?"

- Role-switch questions require a student to look at a situation from the point of view of another character in the dilemma: "Jill would want her to lie, you say. Would the storeowner want her to lie?"

- Universal-consequences questions stimulate students to imagine what would happen if everyone behaved in a certain way: "What would our lives be like if everyone broke laws when it pleased them to do so?"

- Seeking-reason questions are asked to ascertain the reasoning behind the statement of a position: "Why?" (Guidance Associates, 1976a, Handout 11, p. 5)

As the teacher listens to the discussion, he or she should identify reasoning at a particular stage and then encourage a student to respond who has expressed reasoning at a higher stage. The teacher also should prepare questions that stimulate students to consider reasoning that is at a higher level than anyone in the class has expressed. If the teacher knows from past discussions the levels of reasoning usually employed, such "provocative" questions can be prepared in advance.

Step Six: Ask Students to Reevaluate Their Original Positions Individually

After the large-group discussion, the teacher should ask students to review the discussion and answer the following two questions privately: (a) "Now what do you think the main character should do?" and (b) "What is the most important reason for this action?" The teacher should not attempt to get the group to reach consensus about the dilemma or to suggest that one reason or position may be better than another, but the reevaluation is important. The teacher can collect these responses along with the original written position of the student to see if any significant changes occurred. Individual responses should be evaluated according to their stage so that growth over a period of time can be assessed.

To keep the process interesting and stimulating, teachers can and should vary their methods of presenting and discussing moral dilemmas. In the *Values in a Democracy* and *Values in American History* series edited by Fenton and Kohlberg (Guidance Associates, 1976b, 1976c), the following different ways of presenting dilemmas are used: (a) a list of statements about an issue, each followed by "agree," "disagree," or "can't decide," with instructions for students to indicate their position and then write the most important reason for it; (b) one or two paragraphs about an issue with four reasons supporting an action and four opposing it, with instructions for students to choose their preferred reasons; (c) a short description of a dilemma with a list of five arguments at each of five stages supporting an action, which students rank according to their preference; and (d) three arguments supporting a different position on an issue from which the students choose a preferred argument and expand upon it.

With these varied presentations of a dilemma, teachers would need to modify the six-step process. In all of them, however, opportunities should be provided for students to discuss their reasons. The teacher should set up the situation so that students are interacting and being exposed to reasoning at higher stages than their own. In the first presentation, in which students respond to statements indicating their agreement or disagreement, only steps five and six are appropriate, and the procedures at step five should be modified. A way to facilitate discussion in this situation would be to consider each of the five statements in turn, asking students who have taken each position (agree, disagree, can't decide) to state their reasons for the position. As the discussion proceeds, the teacher can ask questions in the same manner outlined previously for this step. Step six is much the same except that students should be asked to choose the statement they prefer and write the major reason for this preference. Other modifications of the process can be made to enhance interest. The major part of each, however, is whole-class discussion of the issues and reasons (step five), with small-group discussions at different times to encourage more interaction among students.

MODIFICATION OF THE BASIC CURRICULUM

Kohlberg's *Moral Dilemma* discussions include mainly content and process modifications that are appropriate for the gifted. To implement these changes effectively, however, the psychological learning environment must be centered on student ideas, permit independence, be open to new ideas and new viewpoints, and be accepting rather than judgmental.

Content Modifications

Discussions of Moral Dilemmas include content modifications appropriate for the gifted due to their focus on moral/ethical issues rather than the usual subject matter content. Because the content is different, the principle of variety is met. However, more important modifications are suggested in the areas of abstractness and complexity. Because the ultimate goal of these discussions is to encourage students to consider ideas at higher stages, which by definition are more abstract, more complex, and more universal, and because gifted children are capable of reaching these stages more quickly than others, discussions should concentrate on these abstract ideas. Guidelines also are given for selecting dilemmas that have no simple solution, dilemmas whose solutions must take into consideration several complex issues with no clear-cut societal solution.

Process Modifications

Process modifications suggested by the method include emphasis on higher levels (stages) of thinking, concentration on reasoning, group interaction, and variety in methods. Open-endedness also is emphasized. Kohlberg suggests a step-by-step procedure for accomplishing these purposes during a discussion. Since the emphasis is on presenting reasoning at levels higher than the students' predominant ones and specific descriptions of the type of thinking at each stage are given, the goal of developing higher levels of thinking should be achieved.

Although Kohlberg's discussion procedures do not emphasize the asking of open-ended questions, the element of provocativeness is included in the entire method. The whole approach is designed to promote cognitive conflict and further thought about a moral issue resulting in positive change or movement through the stages. At step five, a great deal of emphasis is placed on provocative questions, especially "issue-related" questions, "role-switch" questions, and "universal-consequences" questions. Teachers should use these questions to stimulate further and higher level thought from students.

Almost by definition, the procedure makes the process modifications of proof/reasoning and group interaction. The approach is focused on encouraging students to express moral reasoning at higher levels than before the method was introduced, and a basic assumption of the method is that this reasoning reaches higher levels because students have interacted with each other. Those at a lower stage have listened to the reasons presented at higher levels, and since they tend to prefer higher level reasons, they will adopt it. The teacher's major task at steps four (small-group discussion) and five (full-class discussion) is to keep the group's attention focused on a discussion of reasons for actions. Several types of questions recommended at step five are designed to force students to listen and react to the ideas presented by other members of the group (for example, perception-checking questions and interstudent-participation questions).

Variety of methods is accomplished through varied means of presenting and discussing dilemmas. In each different method, the six-step process needs to be modified.

Product and Learning Environment Modifications

The *Moral Dilemma* discussion strategy does not suggest product modifications appropriate for the gifted but does provide one learning environment change. The method makes provisions for developing a learner-centered process. Because the class is divided into small groups for a portion of the time (step four), student talk must be emphasized without the teacher as the center. No opportunity is provided for the teacher to talk during a discussion of this type. Teachers must exercise care, however, to avoid becoming the center of the discussion during step five. The central position can be avoided by (a) liberal use of "perception-checking" and "interstudent-participation" questions to encourage student reaction to student ideas and (b) avoiding a response to every student idea.

Other suggestions for changes in the learning environment are made by Kohlberg's experiments in development of "communities" that govern themselves (Muson, 1979). In these communities, the emphasis is on having group members develop their own rules of government, solve their own problems, and enforce their own rules. According to Kohlberg, the principles of democracy cannot be taught in an autocratic school or institution. These principles must be practiced on a daily basis and developed in a setting in which individuals can observe the effects of their decision making. In most schools, rather than learning democratic principles, students learn obedience to authority and to arbitrary rules made and enforced by adults.

Communities have been developed in several high schools and prisons as an experiment in rehabilitation. Members discuss solutions to their problems based on "fairness and morality." In other words, instead of discussing hypothetical dilemmas, such as the ones used to study moral development, the communities discuss their own real problems. Although the communities have not escaped criticism, Kohlberg views them as a success, especially those operating in high schools. Students have been able to develop a sense of community and govern themselves responsibly. They have their problems, especially when the wishes of the group conflict with state or federal rules and when they conflict with school policy.

Regardless of the criticism, the basic idea of the community applies directly to the development of learning environment changes appropriate for the gifted, especially in the dimension of independence and in the areas of openness and acceptance. With regard to independence, students are encouraged to develop their own management and government rather than relying on the teacher to develop and implement solutions to their problems. The element of openness is present since the students are free to develop and implement their own procedures and to express themselves freely. Teachers present their ideas, but as equal members of groups. The teacher, according to the theory, should present moral reasoning at a higher level than the students so they can be exposed to the highest levels.

Certainly, acceptance is an important part of the process since the teacher must be one of the group and model the kind of behavior expected from students. This behavior includes attempting to understand another person's perspective and ideas, acceptance of the ideas, clarification of the ideas (an important aspect of the *Moral Dilemma* discussions), and challenging the ideas. The challenging is valuable in the Kohlberg strategy since growth is believed to occur through cognitive conflict. As the communities operate for a long period of time and a significant aspect is development of mutual trust, challenging of ideas should be integrated easily.

JUDGMENTS

Advantages

Advantages of the Kohlberg approach seem to be in the area of content changes suggested by the discussion of abstract, complex moral issues. The concentration on ideas and issues of the type suggested by Kohlberg's approach should be not only interesting and stimulating but also valuable in producing the kind of cognitive conflict or disequilibrium that causes growth to occur. Encouraging students to consider these big ideas as early as possible should contribute to higher quality thought about them in the future.

A second advantage is in the possibilities for combining discussions of moral dilemmas with other areas of the curriculum to achieve effective organization for learning value. In social studies classes, for example, when students are studying some of the abstract ideas that form the basis of the democratic system, discussions of historical and current moral dilemmas involving these ideas can bring an added dimension to the student's understanding of the abstraction.

The Kohlberg approach to moral education certainly presents a better alternative than the two previous ones of indoctrination and values clarification for use with gifted students. The indoctrination approach, often seen in the form of behavior modification, has little effect on ethical behavior and no effect on moral reasoning. Values clarification, on the other hand, with its emphasis on a process of examining values, is an important technique to use with gifted students and can help them develop valuable critical thinking skills. However, it does not go far enough in the areas of examination of moral and ethical issues. In the area of personal choice, the approach or the underlying philosophy of values clarification is appropriate. However, in the area of moral and ethical issues, the underlying philosophy of ethical relativism is difficult to accept. The Kohlberg approach goes one step further in recognizing that certain universal ethical principles are important for students to develop.

Disadvantages

The major disadvantages of this approach lie in the process and the ways *Moral Dilemma* discussions are implemented. The use of discussions of moral dilemmas may facilitate growth in moral reasoning. However, the results of research (e.g., Rest, 1974; Sullivan, 1975) are mixed and rather unspectacular. A related weakness is that no structure or sequence is provided for discussions. Through extensive research on the development of children's abstract thinking, Taba (1966) found that both the type and sequence of teacher questions are important in achieving growth in cognitive abilities. Not only the question immediately preceding a child's answer but also the whole sequence of teacher questions and acts leading up to the question determined the quality of thinking exhibited by the answer. This research suggests that a particular sequence of teacher questions might be most valuable for questioning in a Kohlberg discussion. However, Kohlberg discussions have not been developed with the same attention to sequence as have the Taba strategies.

A related disadvantage is in the lack of guidelines for selection of dilemmas. If Kohlberg is right about the developmental sequence of moral reasoning, certain dilemmas might be more appropriate for discussions at particular stages. An optimum sequence of issues (for example, discussing stealing before discussing killing also might be important).

Finally, a major disadvantage of the model is its basis in research involving only boys. Gilligan (1982) presents convincing evidence that women reason differently from men and raises serious questions about the use of a model derived entirely from research on men and boys. Certainly, one can hold discussions about dilemmas, but making judgments about the "level" of reasoning of students is suspect from this perspective.

CONCLUSION

Since the major advantages of the Kohlberg approach are in the area of content modifications and its major disadvantages are in the process area, it could be a valuable approach to use in programs for gifted students when combined with one of the process models, such as the Taba *Strategies*. It also could be combined effectively with a *Creative Problem Solving* approach if moral or ethical problems were selected as the focus of *Creative Problem Solving*. Although research is inconclusive about the validity of Kohlberg's developmental stages, the model does provide a valuable goal for programs for the gifted: the development of sophisticated moral reasoning.

RESOURCES

Background Information

Dabrowski, K., with Piechowski, M. M. (1977). *Theories of levels of emotional development*. Oceanside, NY: Dabor Publications. A multilevel theory of emotional development is presented and explained in this volume and tied to the belief that evolution is a passage from the most simple to the most complex, from the most automatic to the most voluntary. Unlike stage theories of development, this model includes the notion of discontinuity in development as new structures emerge next to, or in place of, old structures rather than developing from old ones. Examples are given of the five levels of development in a number of personality functions, contexts, and disciplines.

Fan-Willman, C., & Gutteridge, D. (1981). Creative thinking and moral reasoning of academically gifted secondary school adolescents. *Gifted Child Quarterly, 25*(4), 149–153.

Gilligan, C. (1982). *In a different voice: Psychological theory and women's development*. Cambridge, MA: Harvard University Press.

Kazemek, F. E. (1989, Spring). *Feminine voice and power in moral education*. Educational Horizons, pp. 76–81. A brief and accessible synthesis of the differences between male and female models of moral thinking. The article includes an extensive bibliography for readers who wish to investigate this issue in more depth.

Power, F. C., Higgins, A., & Kohlberg, L. (1989). *Lawrence Kohlberg's approach to moral education*. New York: Columbia University Press. This book, completed after Kohlberg's death, includes several essays on the concept of the "just community" and the "Blatt effect," the belief that exposure to the next higher stage of reasoning will stimulate student progress to that higher level. Kohlberg's notion that the culture of most schools is nonmoral because competition and individual achievement are emphasized, social conventions are imposed from without, and rules are obeyed out of pragmatic considerations is less well known than his stage theory. A school's moral atmosphere is improved by (a) open discussions with a focus on fairness and morality; (b) cognitive conflict stimulated by exposure to varied perspectives and higher level reasoning; (c) participation in rule making, decision making, and exercise of power and responsibility; and (d) an emphasis on building a sense of community and community values.

Reimer, J., Paolitto, D. P., & Hersh, R. H. (1983). *Promoting moral growth from Piaget to Kohlberg* (2nd ed.). Prospect Heights, IL: Woodland Press. The authors discuss the connections between the moral development theories of Piaget and Kohlberg and point out that Kohlberg's model is, in reality, a theory of moral judgment. They posit that the process of making a choice, in the face of a moral dilemma, is a cognitive process in which an individual reflects on personal values and orders them in a logical hierarchy. Kohlberg's six stages of moral development are presented and analyzed clearly and in some detail.

Instructional Materials and Resources

Dana, N. F., & Lynch-Brown, C. (1991). Moral development for the gifted: Making a case for children's literature. *Roeper Review, 14*(1), 13–16. The authors discuss the theories of Kohlberg and Gilligan as well as a "union" between the two theories and give examples to show how children's literature can be used to stimulate discussions of moral dilemmas and spark moral development.

Field, D. W., & Weiss, J. S. (1987). *Values in selected children's books of fiction and fantasy.* Hamden, CT: Shoestring Press. A rich source of ideas for discussions of moral issues and dilemmas.

Fleisher, P. (1993). *Changing our world: A handbook for young activists.* Tucson, AZ: Zephyr Press. From his experience as a teacher and social activist, the author has prepared a step-by-step guide for young people interested in social justice issues. Suggestions for developing effective leadership skills and historical information about activists also are included.

Lindsey, B. (1988). A lamp for Dogenes: Leadership giftedness and moral education. *Roeper Review, 11*(1), 8–11. This thoughtful discussion of the importance of leadership education (rather than training) for gifted persons includes a chart illustrating parallels between Bloom's *Taxonomy* and Kohlberg's model.

PART THREE
Frank E. Williams: Teaching Strategies for Thinking and Feeling

The Williams model (Williams, 1972) was not developed specifically for use with gifted children. In fact, its major purpose is to provide a model for enhancing the cognitive and affective processes involved in creativity and productivity in all children. The thinking processes of fluency, flexibility, originality, and elaboration, along with the feeling processes of curiosity, risk taking, complexity, and imagination, are developed through the traditional subject matter content. The teacher uses a series of 18 strategies or modes of teaching. For optimum learning to occur, a proper mix of interaction must occur among three basic elements: (a) what children are or can become (pupil behaviors), (b) the curriculum (subject matter content), and (c) what teachers can do with both the curriculum and the students (teacher behaviors). In any teaching situation, all three elements act upon each other. Because of this interaction, the design of any learning experience for any child should consider all three elements.

From this basic philosophy, Williams (1970) developed a morphological model with the following three dimensions: (a) the curriculum, (b) teaching strategies, and (c) student behaviors. As with other morphological frameworks, this model depicts the components as interrelated parts of a whole. No hierarchy of strategies or behaviors is either implied or intended. The framework can be used as a structure for curriculum planning, instruction, and teacher training. In short, it provides a vehicle for intersecting a given subject area with any teaching strategy to produce student behavior that is creative.

ELEMENTS/PARTS

The Williams model (1972) is a morphological one somewhat similar to the *Structure of Intellect* model of human intelligence developed by Guilford (1967). It has three dimensions that interact in any teaching-learning situation (see Figure 11.3).

Dimensions

The Curriculum

This facet includes the traditional subject matter content areas in schools, that is, art, music, science, social studies, arithmetic, and language. The author suggests substituting the content areas used in a particular setting

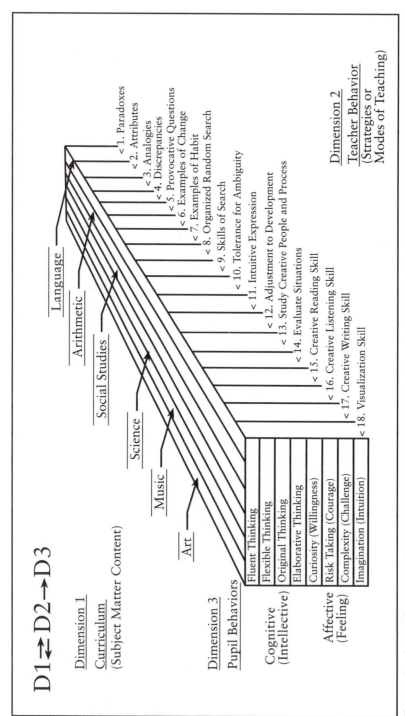

Figure 11.3.   A model for implementing cognitive–affective behaviors in the classroom. From *Classroom Ideas for Encouraging Thinking and Feeling* by F. E. Williams, 1970, Buffalo, NY: D.O.K. Reprinted with permission.

if they are not the same as Williams's areas. In a gifted program, Williams notes, the teacher could substitute areas such as "ecology, marine life studies, man and population growth, psychology, and career development" (Williams, 1972, p.87).

Teaching Strategies

Included in this dimension are the "situations, techniques, or methods" (Williams, 1972, p.87) teachers can use in their classrooms in all of the subject matter areas. The 18 methods or processes have a minimum of overlap when used as they are defined by the author. Following is a list of strategies along with a definition and some examples of each:

- Teach about paradoxes. A paradox is a true situation opposed to common sense, a statement or observation that contradicts itself. Although true in fact, it does not seem to be so. The strategy develops a sensitivity to differences between facts and popular notions.

Examples: In social studies, pose the situation that explorers discovered they could arrive in the West by traveling east. Ask students to think of as many geographical contradictions as possible and try to explain them. In language arts, have students list all the superstitions they can. Have them make a story about one of the superstitions.

- Ask students to look at attributes. Attributes are characteristics of things, that is, inherent properties, conventional symbols, or qualities of items.

Examples: In science, after playing around with magnets, ask students to list all the attributes or qualities of things that are attracted to magnets. Have them list all the qualities of things that are not attracted to magnets. In language arts, have the children list as many adjectives as they can to describe an object the teacher is holding.

- Use analogies. Analogies emphasize similarities between things that otherwise may seem unlike. They make comparisons between these things or between the things and the circumstances surrounding them.

Examples: First, have children brainstorm about the properties and use of traffic signs. Then have them make comparisons between these traffic signs and punctuation marks used in writing (language arts). In social studies, have students make a list of all the fads that existed when their parents were their age and a list of current fads. Ask them to make comparisons between past and present fads to see what common factors can be identified.

- Point out discrepancies. Discrepancies include gaps in knowledge, unknown information, or "missing links."

Examples: Ask children to think of all the things they do not know about people from another country. Have them list all the ways this information could be found. Have children think about life in a glass house. Ask them to make a list of all the ways their lives might be different if they lived in a glass house rather than a regular house.

- Ask provocative questions. These are questions intended to get children excited about inquiry and get them to explore and to discover new knowledge.

Examples: After a science lesson on water and its different forms, ask students whether they would rather be a raindrop or a cloud and why they feel that way. During a unit on living things, ask students to tell all the things they could learn about a tree by looking at its leaves. Then have them answer the question, "What would the world be like if all the trees were destroyed by human carelessness?" (Williams, 1970, p. 41).

- Cite examples of change. Demonstrate to students how dynamic the world is or can be. Provide situations for making substitutions or modifications.

Examples: Discuss the ways people preserve things (for example, freezing fish or bronzing baby shoes). Ask students to think of a list of things that are preserved, kept, or sustained. Then have them think about how and why these things are preserved. Have children develop a list of words by changing only the initial consonant. What is the longest list that can be made?

- Use examples of habit. This strategy develops a sensitivity to the avoidance of rigid or habit-bound thinking through discussing or showing the effects of thinking bound by habits.

Examples: Discuss the habitual use of a base-ten numbering system. After using other bases, have children think of situations in which other bases would be more appropriate. During a unit on transportation, point out the effects of tradition and habit-bound thinking on innovations. Pose questions such as why engines are usually placed at the front of a car, propellers are usually placed on the front of engines, and drive wheels are placed on the rear of a car. Then discuss some results of breaking out of these patterns of thinking.

- Allow for an organized random search. Develop a structure, and use it to lead randomly to another structure. Set ground rules, and allow students to explore within these boundaries.

Examples: Teach students a form such as cinquains. Give a few examples, and then ask them to develop some of their own. The form is the following:

> line 1—one noun
> line 2—two adjectives describing the noun in line 1
> line 3—three words expressing an action
> line 4—four words expressing a feeling
> line 5—one noun that is a synonym of the single noun of line 1

When working with number facts, have students think of all the possible ways to make a certain number.

- Teach the skills of search. This strategy includes teaching several different ways of searching for information including historical search, or looking for ways something has been done before; having students do a trial-and-error search and then describe how it was done; and experimental search, or controlling experimental conditions and reporting the results.

Examples: Have students imagine they are stranded on a desert island. Ask what are all the ways a person could get off the island? After listing all ideas, ask them how they can find more. After talking about seeds and which seeds grow, have students do experiments with different kinds of seeds to see which ones grow.

- Build a tolerance for ambiguity. Provide situations that are challenging and intriguing. Present open-ended situations that do not encourage or force closure.

Examples: Read a story, and stop at an interesting part. Have the students tell or write what they think the ending might be. Emphasize that stories can have many endings, and no "right" way can be found to end a story. Ask students to think about what might happen if certain natural cycles changed (for example, seasons following each other in a different order or ocean tides changing every week).

- Allow for intuitive expression. Use of this strategy encourages the skills of expressing emotions, making guesses based on "hunches," and noticing things through all the senses.

Examples: Show pictures of people expressing different emotions. Have children guess why the person might be feeling that way. Show a film about a natural phenomenon. Have half the students write about it from the point of view of a meteorologist and half of them write about it from the point of view of an artist. Compare the two views.

- Teach not for adjustment but for development. Look at how failures or accidents have been positive, how to learn from mistakes, and how to develop or change rather than simply adjust to things.

Examples: After studying how the government functions and making field trips to government offices, have students design an ideal government. Ask them to decide what qualities ideal governments should have and how these qualities can be achieved. After studying about how scarce and costly paper is in Japan, ask children to imagine that their family is so poor that they cannot buy paper and list all the writing surfaces that could be used in place of paper.

- Have students study creative people and creative processes. In this strategy look at the people who have been recognized for their creativity and examine the processes they used that led to their creativity.

Examples: Have students look at the life of an inventor and an artist. Ask them to consider how these people are similar and how they are different. After the students consider what the people are like as individuals, have them look at the similarities and differences in how the people developed their products. Have the children make a list of all the characteristics they can that relate to an eminent individual, such as Ben Franklin. Ask them to list their own attributes and then compare their characteristics to those of the eminent individual.

- Encourage students to evaluate situations, choose solutions by careful consideration of consequences and implications, and predict from the results of ideas and actions.

Examples: Beginning with a random collection of items, have students predict which ones will sink or float. Have them tell why the prediction was made and then try out items to see whether their predictions were accurate. In social studies, after a unit on exploration showing that movement is always from east to west, have students consider the possible causes and effects of westward movement.

- Develop skills in creative reading. In this strategy, students learn to generate ideas through reading and to read "not what it says, but where it takes you" (Williams, 1970, p. 99).

Examples: During the year, ask students to keep a list of the many expressions used by writers, especially colloquial ones such as "It was raining cats and dogs!" After becoming aware of paradoxes, when students read newspapers, watch TV, or read magazines, they can look for paradoxical situations and keep a list.

- Develop skills in creative listening. Idea generation through listening is emphasized in this strategy. Students are encouraged to listen for information that leads them from one thing to another.

Examples: After each student has created an imaginary animal, have students make up stories about the animals. Have students compose stories in a group setting. The student who created an animal starts a story, then other students add a sentence until each has added one sentence to the story. Have students listen to an audiotape or the teacher's reading of a story. As they listen, they should make two lists. In one list, have them write what information they acquired and, in the other, list what guesses or inferences they can make from what they heard.

- Develop skills in creative writing. In this strategy, students are taught to write their ideas clearly and to express their feelings and emotions through writing.

Examples: In the old activity of writing autobiographies, discuss how a student's life story can be made more interesting. Ask students to generate new ways of organizing the information (that is, use a method different from chronological) and presenting the information (that is, changing the format). As a follow-up to the activity in which students discussed how various items could be preserved or saved, have them write a story about something they would like to preserve and tell why.

- Develop skills in visualization. Give students practice in describing objects or situations from unusual viewpoints or looking at things from an unusual or different perspective. Encourage the expression of ideas in three-dimensional form.

Examples: Discuss dreams and some ideas about why people dream. Also talk about artists and how they make their dreams into pictures and how poets make their dreams into poems. Have students describe five or more of their own dreams by drawing pictures of them. Brainstorm colors that express emotions. After discussing these ideas, while listening to a story or a piece of music, the students can put the emotions expressed by the story or music into an abstract "mood" painting.

Although all of the strategies would be useful at some point in working with creative students, Williams (1970) states that the most effective strategies to use with the more able, highly talented children would be the following: (a) exploring discrepant events, (b) asking and seeking answers to provocative questions, (c) exploring examples of change and habit, (d) developing skills of search, (e) learning how to tolerate ambiguity, (f) teaching for development rather than adjustment, and (g) learning to evaluate situations.

Pupil Behaviors

Student behaviors developed by the strategies through the curriculum are divided into cognitive (intellect) and affective (feeling). Based on research on the behaviors involved in creativity, Williams (1972) identifies eight clusters of behaviors. Following are his descriptions and examples of these behaviors.

List of Thinking Behaviors:

1. Is fluent in thinking. Usually comes up with the most ideas, responses, solutions, or questions. Produces a quantity of ways or suggestions for doing things. Always thinks of more than one answer. A count of these determines how fluent a child is.

Examples:

- The child who has a flow of answers when a question is asked.

- The child who draws several pictures when asked to draw one.

- The child who usually has several ideas about something while others struggle for one idea.

- The child who asks many questions.

- The child who uses a large number of words when expressing himself [or herself].

- The child who always produces more than others in the class.

- The fastest worker in the class, who does more than just the assignment.

2. Is flexible in thinking. Usually is able to produce a variety of ideas, responses, questions, or solutions. Seeks many different directions or alternatives. Has the ability to shift approaches or change direction in thinking about things. A count of the number of changes or categories within which thinking occurs determines how flexible a child is. Fluent children are not flexible if all their ideas are of one kind. Flexible thinkers need not necessarily be fluent, but each idea will be of a different variety.

Examples:

- The child who thinks of various ways to use an object other than its common use.

- The child who has different interpretations of a picture, story or problem other than the one being discussed.

- The child who can apply a principle or concept in subjects other than the one in which it was introduced.

- The child who shifts and takes another point of view or considers situations differently from others in the class.

- The child who, when discussing a situation, will always take a different position from the rest of the class.

- The child who, when given a problem, usually thinks of a number of different possibilities for solving it.

3. Is original in thinking. Usually able to think of novel, unique expressions. Has clever ideas rather than common or obvious ones. His [or her] thinking is unusual and he [or she] chooses to figure things out and express them in new ways. A count of the number of uncommon responses or productions away from the usual determines how original a child is. This may be the child who is neither fluent nor flexible, but after listening to others will think of a new approach that is rarely thought of by the rest

of the class. An original thinker has the capacity to combine pieces of the usual into a new and unusual whole.

Examples:

- The child who likes objects in the room placed off side or prefers asymmetry in drawings and designs.

- The child who is dissatisfied with a stereotyped answer and instead seeks a fresh approach.

- The nonconformist who cannot help being different and always has a new twist in thinking or behavior.

- The child who enjoys the unusual and will rebel against doing things the way everyone else does them.

- The child who deviates from others to do things his [or her] own way.

- The child who, after reading or listening to a problem solution, will go to work on inventing his [or her] own new solution.

- The child who not only questions the old way but will always try to figure out a new way.

4. Is an elaborative thinker. Usually wants to add to or elaborate upon ideas or productions. Loves to stretch or expand upon things. Seeks to embellish materials or solutions by making them more elegant and interesting. The elaborator may not be an originator, but once he [or she] gets hold of a new idea, he [or she] can modify or expand upon it. A count of the number of times he [or she] senses something lacking and adds on details to improve it determines how elaborative a child is.

Examples:

- The child who will add lines, colors, and details to his [or her] own or another child's drawing.

- The child who senses a deeper meaning to an answer or solution by producing more detailed steps.

- The child who takes off with someone else's idea and modifies it.

- The child who will accept an idea or someone else's work but will always want to "jazz it up."

- The child who is uninterested in things that are barren or plain and always attempts to add detail to make them more beautiful. (pp. 35–39)

List of Feeling Behaviors:

1. Is keenly observant and inquisitive by nature. Always curious about people, objects and situations. Likes to wonder, explore, ask questions, and puzzle over things.

Examples:

- The child who questions everything and everyone.
- The child who loves to explore mechanical things.
- The child who constantly searches for "why."
- The child who is more prone to question why things are not done differently than the usually accepted way.
- The child who constantly searches books, maps, pictures, etc., looking for new ideas.
- The child who needs no real push to explore something unfamiliar.
- The child who uses all of his [or her] senses to make sense out of things.
- The child sensitive to problems.
- The child alert to details that produce meaning.

2. Has a very strong imagination. Can visualize and dream about things that have never happened to him [or her]. Can deal with fantasy but knows the difference between that and reality.

Examples:

- The child who can tell a story about a place he [or she] has never visited.
- The child who can feel intuitively something that has not yet happened.
- The child who can predict what someone else has said or done without ever knowing that person.

- The child who can go somewhere in his [or her] dreams without ever leaving the room.

- The child who likes to build images of things he [or she] has never seen.

- The child who can see things in a picture or drawing that no one else has seen.

- The child who can wonder about something that has never happened.

- The child who can make inanimate objects come to life.

3. Is challenged by complexity. Thrives on complicated situations. Likes to tackle difficult problems. Has a preference for "digging in" to intricate solutions and things.

Examples:

- The child who appreciates complex ideas or problems.

- The child who becomes intrigued with messy situations.

- The child who likes to delve into the most complicated task.

- The child who will choose a more difficult way out.

- The child who wants to figure things out for himself [or herself], without help.

- The child who enjoys something harder to do than other children.

- The child who thrives on trying again and again in order to gain success.

- The child who will not give up easily.

- The child who needs harder problems because of the challenge.

- The child who seeks more difficult answers rather than accepting an easy one.

4. Is a courageous risk-taker willing to make guesses. Usually not afraid of failure or criticism. Plays on hunches just to see where they will take him [or her]. Is not bothered by uncertainty, the unconventional, or lack of structure.

Examples:

- The child who will defend his [or her] ideas regardless of what others think.

- The child who will set high goals of accomplishment and not be afraid of trying to reach them.

- The child who will admit to a mistake.

- The child who is willing to try the difficult task.

- The child who really wants to try something new and hard.

- The child who is not concerned by disapproval from classmates or teachers.

- The child who is not easily influenced by friends or teachers.

- The child who prefers to take a chance or a dare. (pp. 70–73)

MODIFICATION OF BASIC CURRICULUM

Process Modifications

The Williams model suggests some modifications of the curriculum to make it more appropriate for gifted students. The major changes are in the areas of process, that is, open-endedness, the use of a discovery approach, freedom of choice, and use of a variety of methods. Perhaps the most important modification is open-endedness. More than any other model, except perhaps Taba's, Williams's approach incorporates open-ended, provocative questions and learning experiences. Several of the teaching strategies (for example, paradoxes, discrepancies, provocative questions, and tolerance for ambiguity) directly address this aspect of teaching methods for the gifted. These strategies require that teachers develop and pose open-ended, stimulating, and challenging questions that could easily interest a gifted student.

Although not addressed quite as directly as the concept of open-endedness, a discovery approach is present in most of the teaching strategies in the model. Most of the ideas included place the teacher in the role of a questioner and the student in the role of the discoverer. The biggest difference between this and traditional discovery approaches is that in the Williams strategies the teacher usually encourages students to "discover" as many ideas (or solutions or principles) as possible rather than discovering a particular idea or principle. Williams also suggests freedom of choice, particularly for the highly able students, by allowing students to choose an area of study and to develop an original product based on that study. The final process modification is suggesting a great variety of methods. Since the 18 different strategies can be used in any content area to encourage eight different behaviors (resulting in a slightly different "twist" to each activity), the result is a great deal of variety in teaching strategies. This should help decrease the possibility that gifted students will become bored.

Content and Product Modifications

In the areas of content and products, the model suggests three modifications. Two of the strategies, organized random search and the skills of search, concentrate on methods used by professionals. In the first strategy, students are taught to use a particular method or structure and to apply it to a different situation, thereby creating something new. In the second, skills of search, students learn various methods that are used by professionals and learn how to apply them. A third strategy also is appropriate and important to use with gifted students—the study of creative people and creative processes. This aspect of creativity, the study of real people and how they were creative, is important to show students the more personal side of creativity. Since the students are likely to be the creators of the future, the study of other eminent individuals may facilitate their success or at least help them adjust to it.

The one product modification suggested by the model is not quite as clear-cut as the content modifications. In one section of the program, Williams suggests that highly able children be allowed to "go off on their own" to develop their creative products. He recommends that the teacher make certain that the final product of independent study "goes further" than a report that is turned in for a grade. The examples of acceptable products (a child's book, an art piece, a research report for a journal, a film) all seem to be transformations rather than summaries. Although he does not address the aspects of audiences and problems, the products recommended are sophisticated.

Learning Environment Modifications

With respect to the learning environment, Williams suggests aspects of all the changes recommended for the gifted. He suggests the development of a learner-centered, independent, open, accepting learning environment by providing a list of ways teachers can both directly and indirectly develop children's creativity. The indirect ways constitute most of those related to the environment, but some of the direct ones can be considered dimensions of the environment. The following recommendations are listed under the environmental dimensions to which they seem to relate most directly.

Learner Centered

- Maintain an attitude of learning with the children. Do not profess to know all the answers and be willing to explore student ideas.
- Treat the questions and ideas of children with a great deal of respect and keep the emphasis on "rightness" or "correctness" to a minimum.

Independence

- Allow children opportunities to help plan projects that involve their environment, such as decorating the room and improving the playground.
- Provide a period of time each day for working with a small group of children and encourage them to plan the use of the time.
- Have a suggestion box for students to tell how they would like the classroom improved.
- Encourage (and even demand) achievement and accomplishment, but only in areas chosen by the student.
- Respect the children, and show that you are confident they will act appropriately and responsibly.
- Avoid allowing overdependency or appearing to reject the child.
- Allow each child to progress at his or her own pace without showing anxious concern about the development of skills and abilities.
- Provide a safe psychological environment that is available to the child when needed, but allow and encourage the child to venture away from it.

Openness

- Be playful, and encourage fantasy and imagination rather than always "bringing them back to reality," even if the task was serious.
- Allow children a free period of time each day to use as they please.
- Show that you believe each child is unique and capable of becoming or being a creative individual.
- Allow noise and messiness in the classroom. Quiet and orderly classrooms do not ensure that learning and creativity are taking place.

Accepting

- When children have new ideas, talk and listen to them in a sensitive manner, sometimes encouraging them to go further with their ideas.

- Listen carefully to children, and attempt to "see things through their eyes."

- Give children honest approval when they produce a product or develop an idea.

- Challenge students by discussing reality, but stimulate them with fantasy.

- Recognize that each child's creative production may be new to him or her even though you may have seen it millions of times.

The environmental dimensions of complexity and high mobility are discussed by Williams mainly in conjunction with his recommendations for the handling of gifted children who are developing independent projects. To assist students in independent study, Williams also recommends that the learning environment be as flexible as possible to allow movement within the classroom and outside. This includes releasing students to work with children from other classrooms and releasing them for certain periods of time each week to work on their own in the library, resource room, or with an expert from outside the school. Children also should be allowed to search for and use media that will assist them in developing their products.

JUDGMENTS

Advantages

The Williams (1972) *Total Creativity Program* has several advantages. The first and perhaps most important is its unique combination of thinking and feeling behaviors. A second related advantage is that the model concentrates on a specific and well-defined set of behaviors. These are observable, measurable behaviors derived from research on the characteristics of creative, productive adults.

Another strength of this model is its emphasis on open-endedness of learning experiences and teacher questions. As discussed earlier, several of the strategies directly address this concept through both open-ended and provocative questions. None of the other approaches discussed in this book provide such helpful guidelines in the development of learning experiences that satisfy this requirement.

Williams also advocates an individualized approach, including assessment and observation of thinking and feeling behaviors, compilation of information, interpretation of profiles, and design of both individual and group learning experiences based on the needs of the children.

Disadvantages

The Williams model also has several disadvantages. First of all, even though the strategies and the total approach have been field-tested in a variety of classrooms, no research is reported on the effectiveness of the strategies. In effect, no research indicates that if teachers do all 18 strategies and attempt to develop the eight behaviors in their students they will actually increase the students' creative behaviors. Data on the effectiveness of the strategies should have been relatively easy to collect during the field testing, but the only data available are on the elements necessary for effective inservice and the frequency of use of the strategies. Data on student gains are conspicuously absent.

A second disadvantage of the model is its lack of empirical or logical "power." The model itself was not derived from a particular theoretical position or set of theoretical principles. Even though the Williams model was derived from Guilford's *Structure of Intellect* model of human intelligence, the only resemblance it bears to this theoretical base is that it is morphological or integrated rather than hierarchical. The thinking behaviors of fluency, flexibility, originality, and elaboration are concepts first developed by Guilford (1967) as part of his definition of divergent thinking but are not a major part of his model of intelligence. One could argue that the subject matter in Williams's model is comparable to the content of Guilford's, the teaching strategies compare to the processes, and the pupil behaviors parallel the products. However, the individual items included in these facts do not appear to be related to those in Guilford's model.

Another weakness of the approach is its lack of comprehensiveness as a total approach. It was not developed for use in programs for the gifted, but as a way to develop creativity in all children. Indeed, Williams advocates using his and other models popular in programs for the gifted to improve education for all children (Williams, 1980). Even though the emphasis on specific behaviors is an advantage, concentration on a limited range of behaviors is a disadvantage. The development of divergent thinking and feeling is not enough. Educators must help gifted children develop a whole range of thinking and feeling behaviors, including divergent ones. For this reason and the fact that only two of the content modifications and one of the product modifications appropriate for the gifted are addressed by the approach, the Williams model must be combined with other models to form a comprehensive program for gifted students.

A final disadvantage is that few materials developed for use in implementing the model are available. If they can be located, however, they are practical and easy to use.

CONCLUSION

Like the other approaches discussed in this book, Williams's model does not provide a comprehensive program for curriculum development for gifted students. However, it offers certain unique features that highly recommend its use in programs for the gifted. The process modifications, individualization, and concentration on the cognitive and affective behaviors necessary for creativity development would be ample justification for its use as a component in a program for the gifted.

If readers decide to implement this approach, however, they are urged to develop procedures for assessing the effectiveness of the strategies, since such data are not available. Use of the needs assessment instruments for evaluation of progress is strongly advised, as is comparison of this method with others to determine the most effective strategies for use with gifted children.

RESOURCES: BACKGROUND INFORMATION

Williams, F. E. (1986). *The second volume of classroom ideas for encouraging thinking and feeling*. East Aurora, NY: D.O.K. This spiral-bound volume has a brief review of the Williams model, more than 200 suggested lessons, plus a supplement to extend selected activities for more able learners. Each idea identifies the cognitive and/or affective behaviors to be encouraged, the curriculum area, and the strategies to be used. Suggestions are very brief but could be developed easily into student task cards for learning centers.

Williams, F. J. (1990). *Curriculum units: Classroom ideas: Vol. 3 for encouraging thinking and feeling*. Buffalo, NY: D.O.K. Subtitled "A new application of the Williams model meeting the needs of today's classroom," this volume features a unit format and includes teaching notes or tips for each unit. Again, the thinking skills to be encouraged, the strategies to be used, and the content area are identified; a brief introduction, activities, conclusion/closure strategies, objectives, and special teaching notes or tips also are included. Thirty-one units (plus eight supplements or extensions) are featured, with titles such as "World Events Watch," "Inductive–Deductive Reasoning," "Myth-Information," "Misguided Trends and Habits," "Analogy through Poetry," and "Statistically Speaking." The units and teaching ideas have been elaborated much more in this volume and are based on more complex content than are the ideas in the first two volumes. For teachers who wish to use the Williams model, this should be a first purchase.

PART FOUR
Two Promising New Approaches
PROBLEM-BASED LEARNING AND THINKING ACTIVELY IN A SOCIAL CONTEXT (TASC)

Two new models are showing great promise for the field and may be included in future volumes. Both are, in many ways, content models but, as both include problem-solving components, they can be considered an integration of content and process.

Problem-Based Learning

This approach, currently used in medical schools, is being tested at the high school level (Gallagher, Stepien, & Rosenthal, 1992; Stepien, Gallagher, & Workman, 1993). Problem-based learning is designed to provide students with guided experience in solving "ill-structured" or "fuzzy" problems. It was designed originally as a way to help medical students model the problem-solving techniques of physicians. Use of this strategy in discipline-based and interdisciplinary programs for gifted students provides practice for them in solving real-world problems in the ways professionals must handle their problems. Teachers act as coaches and tutors rather than as information givers. Students may be given a specific problem-solving strategy to use or may be guided through a more informal approach.

Results of the use of this process have been encouraging (Gallagher et al., 1992) and, judging from the positive effects of similar approaches such as *Future Problem Solving* and *Creative Problem Solving,* one can expect gifted students to benefit from this approach. Gallagher et al. (1992), for instance, found that students involved in the program increased significantly over the control group in their use of one important problem-solving step: problem finding. Studies of the effectiveness of this method and other studies designed to refine and improve it are currently underway (Stepien et al., 1993), including the field testing of eight problem-based science units and the development of a Center for Problem Based Learning.

Thinking Actively in a Social Context (TASC)

This model was developed in a very different context with black students and teachers in Kawa Zulu/Natal schools (Adams & Wallace, 1988, 1991; Wallace & Adams, 1988). However, the model has potential for use in other situations as well (Maltby, 1993). Three theories have been combined in the development of this model: (a) Vygotsky's (1978) belief that the development of higher levels of thinking is based on social transaction; (b) Feuerstein's (1980) theory of cognitive modifiability and the concept of mediated learning experiences; and (c) Sternberg's (1988) triarchic theory of intelligence.

The model provides a flexible framework for designing problem-solving courses according to the needs and experiences of the participants. The general purpose for students is to "make sense of and learn from experience" (Maltby, 1993, p. 45). For teachers, the aim is to improve their ability to facilitate "learning to learn" skills. Underlying principles of the model (Adams & Wallace, 1988) are the following:

1. Adopt a model of the problem-solving process.

2. Identify a set of specific skills and strategies, and give skills training in these.

3. Develop a vocabulary.

4. Give ample practice in both the skills and the strategies, using situations that are significant and relevant to the learners.

5. Give attention to the motivational aspects of problem solving.

6. The progression of teaching is from modeling by the teacher to guided activity by the learner to autonomous action by the learner.

7. Enable the learner to transfer skills and strategies.

8. Emphasize cooperative learning in small groups.

9. Require students to develop metacognitive knowledge.

Future research and current studies in an international context will, no doubt, provide evidence of the success of this exciting approach. Numerous units of study have been developed and are being field-tested.

New curriculum ideas, new thinking and problem-solving models, and new research emphasize the importance of teaching the attitudes and strategies that enable all of us to be lifelong learners.

Chapter 12

Developing a
Comprehensive Approach

The previous chapters have presented a thorough review of each of 10 teaching-learning models and shorter reviews of three more that are currently used in or appropriate for use in developing a curriculum for gifted students. No one model by itself provides a comprehensive approach, and no model by itself should be expected to be a comprehensive approach. The majority of the models reviewed were not developed for use in gifted programs. Most were developed for some specific, well-defined purpose, but educators have used them in a variety of different ways, some appropriate and many inappropriate. Too many educators assume that by using one particular teaching-learning model as the basis for a curriculum, all the needs of the gifted students in that program will be met.

Bloom's *Taxonomy*, for example, was developed for the narrow purpose of classifying educational objectives, according to their complexity, as a way to facilitate communication among professionals about the objectives of instruction. It was never intended as a framework for developing a sequence of questions to guide a discussion, and it certainly was not intended to form the basis of curriculum development for the gifted. Yet it has been used in too many instances as the only curricular modification provided for gifted students. The same is true of the Williams and Guilford models. Although the Williams strategies were developed as ways to stimulate a narrow range of human behaviors (for example, the thinking and feeling behaviors involved in creativity) and Guilford's model was developed as a theory to explain human intelligence, each approach is used by educators as their only curriculum development model for programs for the gifted.

Thus it is important that readers and the authors of the models interpret the comments in this section on assessment of the comprehensiveness of models as an honest attempt to show how a comprehensive curriculum can be developed. Rather than recommending that educators "start all over again" with new models or new approaches, curriculum developers and teachers can begin with existing models or approaches to education of the gifted and move toward an integrated program that incorporates a variety of models adapted to student needs and learning goals. For instance, if a program has used Bloom's *Taxonomy* as a basis for curriculum development, then rather than learning a totally different approach, a more effective strategy might be to build on the previous program, add one or more complementary models, or add components to Bloom's approach.

Critical comments about specific models or approaches in this volume should be interpreted only as criticism of large-scale adoption of the model or approach by educators rather than as criticism of the authors of the models (unless, of course, they have advocated the use of their model as a sole approach to education of the gifted). Authors generally have been clear about the goals of their models and the reasons for their development. Unfortunately many educators often have ignored the underlying assumptions made by the developers and have used the models for many purposes not intended by the authors.

Certainly, not every teacher or program developer will wish to develop a curriculum in which all the modifications recommended by Maker (1982) are incorporated. The number and range of curricular modifications needed in a program will depend on the characteristics of the students. All the recommended curricular changes were designed to build on and extend the present and potential future characteristics of gifted students. Thus, if the students in a particular program do not possess the characteristics that the curricular change was designed to enhance, this particular curricular modification would be unnecessary unless it is seen as a way to develop a particular desirable characteristic that is not present. In addition, other curricular modifications not discussed in this volume may be necessary or desirable because of differing characteristics of the gifted students in the program.

CURRICULUM DEVELOPMENT

Maker (1982) suggests a multifaceted process in development of a curriculum for the gifted that includes: (a) involvement of the key individuals who assess the situation and assist in the formulation of goals and programs, (b) development of a definition of giftedness, (c) assessment of the needs of the students, (d) development of a philosophy, (e) development of program goals, (f) choice of teaching-learning models, (g) development of objectives and strategies, (h) development of evaluation procedures, and (i) development of a plan for curriculum implementation. The process has been adequately described elsewhere. This discussion will assume that program goals include the provision of curricular modifications in all the aspects of content, process, product, and learning environment recommended by Maker (1982) and briefly outlined in Chapter 1 of this volume.

When choosing the teaching-learning models for use in a curriculum for the gifted, the first step is to assess the appropriateness of the existing models for the particular situation. A checklist and questions for this purpose have been presented in Chapter 1 (see Figure 1.1). Each individual familiar with the situation and the models should evaluate the models and compare their ratings to determine those that may be appropriate for the program. A second assessment should then be made to determine the model's comprehensiveness for providing needed modifications of the curriculum. A worksheet designed for this purpose also was presented in Chapter 1 (see Figure 1.2).

ASSESSING THE MODELS

To assist the reader in assessing the comprehensiveness of the teaching-learning models presented in this volume, the worksheet presented in Figure 1.2 has been completed (see Figure 12.1). This assessment provides a summary of material presented in the "Modification of the Basic Curriculum" section in each chapter describing a model. Those who do not understand why a particular assessment was made should review this section in the appropriate chapter. All evaluations are based on whether the model makes direct, specific suggestions regarding how to implement a particular curricular adaptation. Some models indirectly address an idea but do not include specific suggestions. In these cases the model is not listed as making that particular curriculum change.

The column totals in Figure 12.1 provide a summary of the comprehensiveness of the models by giving the total number of modifications provided. As can be seen, the most comprehensive overall are Betts, Parnes, Renzulli, Sharan, Taba, Taylor, Williams, and Treffinger. However, no model makes all recommended modifications. The pattern of check marks also should be examined to determine areas of strength and weakness for each approach. Bruner's approach, for instance, although not one of the most comprehensive in overall ratings, provides most of the content changes needed. Taba's model, although not the most comprehensive overall, provides more of the process changes than any other approach. This information is useful in making decisions about which models can be combined or used together.

The row totals are a third source of information in the worksheet. These totals indicate the number of available models that provide a particular curricular modification. Fewer models provide for content changes, while all except one provide for the process modification of emphasis on

Rate each model on each criterion by placing a ✓ in the column if the modification is made in the model. If modification is not made, leave the space blank.

Curricular Modifications		Betts	Bloom	Bruner	Guilford	Kohlberg	Krathwohl	Parnes	Renzulli	Sharan	Taba	Taylor	Treffinger	Williams	Total	Comments
CONTENT	1. Abstractness	✓	✓	✓	✓	✓					✓				6	
	2. Complexity	✓	✓	✓	✓	✓			✓		✓				7	
	3. Variety	✓	✓		✓		✓	✓	✓	✓	✓	✓	✓	✓	11	
	4. Organization for Learning Value			✓		✓									2	
	5. Study of People	✓									✓				2	
	6. Study of Methods	✓	✓	✓	✓	✓	✓	✓	✓	✓	✓				10	
PROCESS	7. Higher Level Thought	✓	✓	✓	✓	✓	✓	✓	✓	✓	✓	✓	✓		12	
	8. Open-endedness	✓	✓	✓	✓	✓	✓	✓	✓	✓		✓		✓	11	
	9. Discovery	✓		✓	✓	✓			✓	✓		✓	✓	✓	8	
	10. Evidence of Reasoning			✓							✓	✓			3	
	11. Freedom of Choice	✓				✓		✓	✓	✓		✓	✓		6	
	12. Group Interaction	✓						✓		✓	✓	✓		✓	6	
	13. Pacing	✓				✓				✓					3	
	14. Variety	✓			✓			✓	✓	✓	✓	✓	✓	✓	9	

(continues)

Figure 12.1. Sample worksheet for overall curriculum design. Adapted from *Curriculum Development for the Gifted* by J. Maker, 1982, Austin, TX: PRO-ED. Adapted with permission.

Rate each model on each criterion by placing a ✓ in the column if the modification is made in the model. If modification is not made, leave the space blank.

Curricular Modifications

		Betts	Bloom	Bruner	Guilford	Kohlberg	Krathwohl	Parnes	Renzulli	Sharan	Taba	Taylor	Treffinger	Williams	Total	Comments
PRODUCT	15. Result from Real Problems	✓		✓				✓	✓			✓	✓		6	
	16. Addressed to Real Audiences	✓						✓	✓	✓					4	
	17. Transformation	✓	✓	✓	✓			✓	✓	✓		✓	✓	✓	10	
	18. Variety	✓						✓	✓	✓			✓		5	
	19. Self-selected Format	✓							✓	✓			✓		4	
	20. Appropriate Evaluation	✓				✓		✓	✓	✓		✓	✓		7	
LEARNING ENVIRONMENT	21. Learner Centered	✓				✓		✓	✓	✓	✓	✓	✓	✓	9	
	22. Encourages Independence	✓				✓		✓	✓	✓	✓	✓	✓	✓	9	
	23. Openness	✓				✓		✓	✓	✓	✓	✓	✓	✓	9	
	24. Accepting	✓				✓				✓	✓	✓	✓	✓	7	
	25. Complexity	✓							✓	✓				✓	4	
	26. Varied Groupings	✓							✓	✓					3	
	27. Flexibility	✓													1	
	28. High Mobility	✓				✓				✓			✓	✓	5	
	TOTALS	26	6	10	7	15	2	14	19	22	12	15	16	15		

Figure 12.1. *Continued*

higher levels of thinking. Three of the modifications are made only by one or two models. This information can be helpful in suggesting the range of options available for making a certain curricular adaptation.

CHOOSING MODELS

After the appropriateness and comprehensiveness of the different models have been assessed, each educator (or development team) must decide whether to adopt one approach as the basis for curriculum development and incorporate elements to make it more comprehensive, to adopt two or more approaches that are complementary, or to adapt and adopt. Certainly any one of these three options would be appropriate, depending on the situation. If, for example, an earlier assessment showed that only one approach was evaluated highly by those involved (based on its appropriateness, flexibility/adaptability, practicality, and validity), this approach should form the basis of the program. Modifications then could be made to improve its comprehensiveness. In most cases, however, several models would be acceptable, allowing a range of options for different purposes. Combining several models also ensures that variety will be an important aspect of the curriculum and that curricular modifications will be made in more ways than one.

Perhaps the most effective strategy is to employ a combination of options, that is, adopt complementary models and adapt each of them to form a comprehensive approach. With this strategy equal emphasis would be placed on each curricular modification, and the possibility is increased that a well-integrated program will result.

To assist the reader in this task, tables have been developed that summarize for each model the curricular modifications that should be added, suggested changes, and other models that could be combined with the selected model to provide a particular change. In listing other models that can be used with the approach we do not mean to imply that *all* these models be used, just that they are all possibilities. In each separate section describing modifications of a specific model, particular models have been recommended as the most effective complementary ones.

Representative suggestions for changes have been listed in the tables as a quick summary to aid the reader. For example, learning environment modifications that have not been listed as recommendations are essentially the same in many cases and listing them for each model would be repetitious. As educators consider the potential implementation of an approach or model, the specific chapter should be reviewed.

Betts

The *Autonomous Learner Model* was developed specifically as a framework for a comprehensive program for gifted students/learners that will facilitate social, emotional, and cognitive development. The framework includes specific components and suggestions for implementation, but specific processes and strategies to develop creative thinking, problem solving, research skills, and self-regulation processes frequently are implicit. To use Betts' model as a framework for a comprehensive approach to curriculum development, educators must make a variety of adaptations in process dimensions. (See Table 12.1.) A combination of this model with process thinking models, such as Parnes, Taba, and Taylor, and with Treffinger's *Self-Directed Learning* would provide most of the modifications recommended for gifted students. For further information, see Chapter 2.

Bloom

Bloom's *Taxonomy* was not developed as a structure for curriculum development for the gifted. It was intended as a system for classifying educational objectives to facilitate communication among educators. To use Bloom's *Taxonomy* as a comprehensive approach to curriculum development, educators must make a variety of adaptations in content, process, and product dimensions of the curriculum. (See Table 12.2.) None of the learning environment changes have been addressed by the approach, so combination with other models or adaptation is also necessary in this dimension. The major changes are teaching the taxonomy to students and beginning activities at the application level. The taxonomy can be combined or used in conjunction with most of the other models reviewed. For further information, see Chapter 3.

Bruner

Although Bruner's approach was not designed specifically for use with the gifted, it was intended as a model for curriculum design. As such, it makes adaptations in many areas that are recommended for the gifted. The major modifications needed to make Bruner's a more comprehensive approach for use with the gifted are in the areas of process, product, and learning environment. (See Table 12.3.) Although an environment like that recommended for the gifted would be necessary for implementing his approach, Bruner does not make specific recommendations for developing such a climate. His approach to content is highly appropriate for the gifted. Bruner's model is compatible with most other models but best for use with Taba and Renzulli. For further information, see Chapter 4.

Guilford

Guilford's model was not constructed for curriculum development. It was created to explain human intelligence. However, it has been and can be used for curriculum development for the gifted if combined with other models and adapted in certain ways. (See Table 12.4.) The *Structure of Intellect* (SI) theory and SOI applications of the theory make some modifications in the content, process, and product areas but none in learning environment. Guilford's model can be used in conjunction with several other approaches but is best combined with Bruner or Taba, Renzulli, Parnes, and Treffinger. For a further explanation of these ideas, see Chapter 11.

Kohlberg

Kohlberg's theory of moral development and his strategies for *Discussions of Moral Dilemmas* were developed to explain moral/ethical development and to provide a structure for raising levels of ethical development. However, because of its concentration on high levels of ethical behavior and on reasoning, many curricular modifications appropriate for the gifted are made in all areas except products. To provide a comprehensive model, however, it should be used in conjunction with other approaches. (See Table 12.5.) Product adaptations are easily included by encouraging students to develop further products related to moral issues identified during discussions. Kohlberg's approach is compatible with most models but can benefit most from being combined with Taba, Renzulli, Treffinger, or Parnes. For further information, see Chapter 11.

Krathwohl

Like Bloom's, Krathwohl's *Taxonomy* was not created for curriculum development and certainly not for the gifted. It is a system designed for classifying objectives in the affective domain and was developed to facilitate communication between professionals. Of all the models reviewed, Krathwohl's *Taxonomy* makes the fewest curricular modifications for the gifted. However, it can be used in conjunction with other models or adapted to provide a framework for curricular development in the affective area. (See Table 12.6.) No other model provides this addition. Krathwohl's *Taxonomy* is easily combined with Bloom's *Taxonomy*, with Bruner and Taba, with

Renzulli and Parnes, or with Treffinger, Williams, and Taba. For more information, the reader is referred to Chapter 3.

Parnes

Like most of the models reviewed, Parnes's *Creative Problem Solving* (CPS) process was not developed as a curriculum for gifted students. It was designed as a process for developing creative solutions to problems. Because of its emphasis on creativity and the use of creativity in a problem-solving setting, however, CPS provides an important dimension needed in a program for the gifted. Without adaptations, the model provides for most product and learning environment modifications appropriate for the gifted and for some of the content and process changes. When combined or used in conjunction with models like Betts, Taba, or Bruner, it provides a comprehensive approach. (See Table 12.7.) For more information, refer to Chapter 5.

Renzulli

Renzulli's *Enrichment Triad* was designed as a comprehensive framework for program and curriculum development for gifted students. As a framework, it was not intended to provide specific guidelines for curriculum development in all areas. Renzulli, for example, recommends that certain process models be used to develop his Type II activities. Depending on which process models were used, the facilitator would make different process modifications. As recommended by Renzulli, the *Triad* can be used with process models such as Bloom, Parnes, Krathwohl, Guilford, Williams, Taylor, Taba, or Kohlberg. (See Table 12.8.) It also can be used with a content model, such as Bruner's, or with Treffinger's as a way to assist students in developing their Type III investigations. For more information, review Chapter 6.

Sharan and Sharan

The *Group Investigations* model was not developed for gifted students, but it has common roots in developmental theories. Most of the modifications recommended for gifted students are incorporated into the structure of the model. Creative thinking processes, so essential for gifted students, are not specifically included. Recommended changes could be made easily by combining this approach with the Parnes, Taba, and Taylor models and would enhance its value for gifted students. (See Table 12.9.) In addition, including Bruner's principles for content modification would make this collaborative learning model even more appropriate for gifted learners. For further information, see Chapter 7.

Taba

Hilda Taba's *Teaching Strategies* and curriculum development theory were constructed as models for use with all children. However, since the purposes included a major focus on the development of abstract thinking, the Taba model is highly appropriate for use in gifted programs. It makes many of the content, process, and learning environment changes recommended for the gifted but does not provide suggestions for products. These changes can be integrated easily by adapting the model, particularly by using the strategies for different purposes in the development of products. (See Table 12.10.) The Taba *Strategies* also can be used with Renzulli's *Triad* or with Parnes to make these changes. Additional information is contained in Chapter 8.

Taylor

Taylor's *Multiple Talent Model* was developed as a total school model for developing and emphasizing the enhancement of a variety of talents and abilities in all children. The approach also can be used within a categorically funded program for the gifted as a model for the development of a variety of talents in gifted students. As a model for talent development, the approach makes major modifications in the process and learning environment areas of the curriculum. It can be adapted or supplemented by other approaches to provide a comprehensive model. (See Table 12.11.) It is compatible with all other models. The reader should refer to Chapter 9 for more information.

Treffinger

Treffinger's *Self-Directed Learning Model* was not developed as a total approach to curriculum development (or implementation for the gifted). It was designed to provide guidelines for teachers to use in developing an environment where self-directed learning can occur. Since self-direction is a goal of many gifted programs and since independence is a salient characteristic of most gifted students, Treffinger's model is appropriate for use in programs for the gifted. It can be combined with a content model such as Bruner's or Taba's and with several process models that systematically develop higher levels of thinking. (See Table 12.12.) For further information, the reader should consult Chapter 10.

Williams

Frank Williams's *Teaching Strategies for Thinking and Feeling* were developed as strategies for enhancing the cognitive and affective behaviors involved in creativity and are a part of a model for individualizing and humanizing education by concentrating on creativity development. Because of their focus on creativity, the strategies can be highly appropriate for use in gifted programs. Many modifications appropriate for the gifted are made by the model in the areas of learning environment and process, but it needs to be supplemented or adapted to provide necessary content and product modifications. (See Table 12.13.) Williams's strategies can be used effectively with any of the models reviewed. The reader should refer to Chapter 11 for further information.

INTEGRATED APPROACHES

After models have been reviewed and chosen and adaptations made or listed, the student objectives and learning activities must be developed. This process involves reviewing the student needs assessment, program goals, and purposes/provisions of the models.

Each curriculum that is finally designed will be different, even if the same models form the basis, because each developer and each situation will be different. Maker (1982) presents four sample curricula that have integrated a variety of models in the development of comprehensive programs to meet the needs of gifted students. A summary of each of these is not possible in this chapter. A brief example of an integrated approach, a summary of child needs, units and activities, models, and academic areas is presented in Table 12.14.

This curriculum was designed for an elementary resource room program in a middle class school. The emphasis was on development of the following strengths of the gifted students in the program: curiosity, critical thinking, leadership, independence, affective skills, self-expression, and creative thinking. The general approach was a combination of units, special projects, and sharing activities. A range of school subjects was integrated, with units developed to build on rather than duplicate the regular program. Evaluation results showed the curriculum to be highly effective in accomplishing its purposes.

CONCLUSION

In this volume, a wide range of teaching-learning models have been presented that can be helpful in developing a comprehensive curriculum for gifted students. All were designed for different purposes and have different strengths and weaknesses when considered as comprehensive approaches. All have different advantages and disadvantages in a practical sense also. Few have been validated through research as effective programs, and even fewer as effective models for use with the gifted. No comparative research indicates which models are more appropriate than others, but many practitioners are sold on one or more of the approaches. In this collection, we hope that all of you will find at least one that works for you and your students!

TABLE 12.1. Modifying and Complementing Betts's Autonomous Learner Model

Program Goals	Suggested Adaptation of Model	Complementary Models
Organize content around basic concepts and abstract generalizations.	Organize content at all levels of thinking skill development and investigations around complex, abstract content. Encourage students to choose complex content for individual projects.	Bruner Taba
Strive for economy in learning experiences.	Organize activities as above; strive for integrated themes or multiple-purpose activities. Begin activities at the application level of Bloom.	Bloom Bruner Taba
Provide opportunities for students to study creative people and the creative process.	Use the components of Understanding Giftedness and Career Exploration as a framework to study the work and lives of eminent and/or creative persons.	Williams
Cover content areas that are different from the regular curriculum.	Work with content area teachers to compact curriculum and develop in-depth study extensions that will provide opportunities for students to broaden and deepen their understanding of the discipline.	Bloom Bruner Parnes Renzulli Sharan Taba Taylor Treffinger Williams
Provide open-ended activities and ask open-ended questions.	Ask open-ended, provocative questions. Design activities in all components of all dimensions that are open-ended.	Bruner Kohlberg Parnes Renzulli Sharan Taba Taylor Treffinger Williams

(continues)

TABLE 12.1. *Continued*

Program Goals	Suggested Adaptation of Model	Complementary Models
Provide experiences using a discovery approach.	Design the majority of activities using inductive methods or an inquiry approach. Incorporate higher level thinking skills into all activities.	Bloom, Bruner, Renzulli, Sharan, Taba, Taylor, Treffinger, Williams
In all appropriate cases, ask students to explain their reasoning and/or provide support for their answers.	Ask "why" questions at all appropriate times (except when rapid generation of ideas in divergent production is desired). Expect students to provide support for their inferences and conclusions in discussions and written work.	Kohlberg, Taba
Provide opportunities for students to choose topics and methods of studying chosen topics.	Design a variety of learning/thinking/research activities from which students can choose. Teach the inquiry method and encourage students to design independent activities that require higher level thinking.	Bloom, Parnes, Renzulli, Sharan, Treffinger, Williams
Provide structured simulations and group interaction activities in which students can develop leadership and group participation skills.	Use group building and interpersonal development principles also to structure interaction of groups with complex content and real problems. Observe group interaction to evaluate individual progress in leadership and group process skills.	Sharan, Taba
Pace the presentation of new material rapidly.	Move through presentation of new materials/strategies as quickly as possible. If a few students need more time, provide the information in context of group or individual activities.	Renzulli, Taba

(*continues*)

TABLE 12.1. *Continued*

Program Goals	Suggested Adaptation of Model	Complementary Models	
Use a variety of methods.	Incorporate a wide variety of thinking/creativity activities in all components of the model. Encourage students to design individual projects that require creative thinking and problem solving.	Guilford Parnes Sharan Renzulli	Taylor Treffinger Williams
Provide situations that allow students to address real problems.	Encourage students to investigate problems or issues of concern to them. Encourage students to deal with real conflicts or personal problems during discussion and/or coping sessions.	Bruner Parnes Sharan	Taylor Treffinger
Provide situations in which students can direct their products toward real audiences.	Schedule presentations, seminars, and performances at a time when the general public, or invited guests, can attend. Inform students of competitions, markets, and other outlets that publish/present/reward student work.	Parnes Renzulli	Sharan
Provide situations in which student products can be appropriately evaluated; provide for the development of self-evaluation skills.	Teach students the criteria for professional evaluation of products; encourage them to apply the criteria to their own work. Provide opportunities for students to present their work to practicing professionals for evaluation and feedback.	Guilford Parnes Renzulli	Sharan Taylor Treffinger

TABLE 12.2. Modifying and Complementing Bloom's Taxonomy of Cognitive Objectives

Program Goals	Suggested Adaptation of Model	Complementary Models
Organize content around basic concepts and abstract generalizations.	Organize activities at all levels of the taxonomy around complex, abstract content.	Bruner Taba
Strive for economy in learning experiences.	Organize activities around complex, abstract content; begin at the application level of the taxonomy.	Bruner Taba
Provide opportunities for students to study creative people and the creative process.	Use the taxonomy as a structure to design activities for the study of eminent, creative, productive people.	Betts Williams
Cover content areas that are different from the regular curriculum.	Teach the taxonomy to students and encourage them to use it as a way to structure their own investigations.	Betts Bruner Parnes Renzulli Sharan	Taba Taylor Treffinger Williams
Provide open-ended activities and ask open-ended questions.	Ask open-ended, provocative questions. Design open-ended activities at all levels of the taxonomy. Emphasize activities at or above the application level.	Betts Bruner Kohlberg Parnes Renzulli	Sharan Taba Taylor Treffinger Williams
Provide experiences using a discovery approach.	Begin activities at, or above, the application level. Teach students to use inquiry or scientific methods. Provide activities that require inductive thinking.	Bruner Renzulli Taba	Taylor Treffinger Williams

(continues)

TABLE 12.2. *Continued*

Program Goals	Suggested Adaptation of Model	Complementary Models
In all appropriate cases, ask students to explain their reasoning and/or provide support for their answers.	Ask "why" questions, when appropriate, at all levels above simple recall. Encourage students to support answers, inferences, and conclusions.	Kohlberg Taba
Provide opportunities for students to choose topics and methods of studying chosen topics.	Use the taxonomy to design a variety of types of activities from which students can choose. Design open-ended activities at all levels of the taxonomy from which students can choose.	Betts Parnes Renzulli Sharan Treffinger Williams
Provide structured simulations and group interaction activities in which students can develop leadership and group participation skills.	Use the taxonomy as a tool for observing group interaction. Use the taxonomy to develop activities for group interaction and social involvement.	Betts Sharan Taba
Pace the presentation of new material rapidly.	Move through activities and questions at the two lowest levels quickly.	Renzulli Taba
Use a variety of methods.	Design a variety of types of activities at each level of the taxonomy. Incorporate both critical and creative thinking.	Betts Guilford Parnes Sharan Renzulli Taylor Treffinger Williams

(continues)

TABLE 12.2. *Continued*

Program Goals	Suggested Adaptation of Model	Complementary Models	
Provide situations that allow students to address real problems.	Use activities at the analysis level to help students identify and structure real problems for investigation.	Betts Bruner Parnes	Sharan Taylor Treffinger
Provide situations in which students can direct their products toward real audiences.	Teach the taxonomy to students as a tool for the use of audiences to evaluate their products. Encourage students to elaborate on their product syntheses and share them with real audiences.	Betts Parnes	Renzulli Sharan
Provide situations in which student products can be appropriately evaluated; provide for the development of self-evaluation skills.	Teach the taxonomy to students as a tool for self-evaluation of products.	Guilford Parnes Renzulli	Sharan Taylor Treffinger

TABLE 12.3.   Modifying and Complementing Bruner's Structure of a Discipline Approach

Program Goals	Suggested Adaptation of Model	Complementary Models
Organize content around basic concepts and abstract generalizations.	Use a process model to strengthen concept development and to structure inquiry.	Taba
Strive for economy in learning experiences.	Use broad themes and interdisciplinary activities.	Taba
Provide opportunities for students to study creative people and the creative process.	Study significant people related to each basic concept studied. Emphasize people who contributed significantly to our understanding of the concept.	Betts Williams
Cover content areas that are different from the regular curriculum.	Analyze data taught in regular programs according to each key concept and generalization. Teach only that information that students do not know already. Provide opportunities for students to deepen or broaden key ideas.	Betts Bloom Guilford Kohlberg Krathwohl	Parnes Sharan Renzulli Taylor Treffinger
Provide open-ended activities and ask open-ended questions.	Emphasize an inductive approach or inquiry method, and/or structure activities for investigation with open-ended questions. Ask provocative questions in all disciplines.	Betts Bloom Guilford Kohlberg Krathwohl	Parnes Sharan Renzulli Taylor Treffinger Williams

(*continues*)

TABLE 12.3. *Continued*

Program Goals	Suggested Adaptation of Model	Complementary Models	
Provide experiences using a discovery approach.	Provide opportunities for students to investigate phenomena using scientific methods.	Betts Renzulli Taba	Taylor Treffinger Williams
In all appropriate cases, ask students to explain their reasoning and/or provide support for their answers.	Ask questions to discover student's reasoning or support when they have "discovered" a conclusion.	Kohlberg Taba	
Provide opportunities for students to choose topics and methods of studying chosen topics.	Provide options for students to choose areas of study within a particular content and related to the key concepts and generalizations in the content.	Betts Parnes Renzulli	Sharan Treffinger Williams
Provide structured simulations and group interaction activities in which students can develop leadership and group participation skills.	Use simulation games and structured interaction activities. Use computer simulations as tools to help students develop methodological skills in a discipline. Use the methods of anthropologists, sociologists, psychologists, and others who study the behaviors of people as a tool to study group interaction.	Betts Sharan Taba	
Pace the presentation of new material rapidly.	Provide fewer examples of key concepts to be developed than would be required for all students. Use a process strategy to discover what students already know.	Renzulli Taba	
Use a variety of methods.	Encourage the use of a variety of investigative techniques. Make field trips to observe scientists, poets, musicians, artists, and other professionals at work.	Betts Guilford Parnes Sharan	Renzulli Taylor Treffinger Williams

(continues)

TABLE 12.3. *Continued*

Program Goals	Suggested Adaptation of Model	Complementary Models	
Provide situations that allow students to address real problems.	Provide opportunities for students to replicate and/or conduct research in a discipline of their choice using the methodology in that discipline. Use the inquiry method to structure investigation of issues of concern.	Betts Parnes Renzulli	Sharan Taylor Treffinger
Provide situations in which students can direct their products toward real audiences.	Extend students' work by asking "What would the [professional] do with her or his work?" Encourage students to share the results of their work with a variety of real audiences, including classmates. Provide information about possible markets/contests/presentation possibilities.	Betts Parnes	Renzulli Sharan
Provide situations in which student products can be appropriately evaluated; provide for the development of self-evaluation skills.	Extend students' thinking by asking "How would a [professional]'s products be judged?" Provide examples of criteria and standards in professions of interest to students. Study superior products in a discipline to discover the elements that determine (or contribute to) high quality in that discipline.	Guilford Parnes Renzulli	Sharan Taylor Treffinger

TABLE 12.4. Modifying and Complementing Guilford's Structure of the Intellect Model

Program Goals	Suggested Adaptation of Model	Complementary Models
Organize content around basic concepts and abstract generalizations.	Use in conjunction with Bruner or Taba. Use product dimension categories or transformations and implications to judge the abstractness and complexity of generalizations developed.	Bruner Taba
Strive for economy in learning experiences.	Organize learning experiences around abstract dimensions in addition to organizing around SI abilities to be developed.	Bruner Taba
Provide opportunities for students to study creative people and the creative process.	Use in conjunction with Betts or Williams. Teach students the SI theory, dimensions, and categories. Have students use SI categories in all dimensions to examine people, processes, and methods.	Betts Williams
Cover content areas that are different from the regular curriculum.	Use in conjunction with other models. Teach SI theory as a method for analyzing human abilities.	Betts Bloom Bruner Parnes Renzulli	Sharan Taba Taylor Treffinger Williams
Provide open-ended activities and ask open-ended questions.	Use in conjunction with other models. Ask provocative questions about human abilities.	Betts Bloom Bruner Kohlberg Krathwohl	Parnes Sharan Renzulli Taylor Treffinger

(continues)

TABLE 12.4. *Continued*

Program Goals	Suggested Adaptation of Model	Complementary Models	
Provide experiences using a discovery approach.	Use in conjunction with other models. When students have completed an activity, have them identify the SI abilities involved. Exercise SI abilities necessary for discovery learning (e.g., convergent production; figural, symbolic, or semantic content; relations, systems, transformations, implications).	Bruner Renzulli Taba	Taylor Treffinger Williams
In all appropriate cases, ask students to explain their reasoning and/or provide support for their answers.	When activities involve convergent production or evaluation, ask students to explain how they arrived at the answers.	Kohlberg Taba	
Provide opportunities for students to choose topics and methods of studying chosen topics.	Provide a variety of activities, which have been developed to exercise different abilities, from which students can choose. Enable students to participate in the design of their own educational programs.	Betts Parnes Renzulli	Sharan Treffinger Williams
Provide structured simulations and group interaction activities so students can develop leadership and group participation skills.	Use categories in the behavioral dimension to structure observations of the group. Use behavioral dimension categories as pre- and post- measures of effectiveness of group interaction procedures.	Betts Sharan Taba	
Pace the presentation of new material rapidly.	Students pace themselves as they work individually on activities. After group activities, ask for feedback on your pacing of the lesson.	Renzulli Taba	

(continues)

TABLE 12.4. *Continued*

Program Goals	Suggested Adaptation of Model	Complementary Models	
Use a variety of methods.	Avoid tendency to use only SOI workbooks as teaching strategy. Analyze games and learning activities according to the SI abilities involved.	Betts Bloom Parnes Sharan	Renzulli Taylor Treffinger Williams
Provide situations that allow students to address real problems.	As a general strategy for self-understanding of own learning problems, a student can identify the SI abilities that she/he should target for personal improvement.	Betts Bruner Parnes	Sharan Taylor Treffinger
Provide situations in which students can direct their products toward real audiences.	Use in combination with other models.	Betts Parnes	Renzulli Sharan
Provide situations in which student products can be appropriately evaluated; provide for the development of self-evaluation skills.	As a general strategy for product development, identify the SI abilities involved in the development of the product after a student's product has been evaluated by an audience, teacher, or self. Work on identified underlying strengths or weaknesses as a way to improve future products.	Betts Parnes Renzulli	Sharan Taylor Treffinger

TABLE 12.5. Modifying and Complementing Kohlberg's Discussions of Moral Dilemmas

Program Goals	Suggested Adaptation of Model	Complementary Models
Organize content around basic concepts and abstract generalizations.	Present dilemmas that involve abstract and complex ideas. Present dilemmas that involve issues from several different disciplines. Present dilemmas that illustrate the moral/ethical side of key concepts and generalizations that are being developed and studied.	Bloom Sharan Bruner Taba Guilford
Strive for economy in learning experiences.	Select only dilemmas that are excellent illustrations of the themes to be developed.	Bruner Taba
Provide opportunities for students to study creative people and the creative process.	Present moral/ethical dilemmas faced by famous individuals. Compare student resolution of the conflict with the resolution made by the person studied.	Betts Taba Williams
Cover content areas that are different from the regular curriculum.	Present moral/ethical dilemmas faced by investigators and key people in varied disciplines and historical contexts.	Betts Parnes Bloom Sharan Guilford Taylor Krathwohl Treffinger Renzulli Williams
Provide open-ended activities and ask open-ended questions.	Ask questions that enable students to respond thoughtfully in discussions.	Betts Parnes Bloom Sharan Guilford Renzulli Krathwohl Taylor Williams

(continues)

TABLE 12.5. *Continued*

Program Goals	Suggested Adaptation of Model	Complementary Models	
Provide experiences using a discovery approach.	Present dilemmas faced by others. Compare student resolution of conflicts to resolutions of other people.	Bruner Renzulli	Taba Taylor
In all appropriate cases, ask students to explain their reasoning and/or provide support for their answers.	Ask "why" questions whenever appropriate after Step 2.	Taba	
Provide opportunities for students to choose topics and methods of studying chosen topics.	Encourage students to choose moral issues or dilemmas they would like to discuss.	Betts Parnes Renzulli	Sharan Treffinger Williams
Provide structured simulations and group interaction activities in which students can develop leadership and group participation skills.	Provide opportunities for students to role-play famous characters involved in historical moral/ethical dilemmas. Videotape discussions as a basis for analyzing group interaction processes.	Betts Sharan Taba	
Pace the presentation of new material rapidly.	Move through Steps 1 and 2 rapidly; spend more time at later steps.	Renzulli Taba	Treffinger
Use a variety of methods.	Broaden the bases of moral development by including methods suggested by other theorists (e.g., Gilligan, Dabrowski, Piaget).	Betts Guilford Krathwohl Renzulli	Sharan Taba Taylor Williams

(*continues*)

TABLE 12.5. *Continued*

Program Goals	Suggested Adaptation of Model	Complementary Models
Provide situations that allow students to address real problems.	Encourage students to develop products as a result of participation in discussion of moral dilemmas that address a problem or issue of concern to them.	Betts Bruner Parnes / Sharan Taylor
Provide situations in which students can direct their products toward real audiences.	Encourage students to develop products such as original essays about issues or results from original research (e.g., a survey of attitudes toward an ethical issue). Encourage students to develop products that are transformations, then direct their products toward real audiences for presentation and/or publication. Organize seminars that involve students and professionals in the discussion of moral/ethical dilemmas in a discipline/field.	Betts Parnes / Renzulli Sharan
Provide situations in which student products can be appropriately evaluated; provide for the development of self-evaluation skills.	Encourage students to develop defensible criteria for evaluation of products. Encourage students to self-evaluate their products. Encourage students to have their products evaluated by peers/audiences. Encourage students to be self-reflective and evaluate own moral development.	Guilford Parnes Renzulli / Sharan Taylor

TABLE 12.6.   Modifying and Complementing Krathwohl's Taxonomy of Affective Objectives

Program Goals	Suggested Adaptation of Model	Complementary Models
Organize content around basic concepts and abstract generalizations.	Develop abstract generalizations that relate to affective behaviors and values.	Bruner Taba
Strive for economy in learning experiences.	Develop complex generalizations that relate to affective behaviors and values.	Bruner Taba
Provide opportunities for students to study creative people and the creative process.	Analyze the affective behaviors and values of eminent and creative/productive people.	Betts Williams
Cover content areas that are different from the regular curriculum.	Teach the taxonomy to students to use as they conduct investigations. Teach the taxonomy as an educational classification system.	Betts Bloom Bruner Parnes Renzulli	Sharan Taba Taylor Treffinger Williams
Provide open-ended activities and ask open-ended questions.	Ask open-ended questions at all levels of the taxonomy. Design open-ended provocative activities at all levels.	Betts Bloom Guilford Kohlberg	Parnes Sharan Renzulli Taylor Treffinger
Provide experiences using a discovery approach.	Begin activities at the valuing level. Teach the taxonomy to students as a way to structure their own value inquiries.	Bruner Renzulli Taba	Taylor Treffinger Williams

(continues)

TABLE 12.6. *Continued*

Program Goals	Suggested Adaptation of Model	Complementary Models
In all appropriate cases, ask students to explain their reasoning and/or provide support for their answers.	Ask "why" questions when appropriate at all levels except Receiving.	Kohlberg Taba
Provide opportunities for students to choose topics and methods of studying chosen topics.	At each level of the taxonomy, provide a variety of learning activities from which students can choose.	Betts Parnes Renzulli	Sharan Treffinger Williams
Provide structured simulations and group interaction activities in which students can develop leadership and group participation skills.	Use the taxonomy to design group interaction activities. Use the taxonomy as a structure to observe the interaction of a group.	Betts Sharan Taba
Pace the presentation of new material rapidly.	Move through the lower levels rapidly.	Renzulli Taba
Use a variety of methods.	Design a variety of types of activities at each level of the taxonomy.	Betts Guilford Parnes Sharan	Renzulli Taylor Treffinger Williams
Provide situations that allow students to address real problems.	Teach the taxonomy as a way to identify problems to investigate, as a way to analyze underlying ideas or assumptions.	Betts Bruner Parnes	Sharan Taylor Treffinger

(continues)

TABLE 12.6.   *Continued*

Program Goals	Suggested Adaptation of Model	Complementary Models
Provide situations in which student products can be evaluated appropriately and provide for the development of skills in self-evaluation.	Teach the taxonomy to students as a model they can give to real audiences as a format to evaluate their products. Encourage students to share the products of their activities at the characterization level with real audiences.	Betts Parnes Renzulli Sharan Taylor Treffinger
Encourage students to develop products that are transfor-mations rather than summaries of existing information.	Encourage students to develop products that show evidence of the characterization level or, at least, the organization level.	Betts Bloom Bruner Guilford Kohlberg Parnes Renzulli Sharan Taba Taylor Treffinger Williams

TABLE 12.7. Modifying and Complementing Parnes' Creative Problem Solving Model

Program Goals	Suggested Adaptation of Model	Complementary Models
Organize content around basic concepts and abstract generalizations.	Organize content around abstract, complex ideas and select problem situations that relate to those ideas. Problem situations should involve abstract concepts and ideas. Organize content around problem situations and use fact finding as a way to gather information.	Bruner Kohlberg Taba
Strive for economy in learning experiences.	Choose problem situations that do not overlap with content already presented or developed in other ways. Fact finding should involve several content areas or disciplines.	Bruner Kohlberg Taba
Provide opportunities for students to study creative people and the creative process.	Identify problems faced by creative/productive people and use CPS to identify solutions. Compare own solutions to actual solution developed by the individual studied.	Betts Kohlberg Williams
Cover content areas that are different from the regular curriculum.	Identify issues or problems of personal concern in the classroom, school, community, or world. Fact finding activities should be conducted across disciplines.	Betts Bloom Bruner Krathwohl Renzulli
Provide open-ended activities and ask open-ended questions.	Ask provocative questions about issues, concerns, and problems to stimulate student exploration of "the mess."	Betts Bloom Bruner Guilford Kohlberg
		Krathwohl Sharan Renzulli Taylor Treffinger

(continues)

TABLE 12.7. *Continued*

Program Goals	Suggested Adaptation of Model	Complementary Models
Provide experiences using a discovery approach.	Teach the CPS process to students as a tool to structure their own inquiry or discovery learning activities.	Bruner Renzulli Taba / Taylor Treffinger Williams
In all appropriate cases, ask students to explain their reasoning and/or provide support for their answers.	Ask questions calling for support *only* when appropriate (e.g., selection of problem statements, selection of criteria for evaluation, development of action plans). Avoid "why" questions during divergent production phases.	Kohlberg Taba
Provide opportunities for students to choose topics and methods of studying chosen topics.	Teach CPS to students as a strategy for making choices.	Betts Renzulli / Sharan Treffinger Williams
Provide structured simulations and group interaction activities in which students can develop leadership and group participation skills.	Tape a CPS session in a group session and analyze interaction of members of the group. Use CPS as a method to develop solutions to group interaction problems. Design simulations in which participants must solve complex problems in order to bring closure to the activity.	Betts Sharan Taba
Pace the presentation of new material rapidly.	Follow guidelines in Taba.	Renzulli Taba

(continues)

TABLE 12.7. *Continued*

Program Goals	Suggested Adaptation of Model	Complementary Models	
Provide situations that allow students to address real problems.	Conflict situations are naturally occurring problems for which CPS is appropriate. CPS also is a powerful process for students to use to instigate social action on community problems (e.g., polluted areas, disaster relief, changes in rules/laws).	Betts Bruner	Sharan Taylor Treffinger
Provide situations in which students can direct their products toward real audiences.	An essential step of CPS is acceptance finding. Proposed solutions should be presented to appropriate audiences (e.g., policy-making boards, administrators, steering committees, parties to a conflict) who can accept, modify, or reject a proposed solution.	Betts	Renzulli Sharan
Provide situations in which student products can be appropriately evaluated; provide for the development of self-evaluation skills.	Appropriate evaluation is implicit in the acceptance-finding process. Responses from the group(s) to whom a recommendation is presented are one form of real-world evaluation. Students also should be encouraged to reflect on their own participation as a member of the problem-solving group (e.g., What behaviors contributed to group productivity? What factors influenced acceptance/rejection?)	Renzulli Sharan	Taylor Treffinger

TABLE 12.8. Modifying and Complementing Renzulli's Enrichment Triad Model

Program Goals	Suggested Adaptation of Model	Complementary Models
Organize content around basic concepts and abstract generalizations.	Develop abstract, complex generalizations for each content area to be explored. Organize Type I and Type II activities around these generalizations.	Bruner Taba
Strive for economy in learning experiences.	Choose all Type I and Type II experiences very carefully so that key concepts and ideas are illustrated. Expose students to a variety of key ideas in different disciplines.	Bruner Taba
Provide opportunities for students to study creative people and the creative process.	Include, as Type I activities, exposure to biographies and autobiographies of famous individuals who have contributed to the key concepts to be studied. Compare methods of inquiry used by these people with methods now used in various disciplines.	Betts Williams
Cover content areas that are different from the regular curriculum.	Compact the curriculum so that individuals or small groups of students can develop research or production projects with methods and outcomes similar to those used by professionals in a field.	Betts Bloom Bruner Krathwohl Parnes
Provide open-ended activities and ask open-ended questions.	Combine with other process models to meet this objective for Type II activities.	Betts Bloom Guilford Kohlberg Krathwohl Parnes Sharan Taylor Treffinger Williams

(continues)

TABLE 12.8. *Continued*

Program Goals	*Suggested Adaptation of Model*	*Complementary Models*
Provide experiences using a discovery approach.	Combine with other models (e.g., Bruner) to meet this objective for Type II activities.	Bruner Sharan Taba	Taylor Treffinger Williams
In all appropriate cases, ask students to explain their reasoning and/or provide support for their answers.	Ask questions that call for support or reasoning whenever appropriate. However, avoid "why" questions during divergent thinking activities.	Kohlberg Taba	
Provide opportunities for students to choose topics and methods of studying chosen topics.	Encourage students to choose topics or projects for which they have a "passion" or intense interest as Type III activities.	Betts Parnes Sharan	Treffinger Williams
Provide structured simulations and group interaction activities in which students can develop leadership and group participation skills.	Provide a variety of activities to help students develop skills needed to work effectively in a small group. Tape the activities or have "live" observers to give feedback and helpful tips to improve group interaction. Offer minilessons, as needed, on interpersonal skills to individuals or small groups in the context of Type III activities.	Betts Sharan Taba	
Pace the presentation of new material rapidly.	Compact curriculum and remind guest speakers to pace their presentations of material rapidly. Move through Type II activities on "lower levels of thinking" rapidly.	Sharan Taba	
Use a variety of methods.	Teach a variety of process methods of inquiry so that students will have the tools to conduct Type III enrichment.	Betts Guilford Parnes Sharan	Taba Taylor Treffinger Williams

(continues)

TABLE 12.8. *Continued*

Program Goals	Suggested Adaptation of Model	Complementary Models
Provide situations that allow students to address real problems.	Encourage students to investigate real-world problems.	Betts Bruner Taba Taylor
Provide situations in which students can direct their products toward real audiences.	Provide real audiences for student products. Identify possible markets for a variety of student products.	Betts Parnes Sharan Taylor
Provide situations in which student products can be appropriately evaluated; provide for the development of self-evaluation skills.	Teach standards of evaluation for professionals in a field. Help students develop criteria for product evaluation that are similar to those used by professionals. Help students develop procedures for self-evaluation and reflection on their own creative processes.	Parnes Sharan Taylor Treffinger

TABLE 12.9.   Modifying and Complementing Sharan and Sharan's Group Investigations Model

Program Goals	Suggested Adaptation of Model		Complementary Models
Organize content around basic concepts and abstract generalizations.	Broad themes or interdisciplinary topics are recommended. Identify abstract generalizations and key concepts for each topic or theme.		Bruner Taba
Strive for economy in learning experiences.	Ensure that broad themes or topics are developed with complex generalizations and interrelated subtopics for investigation.		Bruner Taba
Provide opportunities for students to study creative people and the creative process.	Identify and investigate creative/productive people who have contributed ideas or impetus to the development of the content to be investigated in a topic or theme study.		Betts Williams
Cover content areas that are different from the regular curriculum.	Design guidelines for small-group investigations that stimulate students to go beyond the regular curriculum to broaden and deepen their understanding of key concepts, key players, and key ideas (generalizations, laws) in chosen subtopics. Use Bruner's approach to identify abstract, complex themes for investigation.	Betts Bloom Bruner Krathwohl Parnes	Renzulli Taba Taylor Treffinger Williams
Provide open-ended activities and ask open-ended questions.	Teach students to ask open-ended questions in discussions so that many, varied ideas are presented before subtopics are chosen. Combine with other process models to meet this objective.	Betts Bloom Guilford Kohlberg Krathwohl	Parnes Renzulli Taylor Treffinger Williams

(continues)

TABLE 12.9. *Continued*

Program Goals	Suggested Adaptation of Model	Complementary Models	
Provide experiences using a discovery approach.	Teach the inquiry method for use by students as they structure their personal or small-group investigations.	Bruner Renzulli Taba	Taylor Treffinger Williams
In all appropriate cases, ask students to explain their reasoning and/or provide support for their answers.	Ask questions that call for support or reasoning whenever appropriate. However, avoid "why" questions during divergent thinking activities.	Kohlberg Taba	
Provide opportunities for students to choose topics and methods of studying chosen topics.	Encourage students to generate many ideas for possible subtopics so that varied choices will be available for small-group investigation. Involve students in discussion of possible broad themes or topics for study.	Betts Parnes Renzulli	Taylor Treffinger Williams
Provide structured simulations and group interaction activities so students can develop leadership and group participation skills.	Provide a variety of group building activities to help students develop skills needed to work effectively in a small group. Offer minilessons, as needed, on interpersonal skills to individuals or small groups in the context of an investigation.	Betts Taba	
Pace the presentation of new material rapidly.	Select nonbook media to ensure valuable experiences for students. Have a variety of books available on the theme/topic. Remind guest speakers to pace their presentations rapidly. During discussions and process development activities, move through those requiring "lower levels of thinking" rapidly.	Renzulli Taba	

(continues)

TABLE 12.9. *Continued*

Program Goals	Suggested Adaptation of Model	Complementary Models
Use a variety of methods.	Teach a variety of process models and methods of inquiry to students so that they will have the tools to conduct small-group investigations.	Betts Guilford Parnes Renzulli Taba Taylor Treffinger Williams
Provide situations that allow students to address real problems.	Encourage students to select subtopics of broad themes that have the potential for investigating real problems (e.g., theme = conflict; subtopics such as terrorism, civil disobedience, gangs, conservation vs. development).	Betts Bruner Kohlberg Taba Taylor Williams
Provide situations in which students can direct their products toward real audiences.	Invite guests to presentations. Facilitate presentations to adult groups away from school as well as to classmates and other students at school.	Betts Parnes Renzulli Taylor
Provide situations in which student products can be appropriately evaluated; provide for the development of self-evaluation skills.	Teach standards of evaluation for professionals in a field. Help students develop criteria for product evaluation that are similar to those used by professionals. Guide students in the preparation of evaluation forms to be completed by members of their audiences. Allow time for tabulating results and reflecting on their presentations.	Parnes Renzulli Taylor Treffinger

TABLE 12.10. Modifying and Complementing Taba's Teaching Strategies

Program Goals	Suggested Adaptation of Model	Complementary Models
Organize content around basic concepts and abstract generalizations.	Develop lessons around key concepts and generalizations that are abstract and complex.	Bruner
Strive for economy in learning experiences.	Teach students to use the strategies to facilitate metacognition, transfer of learning, and understanding of key concepts and abstract generalizations.	Bruner
Provide opportunities for students to study creative people and the creative process.	Use interpretation of data strategy to discuss characteristics of creative/productive people and the causes/effects of these characteristics.	Betts Williams
Cover content areas that are different from the regular curriculum.	Using worksheet suggested by Bruner (Chapter 4), analyze regular curriculum to determine what specific information is being taught and what else needs to be taught.	Betts Bloom Bruner Kohlberg Krathwohl Parnes	Renzulli Sharan Taylor Treffinger Williams
Provide open-ended activities and ask open-ended questions.	Ask questions that facilitate an in-depth understanding of key concepts and an ability to foresee possible effects of phenomena or behavior, and apply generalizations to make reasoned predictions.	Betts Bloom Guilford Kohlberg Krathwohl	Parnes Sharan Renzulli Taylor Treffinger

(continues)

TABLE 12.10. *Continued*

Program Goals	Suggested Adaptation of Model	Complementary Models
Provide experiences using a discovery approach.	Use interpretation of data strategy to evaluate causes/effects of observed phenomena. Use application of generalizations strategy to formulate hypotheses for research.	Bruner Renzulli Taylor Treffinger Williams
In all appropriate cases, ask students to explain their reasoning and/or provide support for their answers.	Develop activities in which students evaluate the reasoning behind their (or other's) inferences and choices.	Kohlberg
Provide opportunities for students to choose topics and methods of studying chosen topics.	Encourage students to choose general topic areas for discussion and plan lessons around those topics. For the resolution of conflict strategy, have students select conflict situations they would like to discuss.	Betts Parnes Renzulli Sharan Treffinger Williams
Provide structured simulations and group interaction activities in which students can develop leadership and group participation skills.	Use role play or simulations to dramatize conflict situations prior to resolution of conflict discussions. Develop discussion skills that will facilitate student interaction in small groups for portions of all strategies.	Betts Sharan
Pace the presentation of new material rapidly.	Focus on key concepts and generalizations; avoid needless repetition.	Renzulli

(*continues*)

TABLE 12.10. *Continued*

Program Goals	Suggested Adaptation of Model	Complementary Models
Use a variety of methods.	Teach the principles underlying each strategy as a means of understanding the steps in the scientific method and other inquiry processes.	Betts Guilford Parnes Sharan Renzulli Taylor Treffinger Williams
Provide situations that allow students to address real problems.	Teach students to use the concept development strategy for organization and reorganization of data, as an aid in selection of a problem or topic area for investigation, and as a tool for writing up results of a study.	Betts Bruner Parnes Sharan Taylor Treffinger
Provide situations in which students can direct their products toward real audiences.	Use the application of generalizations strategy to predict how different audiences might react to a specified product. Use the interpretation of data strategy, with audiences, to form conclusions about the causes and effects of experimental results or new technology.	Betts Parnes Renzulli Sharan
Provide situations in which student products can be appropriately evaluated; provide for the development of self-evaluation skills.	Use all strategies (except resolution of conflict) to develop criteria and procedures for evaluation of products.	Guilford Parnes Renzulli Sharan Taylor Treffinger

TABLE 12.11.   Modifying and Complementing Taylor's Multiple Talents Approach

Program Goals	Suggested Adaptation of Model	Complementary Models	
Organize content around basic concepts and abstract generalizations.	Develop abstract generalizations for each content area to be studied. Develop complex generalizations that integrate several content areas or disciplines. Organize talent development activities around abstract, complex generalizations.	Bloom Bruner	Kohlberg Taba
Strive for economy in learning experiences.	Select talent development activities to develop abstract, complex ideas and talents at the same time. Cultivate knowledge *and* talents, not one without the other.	Bruner Taba	
Provide opportunities for students to study creative people and the creative process.	Compare own plans (decisions) with those made by eminent, productive individuals. Use forecasting activities to predict what might have happened to an eminent individual if she or he had lived in a different place or at a different time.	Betts Williams	
Cover content areas that are different from the regular curriculum.	Involve students in decision making and planning of classroom activities and topics/themes to study. Use productive thinking and communication talents to develop ideas for creative writing, drama, and simulations that will take students beyond the knowledge-based curriculum.	Betts Bloom Bruner Parnes Renzulli	Sharan Taba Treffinger Williams
Provide open-ended activities and ask open-ended questions.	Ask students to think of many, varied, unusual responses to open-ended questions. Involve students in role play, simulations, play writing, construction, and other creative activities.	Betts Bloom Guilford Kohlberg Krathwohl	Parnes Sharan Renzulli Treffinger Williams

(continues)

TABLE 12.11. *Continued*

Program Goals	Suggested Adaptation of Model	Complementary Models
Provide experiences using a discovery approach.	Provide activities in which students use planning, forecasting, and decision-making talents to design procedures for inquiry. Use communication talents to report the results of inquiries to others.	Bruner, Renzulli / Taba, Treffinger, Williams
In all appropriate cases, ask students to explain their reasoning and/or provide support for their answers.	Combine forecasting talent activities with Taba's application of generalizations or interpretation of data strategies. During decision-making, planning, and forecasting activities, ask for reasons or support when appropriate.	Kohlberg, Taba
Provide opportunities for students to choose topics and methods of studying chosen topics.	Have students use productive thinking talent to identify many, varied, unusual subtopics in a broad theme or topic. Have students use decision-making talent to select a subtopic for study and planning talent to organize individual or group study.	Betts, Parnes, Renzulli / Sharan, Treffinger, Williams
Provide structured simulations and group interaction activities in which students can develop leadership and group participation skills.	Videotape group activities for analysis. Use guidelines for communication talent as a structure for observing group interaction or participation. Provide opportunities for students to simulate varied roles in a historical event. Use communication talent to develop group interaction skills.	Betts, Sharan, Taba
Pace the presentation of new material rapidly.	Refer to Taba's discussion techniques for pacing guidelines.	Renzulli, Taba

(continues)

TABLE 12.11. *Continued*

Program Goals	Suggested Adaptation of Model	Complementary Models
Use a variety of methods.	Use each talent (or combination) for varied purposes throughout the school day. Combine all five talents with academic talent to choose a topic and to plan, present, and evaluate independent or small-group studies. Provide activities in which creative thinking talents are emphasized.	Betts Guilford Renzulli Sharan Treffinger Williams
Provide situations that allow students to address real problems.	Use productive thinking talent to identify issues of concern, social problems, and dilemmas in broad topics/themes. Use decision-making talent to select a problem/concern/dilemma for debate and/or investigation.	Betts Bruner Parnes Sharan Treffinger
Provide situations in which students can direct their products toward real audiences.	Encourage students to present products, developed through one or a combination of talents, in public presentations or submit them for publication/display. Provide a list of publications/contests/shows that publish or display student work. Encourage students to contribute creative products also to school publications.	Betts Parnes Renzulli Sharan
Provide situations in which student products can be appropriately evaluated; provide for the development of self-evaluation skills.	Use decision-making talent activities to select criteria for evaluation of products. Use guidelines for communication talent to encourage reflective self-evaluation. Use planning talent to prepare forms that audiences can use to evaluate specific products. Use decision-making talent to evaluate own and classmates' products.	Guilford Parnes Renzulli Sharan Treffinger

TABLE 12.12. Modifying and Complementing Treffinger's Model for Self-Directed Learning

Program Goals	Suggested Adaptation of Model	Complementary Models
Organize content around basic concepts and abstract generalizations.	At teacher-directed level, select and/or develop abstract generalizations and complex ideas as the focus of activities. Organize data (content) around abstract, complex ideas. At levels of self-direction, have student assist in the development and/or selection.	Bloom Kohlberg Bruner Taba
Strive for economy in learning experiences.	At teacher level, select learning experiences integrated across disciplines. Encourage students to select learning experiences for independent study that will be most efficient and effective for teaching a "big" idea.	Bruner Taba
Provide opportunities for students to study creative people and the creative process.	Suggest, as an option, the study of creative/productive people whose work pertains to a big idea being developed.	Betts Williams
Cover content areas that are different from the regular curriculum.	Encourage students to select topics that go beyond the regular curriculum.	Betts Sharan Bloom Taba Bruner Taylor Parnes Williams Renzulli
Provide open-ended activities and ask open-ended questions.	Structure discussions with student to open up a topic for exploration. Combine with a process model for structured development of higher level thinking processes. Offer options at all levels or types of thinking. Encourage students to choose a variety or focus on those they need to use. Avoid premature closure in selection of topic and methods for study.	Betts Parnes Bloom Sharan Guilford Renzulli Kohlberg Taylor Krathwohl

(continues)

TABLE 12.12. *Continued*

Program Goals	Suggested Adaptation of Model	Complementary Models
Provide experiences using a discovery approach.	Encourage students to adopt an inquiry approach to independent study. Combine with guidelines from other models.	Bruner Renzulli Taba / Taylor Williams
In all appropriate cases, ask students to explain their reasoning and/or provide support for their answers.	Ask students to provide reasons/support for their selection of a learning option or study topic. Ask students to explain why they have assessed needs in a particular way.	Kohlberg Taba
Provide opportunities for students to choose topics and methods of studying chosen topics.	Provide a variety of options from which students can choose. Encourage students to move to self-selection of topics as rapidly as possible.	Betts Parnes Renzulli / Sharan Williams
Provide structured simulations and group interaction activities so students can develop leadership and group participation skills.	Encourage students to develop their own methods for observing group interaction. Develop "process seminars" in which students can share their independent learning experiences.	Betts Sharan Taba
Pace the presentation of new material rapidly.	At self-directed levels, students will pace themselves. At teacher-directed level, use suggestions from Taba and ask students for feedback on pacing.	Renzulli Taba

(continues)

TABLE 12.12. *Continued*

Program Goals	Suggested Adaptation of Model	Complementary Models	
Use a variety of methods.	Encourage students to structure independent studies in a variety of ways. Encourage students to use a variety of methods to create products.	Betts Guilford Parnes Sharan	Renzulli Taba Taylor Williams
Provide situations that allow students to address real problems.	At teacher-directed level, design activities that encourage exploration of real problems. At all self-directed levels, offer real problems as an option for independent study.	Betts Bruner Parnes	Sharan Taylor
Provide situations in which students can direct their products toward real audiences.	Encourage students to develop products, following professional guidelines, for presentations to real audiences and/or publication.	Betts Parnes	Renzulli Sharan
Provide situations in which student products can be appropriately evaluated; provide for the development of self-evaluation skills.	Provide teacher-directed activities in which students learn guidelines for product development and criteria for evaluation. Assist the students in developing evaluation instruments for their studies. Provide time for self-evaluation and reflective thinking.	Guilford Parnes Renzulli	Sharan Taylor

TABLE 12.13.   Modifying and Complementing Williams's Strategies for Thinking and Feeling

Program Goals	Suggested Adaptation of Model	Complementary Models	
Organize content around basic concepts and abstract generalizations.	Develop abstract generalizations in each content area to be studied. Develop complex generalizations that integrate content from several disciplines. Organize strategies and development of creative behaviors around complex, abstract generalizations rather than the "general" discipline.	Bloom Bruner Guilford	Kohlberg Sharan Taba
Strive for economy in learning experiences.	Select broad themes or topics to organize interdisciplinary content.	Bruner Taba	
Provide opportunities for students to study creative people and the creative process.	Encourage students to study biographies and autobiographies of people who contributed to the themes/topics to be studied. Ask how an individual might have felt/thought about their contribution to society.	Betts	
Cover content areas that are different from the regular curriculum.	Analyze regular curriculum according to each generalization and key concept. Teach in the special program only that information not taught in the regular curriculum. See worksheet in Chapter 4 for this purpose.	Betts Bloom Guilford Kohlberg Krathwohl	Parnes Renzulli Sharan Taylor Treffinger
Provide open-ended activities and ask open-ended questions.	Use a variety of strategies that incorporate open-ended questions. Provide a variety of open-ended activities to encourage student exploration and thinking development.	Betts Bloom Guilford Kohlberg Krathwohl	Parnes Sharan Renzulli Taylor

(continues)

TABLE 12.13. *Continued*

Program Goals	Suggested Adaptation of Model	Complementary Models	
Provide experiences using a discovery approach.	Follow guidelines suggested by Bruner to structure inquiry processes.	Bruner Renzulli	Taba Taylor
In all appropriate cases, ask students to explain their reasoning and/or provide support for their answers.	Incorporate "why" questions into discussions whenever appropriate. Use strategy recommended by Taba's application of generalizations (make predictions in divergent mode, then go back and ask for reasons later) so creativity will not be inhibited.	Kohlberg Taba	
Provide opportunities for students to choose topics and methods of studying chosen topics.	Encourage students to suggest topics and methods for discussion. Teach the strategies to students and encourage them to lead discussions.	Betts Parnes Renzulli	Sharan Treffinger
Provide structured simulations and group interaction activities in which students can develop leadership and group participation skills.	Use attributes, examples of habit, and intuitive expression as ways to observe and discuss group interaction. Use strategies of search to assist small groups to cooperatively develop topics for group investigations.	Betts Sharan Taba	
Pace the presentation of new material rapidly.	In individual activities, encourage students to pace themselves. In group discussions, follow the suggestions made by Taba.	Renzulli Taba	Treffinger
Use a variety of methods.	Use a wide variety of strategies from the model. Integrate affective and cognitive skill development in most activities.	Betts Guilford Kohlberg Krathwohl	Renzulli Sharan Taba Taylor

(continues)

TABLE 12.13. *Continued*

Program Goals	Suggested Adaptation of Model	Complementary Models
Provide situations that allow students to address real problems.	Encourage students to pursue a topic of interest further and develop an investigation of a real problem. Encourage students to express their feelings about areas of concern.	Betts Bruner Parnes	Sharan Taylor
Provide situations in which students can direct their products toward real audiences.	When students have completed an area of study, developed a product, or conducted an experiment, encourage them to refine the findings for presentation to a real audience.	Betts Parnes	Renzulli Sharan
Provide situations in which student products can be appropriately evaluated; provide for the development of self-evaluation skills.	Encourage students to develop criteria and procedures for evaluation of their own products. Using criteria designed by students as well as that provided by audiences, have all student products evaluated by the student, peers, audience, and the teacher. Allow time for students to reflect on the results of evaluations.	Guilford Parnes Renzulli	Sharan Taylor

TABLE 12.14.   Summary of Child Characteristics, Activities, Models, and Content Areas

Learner Needs	Learning Activities	Models	Academic Areas
Cultivation of natural curiosity	Units—Introduction to diverse, abstract, and complex topics such as Culture, Archaeology, Architecture, Anthropology, Drama, Photography, Painting, Human Body, Chemistry, Electricity, Energy Forms, Astronomy, Career Opportunities, Dance, Genetics, Bioengineering, Molecular Biology, Ecology, Political Science, Economic Geography, Music	Betts Bruner Renzulli Sharan Taba	Fine arts Humanities Language Mathematics Physical education Social studies Science
Development of critical thinking skills	Units—Abstract content and thinking skills designed to elicit higher levels of thinking Activities—Deductive thinking (e.g., Mindbenders), Inductive thinking (e.g., Conceptual Blockbusting), Formal logic (e.g., Syllogisms, Scientific Method)	Betts Bloom Parnes Taba Taylor	Humanities Language Mathematics Philosophy Science Social studies
Development of creative thinking skills	Units—Content and thinking skills integrated and designed to elicit creative thinking and problem solving. Activities—Creative Problem Solving, Future Problem Solving, Synectics, Productive Thinking, Guided Imagery, Scamper, Lateral Thinking, Odyssey of the Mind, Inventive Thinking, Figurative Language, Creative Writing, Integration of Art and Music with Academic Areas, Movement Education	Betts Parnes Renzulli Taba Taylor Williams	Fine arts Humanities Language Mathematics Physical education Science Social studies

(continues)

TABLE 12.14. *Continued*

Learner Needs	Learning Activities	Models	Academic Areas
Development of leadership skills	Units—Content units that integrate group processes and leadership skill techniques into small- and large-group learning. Activities—Group Investigations, Seminars, Role Playing, Body Language, Creative Problem Solving, Conflict Resolution, Group Decision Making, Team Sports, Drama, Simulations, Committees, Student Government, Business Enterprises, Special Events	Betts Kohlberg Parnes Sharan Taba Taylor	Academic clubs Fine arts Humanities Language Mathematics Physical education Science Social studies
Development of independence skills	Units—Integration of goal setting, research skills, library skills, community resource investigation skills, scientific method of research experimentation, evaluation of own products, decision making, and planning with academic content. Activities—Community Surveys, Proposal Writing, Special Events (e.g., Renaissance Fair), Community Problem Solving, Odyssey of the Mind, Database Searches, Opinion Polls, Database Creation, Self-evaluation of both processes and products, Research	Betts Parnes Sharan Renzulli Taba Taylor Treffinger	Fine arts Humanities Language Mathematics Physical education Science Social studies
Development of self-expression	Units—Methods and techniques of self-expression integrated with academic content, Career exploration Activities—Drama, Mime, Creative Writing, Poetry, Photography, Graphic Arts, Sign Language, Dance, Music, Visual Arts, Body Language, Personal Symbols, Publication, Clothing Design, Interior Decoration, Crafts	Betts Kohlberg Krathwohl Renzulli Sharan Taba Taylor	Fine arts Humanities Language Mathematics Physical education Science Social studies Vocational arts

(continues)

TABLE 12.14. *Continued*

Learner Needs	Learning Activities	Models	Academic Areas
Development of affective skills	Units—Integration of affective objectives with content and process objectives Activities—Moral Dilemma Discussions, Sharing Sessions, Values Clarification, Transactional Analysis, Conflict Resolution, Counselor-Led Discussions, Literature Discussion Groups, Reflective Journal Writing, Volunteering and Community Service, Reading Biographies, Role Playing, Simulations, Self-Understanding Exercises	Betts Kohlberg Krathwohl Sharan	Fine arts Humanities Language Mathematics Physical education Science Social studies

References

Adams, H. B., & Wallace, B. (1988). The assessment and development of high school pupils in the third world context of Kwa-Zulu/Natal. *Gifted Child International, 5,* 132–137.

Adams, H. B., & Wallace, B. (1991). A model for curriculum development. *Gifted Education International, 7*(3), 105–113.

Andre, T. (1978, May). *The role of paraphrased and verbatim adjunct questions in facilitating learning by reading.* Paper presented at the annual meeting of the Midwestern Educational Research Association, Bloomington, Indiana.

Aronson, E., Blaney, N., Stephan, C., Sikes, J., & Snapp, M. (1978). *The Jigsaw classroom.* Beverly Hills, CA: Sage Books.

Atwood, B. S. (1974). *Building independent learning skills.* Palo Alto, CA: Education Today.

Ayers, J. D. (1966, February). *Justification of Bloom's taxonomy by factor analysis.* Paper presented at the Annual American Educational Research Association Convention, Chicago.

Barton, B. (1976). *Toward the development of a self-directed learner: A pilot study.* Unpublished master's thesis, University of Kansas, Lawrence.

Begle, E., & Wilson, J. (1970). Evaluation of mathematics program. In The National Society for the Study of Education (Eds.), *Sixty-ninth yearbook.* (Part I, pp. 367–404). Chicago: University of Chicago Press.

Betts, G. (1985). *The Autonomous Learner Model for the gifted and talented.* Greeley, CO: Autonomous Learning Publications and Specialists.

Betts, G., & Knapp, J. (1981). Autonomous learning and the gifted: A secondary model. In A. Arnold (Ed.), *Secondary programs for the gifted* (pp. 29–36). Ventura, CA: Ventura Superintendent of Schools Office.

Beyer, B. K. (1984). Improving thinking skills: Practical approaches. *Phi Delta Kappan, 65*(8), 556–560.

Beyer, B. K. (1987). *Practical strategies for the teaching of thinking.* Boston: Allyn & Bacon.

Bloom, B. S. (1956). *Taxonomy of educational objectives: The classification of educational goals. Handbook I: Cognitive domain.* New York: Longmans, Green & Co.

Bodnar, J. (1974). *Creative problem solving model.* Unpublished manuscript. (Available from Dr. C. J. Maker, Department of Special Education, University of Arizona, Tucson)

Brooks, J. A. (1988). Taba teaching strategies: Effects on higher level cognitive functioning of academically gifted students (Doctoral dissertation, North Carolina State University, 1987/1988). *Dissertation Abstracts International, 49*(10-A), 2908.

Bruner, J. S. (1960). *The process of education.* Cambridge, MA: Harvard University Press.

Bruner, J. (1985, June/July). Models of the learner. *Educational Researcher, 5–9.*

Buros, O. K. (Ed.). (1959). *The fifth mental measurement yearbook.* Highland Park, NJ: The Gryphon Press.

Cafferty, E. (1980). *An analysis of student performance based on the degree of match between the educational cognitive style of the teacher and the educational cognitive styles of the students.* Unpublished doctoral dissertation, University of Nebraska, Omaha.

Callahan, C. M., Covert, R., Aylesworth, M. S., & Vanco, P. (1981). *SEA Test norms and technical manual.* Charlottesville: University of Virginia.

Canedo, M. (1987, February). Presentation at the First National INVENT AMERICA! National Creativity Conference for Educators, Washington, DC.

Canedo, M. (1988). *The inventive thinking project: Project XL. A quest for excellence.* Washington, DC: United States Patent and Trademark Office.

Carter, K. R., & Ormrod, J. E. (1982). Acquisition of formal operations by intellectually gifted children. *Gifted Child Quarterly, 26*(3), 110–115.

Cattell, R. B., & Butcher, H. J. (1968). *The prediction of achievement and creativity.* New York: Bobbs-Merrill.

Chausow, H. M. (1955). *The organization of learning experiences to achieve more effectively the objectives of critical thinking in the general social science course at the junior college level.* Unpublished doctoral dissertation, University of Chicago.

Clark, B. (1983). *Growing up gifted.* Columbus, OH: Charles Merrill.

Cross, J. A., Jr. (1982). *Prevalence in internal locus of control in artistically talented students.* Unpublished research study, University of Alabama, Tuscaloosa.

Dabrowski, K., & Piechowski, M. (1977). *Theories of emotional development.* Oceanside, NY: Dabor Science Publications.

Damon, W. (1984). Peer education: The untapped potential. *Journal of Applied Developmental Psychology, 5,* 331–343.

Dapra, R. A., & Felker, D. B. (1974, September). *Effects of comprehension and verbatim adjunct questions in problem-solving ability from prose material: Extension of mathemagenic hypothesis.* Paper presented at the annual convention of the American Psychological Association, New Orleans.

Davidson, J., & Sternberg, R. J. (1984). The role of insight in intellectual giftedness. *Gifted Child Quarterly, 28*(2), 58–64.

Dempsey, R. D. (1975). Cognitive style differences between gifted and average students. *Dissertation Abstracts International, 36,* 2998B–2999B. (University Microfilms No. 75-29, 379)

Dewey, J. (1938). *Experience and education.* New York: Collier Books.

Dewey, J. (1943). *The school and society* (rev. ed.). Chicago: University of Chicago Press. (Original work published 1902)

Dewey, J. (1944). *Democracy and education: An introduction to the philosophy of education.* New York: The Free Press. (Original work published 1916)

Doise, W., & Mugny, G. (1984). *The social development of the intellect.* Oxford: Pergamon Press.

Dressel, P. L., & Mayhew, L. B. (1954). *General education: Explorations in evaluation.* Washington, DC: American Council on Education.

Dressel, P. L., & Nelson, C. H. (1956). *Questions and problems in science.* Princeton, NJ: Educational Testing Service.

Dunn, R., Dunn, K., & Price, G. E. (1975). *Learning style inventory.* Lawrence, KA: Price Systems.

Eberle, B. (1974). *Classroom cue cards for cultivating multiple talent.* Buffalo, NY: D.O.K.

Education Development Center. (1970). *Man: A course of study (MACOS).* Washington, DC: Curriculum Development Associates.

Educational Testing Service. (1972). *Sequential Test of Educational Progress.* Princeton, NJ: Addison-Wesley.

Ellis, K., & Durkin, M. C. (1972). *Teacher's guide for people in communities (The Taba program in social studies).* Menlo Park, CA: Addison-Wesley.

Ellison, R. L., Abe, C., Fox, D. J., Coray, K. E., & Taylor, C. W. (1976). Using biographical information in identifying artistic talent. *Gifted Child Quarterly, 20*(4), 402–413.

Ellison, R. L., Callner, A., Fox, D. G., & Taylor, C. W. (1971). The identification and selection of creative artistic talent by means of biographical information (Final Rep., Project No. 9-0215). Salt Lake City, UT: Institute for Behavioral Research in Creativity. (ERIC Document Reproduction Service No. ED 054 188).

Ellison, R. L., James, L. R., & Fox, D. G. (1970). *The identification of talent among Negro and white students from biographical data.* Salt Lake City, UT: Institute for Behavioral Research in Creativity. (ERIC Document Reproduction Service No. ED 169 119)

Ellison, R. L., Nelson, D. E., Fox, D. B., & Abe, C. (1978). Utah statewide educational assessment 1978: General report. Salt Lake City, UT: Institute for Behavioral Research in Creativity. (ERIC Document Reproduction Service No. ED 169 119)

Ennis, R. H. (1985). Critical thinking and the curriculum. *National-Forum-Phi-Kappa-Phi Journal, 65*(1), 28–31.

Feldhusen, J. F., & Moon, S. M. (1992). Grouping gifted children: Issues and concerns. *Gifted Child Quarterly, 36*(2), 63–67.

Feldhusen, J. F., & Treffinger, D. J. (1980). *Creative thinking and problem solving in gifted education.* Dubuque, IA: Kendall and Hunt.

Felker, D. P., & Dapra, R. A. (1975). Effects of question type and question placement on problem-solving ability from prose material. *Journal of Educational Psychology, 67,* 380–384.

Feuerstien, R. (1980). *Instrumental enrichment: An intervention program for cognitive modifiability.* Baltimore, MD: University Park Press.

Firestien, R. L. (1990). Effects of creative problem solving training on communication behaviors in small groups. *Small Group Research, 21*(4), 507–521.

Foot, H., Morgan, M., & Shute, R. (Eds.). (1990). *Children helping children.* London: Wiley.

French, J. N., & Rhoder, C. (1992). *Teaching thinking skills: Theory and practice.* New York: Garland.

Gabbert, B., Johnson, D. W., & Johnson, R. T. (1986). Cooperative learning, group-to-individual transfer, process gain, and the acquisition of cognitive processing strategies. *Journal of Psychology, 120*(3), 265–278.

Gagne, F. (1985). Giftedness and talent: Reexamining a reexamination of the definitions. *Gifted Child Quarterly, 29*(3), 103–112.

Gallagher, J. J. (1966). *Research summary on gifted child education.* Springfield, IL: Office of the Superintendent of Public Instruction.

Gallagher, J. J. (1985). *Teaching the gifted child* (3rd ed.). Boston: Allyn & Bacon.

Gallagher, J. J., Aschner, M. J., & Jenne, W. (1967). *Productive thinking in classroom interaction.* Reston, VA: Council for Exceptional Children.

Gallagher, S. A., Stepien, W. J., & Rosenthal, H. (1992). The effects of problem-based learning on problem-solving. *Gifted Child Quarterly, 36*(4), 195–200.

Gardner, H. (1983). *Frames of mind: The theory of multiple intelligences.* New York: Basic Books.

George, W. C. (1976). Accelerating mathematics instruction. *Gifted Child Quarterly, 20,* 246–261.

Getzels, J. W. (1975). Problem-finding and the inventiveness of solutions. *Journal of Creative Behavior, 9,* 12–18.

Getzels, J. W., & Jackson, P. O. (1962). *Creativity and intelligence: Exploration with gifted students.* New York: John Wiley & Sons.

Gilligan, C. (1982). *In a different voice: Psychological theory and women's development.* Cambridge, MA: Harvard University Press.

Graves, N., & Graves, T. (1990). *What is cooperative learning? Tips for teachers and trainers.* Santa Cruz: Cooperative College of California.

Griggs, S., & Price, G. A. (1980). A comparison between the learning styles of gifted versus average suburban junior high school students. *Roeper Review, 3,* 7–9.

Grobman, H. (1962). Some comments on the evaluation program findings and their implications. *Biological Sciences Curriculum Study Newsletter, 19,* 25–29.

Guidance Associates. (1976a). *Teaching training in values education: A workshop* [Sound filmstrip]. White Plains, NY: Author.

Guidance Associates. (1976b). *Values in American history: Conscience in conflict* [Sound filmstrip]. Mount Kisco, NY: Author.

Guidance Associates. (1976c). *Values in a democracy: Making ethical decisions.* Mount Kisco, NY: Author.

Guilford, J. P. (1959). Three faces of intellect. *American Psychologist, 14,* 469–479.

Guilford, J. P. (1967). *The nature of human intelligence.* New York: McGraw-Hill.

Guilford, J. P. (1972). Intellect and the gifted. *The Gifted Child Quarterly, 16,* 175–243.

Guilford, J. P. (1975). Varieties of creative giftedness, their measurement and development. *The Gifted Child Quarterly, 19,* 107–121.

Guilford, J. P. (1977). *Way beyond the IQ.* Buffalo, NY: Creative Education Foundation.

Guilford, J. P. (1988). Some changes in the Structure-of-Intellect Model. *Educational and Psychological Measurement, 48,* 1–4.

Hanley, J. P., Whitla, D. K., Moo, E. W., & Walter, A. S. (1970). *Man: A course of study. An evaluation.* Cambridge, MA: Education Development Center.

Hartshorne, J., & May, M. (1930). A summary of the work of the character inquiry. *Religious Education, 25,* 607–619.

Heath, S. B. (1983). *Ways with words: Language, life, and work in communities and classrooms.* New York: Cambridge University Press.

Hertz-Lazarowitz, R., Sharan, S., & Steinberg, R. (1980). Classroom learning style and cooperative behavior of elementary school children. *Journal of Educational Psychology, 72,* 97–104.

Holland, J. G. (1965). Response contingencies in teaching-machine programs. *Journal of Programmed Instruction, 5,* 474–482.

Hoomes, E. W. (1986). Future Problem Solving: Preparing students for a world community. *Gifted Education International, 4*(1), 16–20.

Hoyt, D. P. (1965). *The relationship between college grades and adult achievement: A review of the literature* (Research Report No. 7). Iowa City, IA: American Testing Program.

Hunt, D. E. (1975). Person–environment interaction: A challenge found wanting before it was tried. *Review of Educational Research, 45,* 209–230.

Hunt, D. E., Butler, L. F., Noy, J. E., & Rosser, M. E. (1978). *Assessing conceptual level by the paragraph completion method.* Toronto: Ontario Institute of Education.

Institute for Staff Development (Eds.). (1971a). *Hilda Taba teaching strategies program: Unit 1.* Miami: Author.

Institute for Staff Development (Eds.). (1971b). *Hilda Taba teaching strategies program: Unit 2.* Miami: Author.

Institute for Staff Development (Eds.). (1971c). *Hilda Taba teaching strategies program: Unit 3.* Miami: Author.

Institute for Staff Development (Eds.). (1971d). *Hilda Taba teaching strategies program: Unit 4.* Miami: Author.

Invent America. Alexandria, VA: United States Patent Model Foundation.

Isaksen, S. G. (1992). *Creative problem solving: A process for creativity.* Unpublished training manual. Buffalo, NY: The Creative Problem Solving Group–Buffalo.

Isaksen, S. G., Dorval, K. B., & Treffinger, D. J. (1994). *Creative approaches to problem solving.* Dubuque, IA: Kendall/Hunt.

Isaksen, S. G., & Parnes, S. J. (1985). Curriculum planning for creative thinking and problem solving. *Journal of Creative Behavior, 19*(1), 1–29.

James, J. (1978). *Sidney Parnes: Creative problem-solving model.* Unpublished manuscript. (Available from Dr. C. J. Maker, Department of Special Education, University of Arizona, Tucson)

Johnson, D., Johnson, R., & Maruyama, G. (1983). Interdependence and interpersonal attraction among heterogeneous and homogeneous individuals: A theoretical formulation and a meta-analysis of the research. *Review of Educational Research, 53*(5), 5–54.

Joyce, B., & Weil, B. (1986). *Models of teaching* (3rd ed.). Englewood Cliffs, NJ: Prentice-Hall.

Jung, C. G. (1923). *Psychological types.* London: Rutledge & Kegan Paul.

Juntune, J. (1979). Project Reach: A teacher training program for developing creative thinking skills in children. *Gifted Child Quarterly, 23*(3), 461–471.

Kagan, S. (1985). Co-op Co-op: A flexible cooperative learning technique. In R. Slavin, S. Sharan, S. Kagan, R. Hertz-Lazarowitz, C. Webb, & R. Schmuck (Eds.), *Learning to cooperate: Cooperating to learn* (pp. 437–462). New York: Plenum Press.

Kant, I. (1965). *Critique of pure reason* (N. K. Smith, Trans.). New York: St. Martin's Press. (Original work published 1929)

Keisel, S. (1979). *The creative problem solving model.* Unpublished manuscript. (Available from Dr. C. J. Maker, Department of Special Education, University of Arizona, Tucson)

Kohlberg, L. (1966). Moral education in the schools: A developmental view. *The School Review, 74,* 1–29.

Kohlberg, L. (1971). Stages of moral development as the basis for moral education. In C. M. Beck, B. S. Crittenden, & E. V. Sullivan (Eds.), *Moral education: Interdisciplinary approaches* (pp. 23–92). New York: Newman Press.

Krathwohl, D. R., Bloom, B. S., & Masia, B. B. (1964). *Taxonomy of educational objectives: The classification of educational goals. Handbook II: Affective domain.* New York: David McKay Co.

Kreitner, K. R. (1981). *Modality strengths and learning styles of musically talented high school students.* Unpublished master's thesis, Ohio State University, Columbus.

Krimsky, J. S. (1982). *A comparative analysis of the effects of matching and mismatching fourth grade students with their learning style preferences for the environmental element of light and their subsequent reading speed and accuracy scores.* Unpublished doctoral dissertation, St. John's University, Jamaica, NY.

Learn Smart: A systematic program of assessment and training tools and materials for the identification of individual learning styles and the improvement of basic and literacy skills, for remediation and enrichment. (1991). San Diego, CA: Key Technologies International.

Lessinger, L. M. (1963). Test building and test banks through the use of The Taxonomy of Educational Objectives. *California Journal of Educational Research, 14,* 195–201.

Lewis, B. A. (1991). *The kid's guide to social action: How to solve the social problems you choose—and turn creative thinking into positive action.* Minneapolis, MN: Free Spirit Press.

Limburg, J. B. (1979). *The taxonomy of educational objectives of the cognitive domain.* Unpublished manuscript. (Available from Dr. C. J. Maker, Department of Special Education, University of Arizona, Tucson)

Lloyd, B. (1984). The longitudinal effects of multiple talent training on 28 second-grade students (Doctoral dissertation, University of Utah, 1984). *Dissertation Abstracts International, 44-A*(12), 3666.

Lloyd, B. C., Seghini, J. B., & Stevenson, G. M. (1974). *Igniting creative potential II.* Sandy, UT: Jordan School District.

Lowman, L. M. (1961). An experimental evaluation of two curriculum designs for teaching first year algebra in a ninth grade class. *Dissertation Abstracts, 22,* 502. (University Microfilms No. 61-2864)

Lundy, R. A. (1978). *Dimensions of learning for the highly gifted student.* Palo Alto, CA: Palo Alto Unified School District. (ERIC Document Reproduction Service No. ED 155 864)

Lüscher, M. (1969). *The Lüscher color test.* New York: Random House.

MacKinnon, D. W. (1962). The nature and nurture of creative talent. *American Psychologist, 17,* 484–495.

MacKinnon, D. W. (1965). Personality and the realization of creative potential. *American Psychologist, 20,* 273–281.

Maehr, M. L. (1976). Continuing motivation: An analysis of a seldom considered educational outcome. *Review of Educational Research, 46,* 443–462.

Maker, C. J. (1979). Developing multiple talents in exceptional children. *Teaching Exceptional Children, 11,* 120–124.

Maker, C. J. (1982). *Curriculum development for the gifted.* Austin, TX: PRO-ED.

Maker, C. J., Redden, M. R., Tonelson, S., & Howell, R. M. (1978). *The self-perceptions of successful handicapped scientists* (BEH Grant No. G00-7701-905). Albuquerque: University of New Mexico.

Maltby, F. (1993). Teaching mathematics through thinking actively in a social context. *Gifted Education International, 9*(1), 45–47.

Mansfield, R. S., Busse, F. V., & Krepelka, E. J. (1978). The effectiveness of creativity training. *Review of Educational Research, 48,* 517–536.

Maslow, A. (1970). *Motivation and personality* (2nd ed.). New York: Harper & Row.

Mayor, J. (1966). *The University of Maryland mathematics project* (Progress Report No. 11). College Park, MD: University of Maryland, College of Education.

McGuire, C. (1963). Research in the process approach to the construction and to analysis of medical examinations. *National Council on Measurement in Education Yearbook, 20,* 7–16.

McKenzie, G. R. (1972). Some effects of frequent quizzes on inferential thinking. *American Educational Research Journal, 9,* 231–240.

McLachlan, J. F., & Hunt, D. E. (1973). Differential effects of discovery learning as a function of student conceptual level. *Canadian Journal of Behavioral Science, 5,* 152–160.

McLean, J. E., & Chisson, B. S. (1980). *Talents Unlimited program: Summary of research findings for 1979–80.* Mobile, AL: Mobile County Public Schools. (ERIC Document Reproduction Service No. ED 198-660)

Meeker, M. N. (1969a). *The structure of intellect: Its interpretation and uses.* Columbus, OH: Charles E. Merrill.

Meeker, M. (1969b). *Advanced SOI divergent production sourcebook.* El Segundo, CA: SOI Institute.

Meeker, M., Meeker, R., & Roid, G. H. (1985). *Structure of the Intellect Learning Abilities Test (SOI-LA) Manual.* Los Angeles: Western Psychological Services.

Milholland, J. E. (1966, February). *An empirical examination of the categories of The Taxonomy of Educational Objectives.* Paper presented at the Annual American Educational Research Association Convention, Chicago.

Mills, C. J., & Durden, W. G. (1993). Cooperative learning and ability grouping: An issue of choice. *Gifted Child Quarterly, 36*(1), 11–16.

Morris, G. C. (1961). *Educational objectives of higher secondary school science.* Melbourne, Australia: Australian Council on Educational Research.

Muson, H. (1979, February). Moral thinking: Can it be taught? *Psychology Today,* pp. 48–58, 67–68, 92.

Myers, I. B., & Briggs, K. C. (1976). *The Myers-Briggs Type Indicator* (2nd ed.). Palo Alto, CA: Consulting Psychologists Press.

Newell, M. (1989). Adapting the Triad Model to serve gifted underachievers. *Gifted Education International, 6*(2), 98–101.

Newman, D., Griffin, P., & Cole, M. (1989). *The construction zone: Working for cognitive change in schools.* New York: Cambridge University Press.

Nielsen, E., & Clark, B. (1978). TAT in action: Project Impact in Polk County, Iowa. *Instructor, 78*(9), 63.

Nielson, A. B. (1984). *Using the Multiple Talent Model to manage independent study projects.* Presentation to the Western Exchange Conference on Gifted Education, Salt Lake City, UT.

Noller, R. B., Treffinger, D. J., & Houseman, E. D. (1979). *It's a gas to be gifted or CPS for the gifted and talented.* Buffalo, NY: D.O.K.

Norris, R., Nielson, E., Clark, B., & Coe, H. (1978). Project Impact: Innovation and motivation in Polk County for the advancement of creative teaching. In C. W. Taylor (Ed.), *Teaching for talents and gifts 1978 status: Developing and implementing multiple talent teaching.* Proceedings of a conference on multiple talent teaching held at the University of Utah, February 15–17, 1977. (ERIC Document Reproduction Service No. ED 172 475)

Olenchak, F. R. (1990). School change through gifted educations: Effects on elementary students' attitudes toward learning. *Journal for Education of the Gifted, 14*(1), 66–78.

Olenchak, F. R., & Renzulli, J. S. (1989). The effectiveness of the Schoolwide Enrichment Model on selected aspects of elementary school change. *Gifted Child Quarterly, 33*(1), 36–46.

Osborn, A. (1963). *Applied imagination.* New York: Scribners.

Osler, S. F., & Fivel, M. W. (1961). Concept attainment: I. The role of age and intelligence in concept attainment by induction. *Journal of Experimental Psychology, 62,* 1–8.

Osler, S. F., & Troutman, G. E. (1961). Concept attainment: II. The effect of stimulus upon concept attainment at two levels of intelligence. *Journal of Experimental Psychology, 62,* 9–13.

Parnes, S. J. (1966). *Programming creative behavior.* Buffalo: State University of New York at Buffalo.

Parnes, S. J. (1967). *Creative potential and the education experience* (Occasional Paper No. 2). Buffalo, NY: Creative Education Foundation.

Parnes, S. J. (1975). *Aha!: Insights into creative behavior.* Buffalo, NY: DOK Publishers.

Parnes, S. J. (1981). *The magic of your mind.* Buffalo, NY: Bearly Limited.

Parnes, S. J. (1987). The creative studies project. In S. Isaksen (Ed.), *Frontiers in creativity research: Beyond the basics* (pp. 156–188). Buffalo, NY: Bearly Limited.

Parnes, S. J. (1988). *Visionizing: State of the art processes for encouraging innovative excellence.* East Aurora, NY: DOK Publishers.

Parnes, S. J., Noller, R., & Biondi, A. (1967). *Guide to creative action.* New York: Scribners.

Paul, R. W. (1985, May). Bloom's taxonomy and critical thinking instruction. *Educational Leadership*, pp. 36–39.

Phelps, E., & Damon, W. (1989). Problem solving with equals: Peer collaboration as a context for learning mathematics and spatial concepts. *Journal of Educational Psychology, 81*(4), 639–646.

Phenix, P. H. (1964). *Realms of meaning*. New York: McGraw-Hill.

Piaget, J. (1963). *The origins of intelligence in children*. New York: Norton. (Original work published 1952)

Piaget, J., & Inhelder, B. (1969). *The psychology of the child*. New York: Basic Books.

Price, G., Dunn, K., Dunn, R., & Griggs, S. (1981). Studies in students' learning styles. *Roeper Review, 4*(2), 38–40.

Proviss, M. (1960). Ability grouping in arithmetic. *Elementary School Journal, 60*, 391–398.

Raths, L. E. (1963). Clarifying values. In R.S. Fleming (Ed.), *Curriculum for today's boys and girls* (pp. 315–342). Columbus, OH: Charles E. Merrill.

Raths, L. E., Harmin, M., & Simon, S. B. (1966). *Values and teaching*. Columbus, OH: Charles E. Merrill.

Rawls, J. (1971). *A theory of justice*. Cambridge, MA: Harvard University Press.

Reis, S. M., & Renzulli, J. S. (1982). A research report on the revolving door on the Revolving Door Identification Model: A case for the broadened conception of giftedness, *Phi Delta Kappan, 63*, 619–620.

Reis, S. M., & Renzulli, J. S. (1985). *Secondary Triad Model: A practical plan for implementing gifted programs at the junior and senior high school*. Mansfield, CT: Creative Learning Press.

Reis, S. M., & Schack, G. D. (1993). Differentiating products for the gifted and talented: The encouragement of independent learning. In C. J. Maker & D. Orzechowski-Harland (Eds.), *Critical issues in gifted education: Vol. III. Programs for the gifted in regular classrooms* (pp. 161–186). Austin, TX: PRO-ED.

Renzulli, J. S. (1977). *The enrichment triad model: A guide for developing defensible programs for the gifted and talented*. Wethersfield, CT: Creative Learning Press.

Renzulli, J. S. (1978). What makes giftedness? *Phi Delta Kappan, 60*, 180–184, 261.

Renzulli, J. S. (1979). *Sample instruments for the evaluation of programs for the gifted and talented*. Storrs, CT: Bureau of Educational Research, University of Connecticut.

Renzulli, J. S., & Gable, R. K. (1976). A factorial study of the attitudes of gifted students toward independent study. *The Gifted Child Quarterly, 20*, 91–99.

Renzulli, J. S., & Reis, S. M. (1985). *The schoolwide enrichment model: A comprehensive plan for educational excellence*. Mansfield Center, CT: Creative Learning Press.

Renzulli, J. S., Reis, S. M., & Smith, L. H. (1981). *The revolving door identification model*. Mansfield, CT: Creative Learning Press.

Renzulli, J. S., & Smith, L. H. (1978). *Learning styles inventory: A measure of student preference for instructional techniques*. Mansfield Center, CT: Creative Learning Press.

Renzulli, J. S., Smith, F. H., White, A. J., Callahan, C. M., & Hartman, R. K. (1976). *Scales for rating the behavioral characteristics of superior students (SRBCSS)*. Wethersfield, CT: Creative Learning Press.

Rest, J. (1974). Developmental psychology as a guide to value education: A review of "Kohlbergian" programs. *Review of Educational Research, 44,* 241–257.

Risemberg, R., & Zimmerman, B. J. (1992). Self-regulated learning in gifted students. *Roeper Review, 15*(2), 98–101.

Roberts, C., Ingram, C., & Harris, C. (1992). The effects of special versus regular classroom programming on higher cognitive processes of intermediate elementary aged gifted and average ability students. *Journal for the Education of the Gifted, 15*(4), 332–343.

Robinson, A. (1991). *Cooperative learning and the academically talented student: Executive summary.* Storrs, CT: National Research Center on the Gifted and Talented.

Roe, A. (1952). *The making of a scientist.* New York: Dodd & Mead.

Rogers, C. (1983). *Freedom to learn for the 80's.* Columbus, OH: Charles Merrill.

Rogoff, B. (1990). *Apprenticeship in thinking: Cognitive development in social context.* New York: Oxford University Press.

Rose, L. H., & Lin, H. (1984). A meta-analysis of long-term creativity training programs. *Journal of Creative Behavior, 11*(2), 124–130.

Ross, J. D., & Ross, C. M. (1976). *The Ross Test of Higher Cognitive Processes.* Novato, CA: Academic Therapy Publications.

Schack, G. D. (1986, April). *Creative productivity and self-efficacy in gifted children.* An expanded version of a paper presented at the 70th Annual Meeting of the American Educational Research Association, San Francisco, CA. (ERIC Document Reproduction Service No. ED 307-732)

Schack, G. D. (1993). Effects of a creative problem solving curriculum on students of varying ability levels. *Gifted Child Quarterly, 37*(1), 32–38.

Schiever, S. W. (1986). *The effects of two teaching/learning models on the higher cognitive processes of students in classes for the gifted.* Unpublished doctoral dissertation, University of Arizona, Tucson.

Schiever, S. W. (1991). *A comprehensive approach to teaching thinking.* Boston: Allyn & Bacon.

Schlichter, C. L. (1981). The Multiple Talent approach in mainstream and gifted programs. *Exceptional Children, 48*(2), 144–150.

Schlichter, C. L. (1986). Applying the multiple talent approach in mainstream and gifted programs. In J. S. Renzulli (Ed.), *Systems and models for developing programs for the gifted and talented* (pp. 352–389). Mansfield Center, CT: Creative Learning Press.

Schneider, B. H. (1987). *The gifted child in peer group perspective.* New York: Springer and Verlag.

Scruggs, T. E., & Mastropieri, M. A. (1988). Acquisition and transfer of learning strategies by gifted and nongifted students. *Journal of Special Education, 22*(2), 153, 166.

Scruggs, T. E., Mastropieri, M. A., Monson, J., & Jorgensen, S. (1985). Maximizing what gifted students can learn: Recent findings of learning strategy research. *Gifted Child Quarterly, 29*(4), 181–185.

Selman, R. (1971). The relation of the role-taking to the development of moral judgment in children. *Child Development, 42,* 79–91.

Sharan, S. (Ed.). (1990). *Cooperative learning: Theory and research.* New York: Praeger.

Sharan, S., Hertz-Lazarowitz, R., & Ackerman, Z. (1980). Academic achievement of elementary school children in small group versus whole class instruction. *Journal of Experimental Education, 48,* 125–129.

Sharan, S., Kussell, P., Hertz-Lazarowitz, R., Bejarano, Y., Raviv, S., & Sharan, Y. (1984). *Cooperative learning in the classroom: Research in desegregated schools.* Hillsdale, NJ: Lawrence Erlbaum.

Sharan, S., & Shachar, H. (1988). *Language and learning in the cooperative classroom.* New York: Springer.

Sharan, S., & Sharan, Y. (1976). *Small-group teaching.* Englewood Cliffs, NJ: Educational Technology Publications.

Sharan, Y., & Sharan, S. (1992). *Expanding cooperative learning through Group Investigations.* New York: Teachers College Press.

Shartzer, C. J. (1972). *Identifying talented children.* Unpublished manuscript, Illinois Department of Education, Springfield. (Available from Dr. C. J. Maker, Department of Special Education, University of Arizona, Tucson)

Shore, B. M., & Dover, A. C. (1987). Metacognition, intelligence, and giftedness. *Gifted Child Quarterly, 31*(1), 37–44.

Short, K. G., & Pierce, K. M. (1990). *Talking about books: Creating literate communities.* Portsmouth, NH: Heinemann.

Slavin, R. (1980). *Using student team learning.* Baltimore, MD: Center for Social Organization of Schools, Johns Hopkins University.

Slavin, R. (1983). *Cooperative learning.* New York: Longman.

Solman, R., & Rosen, G. (1986). Bloom's six cognitive levels represent two levels of performance. *Educational Psychology, 6*(3), 243–263.

Stanford Achievement Test (8th ed.). (1989). New York: Psychological Corporation.

Stanley, J. C., & Bolton, D. T. (1957). Book reviews. *Psychological Measurement, 17,* 631–634.

Starko, A. J. (1988). Effects of the revolving door identification model on creative productivity and self-efficacy. *Gifted Child Quarterly, 32*(3), 291–297.

Stepien, W. J., Gallagher, S. A., & Workman, D. (1993). Problem-based learning for traditional and interdisciplinary classrooms. *Journal for the Education of the Gifted, 16*(4), 338–357.

Sternberg, R. J. (1988). *The triarchic mind: A new theory of human intelligence.* New York: Viking.

Sternberg, R. J. (1990). *Metaphors of mind: Conceptions of the nature of intelligence.* New York: Cambridge University Press.

Sternberg, R. J., & Davidson, J. E. (1986). *Conception of giftedness.* New York: Cambridge University Press.

Stevenson, G., Seghini, J. B., Timothy, K., Brown, K., Lloyd, B. C., Zimmerman, M. A., Maxfield, S., & Buchanan, J. (1971). *Project implode: Igniting creative potential.* Salt Lake City, UT: Bella-Vista-Institute for Behavioral Research in Creativity.

Stewart, E. E. (1981). Learning styles among gifted/talented students: Instructional technique preferences. *Exceptional Children, 48*(2), 134–138.

Stoker, H. W., & Kropp, R. P. (1964). Measurement of cognitive processes. *Journal of Educational Measurement, 1,* 39–42.

Suchman, R. (1965). Inquiry and education. In J. Gallagher (Ed.), *Teaching gifted students: A book of readings* (pp. 193–209). Boston: Allyn & Bacon.

Sullivan, E. V. (1975). *Moral learning: Some findings, issues and questions.* New York: Paulist Press.

Suppes, P. (1969). *Sets and numbers: Teacher's handbook for book 1* (rev. ed.). New York: Random House.

Taba, H. (1962). *Curriculum development: Theory and practice.* New York: Harcourt, Brace & World.

Taba, H. (1964). *Thinking in elementary school children* (U.S.O.E. Cooperative Research Project, No. 1574). San Francisco: San Francisco State College. (ERIC Document Reproduction Service No. ED 003 285)

Taba, H. (1966). *Teaching strategies and cognitive functioning in elementary school children* (U.S.O.E. Cooperative Research Project No. 2404). San Francisco: San Francisco State College.

Tallent, M. K. (1985). *Effects of the Future Problem Solving program on gifted students' ability to solve futuristic problems* (Doctoral dissertation, University of Texas). *Dissertation Abstracts International, 47,* 843A.

Tallent-Runnels, M. K., & Yarbrough, D. W. (1992). Effects of the Future Problem Solving program on children's concerns about the future. *Gifted Child Quarterly, 36*(4), 190–194.

Tannenbaum, R. (1982). *An investigation of the relationships between selected instructional techniques and identified field independent cognitive styles as evidenced among high school students enrolled in studies of nutrition.* Unpublished doctoral dissertation, St. John's University, Jamaica, NY.

Tatsuoka, M. M., & Easley, J. A., Jr. (1963). *Comparison of UICSM vs. traditional algebra classes on COOP algebra test scores* (Research Report No. 1). Urbana, IL: University of Illinois Committee on School Mathematics.

Taylor, C. W. (1947). A factorial study of fluency in writing. Unpublished doctoral dissertation, University of Chicago.

Taylor, C. W. (1967). Questioning and creating: A model for curriculum reform. *Journal of Creative Behavior, 1*(1), 22–23.

Taylor, C. W. (1968a). The multiple talent approach. *The Instructor, 77,* 27, 142, 144, 146.

Taylor, C. W. (1968b). Be talent developers as well as knowledge dispensers. *Today's Education, 57,* 67–69.

Taylor, C. W. (1968c, May). *The highest talent potentials of man.* Presentation to the 15th Annual Conference of the National Association for Gifted Children, Chicago, IL.

Taylor, C. W. (Ed.). (1978, February). *Teaching for talents and gifts 1978 status: Developing and implementing multiple talent teaching.* Proceedings of a conference on multiple talent teaching, University of Utah. (ERIC Document Reproduction Service No. ED 172 475)

Taylor, C. W. (1986a). Cultivating simultaneous student growth in both multiple creative talents and knowledge. In J. S. Renzulli (Ed.), *Systems and models for developing programs for the gifted and talented* (pp. 307–351). Mansfield Center, CT: Creative Learning Press.

Taylor, C. W. (1986b). The growing importance of creativity and leadership is spreading gifted and talented programs world-wide. *Roeper Review, 8,* 256–263.

Taylor, C. W., Allington, D., & Lloyd, B. (1990). Multiple creative talent totem poles: Their uses and transferability to non-academic situations. In C. W. Taylor (Ed.), *Expanding awareness of creative potentials worldwide* (pp. 35–55). Salt Lake City, UT: Brain-Powers Press.

Terman, L. M. (Ed.). (1959). *Genetic studies of genius: Vol. 1. Mental and physical traits of a thousand gifted children.* Palo Alto, CA: Stanford University Press.

Terman, L. M., & Oden, M. (1959). *Genetic studies of genius: Vol. 5. The gifted group at mid-life.* Palo Alto, CA: Stanford University Press.

Thurstone, L. L. (1935). *The vectors of mind.* Chicago: University of Chicago Press.

Thurstone, L. L. (1947). *Multiple factor analysis: A development and expansion of The vectors of mind.* Chicago: University of Chicago Press.

Torrance, E. P. (1972). Can we teach children to think creatively? *Journal of Creative Behavior, 6*(4), 236–262.

Torrance, E. P. (1974). *Torrance Tests of Creative Thinking: Norms-technical manual.* Lexington, MA: Personnel Press.

Torrance, E. P. (1977). Today's students' images of the future. In S. L. Carmean & B. L. Grover (Eds.), *Creative thinking* (pp. 5–21). Bellingham, WA: Western Washington University.

Torrance, E. P., Williams, S., & Torrance, J. P. (1977). *Handbook for training future problem solving teams.* Athens, GA: University of Georgia, Department of Educational Psychology.

Trautman, P. (1979). *An investigation of the relationship between selected instructional techniques and identified cognitive style.* Unpublished doctoral dissertation, Wayne State University, Detroit, MI.

Treffinger, D. J. (1975). Teaching for self-directed learning: A priority for the gifted and talented. *The Gifted Child Quarterly, 19,* 46–59.

Treffinger, D. J. (1978). Guidelines for encouraging independence and self-direction among gifted students. *Journal of Creative Behavior, 12*(1), 14–20.

Tyler, L. L. (1966). The taxonomy of educational objectives: Cognitive domain. Its use in evaluating programmed instruction. *California Journal of Educational Research, 17,* 26–32.

United States Patent Model Foundation. (n.d.). *INVENT AMERICA! Teachers' classroom guide.* Washington, DC: Author.

Virostko, J. (1983). *An analysis of the relationships among student academic achievement in mathematics and reading, assigned instructional schedules, and the learning style preferences of a New York suburban school's third, fourth, fifth and sixth grade students.* Unpublished doctoral dissertation, St. John's University, Jamaica, NY.

Vygotsky, L. S. (1978). *Mind in society: The development of higher psychological processes.* Cambridge, MA: Harvard University Press.

Wallace, B., & Adams, H. B. (1988). Assessment and development of potential of high school students in the third world context of Kwa Zulu/Natal. *Gifted Education International, 5,* 72–78.

Wallace, W. L. (1962). The BSCS 1961–62 evaluation program: A statistical report. *Biological Sciences Curriculum Study Newsletter, 19,* 22–24.

Wallach, M. A. (1976). Tests tell us little about talent. *American Scientist, 44,* 57–63.

Wallach, M. A., & Kogan, N. (1965). *Modes of thinking in young children.* New York: Holt, Rinehart and Winston.

Wallen, N. E., Durkin, M. C., Fraenkel, J. R., McNaughton, A. J., & Sawin, E. I. (1969). *The Taba curriculum development project in social studies.* Menlo Park, CA: Addison-Wesley.

Ward, V. S. (1961). *Educating the gifted: An axiomatic approach.* Columbus, OH: Charles E. Merrill.

Wasson, F. R. (1980). *A comparative analysis of learning styles and personality characteristics of achieving and underachieving gifted elementary students.* Unpublished doctoral dissertation, Florida State University, Tallahassee.

Watts, G. H., & Anderson, R. C. (1971). Effects of three types of inserted questions on learning from prose. *Journal of Educational Psychology, 62,* 387–394.

Webb, J. T., Meckstroth, E. A., & Tolan, S. (1982). *Guiding the gifted child.* Columbus, OH: Ohio Psychology Publishing.

Wechsler, D. (1974). *Wechsler intelligence scale for children (rev.).* New York: Psychological Corporation.

Wheeler, R. (1980). An alternative to failure: Teaching reading according to students' perceptual strengths. *Kappa Delta Pi Record, 17*(2), 59–63.

Williams, F. E. (1970). *Classroom ideas for encouraging thinking and feeling* (2nd ed.). Buffalo, NY: D.O.K.

Williams, F. E. (1971). Models for encouraging creativity in the classroom. In J. C. Gowan & E. P. Torrance (Eds.), *Educating the ablest: A book of readings on the education of gifted children.* Itasca, IL: F. E. Peacock Publishers.

Williams, F. E. (1972). *A total creativity program for individualizing and humanizing the learning process.* Englewood Cliffs, NJ: Educational Technology Publications.

Wilson, S. H., Greer, J. F., & Johnson, R. M. (1973). Synectics: A creative problem-solving technique for the gifted. *The Gifted Child Quarterly, 17,* 260–267.

Zimmerman, B. J., & Martinez-Pons, M. (1990). Student differences in self-regulated learning: Relating grade, sex, and giftedness to self-efficacy and strategy use. *Journal of Educational Psychology, 82*(1), 51–59.

Zinn, K. L. (1966, February). *The use of the taxonomy and computer assistance in assembling sets of objectives, test items, and diagnostic test sequences.* Paper presented at the Annual American Educational Research Association Convention, Chicago.

Author Index

Subject Index

DATE DUE

DEC 0 8 1998		
JY 14 '99		
MAY 0 8 2000		
OC 2 0 01		